The Philippine Council of Evangelical Churches

Its Background, Context, and Formation among Post-World War II Churches

Raymundo Go

© 2019 Raymundo Go

Published 2019 by Langham Academic (Previously Langham Monographs)
An imprint of Langham Publishing
www.langhampublishing.org

Langham Publishing and its imprints are a ministry of Langham Partnership

Langham Partnership
PO Box 296, Carlisle, Cumbria, CA3 9WZ, UK
www.langham.org

ISBNs:
978-1-78368-589-9 Print
978-1-78368-590-5 ePub
978-1-78368-592-9 PDF

Raymundo Go has asserted his right under the Copyright, Designs and Patents Act, 1988 to be identified as the Author of this work.

All rights reserved. No part of this publication may be reproduced, stored in a retrieval system or transmitted, in any form or by any means, electronic, mechanical, photocopying, recording or otherwise, without the prior written permission of the publisher or the Copyright Licensing Agency.

Requests to reuse content from Langham Publishing are processed through PLSclear. Please visit www.plsclear.com to complete your request.

All Scripture quotations, unless otherwise indicated, are taken from the Holy Bible, New International Version®, NIV®. Copyright ©1973, 1978, 1984, 2011 by Biblica, Inc.™ Used by permission of Zondervan.

British Library Cataloguing-in-Publication Data
A catalogue record for this book is available from the British Library

ISBN: 978-1-78368-589-9

Cover & Book Design: projectluz.com

Langham Partnership actively supports theological dialogue and an author's right to publish but does not necessarily endorse the views and opinions set forth here or in works referenced within this publication, nor can we guarantee technical and grammatical correctness. Langham Partnership does not accept any responsibility or liability to persons or property as a consequence of the reading, use or interpretation of its published content.

This study is dedicated:

To Lut, my wife and inspiration. I thank her for the love and support she gave in helping produce this work especially during those difficult times.

To my colleagues at the International Graduate School of Leadership, my friends and co-laborers who gave me the time and their support to complete my PhD studies.

To my students whose questions and opinions helped me see the importance of "looking into the past."

To Dr Frank Pardue for guiding me and verifying my historical data.

To Theresa Huculak for editing the work.

To my mentor, Fr. Antonio de Castro, SJ, whose wisdom and insights helped shape the final presentation of historical data and its analysis.

And ultimately to God who gave me the ability to write and to appreciate his church in the Philippines.

Contents

List of Abbreviations xiii
Foreword xvii

Chapter 1 1
General Introduction
    Background of the Study 1
    Statement of the Problem 4
    Outline of the Study 4
    Scope and Limitations 6
        Scope 7
        Limitations 7
    Significance of the Problem 7
    Methodology 8
    Review of Related Literature 9
    Conclusion 10

Chapter 2 13
The Modernist/Liberal-Fundamentalist Controversy and the Fundamentalist/Evangelical Controversy in North America (1800–1960)
    The "Awakenings" and Evangelicalism (1700s–1800s) 14
    Personal Repentance 15
        Growth in Numbers 16
        Itinerant Evangelists 16
        Growth in Missions 17
    Social Reformations 17
        The Establishment of Educational Institutions 18
        The Abolitionist Movement 19
        Establishment of Social Institutions 20
    Modernist-Fundamentalist Controversy (1800s–1920s) 20
        The Rise of the Modernist Movement (Mid-1800s) 21
    The Rise of the Fundamentalist Movement (Late 1800s) 26
    The Gap Widens Between the Factions (1900–1920) 28
        The Federal Council of Churches (1908) 29
        World Missionary Conference in Edinburgh (1910) 30
        Fundamentalist Books and Publications (1910–1915) 31
    Liberalism Gains Popularity (1920s–1940s) 32

  The Growing Secularism of America 32
  Public Support for the Liberal Cause 33
  Christian Institutions Become Liberal... 34
 Reconsolidation of Fundamentalism (1930–1940).............................. 34
  The Establishment of Reformed Institutions............................. 35
  The Rise of Pentecostalism (1900–1930s) 37
  The Surge in Proclamation Ministry 39
 The Rise of Evangelicalism (1940s–1950s) 43
  Key Characteristics of the Evangelicals.. 46
 Fundamentalist-Evangelical Controversy (1950s–1980s)................... 52
 Conclusion 53

Chapter 3 55
Protestantism in the Philippines: From Inception to the
Post-World War II Era (1890s–1950s)
 The Arrival of Protestantism in the Islands (1900s) 55
  Missionary Boards Conference in New York (1898).................. 56
  The Evangelical Union (1901) 58
  Early Proclamation and Reform Efforts 66
 Mergers and Schisms Among Pre-War Protestant Churches
 (1910–1920s) 69
  The IEMELIF (1909) 70
  The Evangelical Church of the Philippines (Independent
   Presbyterian) (1914)... 73
  The Union Church of Manila (1914).. 74
  The Evangelical Christian Church of the Philippine Islands
   (1915)... 75
  The United Church of Manila (1924) 76
  The United Evangelical Church in the Philippines Islands
   (1929).. 77
  The National Christian Council (1929) 78
  The UNIDA (1932) 79
  The Philippine Methodist Church (1933).................................. 80
  The Philippine Federation of Evangelical Churches (1938)........ 81
 Fundamentalism in the Philippines.. 82
  Schisms Caused by Modernist-Fundamentalist Controversy
   (1920s) 82
  The Arrival of Fundamentalist/Conservative Churches 84
  Baptist Separation Issues in Iloilo (1930s).................................. 89
  Fundamental Baptist Churches Growth and Expansion
   (late 1930s to 1940s).. 91

    Wartime Union and Activities (1942–1946) 92
        Religious Section of the Japanese Imperial Army.......................94
        Forced Agreement at the Manila Hotel 95
        Federation of Evangelical Churches in the Philippines
            and the Evangelical Church of the Philippines 96
        Wartime Fundamentalist Efforts 98
    Immediate Post-War Period (1946–1948) 99
        Mergers and Unions among Mainline Protestant Churches 100
        Mergers and Arrival among Fundamentalist/Conservative
            Churches..102
    Conclusion 110

Chapter 4 113
The Formation of the Philippine Council of Evangelical Churches (1960s)
    Transitions and Changes (1950s) 114
        The Arrival of New Fundamentalist/Evangelical Churches
            in the Post-War Period..114
        Developments within the Pre-War Mainline
            Protestant Churches 120
        Differences Between the Pre-War Mainline Protestants
            and the Fundamentalist/Evangelical Churches 125
        Summary...129
    The Formation of PCEC (1960s) 129
        The Philippine Council of Fundamental Churches (1964).......131
        Philippine Council of Fundamental-Evangelical
            Churches (1964) 134
        The Philippine Council of Evangelical Churches (1969)..........142
        PCEC's Directions and Emphasis (Late 1970s–1990s) 146
    Conclusion 156

Chapter 5 157
Analysis and Synthesis of the Formation and Developments within PCEC Using Hiebert's Bounded versus Centered Set Categories
    Bounded versus Centered Set Unions...159
    Applying Hiebert's Categorization to the Post-War Councils
        in the Philippines..160
        Two Councils in Contrast...160
        Summary...170
    PCEC in the Lens of Hiebert's Model...171
        PCEC's Early Years – Bounded Set (1964–1966)......................171

       PCEC's Transitional Period (1966–1980s) 174
       PCEC as a Centered Set Union (1978–1990s) 182
       PCEC as a Centrist Organization 185
       Summary 185
   Conclusion 186

Chapter 6 187
Recommendations and Conclusion
   Introduction 187
   A Summary of Findings 187
   Recommendations 189
   Recommendations for Further Study 190
       The Adjustments Taken by the Roman Catholic Church 190
       Historical Developments within the Mainline
           Protestant Churches 190
       The Present Condition of the Fundamentalist Churches 191
       The Current Trends and Developments within the
           Mega-Churches 191
       Dialogue between the Evangelicals and the Roman Catholic
           Churches 191
       The Possibility of a Future Unification among the Religious
           Leaders of the Country 191
       The Future for PCEC and Its Constituents 192
   Conclusion 192

Appendix A 195
PCEC Timeline

Appendix B 201
PCEC Constitution and By-Laws

Appendix C 213
Aragon's List of Attendees Who Initiated the Formation of PCEC

Appendix D 215
Interview with Fred Magbanua, Jr

Appendix E 229
Interview with Mariano Leones

Appendix F 237
Interview with Eliseo Capile

Appendix G 241
    Interview with Pio Tica

Appendix H 265
    Interview with Ebenezer Nacita

Appendix I 275
    Correspondence with Faustino Ruivivar, Jr (6 June 2010)

Appendix J 279
    Correspondence with Faustino Ruivivar, Jr (7 June 2010)

Appendix K 283
    Correspondence with Faustino Ruivivar, Jr (8 June 2010)

Appendix L 285
    Correspondence with Faustino Ruivivar, Jr (9 June 2010)

Appendix M 289
    Correspondence with Faustino Ruivivar, Jr (12 June 2010)

Appendix N 291
    Correspondence with Faustino Ruivivar, Jr (19 June 2010)

Appendix O 293
    Correspondence with Faustino Ruivivar, Jr (16 August 2010)

Appendix P 297
    Correspondence with Felipe Ferrez, Jr (11 June 2013)

Appendix Q 299
    Interview with Agustin B. Vencer

Glossary 333

Selected Bibliography 335

List of Abbreviations

ABCL	Association of Baptist Church in Luzon
ABCLVM	Association of Baptist Churches in Luzon, Visayas, and Mindanao
ABCCOP	Alliance of Bible Christian Communities of the Philippines
ABEO	Association of Baptists for the Evangelism in the Orient
ABFMS	American Baptist Foreign Mission Society
ABWE	Association of Baptists for World Evangelism
AFBCP	Association of Fundamentalist Baptist Churches of the Philippines
AG	Assemblies of God
BABC	Bukidnon Association of Baptist Churches
CAMACOP	Christian and Missionary Alliance Churches of the Philippines
CBAP	Conservative Baptist Association of the Philippines
CBFMS	Conservative Baptist Foreign Mission Society
CCWM	Congress on the Church's Worldwide Mission
C-GRIP	Church Growth Research in the Philippines
CIM	China Inland Mission
CMA	Christian Missionary Alliance
CORE	Christian Organized for Renewal and Evangelism
CPCM	Commission on Philippine Chinese Mission
DAWN 2000	Discipling A Whole Nation Movement 2000
DEI	Doane Evangelistic Institute

ECP	Evangelical Church of the Philippines
ECP-IP	Evangelical Church of the Philippines (Independent Presbyterian)
EFMA	Evangelical Foreign Missions Association
EXCOM	Executive Committee
FBCM	First Baptist Church of Manila
FEBC	Far East Broadcasting Company
FEBIAS	Far Eastern Bible Institute and Seminary
FECCC	Far Eastern Council of Christian Churches
FECP	Federation of Evangelical Churches in the Philippines
FEGC	Far Eastern Gospel Crusade
GCMCA	General Conference of the Methodist Church of America
GI	lit. Government Issue, refers to the US military servicemen
ICCC	International Council of Christian Churches
ICFG	International Church of the Foursquare Gospel
IEMELIF	*La Iglesia Evangelica Metodista en las Islas Filipinas*
IFI	*Iglesia Filipina Independiente* (Philippine Independent Church) aka. The Aglipayans
IFMA	Interdenominational Foreign Mission Association
LICWE	Lausanne International Congress on World Evangelism
MEI	Manila Evangelistic Institute
NAE	National Association of Evangelicals for United Action
NCCP	National Council of Churches in the Philippines
NEA	National Evangelical Association
NECCOM	National Ecumenical Consultative Committee
NEF	New England Fellowship
NIV	The New International Version
NPA	National People's Army

OMF	Overseas Missionary Fellowship
PABWE	Philippine Association of Baptists for World Evangelism
PBTS	Philippine Baptist Theological Seminary
PCEC	Philippine Council of Evangelical Churches
PCFC	Philippine Council of Fundamentalist Churches
PCFEC	Philippine Council of Fundamentalist and Evangelical Churches
PEC	Philippine Episcopal Church
PFCC	Philippine Federation of Christian Churches
PFEC	Philippine Federation of Evangelical Churches
PHILRADS	Philippine Relief and Development Services
PMC	Philippine Methodist Church
RCC	Roman Catholic Church
SBC	Southern Baptist Convention
SEC	Securities and Exchange Commission
UCCP	United Church of Christ in the Philippines
UCM	Union Church of Manila
UECPI	United Evangelical Church in the Philippines Islands
UNIDA	United Evangelical Church of the Philippines or *La Iglesia Evangelica Unida de Filipinas*
VFFBC	Visayas Fellowship of Fundamental Baptist Churches
WCC	World Council of Churches
WEF	World Evangelical Fellowship
YMCA	Young Men's Christian Association

Foreword

During certain events such as weddings and other family celebrations, one gets to meet different people and hear about stories regarding their lives and relationships to each other. While it is easy to keep track of details in a smaller gathering, a larger group becomes a greater challenge especially when one tries to recall personal details and relationships. Similarly, the evangelical community within the Philippines has grown in number through the years and it can be quite challenging to identify the relationships of one church to another.

This monograph is an attempt to historically trace the relationships of the different churches within the Philippines and to understand the motivations behind some of the cooperative and conciliar efforts among them. It introduces the context behind some of the approaches and predispositions of these Filipino Christians by showing their western roots. The victories and difficulties that these Christian leaders experienced to gain a "voice" are recounted to give this new generation of Christian leaders an example to study as they develop their own plans for the future of Christianity in our beloved country.

Another contribution of this book is its effort to preserve the details of the past. As the memories of past events of the last one hundred years begin to fade with the passage of time, this monograph is an effort to preserve some of the details that happened within Christianity in Philippines. Sadly, most of the records are unavailable for careful study as these details have not been written down, have been misplace or lost, and have been simply forgotten. Thus, the appendices offer a valuable resource as personal interviews with some of the leaders (three of whom are no longer with us) of these churches and movements recall the past.

This book is important for Filipino Christians who wants to understand their spiritual roots, to see the values and visions of their forebears and to give them a hope that the same God who guided the leaders in the past is still at work today within the churches in the Philippines. Let it be a vanguard for other books and papers that would chronicle the rich Christian heritage that we have as Filipinos and as God's people.

Tom Roxas
President, International Graduate School of Leadership
Quezon City, Philippines

CHAPTER 1

General Introduction

In the early 1960s, several Filipino fundamentalist and evangelical leaders met in the First Baptist Church of Manila (FBCM) to discuss the possibility of establishing a council of churches that would adequately represent their theology and ministry philosophy. While their action was not uncommon, their decision was, to some extent, intriguing since it would have been easier and more convenient to simply join the pre-war Filipino Protestant churches that had recently merged to form the National Council of Churches in the Philippines (NCCP) in 1963;[1] instead they chose to form the Philippine Council of Evangelical Churches (PCEC).

Background of the Study

In order to understand the reason for their alternative choice, it is important to view this in light of Philippine Protestantism's history and context.

One of the foremost desires of most Christians is to fulfill the prayer of the Lord Jesus for unity (John 17:21).[2] While churches and Christian organizations have made great strides in the past to fulfill this prayer, it continues to be an elusive dream. From a brief survey of the history of Christianity in the Philippines, there have been several efforts to fulfill this dream by establishing a united and organic Filipino Protestant church. At the eve of Protestantism's arrival in 1899, several American missionary organizations

---

1. For details on the establishment of the UCCP and the NCCP, see T. Valentino Sitoy, Jr, *Comity and Unity: Ardent Aspirations of Six Decades of Protestantism in the Philippines (1901-1961)* (Quezon City, Philippines: National Council of Churches in the Philippines, 1989).

2. An example of such an effort to call for the "reunification" of the Christian Church is the papal declaration of John Paul II *Ut Unum Sint* in 1995.

began to initiate strategies and agreements to find a way to unite the fruit of their efforts and to form a single Filipino church. As a result of this desire for cooperative efforts, these early western missionaries established the Evangelical Union in 1901 to guide its members in unity and cooperation through the Comity Agreement (e.g. adoption of a common name – *Iglesia Evangelica*, the division of the archipelago into distinct areas, etc.).[3]

However, this cooperative effort had its own difficulties as conflicts persisted due to the continued competition and rivalry among its member parties. For example, the theological and practical distinctions among these groups became a major hindrance in the planned union among the "fruit of the labors." In addition, the confusion and violation of the territorial divisions previously agreed upon by the comity members proved to be a continued strain in the relationship among these Protestant churches.[4]

While efforts by comity members to settle their differences and difficulties continued, by the 1920s and 1930s, this dream of a unified organic Filipino church was adopted and acquired by several Filipino leaders and their churches. Although there had been successful mergers (e.g. United Church of Manila – 1924; the UNIDA – 1932; and the United Church of Christ in the Philippines – 1948), the goal of forming an all-inclusive unified Filipino Protestant church was beyond their abilities as each of these churches were unwilling to give up their commitment to their particular theology, tradition, and praxis.

Thus, the less strenuous option of forming conciliar union became the accepted alternative, since this arrangement could fulfill the requirement of unity and cooperation while allowing each member to continue their distinctives and autonomy (e.g. National Christian Council – 1929; Philippine Federation of Evangelical Churches – 1938; and the Philippine Federation of Christian Churches – 1949). As a result, by 3 March 1950, the Comity Agreement was dissolved when its member organizations felt that the agreement was already obsolete, its provisions and rulings were often disregarded, and several councils followed this to achieve the desired goal.[5]

---

3. Sitoy, *Comity and Unity*, 10.

4. Sitoy, 23–39.

5. Richard L. Deats, *The Story of Methodism in the Philippines* (Manila: G. Rangel & Sons, 1964), 109–111.

In 1963, several of these mainline Filipino Protestant churches formed the National Council of Churches in the Philippines (NCCP) to fulfill the dream of finally uniting all the churches in the Philippines. Efforts to unify these churches by "dissolving" the denominational distinctives were initiated so that "within the first two years of its existence, the NCCP also sponsored a thorough study on interdenominational worship services and held a national conference on the life and mission of the Church."[6]

While there was some excitement over the formation of the NCCP, several fundamentalist and evangelical leaders remained unwilling to enlist themselves in the newly formed council. Their decision was not made for a lack of passion for unity;[7] instead, it was born out of a conviction that the formation of a parallel council was a better alternative since it could represent their conservative theology and views – as some perceived that several members of the NCCP were too "modernist" or "liberal" in their theology and praxis.[8] This "tension" that exists among these churches and mission organizations can ultimately be traced back to the "modernist/fundamentalist" controversy and even the "fundamentalist/evangelical" controversy in the United States during the nineteenth and twentieth centuries, respectively.

---

6. Sitoy, *Comity and Unity*, 130.

7. In an article written by Rev Agustin B. Vencer, Jr, PCEC's former General Secretary, he makes a strong case against the apparent divisions among the Body of Christ and calls it "scandalous" and a "stumbling block" (Agustin B. Vencer, Jr, "Evangelical Unity and Cooperation in Asia: A Biblical Basis," *Evangelical Thrust* 10, no. 1 [January 1983], 20). He further adds that "disunity is a satanic ploy that saps our strength so that we have little left for the furtherance of the Gospel" (Vencer, "Evangelical Unity," 20). In fact, the decision to establish a parallel council brought several problems to Protestantism. For one, it did not end the gap between the old pre-war churches and these fundamentalist/evangelical churches and organization. It also alienated some key sectors of society which had strong ties with the NCCP. For example, anyone who would want to serve as a Protestant chaplain in the armed forces of the Philippines must get an endorsement from the NCCP. This has prevented evangelical pastors from joining the chaplaincy service since they belong to the "opposing" council ("Topic: Army Chaplain," *Philippine Defense Forum*, accessed 18 June 2012, http://www.timawa.net/forum/index.php?topic=19859.0).

8. Averell U. Aragon, "The Philippine Council of Evangelical Churches," in *Chapters in Philippine Church History*, ed. Anne C. Kwantes (Manila, Philippines: OMF Literature, 2001), 372.

Statement of the Problem

As a result, an understanding of the historical context and issues that confronted the founding members of PCEC can help explain the "path" that they took and the decisions that they made. Hence, this study attempts to answer the question, "What caused a group of post-World War II churches to refrain from uniting with the newly established National Council of Churches in the Philippines (NCCP) and to form their own parallel council, the Philippine Council of Evangelical Churches (PCEC)?"

Outline of the Study

In order to adequately address and explain the reason for the inquiry, this study will take the following course:

Chapter 1 serves as the introduction. It provides the following: the statement of the problem, scope and limitations, significance of the problem, and methodology.

Chapter 2 is entitled the "The Modernist/Liberal-Fundamentalist Controversy and the Fundamentalist/Evangelical Controversy in North America (1800–1960)." This chapter examines the particular events that took place in North America that led to the emergence of the modernist/liberal-fundamentalist controversy and the resulting Protestant "landscape" in the aftermath of the debate prior to the Second World War. It recounts the accomplishments and developments within the two major divisions (i.e. the modernist/liberal side versus the fundamentalist side) as the gap widened between the two. It also recounts the background that paved the way for the rise and the formation of the National Evangelical Association (NEA) in the post-World War II era. It also briefly narrates the resulting controversy among these non-mainline Protestant churches as their emphases and policies began to cause schisms, which broke these churches into two further groups; namely, the evangelicals and fundamentalists.

Chapter 3 is entitled "Protestantism in the Philippines: From Inception to the Post-World War II Era (1890s–1950s)." This brief historical account describes the arrival of the early North American Protestant missionaries and the establishment of Protestantism in the Philippines. It describes their efforts to balance both evangelism and social transformation as they sought to someday replace Roman Catholicism as the main religion of the Philippines. As Philippine Protestantism entered its second decade, calls for autonomy and independence began to influence these Filipino churches and their leaders. As a result, several mergers and schisms took place within the period as Filipino Protestants sought to form an independent national church. In addition, several new denominations and councils were formed. This chapter also introduces the arrival of the modernist/liberal-fundamentalist controversy in the country and the resulting schisms among these missionary organizations and churches. It also recounts the arrival of several fundamentalist/conservative churches during the pre-war period. The chapter also discusses the events that took place among the mainline Protestant churches and the fundamentalist/conservative churches both during and immediately after the war in the Pacific, recalling the mergers and unions among the mainline Protestant churches and the mergers and arrival of several fundamentalist/conservative churches.

Chapter 4, "The Formation of the Philippine Council of Evangelcial Churches (1960s)" is divided into two sections, where the first section discusses the historical context of the second section, which is the actual formation of the Philippine Council of Evangelical Churches (PCEC). The first section discusses the arrival of several fundamentalist/evangelical churches and missionary organizations (e.g. western missionaries who were expelled from China) in the 1950s. It also recalls several developments within the mainline Protestant churches leading up to the establishment of the National Council of Churches in the Philippines (NCCP) in 1963. The section also includes the differences between the fundamentalist/evangelicals and the mainline Protestant churches, ending the section with a brief summary. The second section recalls the actions and the motivations that led a group of Filipino evangelicals to form a parallel council – the PCEC. It discusses briefly the perceived differences between the two councils which provided a basis for their separation from one another. It also narrates the struggle between the fundamentalists and the evangelicals within the PCEC which eventually led to its own schism. This would be followed by the changes that took place within the council as a result of the departure of the fundamentalists, the efforts by the evangelicals to redefine and refocus their efforts resulting in major changes during the leadership of Dr Agustin B. Vencer, Jr.

Chapter 5 is entitled "Analysis and Synthesis of the Formation and Developments within PCEC Using Hiebert's Bounded versus Centered Set Categories." A brief description of Paul Hiebert's bounded and centered set categories is provided, which the remaining section employed to evaluate the actions and choices of these Filipino Protestants. The Association of Fundamentalist Baptist Churches of the Philippines (AFBCP), the PCEC, and the NCCP are assessed in light of Hiebert's categories to show the differences between a bounded set union and a centered set union. The chapter also shows that the direction and emphasis of the PCEC during its early years (1964–1975) were consistent with a bounded set union, as it was influenced by its association with the fundamentalist leaders who had helped establish this council of churches. This is followed by a brief discussion of the events and the reasons to explain why during the 1960s and the 1970s the PCEC, which had initially sided with the fundamentalists, shifted itself to a centered set union under the leadership of Dr Vencer and redefined the council's relationship with the NCCP and the other religious groups in the country. It shows that the resulting changes in its purposes were consistent with a centered set union. Under Dr Vencer's leadership, "knowing and making Jesus Christ known" became the council's center where proclamation and social engagement/transformation became the focus of the PCEC. Finally, the chapter ends with the PCEC's definition and declaration of the council's centrist position.

Chapter 6 serves as the Conclusion. It summarizes all the findings by evaluating historical data that has been presented and the lessons learned from the formation of the PCEC. It also offers several recommendations as a result of the study.

Scope and Limitations

This study evaluates the events and issues that served as the historical context of these evangelical leaders during the post-war period. It also studies the motivations and the rationale of the PCEC's leaders as they sought to define the council's identity in the light of the current needs and trends within the Philippine society and the world.

Scope
This study explores the historical background and contexts that became the basis by which the PCEC was formed; namely the theological arguments and positions, the desire to gain a strategic position in society, and other historical events that guided the decisions of the leaders of this council. It includes a summary of events in North America, the primary sending country of Protestant missionaries to the Philippines, which explains the schism that formed along the fundamentalist and modernist/liberal lines. It also studies the emergence of evangelicalism from among the member churches within the fundamentalist movement in the 1940s. This paper explores the early beginnings of the Protestant movement within the Philippines, tracing its development through the different missionary groups that came and formed the NCCP. Finally, it examines the arrival and the establishment of evangelical churches and missionary agencies in the post-World War II period and the resulting formation of the PCEC and the reasons for the changes instituted by Dr Vencer in the late 1970s which redirected and refocused the efforts and emphasis of the Council.

Limitations
This dissertation does not discuss each and every denomination that emerged from the schisms in North America and it only refers to a few representative churches that were directly involved in the growth and establishment of the Protestant church in the Philippines. It also does not discuss the condition and the growth of the Roman Catholic Church in the Philippines from the onset of the Protestant period (1899) to the present, and the other independent churches that were established in the Philippines (e.g. the *Iglesia ni Kristo*) that had no direct connection to the formation of the PCEC. Finally, it limits itself by simply summarizing the growth and establishment of the PCEC from 1970 to its current condition. The focus is primarily on its founding, internal struggles among its leaders, its early years and the shift in direction during the leadership of Dr Vencer.

Significance of the Problem
This study can provide a fresh understanding of the historical contexts that influenced and guided the early founders of the PCEC to form their

own council, which can account for the apparent factionalism among the Protestant churches in the Philippines. Employing Hiebert's categories helps provide an understanding of the actions and characteristics of these evangelicals that led them to unite, but at the same time reject union with the modernist/liberal and the fundamentalist groups. Further, it can enlighten and help explore the possibility of a future merger among these groups since this study provides the rationale for this dividedness, which can be reassessed in light of the current developments among the Filipino churches.

Methodology

This work is a descriptive narrative of key events that took place and became the historical context by which the PCEC was formed, using historical analysis and analytical interpretations of these events. The work is a qualitative study as available resources and persons were used to determine the facts presented. Thus, information from resources such as personal interviews, emails, websites, archives, formal documents, news reports, and other official literature from churches and organizations that are connected with both the PCEC and the NCCP were studied and consulted.

Although there is an abundance of written sources that account for the growth of the Roman Catholic Church and the Mainline Protestant churches connected with the NCCP in the Philippines, there has been a limited number of books that narrate the history of evangelicalism in the Philippines. Part of the challenge in this study was to locate the limited number of archives, records, and other historical documents that survived and were preserved.[9] As for this apparent scarcity of material, there are several reasons for this: first, the evangelical movement in the Philippines is a relatively recent entity and few have taken the time to write their memoirs or chronicle the events that took place right after World War II; second, these churches and mission organizations were very active and were often so preoccupied with their efforts that they failed to record their efforts; and finally, most did

---

9. At the present, the research material gathered for this study came from personal collections and from old church files. Several yearbooks obtained from libraries and other sources also helped in giving details to key events such as names, locations, and other details. Unfortunately, majority of the original documents were either damaged or lost since there was no intentional effort to preserve them.

not consider their actions and words worthy of cataloguing as they did not reckon their actions to be extraordinary or remarkable.[10]

As a result, much of the crucial information and detailed accounting of their accomplishments were forgotten and remained undocumented.[11] Some of the details given in this study are based on the recollection of individuals which have been gathered to form a narrative as indicated in their corresponding footnotes. As a result, some of the narrative written in this work is a reconstruction of information and material gathered from available sources.[12]

Review of Related Literature

The following is a brief review of works that have been used in this study. These sources proved invaluable in providing the necessary framework to piece together the details to complete the historical "picture" of Protestantism in the Philippines.

The book entitled *Comity and Unity: Ardent Aspirations of Six Decades of Protestantism in the Philippines (1901–1961)* by Valentino Sitoy, Jr is a brief chronicle of key events that took place from the arrival of the first North American Protestant missionaries in 1899 to the formation of the NCCP in 1963. It followed the efforts of these western and Filipino leaders in seeing the fulfillment of their aspirations to form a unified and autonomous Filipino church. It provided abbreviated details of the varied attempts of several councils and churches to unite through organic union, cooperatives, or conciliar cooperation. Sitoy's primary focus was to narrate the path taken

---

10. During the interviews and consultation with some of the sources, most of these individuals did not consider their efforts as remarkable but merely a continuing affirmation and commitment to what they considered as their basic beliefs and praxis that was seem within the first-century church.

11. There are many details and information that have been "lost" as these have been forgotten or those who could possibly answer the inquiry are no longer available. In an email that was sent to the author on 9 June 2010, Dr Faustino Ruivivar, one of the earliest members of PCEC, wrote that it was unfortunate that he could no longer "recall" those who were in the very first meeting and even its exact location (See Appendix L).

12. For more details, see chapter 4 on the Formation of PCEC and other information in the appendices. In addition, this work attempted to avoid gathering erroneous data. Several guidelines were observed: first, the information gathered must have been verified by at least another person or document; second, the details must be cross-checked with actual historical facts gathered from reliable sources; and third, efforts are made to reconcile discrepancies and conflicting details.

towards the formation of the NCCP; it does not provide adequate analysis of the effects of the modernist-fundamentalist controversy in North America on the Philippine Protestant churches. Thus, this work employed the details of Sitoy's book as "milestones" and added supplemental information on the arrival and emergence of fundamentalist/evangelical groups within the Protestant landscape of the Philippines.

The short chapter entitled "The Philippine Council of Evangelical Churches" written by Averell Aragon found in *Chapters in Philippine Church History* gives an account of the emergence of the PCEC from the initial meeting of several leaders in 1964 to PCEC's recent accomplishments. It provides details of how these evangelical leaders struggled and triumphed in the formation of the council which was initially called the Philippine Council of Fundamentalist Churches (PCFC) and the internal struggle which changed this group to its present composition and name, PCEC. It also gives the list of accomplishments by the said group. Thus, this study employed several details provided by Aragon's work. However, Aragon's work limited itself to the efforts of the evangelicals and does not give a full account of the NCCP and the fundamentalists' role in the formation of the PCEC. Hence, this study provides some additional details to "complete" the narrative. While, Aragon's work mentions some of the changes that took place in the later years of the council (e.g. the PCEC's membership in the National Ecumenical Consultative Committee, the establishment of PHILRADS, etc.); it does not provide the rationale for these actions and the changes that took place as part of the council's evolution.

Conclusion

In 1963, a group of fundamentalist and evangelical leaders were prompted by the formation of the NCCP to establish their own parallel council which they believed would represent their beliefs and convictions. The conciliar union forged between the fundamentalists and the evangelicals is an amazing accomplishment as its leaders were able to work out their differences and work together. However, their divergent emphases and directions continued to pull the council apart so that this fragile union began to disintegrate and eventually break apart, leaving behind the evangelicals to redefine the council's purpose. It was under the leadership of Dr Vencer that the council became a centered set union. The PCEC was a product of its history, tradition, and the needs of the time. It is clear that these factors influenced its leaders as they established, redefined, and developed the council to its current form and function.

CHAPTER 2

The Modernist/Liberal-Fundamentalist Controversy and the Fundamentalist/Evangelical Controversy in North America (1800–1960)

A survey of Philippine Protestantism reveals factions and autonomous congregations among these churches and organizations.[1] While there have been efforts to establish a unified organic Philippine church; differences in theology, traditions, praxis, and other issues have become major obstacles to that goal. As a result, conciliar unity became an alternative utilized by these churches to achieve harmony and cooperation where mergers proved to be difficult.[2]

In 1963, several mainline Protestant churches agreed to "lay aside" their differences to establish a cooperative council – the National Council of Churches in the Philippines (NCCP).[3] While the possibility of finally see-

---

1. Among these churches and organizations, distinctions are made by names that they adopt to refer to themselves (e.g. protestants, evangelical, fundamental, etc.). This is a common characteristic that can be observed in other countries as well. Fuller states, "There are about 23,000 denominations in the World, each claiming to proclaim Christ as the only way," (W. Harold Fuller, *Global Crossroads: Focusing the Strength of Local Churches* [Mandaluyong City, Philippines: OMF Literature, 1998], 16).

2. For a brief survey of the efforts of several mainline protestant churches in the Philippines to form a council, see Sitoy, *Comity and Unity*.

3. Its founding members were initially from seven Filipino churches; namely, the *Iglesia Filipina Independiente* (the Philippine Independent Church), Episcopal Church of the Philippines, United Church of Christ in the Philippines, United Methodist Church of the Philippines, Convention of Philippine Baptist Churches, *Iglesia Evangelica Metodista En Las Islas Filipinas*, and the *Iglesia Unida Ekyumenikal*.

ing national cooperation and solidarity among these Protestant churches and organizations was within reach, several evangelical[4] and fundamentalist leaders remained unwilling to join the NCCP and instead formed a parallel council – the Philippine Council of Evangelical Churches (PCEC).

To appreciate the raison d'être of the PCEC, it is important to understand the historical and theological roots of the modernist-fundamentalist controversy and the fundamentalist/evangelical controversy among the Protestant churches and organizations in the United States of America. Although these controversies took place in North America, they strongly influenced the Filipino churches as these attitudes and perspectives were "passed on" and "inherited" by their adherents in the Philippines. This chapter seeks to follow the key events in North America which brought about these Protestant controversies and divisions.

The "Awakenings" and Evangelicalism (1700s–1800s)

By the eighteenth century, revivalist movements were taking place in Germany,[5] England, and the North American colonies. The spiritual move-

---

4. While the term "evangelical" could be applied to any branch within Christendom that places a strong emphasis on the preaching of the gospel or *euangelion*, the name *evangelische* (evangelical) was used to describe Luther's church during the Protestant Reformation period (Frank S. Mead and Samuel S. Hill, *Handbook of Denominations in the United States*, new 9th ed., [Nashville: Abingdon, 1990], 254). However, the name has been adopted to refer to American evangelicalism which came out of the revivalist movement during the Great Awakening. Unlike the Puritans that were involved in English politics, the evangelicals were unencumbered by this concern as they saw that the proclamation of the gospel was their primary task. However, they were "not detached from politics, as the Pietists were" as their later involvement in societal issues reveal their passion for the transformation of society (Bruce L. Shelley, *Church History in Plain Language*, updated 2nd ed. [Nashville, TN: Thomas Nelson, 1995], 332). Today, the name has been commonly used to refer to a group of conservative churches in North America (and their progeny in the rest of the world) that banded together during the mid-twentieth century and that seeks to return to the values of the Great Awakenings.

5. For example, Lutheranism was experiencing its own form of revivalism, which is commonly referred to as Pietism or the Pietist movement in Germany during the seventeenth century. As Cairns describes the movement, it was "an internal evangelical corrective to the cold orthodoxy of the seventeenth-century Lutheran church . . . [it] emphasized an internal, subjective, and individual return to Bible study and prayer" (Earle E. Cairns, *Christianity Through the Centuries: A History of the Christian Church*, 3rd ed., rev. and expanded [Grand Rapids: Zondervan, 1996], 383). For further details on the movement, see Paul E. Pierson, *The Dynamics of Christian Mission: History through a Missiological Perspective* (Pasadena, CA:

ments which took place in North America and in England were commonly referred to as the Great Awakenings. Revivalist movements were taking place in the midst of the non-conformist churches (i.e. Baptist, Presbyterians, and Congregationalists)[6] in the New World and among the Anglican churches in England; independent preachers like Jonathan Edwards held revival meetings in Massachusetts and the other colonies, which spread to England as John Wesley and George Whitefield were influenced by the revivals in the colonies.[7] This sudden revitalization and renewal of faith greatly affected the church and society in the New World and England such that the phenomena were referred to as the "awakenings" or revivals.

Personal Repentance

Prior to these revivalist movements, there was an overall spiritual "lethargy" among the American colonies and England. For example, during the eighteenth century, "alcoholism was at an all-time high, capital punishment was used routinely for trivial crimes, slavery was practiced throughout the

---

William Carey International University Press, 2009), 177–186; Mark A. Noll, "Pietism," in *Evangelical Dictionary of Theology*, 2nd ed., Baker Reference Library, ed. Walter A. Elwell (Grand Rapids: Baker, 2001), 955–956. While Pietism would have its influence in North American Protestantism; for the sake of brevity, this study would not elaborate on its growth and influence.

6. Even from the beginning, Protestantism in North America was divided among the varied denominations which were brought by the migrants from the Old World. Some followed state religions such as Anglicanism while others subscribed to separatist groups such as the Puritans and the Quakers. Each church/denomination had its own doctrine, church life, and government (Mead and Hill, *Handbook of Denominations*, 254).

7. In fact, it was the First Great Awakenings in the American colonies that motivated and inspired John Wesley to take upon the task of preaching the gospel in England after reading Jonathan Edwards' *A Faithful Narrative of the Surprising Work of God in the Conversion of Many Hundred Souls in Northampton* published in 1737. It was this essay and other reports of revivals in the American colonies (as early as 1725), which helped stir revivals in in England. One of those who personally experienced the revivalist movement in the colonies, George Whitefield, was "considered the greatest English-speaking preacher of his day" and was reported to have "preached out of doors to crowds as large as thirty thousand" (Pierson, *Dynamics of Christian Mission*, 214). He had crossed the Atlantic to make at least "seven visits between 1738 and 1769" where he experienced great success in seeing many turn from a life of immorality back to God (Cairns, *Christianity Through the Centuries*, 368). In 1739, Whitefield and Wesley began their revival movement in England, starting among the coal miners of Bristol. Thus, "the Great Awakening in New England had a direct influence upon the Wesleyan revival in the mother country" (Cairns, *Christianity Through the Centuries*, 336).

British Empire, [and] the churches were out of touch."[8] However, in the midst of this spiritual lethargy, the revivalist movement or the "awakenings" began to influence society, spurring spiritual growth and personal devotion among the populace.

Growth in Numbers

From having few attendees, these New England churches became swamped with new committed members as whole communities turned to God. All the churches experienced growth in the number of new congregations formed. This led to the need to recruit and train more pastors and spiritual leaders. Overall, there was an increase in the number of worshippers in the different churches. Cairns gives this example,

> Between thirty and forty thousand people and 150 new churches were added to those in New England alone out of a population of three hundred thousand. Thousands more came into the churches in the southern and middle colonies. A higher moral tone was noticed in the homes, work, and amusements of the people.[9]

Itinerant Evangelists

Another feature of this period was the ministry of itinerant and lay preachers who went from town to town, colony to colony to preach the gospel with those who were willing to listen. While Wesley, Whitefield, and Edwards were ordained ministers, the laity became involved as there were those who simply took up the task of preaching the gospel and traveled on horseback, gathering people in churches, tents, and even in open fields. While there were some rejections, the majority of the responses to their efforts were positive. As the momentum grew, the number of preachers and their audiences grew; at times, they would gather in open fields when the local churches were either unable or unwilling to accommodate them.[10] In fact, during the

---

8. "Patterns of Spiritual Renewal," *Christian History and Biography* 23 (July 1989), from *Christian History: The Entire Collection of "Christian History and Biography" Magazine*, CD-ROM (Carol Stream, IL: Christianity Today International, n.d.).

9. Cairns, *Christianity Through the Centuries*, 368.

10. For a brief list of evangelists that were involved in the First Great Awakening, see "Jonathan Edwards: A Gallery of Friends, Foes and Followers," *Christian History and Biography*

First Great Awakening (1730–1740), the revivals were spreading so quickly among the different territories that it became somewhat ecumenical since it did not distinguish between one church over another.

Growth in Missions

As the burden to bring the gospel to the "lost" became a topic among these churches, individuals began volunteering to serve as missionaries to reach the West and the Native American Indian tribes.[11] In fact, a strategy was developed by these churches to reach the different Native American tribes through the American Indian converts who were trained in seminaries that enabled them to reach out to their fellow tribesmen. For example, Rev Eleazer Wheelock established the Moor's School in 1754 with the specific task of recruiting and training Native Americans to become evangelists and ministers, and "the school was moved to Hanover, New Hampshire in 1769 and renamed Dartmouth College."[12] This passion for evangelism and missions was common among those who were involved in these revivals.

By the Second Great Awakening (1795–1830), calls for foreign missions began as students responded to the call of bringing the gospel to the nations. In 1806, a group of college students held regular prayer meetings where they beseeched God for a revival among the colleges. During one stormy day, Samuel Mills and several students continued their prayer meeting inside a haystack which resulted in their commitment to serve God as missionaries to foreign nations. In time, the American Board of Commissioners for Foreign Missions (ABCFM) was formed in 1810 which started the cross-cultural missionary effort of America.[13]

Social Reformations

The effects of the awakening were not limited to spiritual or religious activities. As individuals and whole communities became spiritually renewed,

---

8 (October 1985) from, *Christian History: The Entire Collection*.

11. These spiritual movements spread from New England in the east and "also grew the later revivalism of the American frontier" (Millard J. Erickson, *The Evangelical Left: Encountering Postconservative Evangelical Theology* [Grand Rapids: Baker Books, 1997], 17).

12. "In the Wake of the Great Awakening," *Christian History and Biography* 23 (July 1989) from, *Christian History: The Entire Collection*.

13. Pierson, *Dynamics of Christian Mission*, 215–216.

several calls and efforts were made to see their faith manifested in the reformation of their communities. Thus, North America saw major social developments as those who were "awakened" became active in helping address social issues and enacting social reforms, which coincided with America's efforts to establish itself as a modern nation through the creation of key institutions.[14] A few examples are listed below.

The Establishment of Educational Institutions

The surge to build educational institutions in North America coincided with the resulting effects of the revivalist movement.[15] In fact, several universities (e.g. the University of Pennsylvania – 1740, the Brown University – 1764, Rutgers University – 1766, and Princeton Theological Seminary – 1812) were founded not only to provide better secular education to the American people but to also help fill the demand for local ministers and missionaries to lead the newly established churches in the country and help with its expansion.[16] Since the majority of the academe were originally from the clergy, most of these universities and colleges were established by Christian faculty and administrators who held to the ideals and theology of the "Great Awakenings."[17] These institutions provided support in helping spread and further Christian values and education within the American society as they produced the theological educators and leaders of the evangelical movement, even providing some of the political leaders of the fledgling United States of America. For example, Princeton Theological Seminary (founded in 1812) was initially led by strong Christian leaders who helped produce

---

14. These spiritual renewal movements had a strong impact on American society resulting in succeeding movements such as "the temperance crusade where, church leaders . . . provided the initial impulse . . . nearly all the campaigns were pervaded by appeals to 'Christian principles'" (Sydney E. Ahlstrom, *A Religious History of the American People* [New Haven; London: Yale University Press, 1972], 640).

15. In fact, six out of the nine colonial colonial colleges were founded during the Great Awakening (1730–1770). These are, College of New Jersey – 1746, King's College – 1754, College of Philadelphia – 1755, College of Rhode Island – 1764, Queen's College – 1766, and Dartmouth College – 1769 ("Spiritual Awakenings in North America: Did You Know?," *Christian History and Biography* 23 [July 1989] from, *Christian History: The Entire Collection*).

16. Some of these universities and colleges were initially centers for Christian values and knowledge during this period. As Ahsltrom observes, "in view of the country's dominant Protestant ethos, and the fact that the clergy was still the leading intellectual class, these universities were rarely secular in spirit" (Ahlstrom, *Religious History*, 641).

17. Erickson, *Evangelical Left*, 17.

some of the leading Presbyterian theologians, pastors, and missionaries in North America for almost a century.[18]

The Abolitionist Movement

Although many Westerners in the 1700s disagreed and abhorred the practice of slavery, the main difficulty and hindrance in ending this inhuman trade came "from merchants whose income was threatened . . . [and who had used] political obstacles" to prevent its abolition.[19] In the eighteenth century, the effects of revivalism in England moved several individuals to take up the cause of the abolitionist movement. Former slave-owner John Newton, together with William Wilberforce and his evangelical party were instrumental in the campaign against slavery in the United Kingdom.[20] Despite several setbacks, slavery was finally abolished with the passing of the Slave Trade Act of 1807. In the following year, the United States passed its own law banning the slave trade. While evangelicals cannot solely claim this achievement, the fact was that the abolitionist movement and Christianity "had struck a close and powerful alliance that would soon wield great political influence" in America's future.[21]

---

18. Mark A. Noll, "Princeton Theology, Old," in *Evangelical Dictionary of Theology*, 2nd ed., Baker Reference Library, ed. Walter A. Elwell (Grand Rapids: Baker, 2001), 955–956. This is exemplified by Princeton Seminary's first professor; Archibald Alexander is described as "a person of piety and Christian warmth . . . his main emphases in theology were the reliability of Scripture and the ability of human reason to understand Christian truth" (Noll, "Princeton Theology," 955). Ahlstrom describes this as the "great age of the church college" where graduates from Princeton and Yale helped spread the Christian values to the rest of America as they founded other educational institutions such as "academies, colleges, seminaries, and universities, and staffing their faculties" (Ahlstrom, *Religious History*, 641).

19. David Bebbington, "Abolition: William Wilberforce," in *More Than Conquerors: Portraits of Believers from All Walks of Life*, ed. John Woodbridge, (Quezon City, Philippines: Pick Source, 2003), 261.

20. John Newton was an English sailor who was involved in the slave trade, a common practice and an integral part of trade by most European nations at that time. After having a life-changing experience during a severe storm that almost sank his vessel, he returned to England a changed man. He avoided profanity, gambling, and drunkenness. He eventually gave up the slave trade and retired to become an Anglican priest and is known for his composition of *Amazing Grace*. He became involved with the revival meetings in London "associated with George Whitefield and the Wesleys" (D. B. Hindmarsh, "Newton, John," in *Biographical Dictionary of Evangelicals*, ed. Timothy Larsen [Downers Grove, IL: InterVarsity Press, 2003], 477).

21. Ahlstrom, *Religious History*, 653.

Establishment of Social Institutions

Several institutions were also formed during this period which was indirectly due to the influence of evangelicalism. In the area of literacy and education, the growing desire for understanding the teachings of the Bible and Christianity added to the impetus of these sectors. The American Bible Society was established in 1816, harnessing the power of the printing press which not only spread God's word but also addressed the problem of illiteracy.[22] Another institution that helped the growth of education was the American Sunday School Union which was founded in 1817. The American Temperance Society was formed in 1826 to address the growing addiction to alcoholic beverages which was blamed as the cause of criminality and other social ills. Other humanitarian institutions (e.g. hospitals and more humane prisons) and human rights crusades (i.e. for women's rights) were established.[23]

Therefore, the 1700s and the 1800s mark the height of evangelicalism's influence in society as churches became involved in both the proclamation of the gospel and the alleviation of negative social conditions. The need to address societal ills was not initially seen as a separate task but as "part of a rich Judeo-Christian heritage of response to human need, with roots in the OT and NT, and with antecedents in every era of church history."[24] Personal repentance and social reformation were not seen as an "either-or" situation but as mutually supportive.

Modernist-Fundamentalist Controversy (1800s–1920s)

As evangelicalism was experiencing these great strides; gradual changes within the American culture and theological inclinations began to affect the spiritual condition and outlook of these mainline Protestant churches,

---

22. Richard V. Pierard and Walter A. Elwell, "Evangelicalism," in *Evangelical Dictionary of Theology*, 2nd ed., Baker Reference Library, ed. Walter A. Elwell (Grand Rapids: Baker, 2001), 407.

23. See Ahlstrom, *Religious History*, 635–647.

24. Norris A. Magnuson, "Social Gospel," in *Evangelical Dictionary of Theology*, 2nd ed., Baker Reference Library, ed. Walter A. Elwell (Grand Rapids: Baker, 2001), 1118.

eventually threatening and weakening the unity and cooperative spirit among these churches.²⁵

The Rise of the Modernist Movement (Mid-1800s)

Originally, the churches in North America were from diverse religious backgrounds depending on the colonists that had migrated to the New World; for example, "Baltimore, Maryland, was predominantly Roman Catholic; Pennsylvania was predominantly Quaker, Lutheran, and Presbyterian; New Jersey was predominantly Presbyterian and Dutch Reformed."²⁶ Despite these differences, these churches held to conservative values and theology which were relatively free from the influence of the Enlightenment due to the geographical isolation of North America from Europe and due to the influence of the Awakenings during its early years as a nation.²⁷ As Shelley describes these churches,

> Prior to 1880 most New England ministers held to the sovereignty of God; to the innate depravity of mankind (which they traced to the sin of the first man); to the atonement of Jesus Christ, the ground of man's forgiveness of sin; to the Holy Spirit as essential to conversion; and to the eternal separation of the saved and lost in heaven or hell.²⁸

However, American Protestantism began to change as the influence of the Enlightenment "entered" the churches and the seminaries in America. Among its sources was the influx of European immigrants who brought their own religious and philosophical traditions to America.²⁹ Another source for these "innovations" in theology was the influence of seminary professors and theologians who had been exposed to the modernist/liberal theology

---

25. Gary B. McGee, "Evangelical Movement," in *Evangelical Dictionary of World Missions,* Baker Reference Library, ed. A. Scott Moreau (Grand Rapids: Baker, 2000), 338.

26. Pierson, *Dynamics of Christian Mission,* 209.

27. While the Enlightenment would eventually influence both Roman Catholicism and Protestantism, the Great Awakenings that took take place in England and America preserved the conservatism of these Protestant churches for the moment and kept the "evangelical" faith alive (Pierard and Elwell, "Evangelicalism," 407).

28. Shelley, *Church History,* 403.

29. Cairns, *Christianity Through the Centuries,* 379–380. For further details, see Ahlstrom, *Religious History,* 749–762.

when they traveled to Europe to complete their postgraduate studies. These "new" and "innovative" philosophical and theological concepts that gained popularity in America in the late nineteenth century were developed through the interaction between the Enlightenment and Protestant theology in Western Europe, especially in Germany where historic-literary criticism or higher criticism began to question the former affirmations of the Christian faith. The modernist or liberal theology which was the result of the amalgamation was initially referred to as the "New Theology" while their former teachings were called "Old Theology."[30]

The New Theology came as a result of the influence of German philosophers and theologians among the churches in North America where reason and science interacted with Christian traditions and theology.[31] In this new theological method, "the Enlightenment championed the scientific method, where everything—including the Bible—was subject to rational, empirical analysis."[32] Several emphases caused alarm among the conservatives as follows.

The Nature of God

God is more immanent than transcendent. The Old Theology affirmed God's distinction from the cosmos (i.e. the sovereignty of God, the omnipotence of God, etc.) where he is beyond the laws of nature and that "miracles" are supernatural events where God intervenes or suspends these natural laws. In contrast, the New Theology gives more weight to the immanence of God where he is no different from his creation so that he operates within the

---

30. Shelley, *Church History*, 403.

31. This resulted in a new approach in theological formulation which assumes the ascendancy of science and rationality. For example, Cairns observes, "Kant held to two levels of truth and confined the Bible to phenomenal history as the subjective record of man's consciousness of God. The Bible was to be studied as a human book by scientific methods rather than as a revelation from God" (Cairns, *Christianity Through the Centuries*, 460). For the modernist Christian, it was necessary for Christianity to accommodate the advances gained by the Enlightenment. It is assumed that the problem within the church and its leadership was its continued unwillingness to open its eyes to the truths of science and rational thought. "Bemoaning the decline of evangelicalism in the wider church, liberal evangelicals have seen a major reason as being a lack of sensitivity to the modern age and its thought forms" (Robert K. Johnston, "Liberal Evangelicalism," in *Evangelical Dictionary of Theology*, 2nd ed., Baker Reference Library, ed. Walter A. Elwell [Grand Rapids: Baker, 2001], 682).

32. Harold Carl, "User-Friendly Faith," in *Christian History and Biography* 55 (July 1997) from, *Christian History: The Entire Collection*.

boundaries of nature and science. Within this worldview, the natural world is perceived as a perfect "closed system" created by God/Creator which is completely controlled by the laws of nature often depicted as "a machine or mechanism . . . operated by inflexible natural laws."[33] Thus, adherents of the New Theology were skeptical of the supernatural elements of Christianity; biblical accounts of miracles and supernatural events were often questioned and relegated to the status of a myth.[34] As a result, churches and other ecclesiastical bodies were being influenced by these new trends which affected their praxis.[35]

The Authority of the Scriptures

The Bible was no longer assumed to be of divine origin and authorship, but simply a product of human effort. The authority and origin of Scriptures came under the scrutiny of reason and science which paved the way for the discipline of biblical criticism. Modernist/liberal theologians began to question the Bible's ability to present scientific and historical facts.[36] For example, the biblical account of Moses's efforts to free the Israelites was seen as a call

---

33. Cairns, *Christianity Through the Centuries*, 377. This concept was adopted by the modernist who saw the world as a "closed system" that can't be opened or "reordered" by anyone even a "transcendent being" (James W. Sire, *The Universe Next Door: A Basic Worldview Catalog*, 5th ed. [Downers Grove, IL: InterVarsity Press, 2009], 70).

34. By the early 1900s, the biblical accounts such as the creation narrative, Noah's flood, the parting of the Red Sea, Jesus walking on water, and other such miraculous events recorded in the Scriptures were being doubted as matter-of-fact. Some of the modernist/liberal theologians of this period held a "bias" which was characterized by a "growing rejection of the miraculous, not only by scientists, but even among theologians" (George M. Marsden, *Fundamentalism and American Culture: The Shaping of Twentieth-Century Evangelicalism, 1870-1925* [New York: Oxford University Press, 1982], 116).

35. For more details on the liberal view on God's immanence, see Millard J. Erickson, *Christian Theology*, unabridged, 1-vol. ed. (Manila, Philippines: Christian Growth Ministries, 1995), 304–311.

36. For example, Friedrich Schleiermacher, German theologian and "recognized founder of modern Protestant theology" questioned the supernatural origin of the Bible ("Schleiermacher, Friedrich [Ernest Daniel]," in *The New Encyclopaedia Britannica: Micropaedia Ready Reference*, 15th ed., vol. 10 [Chicago: Encyclopaedia Britannica, 1994], 522). He denied that the Bible is the basis of faith "since faith is needed to read it" and denied its divine inspiration by affirming that the "Scriptures inspiration [came] from the 'spirit of the community'" (Geoffrey W. Bromiley, *Historical Theology: An Introduction* [Grand Rapids: Eerdmans, 1978], 380). For Schleiermacher, Christianity is neither unique nor superior from the other religions since it is another expression of the "inner religion" that seeks to reach the "Highest Being" (Bromiley, *Historical Theology*, 366). In the end, he encouraged his "readers to let whatever type of religion develops in them flourish" (Bromiley, *Historical Theology*, 367).

for the liberation of the oppressed, thus the supernatural elements no longer mattered since the important part was the human author's task of inspiring his readers. The Christian Bible was now viewed on the same level as any other ancient literature.[37] As such, it was to be critically studied, its assertions scrutinized and "interpreted in the same manner as other important historical documents."[38]

As the narratives found within the biblical account were no longer perceived as actual/historical events, doubts emerged whether the Bible could be a reliable source of propositional truths; instead the Bible's stories were to be simply taken as a source of inspiration for its readers. For example, those who struggled with oppression and injustice could see the actions of Moses in Exodus as a source of spiritual inspiration for liberation theology.

Thus, the basis for truth had shifted from the teachings of the church and the Scriptures to the authority of human reason and science. In time, the act of knowing God became subjective. The possibility of fully knowing God was further questioned. For example, Immanuel Kant's epistemology excluded God from the reach of man. While Kant did not desire to remove God from the equation, "his closing of man to the knowledge of God hypnotized his contemporaries into acceptance not only of God's incompetence in communication but also of his virtual non-existence."[39]

Future Things
According to the modernists, it is humanity's destiny to someday achieve perfection and bliss. No longer enslaved by superstitious beliefs of the past, humanity is free to achieve its highest potential. The optimism brought by the promise of the Enlightenment and later coupled with the adaptation of Darwin's Theory of Evolution created a sense of hope that humanity was

---

37. For example, Albrecht Ritschl, a nineteenth-century German theologian, "rejected everything supernatural about Christianity and proposed that the Christian faith be based solely on its historic foundations. Traditional creeds were distrusted. Instead of Christianity shaping culture, culture was to reshape Christianity" (Robert J. Choun, "Liberalism," in *Evangelical Dictionary of Christian Education*, Baker Reference Library, ed. Michael J. Anthony [Grand Rapids: Baker Academic, 2001], 428).

38. Ahlstrom, *Religious History*, 772.

39. Bromiley, *Historical Theology*, 362.

on the verge of perfection.[40] The discoveries of science, the development of philosophy, and other such achievements promised a bright future for humanity. The problems of society were caused by human inadequacy and failure, not by a personal rebellion against a holy God or by the afflictions caused by spiritual beings (i.e. demons or angels).

Hence, there were those who began to advocate that the "solutions" to these man-made societal problems would be provided by human knowledge and science; not by superstition or religion which was judged as obsolete and inadequate. Modernist theologians saw humanity as evolving, "God wasn't saving a sinful humanity; he was perfecting an incomplete and immature humanity."[41] Thus, the concept of heaven was transformed from a future immaterial eschatological promise to a near-future utopian society where acts of oppression and social injustice will be overcome by humanity. In addition, other traditional doctrinal affirmations were questioned such as the deity of Christ, the reality of the resurrection, the substitutionary atonement, and other doctrines.

Therefore, adherents of the New Theology slowly shifted their emphasis and priorities to social reforms and lessened their efforts in the proclamation of the gospel. The alleviation of poverty, the emphasis on education, crusades against injustice, and other such campaigns were aimed at achieving a brighter future for humankind. Thus, the dual-approach to ministry gradually became two separate activities where social reforms took precedence over evangelism, the latter being perceived to be irrelevant and antiquated in a modern world.

---

40. This fusion between evolution and eschatology can be seen in the efforts of several theologians of the period. As Pannenberg explains this perspective, "salvation history was seen as a continuation of evolution, which reached its culmination in Jesus Christ as the new man" (Wolfhart Pannenberg, *Systematic Theology*, vol. 2, trans. Geoffrey W. Bromiley [Grand Rapids: Eerdmans; Edinburgh: T & T Clark, 1994], 120–121). A well known example of this is Teilhard de Chardin's view on eschatology where evolution and Christianity is harmonized in his concept of the "Christ-Omega." As Latourelle explains, "Teilhard speaks of critical points, stages, crises, critical thresholds, critical stages, mutations, emergences, new orders, and discontinuities . . . another decisive leap in which the vital drive reaches its completion: this point is Christ-Omega" (René Latourelle, "Teilhard De Chardin, Pierre," in *Dictionary of Fundamental Theology*, eds. René Latourelle and Rino Fisichella [Makati, Philippines: St. Pauls, 1994], 1028).

41. Carl, "User-Friendly Faith," *Christian History: The Entire Collection*.

The Rise of the Fundamentalist Movement (Late 1800s)

As the popularity of the modernist movement and its New Theology spread across North America, its strength and influence became stronger and more pronounced as churches and seminaries held to modernists/liberal views and theology. Cairns describes the influence of this theological development in this way, "According to these men, Christ was a man who died a martyr's death, and one need only follow His example to be saved. Ministers who were trained in German philosophy, evolution, and biblical criticism introduced these ideas to the laity in the pew. By 1880 it was clear that theological liberalism was opposed to Reformation orthodoxy."[42] The New Theology began to reshape the theology and praxis of the Baptists, Presbyterians, Congregationalists, and other mainline Protestant denominations in the United States, which unsettled many of the conservatives within these churches who disagreed with the modernist movement. They were further alarmed when many of their conservative views were challenged and soon became unpopular. As Ahlstrom observes, the late nineteenth century became "a confrontation between traditional orthodoxies and the new grounds for religious skepticism."[43]

In the midst of these growing ecclesiastical and theological tensions, the summer Bible institutes movement became popular among the conservatives. As these conservative Christians began losing influence and authority, pre-millennialism became popular as many interpreted the events within the churches and the seminaries as eschatological signs; many believed "that Christ's return was imminent and society would inevitably get worse."[44] Thus, summer Bible institutes and conferences became a popular venue to hold discussions on eschatology and pre-millennialism. One of its initiators was Dwight L. Moody, considered the most influential evangelist of the 1800s.[45] Through his initiative and contacts, he was able to bring speakers

---

42. Cairns, *Christianity Through the Centuries*, 479.
43. Ahlstrom, *Religious History*, 783.
44. Shelley, *Church History*, 432.
45. For more details, see James F. Findlay, *Dwight L. Moody, American Evangelist: 1837-99* (Chicago: University of Chicago Press, 1969), David Maas, "The Life and Times of D. L. Moody," in *Christian History and Biography* 25 (January 1990) from, *Christian History: The*

to Northfield, Massachusetts from 1880 to 1899 for "summer conference sessions that attracted men of all persuasions and changed the character of American Protestantism."[46] Being encouraged by Moody's summer Bible conferences, Presbyterian minister James H. Brooks started his own annual Bible conference in July 1876 at Swampscott, Massachusetts, which became known as the Niagara Bible Conference in 1890.[47]

While these annual camps/conferences were originally intended to promote and discuss pre-millennialism, it soon became apparent that these conferences served as a venue and "refuge" for conservative Christians from across denominational lines. The growing modernist influence and religious trends in North America were interpreted as a fulfillment of the apostasy that was connected with the "last days." As Ahlstrom points out,

> Animating this new impulse was a two-fold conviction that the whole Christian world, including the United States and Canada, was falling into apostasy and heresy so deeply and decisively that it could only mean the approach of the Last Days; and that, therefore, nothing was more directly needed than preaching of the hard facts drawn from God's Word. . . . They searched out God's whole "pattern for the ages," and gradually, a distinct system of dispensational premillennialism unified this intense "bible study" movement and informed its conferences.[48]

Responding to the threat of apostasy, delegates from the Niagara Conference in 1895 drew up a list of basic beliefs which they believed were the core doctrinal statements that a genuine Christian should affirm and defend. The list which eventually became fourteen statements of faith was initially known as the "Five Fundamentals of Niagara" which addressed "the inspiration of the Bible, the depravity of man, redemption through Christ's blood,

---

Entire Collection; Paul Moody, *My Father: An Intimate Portrait of Dwight L. Moody* (Boston: Little, Brown & Co., 1938); John C. Pollock, *Moody: A Biographical Portrait of the Pacesetter in Modern Mass Evangelism* (New York: Macmillan, 1963).

46. Ernest R. Sandeen, *The Roots of Fundamentalism: British and American Millenarianism, 1800-1930* (Grand Rapids: Baker Books, 1970), 172.

47. George W. Dollar, *A History of Fundamentalism in America* (Greenville, SC: Bob Jones University Press, 1973), 28.

48. Ahlstrom, *Religious History*, 808.

the true church made up of all believers, and the coming of the Lord to set up His reign."[49]

In time, the "list" became a demarcation line for establishing fellowship by these conservatives who either "broke away" or "rejected" from their midst those who could not agree with these statements of faith; reckoning them as apostates or even as unbelievers.[50] Thus, the title "fundamental" and "fundamentalists" became the moniker of those who affirmed and were committed to re-establish the Old Theology in North America. As the modernist/liberal Christians emphasized the "social gospel," these fundamentalist asserted that their message was the "pure gospel."

Thus, what had simply begun as a doctrinal affirmations to determine the basis for fellowship soon became the "battle-lines" by which the modernists/liberals and the fundamentalists divided the churches, missionary boards, and seminaries. "Skirmishes" erupted as the fundamentalists sought to preserve and/or regain these Christian institutions from the modernists/liberals. As Erickson describes the conflict,

> Gradually the nature of fundamentalism began to change. As liberalism became more vocal and influential in the various denominations, emphasis switched from affirmation of and argumentation for fundamental doctrines to criticism and rebuttal of the teachings of more liberal theologians. Fundamentalists sought to distinguish their own views from those of the liberals.[51]

The Gap Widens Between the Factions (1900–1920)

As churches and Christian institutions sided with either the modernist/liberals or conservative/fundamentalists, developments within Protestantism in North America further exacerbated the tensions and widened the gap between the two camps. The following are some of these events.

---

49. Dollar, *History of Fundamentalism*, 72.

50. They saw that this was the current application of the biblical admonition, "do not be yoked [or bound] together with unbelievers" in 2 Cor 6:14.

51. Erickson, *Evangelical Left*, 19.

The Federal Council of Churches (1908)

Initially conceptualized as a means to foster collaboration among the divided churches, the Interchurch Conference of Federation was held in New York in November 1905, with thirty churches exploring the possibility of forming a federation that would "promote the spirit of fellowship, service, and cooperation."[52] Thus, in December 1908 the Federal Council of the Churches of Christ in America (renamed Federal Council of Churches or FCC) was formed with the following objectives:

> 1. To express the fellowship and catholic unity of the Christian Church.
>
> 2. To bring the Christian bodies of America into united service for Christ and the world.
>
> 3. To encourage devotional fellowship and mutual counsel concerning the spiritual life and religious activities of the churches.
>
> 4. To secure a larger combined influence for the churches of Christ in all matters affecting the moral and social condition of the people, so as to promote the application of the law of Christ in every relation of human life.
>
> 5. To assist in the organization of local branches of the Federal Council to promote its aims in their communities.[53]

While the FCC was not originally established as a modernist federation, the fundamentalists perceived it as such when the liberals supported its formation and especially "in 1912 when liberals set up a commission on evangelism in the Federal Council."[54] While the liberal movement benefited from the popularity and credibility gained by the FCC, the fundamentalists chose to separate from the Council.

---

52. "Federal Council of the Churches of Christ in America Record, 1894-1952," accessed 25 June 2013, http://www.history.pcusa.org/collections/findingaids/fa.cfm?record_id=NCC18.

53. "Federal Council of the Churches of Christ in America Record."

54. Cairns, *Christianity Through the Centuries*, 480.

World Missionary Conference in Edinburgh (1910)

Although unrelated to the controversy being argued among the modernists and the fundamentalists, a growing concern on the state of the missionary endeavor prompted the convening of several international conferences which addressed the issues and needs for their efforts. The first international conference was held in 1860 at Liverpool which was followed by several more conferences. This led to the 1910 World Missionary Conference in Edinburgh, Scotland which is considered the beginning of Protestant ecumenism where the different churches and mission organizations involved in missions pledged cooperation and unity among themselves.[55]

As the Protestant missionary movement experienced growth and expansion with acquisition of new colonies (e.g. Cuba, Philippines, etc.) and further expansion of older missionary territories (i.e. China, Africa, South America, etc.), these Western missionaries in the field saw the problems and difficulties caused by the growing schisms within American Protestantism.[56] The need for a consolidated effort, a unified message, and inter-agency cooperation brought about several international and inter-denominational conferences held in London (1878 and 1888) and in New York (1900). The concept of cooperative efforts was nothing new to the American missionary effort. Comity agreements existed among different countries, such as the Philippines, Korea, etc. However, the conference aimed at taking the next step towards organizational mergers and the formation of ecumenical bodies.

The 1910 World Missionary Conference, aimed at discussing the future direction of missions and the evangelization of the world, was led by John R. Mott.[57] During the conference, delegates were confronted by the need to

---

55. It must be noted that the 1910 World Missionary Conference was not supporting either the liberal or fundamentalist cause. The modernist-fundamentalist controversy was still in its early stages and only a few denominations and missionary organizations were affected by this issue at this point in time. It was in the post-World War I era that the controversy would become a major issue and source of conflict among Protestant churches and mission agencies.

56. According to Erickson, "missionaries were the first to sense that the divisions among the churches constituted an obstacle to the work of evangelization" (Erickson, *Christian Theology*, 1138).

57. John R. Mott was a veteran missionary who was among the "Mount Hermon Hundred" and the chairman of the Student Volunteer Movement for Foreign Missions. For more details, see Brian Stanley, "Mott, John Raleigh," *Biographical Dictionary of Evangelicals*, ed. Timothy Larsen (Downers Grove, IL: InterVarsity Press, 2003); Howard C. Hopkins, *John R. Mott: A Biography* (Grand Rapids: Eerdmans, 1979), Robert C. Mackie, *Layman*

set aside their differences for the furtherance of the work; thus giving birth to the modern ecumenical movement. For example, the Chinese delegate Cheng Ching Yi presented the plans of the Christian Federation of China to form a united inter-denominational Christian Church in their mission field.[58]

While the implementation of the Edinburgh Conference was put on hold during World War I, ways and means to foster cooperation and ecumenism among these churches were further discussed.[59] And after the conflict, several conferences – the Faith and Order Conference in Switzerland (1927) and the Life and Work Conference in Oxford (1937) – were held to further their efforts on cooperation and unity.

While seen as a triumph in church cooperation by many, there were those who were cautious and/or uncomfortable with some of the resolutions of the Edinburgh Conference of 1910.[60] Despite the varied reactions to these developments, the issue of ecumenism and cooperative efforts was now a major issue among the different Protestant churches and missionary groups.

Fundamentalist Books and Publications (1910–1915)

On the fundamentalist's side, their response to the growing influence of liberalism in North America was to devote their efforts to correcting the New Theology through the publication and distribution of Fundamentalist books and materials. Reuben A. Torrey and Amzi C. Dixon were able to solicit the financial support from two wealthy oil men, Lyman and Milton Stewart, to finance the publication of a twelve-volume set entitled *The Fundamentals* which featured articles aimed to promote their conservative

---

Extraordinary: John R. Mott 1865-1965 (New York: Association Press, 1965), Richard Pierard, "Evangelizing the World in a Generation: John Mott," in *More Than Conquerors: Portraits of Believers From All Walks of Life*, ed. John Woodbridge (Quezon City, Philippines: Picksource, 2003), 290–294.

58. Virtual Museum of Protestantism, "The 1910 World Missionary Conference , Which was Held in Edinburgh," accessed 5 July 2018, https://www.museeprotestant.org/en/notice/la-conference-missionnaire-mondiale-edimbourg-1910/.

59. For details see Erickson, *Christian Theology*, 1137–1142.

60. One example was the Conference's resolution "that Latin America was not to be considered as a mission field" a result of the insistence of the Anglican Church (J. Herbert Kane, *Understanding Christian Missions,* 4th ed. [Grand Rapids, Baker, 1986], 230). This attitude of the Anglican church towards the Roman Catholics is consistent with their view that the Roman Catholic Church is a sister communion and that efforts to evangelize their members is a form of proselytizing.

theological convictions.⁶¹ The first volume was printed in 1910 and the last volume was published in 1915. Three hundred thousand sets were given "free of charge to seminary professors and students, pastors, and Y.M.C.A secretaries in the United States, Canada, and Great Britain."⁶² In addition, other books (e.g. W. E. Blackstone's *Jesus Is Coming*) and magazines (e.g. *The Sunday School Times*, *Moody Monthly*, *Christian Standard*, etc.) were published to promote the fundamentals of the faith and win these Christian leaders back to their side.

Liberalism Gains Popularity (1920s–1940s)

By the early twentieth century, American Protestantism was being torn apart by the modernist-fundamentalist controversy which resulted in a dichotomy where social reforms became exclusive to the modernists and the ministry of proclamation became solely identified with the fundamentalists. As both camps held key positions among the denominations, seminaries, mission boards, and other organizations, the controversy affected these institutions and their efforts. While the theological conflict was suspended during World War I; by the end of the conflict, "Baptists, Presbyterians, Methodists, and the Disciples of Christ launched their own war of words over the values and dangers of liberal theology in the churches."⁶³

Despite their efforts, the fundamentalists continued to lose their "voice" in society and were soon disregarded by the public while the modernist/liberals gained popularity not only among the mainline Protestant churches but within American society. The following were some of the factors that helped bring about this situation.

The Growing Secularism of America

The post-World War I era brought about growth in the United States. As America experienced growth in business, finance, and technology, the standard of living grew so that luxury and leisure became the norm of every American home. It was also a period of urbanization where new cities grew

---

61. Cairns, *Christianity Through the Centuries*, 480–481.
62. Cairns, 481.
63. Shelley, *Church History*, 433.

and the slow-paced life of the past gave way to advancement in technology and media with the advent of the age of industrialization. Greatly promoted by the growing movie and radio industry, entertainment, sports, and other leisure events began to supersede Sunday worship and other religious activities.[64] This shift in religious and moral values affected the spirituality of the masses and church attendance diminished. The fundementalist's influence over their society's moral and intellectual values began to weaken. Thus, the 1920s was described as "a lamentable season of excess, ballyhoo, and moral degeneration" where the spirituality of the previous generation appeared to fade into the background.[65]

Public Support for the Liberal Cause

In response to the shift towards the New Theology, the fundamentalists employed their connections to influence legislation in some of the conservative states to compel the youth to return to their spiritual roots and Christian truths. In 1925 the Florida legislature "required daily Bible readings in all public schools" while a ban on the teaching of evolution in public schools was enforced in Tennessee and Texas.[66]

Unfortunately, these actions did more harm than good to the fundamentalist cause as eventually public opinion turned against them. The liberals took advantage of this situation to further their cause as public sentiment slowly turned to their side. An example of this was the *State of Tennessee vs. John Thomas Scopes* trial or the "Scopes monkey trial" where a biology teacher was brought to court for teaching evolution in school.[67] The trial soon became an opportunity for the liberals to state their case to the American public. Although the fundamentalists won the case, their victory

---

64. Radio and Hollywood began to shape the hearts and minds of the American people. For details see Guy Gugliotta, "How Radio Changed Everything," *Discover*, 31 May 2007, accessed 3 July 2018, http://discovermagazine.com/2007/jun/tireless-wireless; Dan Fletcher, "A Brief History of NBC," *Time Entertainment*, 4 December 2009, accessed 3 July 2018, http://www.time.com/time/arts/article/0,8599,1945408, 00.html.

65. Ahlstrom, *Religious History*, 895.

66. Mark Galli, "Did You Know: The Frenzied Twenties," *Christian History and Biography* 55 (July 1997) from, *Christian History: The Entire Collection*.

67. For details see David Goetz, "The Monkey Trial," *Christian History and Biography* 55 (July 1997) from, *Christian History: The Entire Collection*.

was short-lived because they were portrayed by the press as "narrow-minded ignoramus . . . [and as] opponents of academic freedom."[68]

Christian Institutions Become Liberal

North American seminaries and Bible schools were also affected by the modernist/liberal values (e.g. Andover Seminary, Southern Baptist Theological Seminary, Princeton Theological Seminary, etc.). Those who went to Europe to complete their academic degrees were affected by the liberal theology. As Pierard observes, "by the 1890s most of the major theologians had studied in Germany, and many of them had come to accept the principles of higher criticism and Darwinism."[69] For example, J. Gresham Machen experienced "a crisis of faith" as he interacted with what he was learning from the center of Protestant theology in Germany.[70]

Liberal thought and perspectives began to influence these key institutions which had formerly been established bastions of conservative evangelicalism. For example, Princeton Theological Seminary was considered a premier Presbyterian seminary and a stronghold of fundamentalist teachings of conservatives such as B. B. Warfield and Charles Hodge. The controversy and resulting schism erupted when the conservatives suspected that the delay and rejection of a candidate to the Princeton's Board was due to his strong support of fundamentalist views. In response, board members, faculty, and students who considered themselves as fundamentalist withdrew from Princeton in 1929 and formed the Westminster Seminary in Philadelphia "to carry on the tradition of orthodox scholarship."[71]

Reconsolidation of Fundamentalism (1930–1940)

Although the fundamentalists lost their influence both within the mainline Protestant churches and in mainstream society from the turn of the century up to the 1920s, this trend would change as the effects of the Great

---

68. Erickson, *Evangelical Left*, 20.

69. Richard V. Pierard, "Liberalism, Theological," in *Evangelical Dictionary of Theology*, 2nd ed., Baker Reference Library, ed. Walter A. Elwell (Grand Rapids: Baker, 2001), 684.

70. Daryl Hart, "Christianity v. Liberalism: J. Gresham Machen," in *More Than Conquerors: Portraits of Believers from All Walks of Life*, ed. John Woodbridge (Quezon City, Philippines: Pick Source, 2003), 333.

71. Erickson, *Evangelical Left*, 21.

Depression spurred growth among the fundamentalist churches and ushered in a period of consolidation. The following were some of the factors that prepared the fundamentalists to respond effectively to the challenges of this period.

The Establishment of Reformed Institutions

The fundamentalists reacted to their diminishing hold and influence among the churches and Christian institutions in North America by abandoning these old ecclesiastical bodies and creating "reformed" substitutes as alternatives to those that had become modernist/liberal.

On the church/denominational level, the fundamentalists established "reformed" versions of these churches and began to compete with the older institutions. While there were churches that had separated from the modernist/liberal churches in the nineteenth century, several key churches were formed in the 1930s. These "alternatives" were created in response to the growing gap between the modernist/liberals and the fundamentalists. These fundamentalist leaders not only considered liberalism as another religion, they saw it as a contradiction to the historic Christian faith.[72] Thus, it was imperative for the fundamentalists to separate from the liberals. If they were unable to expel the liberals, the fundamentalists abandoned these mainline Protestant churches to form their own fundamentalist counterparts. For example, on 11 June 1936, the Presbyterian Church of America was established when John Gresham Machen and three hundred individuals broke fellowship from the Presbyterian Church (USA); Machen's new church was composed of ex-Princeton fundamentalists and "millenarian Christians."[73]

This resurgence also affected seminaries and missionary training institutions. Several fundamentalist seminaries were established during this period. The Dallas Theological Seminary was a fundamentalist seminary established by Lewis Sperry Chafer in 1924 which "became a center of dispensational pre-millennialism."[74] In 1927, Bob Jones University was established in

---

72. Machen believed that "liberalism was not a variety of Christianity but was an entirely different religion." (Hart, "Christianity v. Liberalism," 335).

73. Sandeen, *Roots of Fundamentalism*, 259. Eventually, the Presbyterian Church of America would divide into two churches; namely, the Bible Presbyterian Church and the Orthodox Presbyterian Church (Mead and Hill, *Handbook of Denominations*, 200–201).

74. Cairns, *Christianity Through the Centuries*, 481.

Florida (later transferred to Tennessee in 1933 and then to South Carolina in 1947). It was founded by the fundamentalist-evangelist Bob Jones Sr who felt a burden "to provide an alternative . . . a school to which 'no evolutionist need apply.'"[75] And as mentioned above, when Machen left Princeton in 1929, these dissenters formed the Westminster Seminary in Philadelphia.[76]

On the missionary organization level, several fundamentalist mission boards were formed as their mother churches experienced schisms as a result of the growing modernist/liberal-fundamentalist controversy. An example of this is the schism experienced by the American Baptist Foreign Mission Society (ABFMS) which produced several fundamentalist missionary organizations such as the Association of Baptists for the Evangelism in the Orient (ABEO).[77] After World War I, tensions grew within the American (Northern) Baptist Convention when several churches became uncomfortable with what they considered the "infiltration of liberal and modernist tendencies and teaching" within the Convention.[78] In the 1920s, these churches formed the "Fundamentalist Fellowship" within the American Baptist Churches which adhered to a more fundamentalist interpretation of the Bible and began operating their own missionary board and churches. The disagreement worsened with the decision of the ABFMS to implement an "inclusive" approach by sending missionaries without regard as to whether the missionary candidate was a liberal or fundamentalist.[79] The tensions worsened as differences of theology and praxis affected the missionary work when one group would set their extremist policies to the detriment of the other group within the same mission field. Due to irreconcilable differences, the fundamentalist groups pulled out of the ABFMS.

---

75. Barry Hankins, "Jones, Bob, Sr.," in *Biographical Dictionary of Evangelicals*, ed. Timothy Larsen (Downers Grove, IL: InterVarsity Press, 2003), 336.

76. Hart, "Christianity v. Liberalism," 335.

77. More will be mentioned about ABEO in the later chapters. Missionaries from the American (Northern) Baptist Convention (ABC) were the first Baptist missionaries in the Philippines that were sent through the American Baptist Foreign Missionary Society (ABFMS) in 1900 (Elaine J. Kennedy, *Baptist Centennial History of the Philippines* [Makati City: Church Strengthening Ministry, 2000], 24–25).

78. Mead and Hill, *Handbook of Denominations*, 45.

79. Mead, 45.

The Rise of Pentecostalism (1900–1930s)

In the midst of the modernist-fundamentalist controversy, another movement began in North America that emphasized a personal spiritual renewal which could be appropriated through the baptism of the Holy Spirit.[80] Although affirming the fundamentals, their main focus was on a life lived in the power of the Holy Spirit which manifests itself in the practice of grace gifts (e.g. speaking in tongues, healings, and etc.). As Mead describes,

> Ardently fundamentalist, its theology is Arminian; there is strong belief in the infallibility and inspiration of the Bible, the fall and redemption of the human race, baptism in the Holy Spirit, a life of holiness and separation from the world, divine healing, the second Advent of Jesus and his millennial reign, eternal punishment for the wicked, eternal bliss for believers.[81]

The earliest record of modern Pentecostalism in America was when the "Midwestern Methodist and other Christians associated with the Holiness movement" became fascinated with the possibility of "divine healing" and "speaking in tongues."[82] During this period, an eighteen-year-old Methodist named Charles F. Parham believed that God could give the gift of tongues to spirit-baptized believers for the purpose of evangelism.[83] As a result of this conviction, Parham established a Bible school in Topeka, Kansas in 1900. On 1 January 1901, Parham had reportedly prayed and laid his hands on his student Agnes Ozman who had requested that she be baptized by the

---

80. Wayne A. Grudem, *Systematic Theology: An Introduction to Biblical Doctrine* (Grand Rapids: Zondervan, 1994), 764–765.

81. Mead and Hill, *Handbook of Denominations*, 189.

82. Ted Olsen, "American Pentecost: The Story Behind the Azusa Street Revival, the Most Phenomenal Event of Twentieth-century Christianity," in *Christian History and Biography* 58 (April 1998) from, *Christian History: The Entire Collection*.

83. He believed that God could supernaturally enable spirit-baptized believers to speak a real foreign language, Xenolalia (i.e. foreign and unknown to the speaker but a real earthly language that the listener understands) so that these missionaries could rapidly evangelize the world and usher in the return of Christ (Mark Galli, "The Rise of Pentecostalism: Did You Know," in *Christian History and Biography* 58 (April 1998) from, *Christian History: The Entire Collection*).

Holy Spirit. This resulted in the manifestation of the *glossolalia* for her and those who were in attendance.[84]

In 1906, William J. Seymour, an African-American student of Parham, led a small congregation that began to manifest "speaking in tongues" with others being "slain under the power of God" or entranced in an old abandoned church in 312 Azusa Street in Los Angeles, California. As a result, the emerging Pentecostal movement was called the Azusa Street Revival. With the movement rapidly growing in numbers, its adherents saw the need to organize their churches into a council to avoid extremes and consolidate their efforts. Thus, in April 1914, three hundred delegates established the General Council of the Assemblies of God (AG) with the following objectives: "to promote unity and doctrinal stability, establish legal standing, coordinate the mission enterprise, and establish a ministerial training school."[85]

Aside from having similar doctrines, these Pentecostals were similar to the fundamentalists as they banned "traditional vices like alcohol, tobacco, and the movies, they have targeted chewing gum, short-sleeved dresses, soft drinks, and neckties."[86] In addition they were as committed to evangelism and missions as the fundamentalists. It is probably this passion for evangelism which explains the growth which both groups experienced during the Great Depression.[87] Thus, by the early 1920s, the AG established "missionary agencies" with the goal of spreading their Pentecostal teachings both at home and overseas.[88]

Another Pentecostal group that came out of the Azusa Street Revival was the International Church of the Foursquare Gospel (ICFG) in America which is distantly related to the AG since its founder was a former AG pastor. The ICFG was established as a result of the work of Aimee Semple McPherson; different from the contemporary "fire and brimstone" preachers of that day, McPherson's messages were filled with God's love. She would

---

84. For details see Apostolic Archives International, "Agnes Ozman - My Personal Testimony," Apostolic Faith April, 1951, accessed 6 July 2018, http://www.apostolicarchives.com/articles/article/8801925/173171.htm.

85. General Council of the Assemblies of God, "History," accessed 27 May 2010 https://ag.org/About/About-the-AG/History.

86. Galli, "The Rise of Pentecostalism," *Christian History: The Entire Collection*.

87. Ahlstrom, *Religious History*, 920.

88. Galli, "The Rise of Pentecostalism," *Christian History: The Entire Collection*.

often summarize her sermon into four major points, thus her messages became known as "The Foursquare Gospel" from which they derived their name. Mead explains that through "her great speaking ability and faith in prayer for the sick, Mrs. McPherson attracted thousands to her meetings."[89] Mrs McPherson was able to build the Angelus Temple in California in January 1923 and owned and operated a radio station which spread their message across America.[90]

Thus, Pentecostalism alongside fundamentalism became increasingly popular during the 1930s. Part of the growth could be attributed to the spirituality and religious experience that Pentecostalism offers (e.g. speaking in tongues, prophetic utterances, healing ministry, casting out of demons, and other miraculous signs). The crises and the upheavals of their times were seen as harbingers of the *eschaton* and the special manifestations of the Holy Spirit in the Pentecostal meetings validated their claims as the hope for those who are lost during these "dark times."[91]

The Surge in Proclamation Ministry

Frequently used by the revivalist preachers during the Awakenings, tent-meetings became a common sight as it was the method preferred by fundamentalist and Pentecostal preachers to spread the gospel message during the 1930s, especially during the Great Depression. As Americans were "brought to their knees" when they lost their homes and even their loved ones, these preachers redoubled their efforts to reclaim the "lost territories." Seeing the spiritual hunger of their audiences, they became passionate with

---

89. Mead and Hill, *Handbook of Denominations*, 111.

90. For details see Matthew Avery Sutton, *Aimee Semple McPherson and the Resurrection of Christian America* (Cambridge: Harvard University Press, 2009); Chas H. Barfoot, *Aimee Semple McPherson and the Making of Modern Pentecostalism, 1890-1926* (New York: Routledge, 2014); Daniel Mark Epstein, *Sister Aimee: The Life of Aimee Semple McPherson* (New York: Harcourt, 1994).

91. Many saw the events of their time as a sign of the End Times. For example, World War I or the Great War was seen as the fulfillment of the prophecy of wars and rumors of wars in Matthew 24:6. The growing spiritual coldness and secularism of American society was seen as the great apostasy promised in 2 Timothy 3:1–4. The rise of liberalism was also seen as examples of the false teachers that would increase as promised in 2 Peter 2:1–3. On the other hand, the practice of speaking in tongues and uttering prophecies by the Pentecostals was seen as the fulfillment of the prophecy in Joel 2:28–32.

their proclamation ministries, conducting "fiery" revival tent-meetings.[92] As Ahlstrom describes this period, "During the 1930s conservative revivalistic Christianity would flourish. The number of Bible institutes grew from 49 in 1930 to 144 in 1950; radio evangelists prospered (most sensationally, Charles E. Fuller's 'Old Fashioned Revival Hour' emanating from Los Angeles), and independent Fundamentalist congregations became increasingly numerous."[93]

Thus, although they continued to remain the minority compared to the mainline denominations, the fundamentalists and the Pentecostals experienced growth in numbers. However, one of the characteristics of these early fundamentalist and Pentecostal churches was their extremist and exclusivist nature which often resulted in further division as they separated from each other over finer details and doctrines. For example, due to their differences in theology and praxis, the fundamentalists and the Pentecostals were unable to form any cooperative efforts prior to the 1950s as they disagreed on the validity of the gifts of healing today.[94]

While these "fragmentations" and schisms weakened their influence in society; they did help in spreading their values and formed a subculture within the American society which continued to draw the "disconnected" and "dissatisfied" conservatives to their side.

World Council of Churches (WCC)

As the last decade before World War II drew to a close, the liberals were able to establish cooperative relationships with other countries; so that immediately after World War II, the World Council of Churches (WCC) was formed in 1948 in Amsterdam.

---

92. Both Charles E. Fuller and William Franklin "Billy" Graham experienced a spiritual conversion after hearing the gospel in a fundamentalist meeting during the early twentieth century.

93. Ahlstrom, *Religious History*, 913. As Ahlstrom observes, "among the Fundamentalist and in the Holiness and Pentecostal churches . . . a revival took place. . . . Between 1926 and 1936 for example, the Church of the Nazarene grew from 63,558 to 136,227 and the Assemblies of God from 47,950 to 148,043 . . . [while] large mainstream denominations were experiencing a drastic decline in congregational giving and were barely holding their own in membership" (Ahlstrom, *Religious History*, 920).

94. While healing ministries are quite common among Pentecostals, most Fundamentalist Baptists do not practice it. As Rev Nacita writes, "we believe that today no one possesses the gifts of healing and miracles as the apostles had in their time" (Ebenezer T. Nacita, *Celebrating God's Mercy and Grace Through the Years . . . and Beyond: Church Anniversary Program* [Quezon City, Philippines: n.p., 2003], 45).

There were at least three major developments that followed Edinburgh 1910 which led to the formation of the WCC. First was the formation of the International Missionary Council (IMC) in 1921 which aimed to unify all protestant missionary efforts. It was more of a coordinating body which held several meetings among missionary agencies; namely, Jerusalem in 1928 and Madras, India in 1938. The IMC steadily became ecumenical in its stance as it "would not deal with ecclesiastical or doctrinal questions . . . united in the belief that Christians had the duty to bear witness to the gospel of Jesus Christ among peoples of all nations."[95] The second major development towards ecumenism was the Life and Work Movement which was launched in Stockholm in 1925. It was in this movement that the focus began to shift towards social concern.[96] The third was the World Conference on Faith and Order held at Lausanne in 1927 and at Edinburgh in 1937. The focus was on theological unity; as Cairns states, "the idea of unity in diversity seems to have been uppermost in the minds of leaders as they discussed the common faith, the sacraments, and the nature of the church."[97] These three developments paved the way for greater openness and support in the ecumenical movement. By 1937, delegates from the Life and Work Movement and Faith and Order began calls for a unified body which would embody their ecumenical values. Due to the delay caused by World War II, their desire to form a unified body was only fulfilled in 1948 with the formation of the World Council of Churches at Amsterdam.

By 1961, the IMC merged with the WCC as its missionary arm. While some of WCC's members and leaders might have had inclinations towards liberalism as seen its gradual shift from evangelism towards social and political concern, it was not until the WCC conference at Uppsala in 1968 that this ecumenical body shifted its focus "exclusively on political and social concerns."[98] As an observer, Billy Graham gave his understanding to this shift in commitment, "the 1968 Fourth Assembly of the World Council of Churches . . . tended to redefine the good news of the Gospel in terms of restructuring society instead of calling individuals to repentance and faith

---

95. Pierard, "Evangelizing the World," 294.
96. Pierson, *Dynamics of Christian Mission*, 264.
97. Cairns, *Christianity Through the Centuries*, 474.
98. Pierson, *Dynamics of Christian Mission*, 265.

in Christ."⁹⁹ As a result, most fundamentalists rejected the WCC as a liberal council due to its ecumenical nature and its cooperation with churches and religious groups that were not in congruence with fundamentalist theology.

International Council of Christian Churches (ICCC), 1948

In response, the fundamentalists formed their own council – International Council of Christian Churches (ICCC) – as a counterpart to the WCC.¹⁰⁰ Eleven days before the WCC would convene its assembly in Amsterdam, 150 delegates from twenty-nine countries and thirty-nine churches formed the ICCC under the leadership Carl McIntire.¹⁰¹

While the fundamentalists were not opposed to the idea of mergers and ecumenical councils, they felt that the WCC was furthering the cause of the modernist-liberalists. They were convinced that the proper response was a "militant opposition to the World Council of Churches, to Communism, and to defections from orthodox Christianity."¹⁰² For these churches, they saw that the issue was the preservation of the purity of the gospel as seen in their congress' theme, "The Christ of the Scriptures." In his speech, McIntire states, "the ICCC became a fellowship of evangelical churches to promote a revival of Bible Christianity and to warn against the unbelief and its consequences inside the house of God. These questions concerned all Christian churches over the world."¹⁰³ In line with its purpose to counter the WCC, the ICCC helped established parallel councils, mission boards,

---

99. Billy Graham, *Just as I Am: The Autobiography of Billy Graham* (San Francisco: HarperCollins, 1997), 568.

100. For more details see ICCC.Org, "A Short History of FECCC," accessed 27 May 2013, http://www.iccc.org.sg/FECC.html.

101. Carl Curtis McIntire (1906–2002) was one of the students who joined John Gresham Machen when the fundamentalists abandoned Princeton to established Westminster Seminary. He is well known for his strong response to the growing liberalism. He played a critical role in the development of fundamentalism in the Philippines during the post-World War II era. He was eventually ousted from the Presbyterian Church for his part in "the Independent Board for Presbyterian Foreign Missions, which Machen had created as an alternative to the increasingly liberal Presbyterian Board of Foreign Missions" (David K. Larsen, "McIntire, Carl," in *Biographical Dictionary of Evangelicals*, ed. Timothy Larsen [Downers Grove, IL: InterVarsity Press, 2003], 394).

102. Biblicaltraining.org, "International Council of Christian Churches," accessed 6 July 2018, https://www.biblicaltraining.org/library/international-council-christian-churches.

103. Carl McIntire, "A Critique of the World Council of Churches by the International Council of Christian Churches," speech given in August 1948, *CarlMcIntire.org*, accessed 6 July 2018, http://www.carlmcintire.org/speeches-critique.php.

churches and periodicals. For example, in response to the establishment of the East Asia Christian Conference that was sponsored by the WCC, the ICCC established the Far Eastern Council of Christian Churches in the Philippines.[104]

The Rise of Evangelicalism (1940s–1950s)

During the mid-1940s, a new group of progressive fundamentalist leaders became dissatisfied with the *status quo ante* where the modernist/liberals had the political voice while the fundamentalists were ignored and were isolated from the rest of society. As a result, fundamentalist pastors like Rev Harold John Ockenga of the famous Park Street Church in Boston felt that their call was to maintain the fundamentals of the faith while being actively engaged in the propagation of the gospel and the transformation of society.[105] They believed that if they were to effect lasting change in their society, they must have a united "voice" that would be credible and would be heard by the rest of their countrymen. This new breed of fundamentalist leaders were committed to the restoration of the balance between proclamation and social engagement without sacrificing their fundamentalist dogmas.

Hearing about Rev Ockenga's vision, Rev J. Elwin Wright of the New England Fellowship (NEF) approached him with the idea of forming a small

---

104. Nacita, *Celebrating God's Mercy*, 13–14.

105. Harold John Ockenga (1905–1985) dedicated his life to Christ in an old-fashioned Methodist camp meeting at the age of eleven. At age seventeen, he rededicated his life and fully surrendered it to God. As Rosell describes the experience, "He received assurance of his own salvation. He experienced what Wesleyans call the 'second blessing'—an experience of sanctification. And he was called by God to be a preacher of the Word" (Garth M. Rosell, "America's Hour Has Struck," in *Christian History and Biography* 92 (September 2006) from, *Christian History: The Entire Collection*. His arrival in Princeton Theological Seminary coincided with the height of the conflict between the fundamentalists and the modernists. Even though he was elected student body president in his final year, he chose to transfer to the newly formed fundamentalist Westminster Theological Seminary where he graduated with honors in 1930. In 1936, Ockenga became the pastor of Park Street Church in Boston where he established a reputation for "his intellectual sermons, cultural sophistication, organizational genius and quick mind" for almost thirty years (A. Donald MacLeod, "Ockenga, Harold John," in *Biographical Dictionary of Evangelicals*, ed. Timothy Larsen [Downers Grove, IL: InterVarsity Press, 2003], 483). Aside from his role in establishing the National Association of Evangelicals, Ockenga was constantly involved in the growth of the evangelical cause throughout the rest of his life; having served in "an advisory role in the 1966 Berlin Conference on Evangelism and the 1974 Lausanne Conference on World Evangelization" (MacLeod, "Ockenga," 484).

cooperative network of fundamentalist leaders and churches who shared common values and sentiments for mutual encouragement and support. The initial meeting was held at the Moody Bible Institute in 1941 by a group of pastors from New England, which included Ockenga and Wright.[106]

Soon thereafter, the NEF gained popularity among other conservative and fundamentalist Christian leaders throughout the United States who began a call for the establishment of a national fellowship that would encompass all like-minded conservatives Christians throughout the United States for the purpose of unity and a common voice. During the same period, Charles E. Fuller's radio ministry was being threatened with closure by mainline Protestant denominations.[107] Realizing that a national organization could help save his radio show, Fuller allowed Ockenga to use his radio

---

106. By 1937, there were over one-thousand churches who took part in NEF sponsored activities. The NEF began as an organization that held "summer camp meetings and annual conferences for ministers and Christian workers" from different denominations (e.g. Baptists, Episcopalian, Methodists, Pentecostals, Presbyterians, and etc.) (Kurt Berends, "Wright, James Elwin," in *Biographical Dictionary of Evangelicals*, ed. Timothy Larsen [Downers Grove, IL: InterVarsity Press, 2003], 752).

107. Charles Edward Fuller (1887–1968), graduated in 1910 with a degree in chemistry and worked in California's "orange industry" (Philip Goff, "Fuller, Charles Edward," in *Biographical Dictionary of Evangelicals*, ed. Timothy Larsen [Downers Grove, IL: InterVarsity Press, 2003], 245). In 1916, he converted to fundamentalism after hearing the message of "former wrestler and boxer" Paul Rader (Bruce L. Shelley, "Old Fashioned Revivalist: Charles E. Fuller," in *More Than Conquerors: Portraits of Believers from All Walks of Life*, ed. John Woodbridge [Quezon City, Philippines: Pick Source, 2003], 170). Leaving a stable job, he entered the Bible Institute of Los Angeles (BIOLA) where he completed his studies in 1921. He initially served in a Presbyterian church but became dissatisfied with its modernist disposition that he took the small Bible class that he started and established the Calvary Church, an independent, non-denominational church (Shelley, "Old Fashioned Revivalist," 172). It was when he was asked to substitute for the regular preacher on a local radio broadcast that he saw Radio's potential for the propagation of the gospel (Daniel P. Fuller, *Give the Winds a Mighty Voice: The Story of Charles E. Fulle*r [Eugene, OR: Wipf & Stock, 1972], 74). By 1931, Fuller's first radio programs "The Pilgrims' Hour" and "Heart to Heart Talks" went on air over seven stations on the Columbia Broadcasting System (CBS) (Shelley, "Old Fashioned Revivalist," 172). In time, Fuller's radio ministry was opposed by both the modernist and the fundamentalist groups. From the modernist side, the mainstream protestant churches lobbied to block Fuller and other conservatives from getting "air time" (Goff, "Fuller, Charles," 245). While the "ultra-right-wing fundamentalists" were condemning Fuller for his unwillingness to exhort his listeners to separate from the modernists. As a moderate, Fuller advocated that his conservative listeners should lay aside their differences with like-minded "liberal" Christians; and even, challenging them to remain in these "liberal" denominations so as to effect change from within (Goff, "Fuller, Charles," 246). He is best remembered for the "Old Fashioned Revival Hour" which lasted for thirty years. Fuller supported several evangelical organizations such as the Navigators, New Life, Wycliffe Bible Translators and Youth for Christ (Shelley, "Old Fashioned Revivalist," 172).

show to broadcast an invitation to all interested church leaders to attend the first "National Conference for United Action among Evangelicals" in St. Louis, Missouri.

During the St. Louis Conference in April 1942, 147 conservative Christian leaders were stirred by the messages given by Harold Ockenga (Park Street Church in Boston), William Ayer (Calvary Baptist Church in New York), Stephen Paine (Houghton College), and Robert G. Lee (Bellevue Baptist Church in Memphis). Ockenga called upon those who shared his convictions to unite and speak boldly to a world that had already discredited and dismissed conservative Christianity. In his fiery message to the delegates, he challenged these Christian leaders to work together so that conservative Christianity could reassert and reclaim its place in American society. As Rosell describes Ockenga's challenge,

> Rather than a continuation of the fundamentalists' strategy of withdrawal, here was a challenge to reengage the culture and its institutions. Instead of retreat, here was a call to advance the gospel throughout the world. In place of discouragement and fear, here was a new hope for spiritual power and refreshment. Rather than endless argumentation and division, here at last was the possibility of united evangelical action.[108]

The challenge to unite the fragmented conservative churches was finally answered by a unanimous vote from the delegates to form the "National Association of Evangelicals for United Action," despite some opposition from the McIntire and the ACCC.[109] The moniker "evangelical" was chosen since the title "fundamentalist" had gained a negative connotation at that

---

108. Rosell, "America's Hour Has Struck," *Christian History: The Entire Collection*.

109. McIntire believed that these churches should just join the American Council of Christian Churches (ACCC) whose main purpose was "to dispute the claim of the Federal Council to speak for all Protestants" (Cairns, *Christianity Through the Centuries*, 471). "His request had been placed on the table at the earlier Chicago meeting, but in St. Louis the participants declined McIntire's invitation, believing that a more positive presentation of the gospel was needed. While they all shared serious reservations about the FCC, the participants did not feel that militant opposition and direct confrontation with the well-established Protestant council was the best strategy" (National Association of Evangelicals, "History," accessed 15 April 2011, https://www.nae.net/about-nae/history/).

time, and so that the name would define their purpose as a movement.[110] As Ahlstrom describes the movement,

> It [NAE] was founded in 1942 by a group of diverse conservatives who were dissatisfied with the politically oriented and rabidly exclusivist American Council of Churches which Carl McIntire had organized during the preceding year. Though agreeing with McIntire that conservatives needed to counter the Federal Council of Churches with some corporate expression, many evangelicals wanted a less divisive and more constructive association.[111]

Although their fellow fundamentalists continued to question their actions and the mainline Protestant churches dismissed the NAE as a "flash in the pan," the movement eventually gained momentum and its own unified voice. It was a victory for these progressive conservatives – evangelicals who saw the possibility that orthodox Christianity could once more influence their country and help guide its direction and policies, and re-establish conservative Christian values. The following year, the name was shortened to National Association of Evangelicals (NAE). Ockenga served as its first president while Wright served as NAE's first executive secretary.

Key Characteristics of the Evangelicals

The new evangelical movement of the 1950s had several characteristics that were inherited from their predecessors which they adapted to fit their goals and purposes.

Commitment to Theological Training

Similar to the fundamentalists of the 1930s, these evangelicals saw the indispensability of forming educational centers that would not only strengthen their theological base but would also develop the future leaders and

---

110. For example, when Billy Graham was asked whether he was a fundamentalist or not, he openly admitted that he was in terms of his faith and his affirmations of the fundamentals. However, he adds, "if by fundamentalist you mean 'narrow', 'bigoted', 'prejudiced', 'extremist', 'emotional', 'snake handler', 'without social conscience'—then I am definitely not a fundamentalist" (Robert P. Ramey, "Pathfinder in Evangelism: Billy Graham," in *More Than Conquerors: Portraits of Believers from All Walks of Life*, ed. John Woodbridge [Quezon City, Philippines: Pick Source, 2003], 190).

111. Ahlstrom, *Religious History*, 958.

missionaries of the movement. An example of this is creation of the Fuller Theological Seminary in 1947, named after Charles Fuller's father whose endowment helped start the school. This seminary was the amalgamation of John Ockenga's and Charles Fuller's resources.[112] When Fuller heard of Ockenga's efforts in Boston, he suggested that they merge their efforts to form a conservative Christian seminary. It fulfilled Fuller's dream of a school for evangelists and Ockenga's aspiration to form a conservative evangelical alternative to Princeton Theological Seminary. When Fuller Theological Seminary opened its doors, Carl F. H. Henry, Wilbur Smith, Everett F. Harrison, and Harold Lindsell served as its faculty and classes started in September 1947 with Ockenga serving as its first president.[113] Fuller continued to support the seminary by using his popularity to promote and provide resources for the school.[114] In time, several conservative seminaries were established throughout North America.[115] One key innovation in seminary education was the establishment of accrediting institutions such as the Association for Biblical Higher Education (ABHE) established in 1947 which helped in regulating the curriculum and helped in the accreditation of these theological institutions.[116]

Commitment to Fundamentalist Theology

The evangelicals continued the theological convictions and teachings of their fundamentalist predecessors. In fact, they understood that this was

---

112. By his own initiative, Ockenga hosted several biblical and theological conferences in his church from 1944 to 1947 which drew scholars like Carl F. H. Henry from Boston University and Edward J. Carnell from Harvard University. At the same time, Charles Fuller hosted his own theological classes on his radio program the "Pilgrims' Hour" since he lacked qualified faculty to run the Christian college he envisioned.

113. Shelley, "Old Fashioned Revivalist," 174. Ockenga elected to remain as the senior pastor of Park Street Church; as a result, he had to commute from Boston to Los Angeles (MacLeod, "Ockenga," 483).

114. "Charles Fuller's broadcasting ministry funded Fuller Seminary, and his reputation with ordinary evangelicals protected the scholars who worked there" (Michael S. Hamilton, "Evangelical Entrepreneurs: The Parachurch Phenomenon," in *Christian History and Biography* 92 [September 2006] from, *Christian History: The Entire Collection*).

115. An example is the evangelical Gordon-Conwell Theological Seminary which was established in 1969 as a result of the merger of Gordon Divinity School of Boston and the Conwell School of Theology of Temple University in Philadelphia (MacLeod, "Ockenga," 483–484).

116. For more information, see Association for Biblical Higher Education, "Our History," accessed 5 July 2013, http://www.abhe.org/pages/NAV-OurHistory.html.

one area that they could not compromise. For example, Carl Henry affirmed evangelicalism's commitment to biblical inerrancy and the authority of Scriptures through his magnum opus entitled *God, Revelation, and Authority* (1983).[117] However, the evangelicals included a stronger theological basis for the Christian's social engagement that was not connected or limited to the humanist values of the modernists/liberals. It is in this area that Carl F. H. Henry became evangelicalism's key theologian.[118] Dr Henry provided the theological and biblical basis of the tenets of evangelicalism through his works; *The Uneasy Conscience of Modern Fundamentalism* (1947) was his first major work where he explained the "basis for positive engagement with society and culture without the theology of the 'social gospel' movement."[119] One major difference in evangelicalism's theological process was "its effort to overcome the powerful anti-intellectual and anti-scientific spirit that had discredited the older fundamentalism."[120]

Commitment to Evangelism

As their movement's name implied, the ministry of proclamation became an integral part of the evangelicals' program, a practice that they inherited from the fundamentalists in the past. While the movement was able to produce several popular evangelists (e.g. Charles Fuller, Dawson Trotman, Luis Palau, Joon Gon Kim, etc.), one of the most well-known in the late

---

117. Other titles include *Remaking the Modern Mind* (1948), *Giving a Reason For Our Hope* (1949), *Fifty Years of Protestant Theology* (1950), *The Drift of Western Thought* (1951), *Christian Personal Ethics* (1957), *Basic Christian Doctrines* (1962), *Christian Faith and Modern Theology* (1964), *Jesus of Nazareth: Savior and Lord* (1966).

118. Carl Ferdinand Howard Henry (1913–2003) had no religious instruction at home and "considered himself a virtual pagan prior to his personal conversion to Christ in the summer of 1933" (Timothy George, "Henry, Carl Ferdinand Howard," in *Biographical Dictionary of Evangelicals*, ed. Timothy Larsen [Downers Grove, IL: InterVarsity Press, 2003], 297). Although he had a good career in journalism, Henry experienced a personal conversion through Gene Bedford who led him to a personal faith in Christ. As a result, Henry left journalism and entered Wheaton College in 1935. During his studies, he was mentored by Gordon Clark, a fundamentalist Presbyterian "whose emphasis on propositional truth and the rationality of belief in God" influenced the doctrinal convictions of Henry (George, "Henry, Carl Ferdinand Howard," 297). In 1947, he was invited to teach in the newly established Fuller Theological Seminary where he taught theology, philosophy, and ethics; and served as dean for a time

119. George, "Henry, Carl Ferdinand Howard," 298.

120. Ahlstrom, *Religious History*, 958–959.

twentieth century is William "Billy" Franklin Graham, Jr who became the movement's spokesperson and ambassador of goodwill.

Although he was virtually unknown in the 1940s, by the following decade, this southern Baptist preacher became a household name in America. The "tipping point" took place in 1949, when he conducted his three-week revival meetings in Greater Los Angeles. While the first few meetings of the evangelistic crusade had "modest results," towards the end of its three-week stint several important and popular individuals became "converted." One of these was Stuart Hamblen, a popular radio star, who attended Billy Graham's meeting where he experienced a "dramatic conversion." Soon the revival meetings became a buzzword around town, drawing people to the crusades. Another factor that helped was the media exposure Billy Graham received when William Randolph Hearst, the owner of two major national-circulated newspapers, sent his reporters and photographers to cover the remaining revival meetings. Graham's popularity grew and opportunities to spread the message of evangelicalism spread not only throughout America but also in foreign countries which eventually helped mobilize the Lausanne Movement.

Commitment to Address Social Issues
In their effort to restore the voice of conservative Christianity in American society, the evangelicals engaged themselves in issues that were pertinent to their times. This was a departure from the fundamentalist approach that limited Christianity's involvement to spiritual issues only. *Christianity Today*, which serves as evangelicalism's main periodical, addressed controversial issues such as the Vietnam War, homosexuality, racism, and other societal issues. At the height of the civil rights movement in the 1950s, Billy Graham not only spoke against segregation but was one of the first to support integrated seating in his crusades and jointly preached with Rev Martin Luther King, Jr in a 1957 rally in New York.[121] The evangelicals spoke for or against the social issues of their time.

---

121. His evangelistic crusade in Chattanooga, Tennessee in 1953 was the "first deliberately integrated crusade held in any southern city" (Ramey, "Pathfinder in Evangelism," 190–191).

Commitment to Expansion

The time of isolationism for these conservative Christians was finally over. And as their reputation and accomplishments spread, conservative Christians from other nations began to follow their example and ushered calls to form a global network among evangelicals throughout the world. This helped start the World Evangelical Fellowship (WEF) which was established in 1951.[122] Another factor that helped expand evangelicalism's influence was the international congresses that were held in the later part of the twentieth century. These conferences fostered unity among conservative Christians and strengthened their movement.

World Congress on Evangelism

In 1966, Dr Henry and Billy Graham convened the World Congress on Evangelism (WCE) in West Berlin; this was a crucial event as Protestant evangelical leaders from around the globe gathered for the first time to establish stronger ties which enabled partnerships and mutual benefits.

Although planned and coordinated by the Americans, more than 1,200 delegates from a hundred different countries participated. It was clear that the congress was aimed not in providing evangelistic training but in presenting papers which discussed the concerns of evangelicalism's commitment towards world evangelization. "Papers at the conference gave many indications of the explosive growth of the church in Africa, Asia and Latin America and the shifting center of gravity of the church from the Western to nonwestern cultures,"[123] the Congress' main goal was to remind its delegates of the continuing task of evangelization.

---

122. In 1946, Elwin Wright visited Europe where he found churches that had a common desire to form a global coalition similar to the NAE. Wright and Clyde W. Taylor held exploratory meeting in Clarens, Switzerland to discuss a possible merger. Thus in August 1951, an International Convention of Evangelicals was held in Holland which created the World Evangelical Fellowship (W. Harold Fuller, *People of the Mandate: The Story of the World Evangelical Fellowship* [Grand Rapids: Baker, 1996], 31). PCEC joined the WEF in 1974 and had greatly benefited from this relationship. According to Vencer, it was at "the 6th PCEC National Assembly held on November 22, 1974 [when] PCEC voted to become a member of the World Evangelical Fellowship" (Agustin B. Vencer, "The Evangelicals in the Philippines: A Brief History of the Philippine Council of Evangelical Churches," *Evangelicals Today and Asia Ministry Digest* 21, no. 8 [August 1994], 17). In fact, in 1992, Vencer became the International Director of WEF (Fuller, *People of the Mandate*, 7).

123. Lausanne Movement, "1966 World Congress on Evangelism," accessed 20 May 2011, http://www.lausanne.org/berlin-1966/overview.html.

As Billy Graham writes, "Our goal is nothing short of the evangelization of the human race in this generation."[124] When asked about the Congress' accomplishment; Graham states, "Beyond forging a new unity among evangelicals, the Congress served as a catalyst for a number of new efforts in evangelism."[125] Thus, evangelicalism's theology of evangelism was reemphasized

International Congress on World Evangelism Lausanne '74
The WCE was followed by other conferences such as the International Congress on Evangelism. These events strengthened and unified the evangelical "voice" throughout the world. This was followed by another international congress held at Lausanne, Switzerland in 1974 designated as the International Congress on World Evangelization (ICWE) which most evangelicals refer to as Lausanne '74 which produced the Lausanne Covenant as drafted and approved by its delegates.

The ICWE was held from 16–25 July 1974, with 2,473 delegates from 150 countries. The theme of the congress was "Let The Earth Hear His Voice." In his opening address, Billy Graham recalls that he had "underlined the single focus" of the Congress: "Here at Lausanne, let's make sure that Evangelization is the one task which we are unitedly determined to do."[126] The congress further developed the theology on evangelism, which was reaffirmed during the World Congress on Evangelism at West Berlin in 1966 where "plenary addresses explored the Bible's teaching on evangelism, including such topics as the nature of God, the work of Christ, conversion, the uniqueness of Christ, the lostness of humanity, the mission of the Church, and the authority of the Bible."[127]

The congress resulted in a call for united effort among all evangelicals with a common purpose of world evangelization. In addition, the Lausanne Covenant was adopted by many of its delegates for their churches and mission organizations.[128] Another result of this congress was the formation of a

---

124. Graham, *Just as I Am*, 565.
125. Graham, 566.
126. Graham, 571.
127. Graham, 572.
128. The Lausanne Movement, "Lausanne I: The International Congress on World Evangelization," accessed 20 May 2011, http://www.lausanne.org/en/gatherings/global-

permanent body called the Lausanne Committee for World Evangelization whose task is "to carry on the vision and work of Lausanne."[129]

In time, similar meetings and congresses were held in India, Hong Kong, Singapore, Cuba, and in Manila to further the advances made in ICWE.

Fundamentalist-Evangelical Controversy (1950s–1980s)

As the evangelicals grew in number and began "moving" within American society through their engagement of social issues, they were criticized by both the modernists and the fundamentalists. For example, Billy Graham's efforts and messages were criticized as naïve and obsolete by the modernists; while, the fundamentalists considered him a "compromiser" for his ecumenical approach in his ministry.[130] Although largely criticized by some liberals, as mentioned earlier, the main opposition for the formation of the NAE came from McIntire who wanted the evangelicals to join the ACCC in their commitment to separation and fundamentalism.

However, it was clear that evangelicalism's leaders and theologians did not agree with the old fundamentalist's way. Thus, tensions grew and an ever-widening gap increased between the fundamentalists and the evangelicals, affecting relationships between their member churches. The fundamentalists like McIntire were affronted by the evangelicals' choice to work with groups that they considered "liberal."[131] As a result, McIntire and the ACCC openly opposed the evangelicals as they called on other conservative Christians to

---

congress/lausanne-1974.html.

129. Graham, *Just as I Am*, 573.

130. Billy Graham had a growing tension with several fundamentalist leaders such as Carl McIntire, Bob Jones, and John R. Rice. The strain reached its peak during an evangelistic crusade in the late 1950s, when Graham accepted the invitation "to hold a crusade in New York from the broadly representative Protestant Council of Churches, aligned with both the National and World Councils of Churches, fundamentalists attacked him in repeated editorials and articles in their publications" (William Martin, "The Riptide of Revival," in *Christian History and Biography* 92 (September 2006) from, *Christian History: The Entire Collection*.

131. For example, Billy Graham was always willing to work with any church, denomination, and Christian organization that could help with his crusades. The BGEA partnered with the Roman Catholic Church as they conducted crusades in several countries (Religious Tolerance.Org, "Cooperation between Roman Catholics and Conservative Protestants," accessed 15 May 2011, http://www.religioustolerance.org/ chr_caev.htm).

boycott Billy Graham's Crusade, *Christianity Today*, and evangelical seminaries (e.g. Wheaton College, Fuller Theological Seminary, etc.). These fundamentalists "believed they differed from evangelicals and neoevangelicals by being more faithful to Bible-believing Christianity; more militant against church apostasy, communism, and personal evils."[132] Being evangelicalism's most popular representative, Billy Graham was criticized harshly by these fundamentalist leaders which saw his actions as a form of compromise. Thus, the fundamentalists and the evangelicals parted ways, as seen in McIntire's act of joining the protesters outside the Lausanne Conference in 1974.[133]

Conclusion

These events that took place in North America explain the reason for the schisms and the controversies within Protestantism in the United States. While they were divided even during the foundation of the nation, through the influence of the Awakenings these churches shared common doctrines and values that were referred to as the Old Theology, which had the dual emphasis on personal repentance and social transformation. However, as the culture of America changed and as a result of the influence of the Enlightenment; these churches were divided over the modernist/liberal-fundamentalist controversy. While the modernist/liberals were able to gain public affirmation, the fundamentalists chose to separate and withdrew from society. This soon changed in the post-World War II era when several fundamentalist leaders desired to regain conservative Christianity's voice in American society. While they were able to achieve this goal, sadly,

---

132. C. T. McIntire, "Fundamentalism," in *Evangelical Dictionary of Theology*, 2nd ed., Baker Reference Library, ed. Walter A. Elwell (Grand Rapids: Baker, 2001), 474.

133. It is unfortunate that the fundamentalist and the evangelicals broke away from each other. These schisms brought much pain and discouragement to the evangelicals, as Billy Graham expressed his feelings on the matter,
> Much more painful to me, however, was the opposition from some of the leading fundamentalists. Most of them I knew personally, and even if I did not agree with them on every detail, I greatly admired them and respected their commitment to Christ. Many also had been among our strongest supporters in the early years of our public ministry. Their criticism hurt immensely, nor could I shrug them off as the objections of people who rejected the basic tenets of the Christian faith or who opposed evangelism of any type. Their harshness and their lack of love saddened me and struck me as being far from the spirit of Christ.

Graham, *Just as I Am*, 302.

fundamentalism experienced its own schism as the fundamentalists and the evangelicals became divided. What is unfortunate was that these divisions and factionalism were passed on by these American churches to the churches and organizations that they had started in the other nations. It is these schisms that influenced the actions of the Filipino churches when it came to the issue of unity and cooperation among the Protestant churches in the Philippines. This was the predisposition that the Filipino Protestant leaders had to contend with as they struggled to form conciliar unions. The next chapter follows the efforts of the Filipino churches to form united churches and cooperative unions despite the biases of the past.

CHAPTER 3

Protestantism in the Philippines: From Inception to the Post-World War II Era (1890s–1950s)

While Protestantism in North America was beginning to experience tensions and schisms brought about by the growing modernist/liberal-fundamentalist controversy, the Philippines was relatively spared as the early American missionaries were unaffected by it. It was only during the 1920s and 1930s that the controversy was "felt" as several mission organizations and their churches experienced divisions and tensions. Its arrival coincided with the difficulties and troubles that arose as a result of the efforts of some Filipino churches and their leaders to gain autonomy through conciliar unions, mergers, and even schisms. This chapter examines briefly the history of Philippine Protestantism from its inception until immediately after World War II.

The Arrival of Protestantism in the Islands (1900s)

On 1 May 1898, Admiral George Dewey of the United States Navy defeated the Spanish Naval Armada in Manila Bay, heralding the end of more than three centuries of Spanish colonial rule and inaugurating the American colonization of the Philippines. As the United States military forces captured Manila, North American Protestantism entered the country. It was on Sunday 28 August 1898, that the first Protestant worship service was held "in an old Spanish dungeon facing the bay" inside the walled city of Intramuros, by Chaplain George Stull (Methodist-Episcopal) where American personnel and several Filipinos joined together in worship.[1]

As the Philippines became a colony of the United States, there were three prevailing opinions on what should be done regarding the faith of the Filipinos. The first was from those who belonged and supported the Roman Catholic faith; they affirmed that the Filipinos already had their own form of Christianity (i.e. Roman Catholicism) and that it was no longer necessary for America to change or replace it.[2] On the other side, the mainline Protestant churches and organizations interpreted the political events as a divine sign that they must immediately begin efforts to proclaim the gospel message to the Filipinos.[3] Finally, the Episcopalians were convinced that the missionary efforts in the Philippines and other new colonies should only be limited to and focused on those who were of another religion or of pagan faith.[4]

Eventually, all three groups found themselves working among the Filipinos at the beginning of the twentieth century. Among those of the second group, the first to mobilize their missionary teams were the Presbyterians who were soon followed by the Baptists, Methodists-Episcopalians, Congregationalists, Reformed, and the Christian and Missionary Alliance.[5]

Missionary Boards Conference in New York (1898)

While there was eagerness to begin the work, some of these American missionary boards decided to be more deliberate in their approach. One important strategy that was being considered was the establishment of a missionary council or federation, whose members were to be bound by a comity agreement to ensure that their efforts would be efficient and economical.[6]

---

1. Richard L. Deats, *The Story of Methodism in the Philippines* (Manila: G. Rangel & Sons, 1964), 3.

2. Arthur Judson Brown, *New Era in the Philippines* (New York, NY: Fleming H. Revell, 1903), 152.

3. Rev George F. Pentecost, Chairman of the Standing Committee on Foreign Missions, believed that it was the will of God that the Philippines was given to America and that their missionary efforts must soon begin. For his actual words in the minutes of the General Assembly of the Presbyterians in 1898, see Maurice W. Armstrong, Lefferts A. Loetscher, and Charles A. Anderson, *The Presbyterian Enterprise* (Eugene, OR: Wipf & Stock, 2001), 266.

4. Sitoy, *Comity and Unity*, 16–17.

5. Sitoy, 10.

6. For details, see n.a. *The Church: Volume 4, Issue 4* (n.p.: Church Publication Company, 1897), 493.

The rationale was that potential rivalry and conflict among the different missionary groups would be avoided if the council/federation could lay out procedures for conflict resolution, coordinate the missionary teams, and adjudicate between territorial claims and conflicts.[7]

Accordingly, it was the Presbyterian missionary board who took the initiative to call for a conference among foreign mission boards (i.e. Congregational, Baptist, Methodist, Episcopal, and the Reformed) that had expressed an interest in missionary work in the three new mission fields; namely, Puerto Rico, Cuba, and the Philippines. William R. Richards, Chairman of the Committee on China (Presbyterian), summarized the motivation for calling the meeting, "We believe that the new situation thus providentially forced upon us affords us excellent opportunity not only for beginning this work but for beginning it right from the view-point of Christian fellowship and the economical use of men and money."[8]

Thus, on 13 July 1898, inside the Presbyterian board room in New York City, several missionary boards met to finalize and coordinate their plans to begin the missionary efforts in these newly acquired colonies. For the work in the Philippine Islands, it was the Presbyterians, the Methodist-Episcopalians and the Baptists (Northern Convention) who were among the very first to express their desire and commitment to the work. It was the Presbyterians who announced their capability to immediately embark on their missionary work in Manila and Iloilo while the Methodist-Episcopalians and the Northern Convention Baptists were unable to immediately respond due to financial constraints.[9] Given that there was no verbal dissent from the two churches regarding Presbyterians' stated plans to start their missionary efforts in Manila and Iloilo, they interpreted this as a binding claim.[10]

By the end of the meeting, several resolutions were established by these missionary boards. Among these were the following:

---

7. The principle of comity had earlier been developed and applied in an inter-mission cooperation both in Japan and in Korea. For details, see Sitoy, *Comity and Unity*, 6–7.

8. Brown, *New Era*, 176.

9. The Presbyterians were ready as several of their churches enthusiastically responded to the challenge of sending missionaries to the Philippines. In fact, a pastor had actually raised and handed over $1,000 to support the missionary effort (Brown, *New Era*, 176).

10. Sitoy, *Comity and Unity*, 5.

1. That each of the Boards mentioned appoint a committee of two on the field or fields which it thinks of entering, each group of committees to confer with a view to a frank and mutual understanding as to the most effective and equitable distribution of the territory and work under the several Boards.

2. That the committee takes early steps to secure available information regarding these various islands as missionary fields, and that all information thus obtained be shared with the other committees concerned, with a view to subsequent action.[11]

As intended, these resolutions were aimed at avoiding needless duplication and rivalry by agreeing to divide the territories among these missionary groups and to foster cooperation among these groups; avoiding circumstances that might lead to unnecessary financial drain, "friction" among the missionaries, and confusion among the new believers. This agreement was hailed as a major accomplishment, as Brown comments,

> It is a great thing that, for the first time in the history of the world, so far as we know, before occupying a new field, the representatives of the various Boards sat down to consider fraternally the situation, to pray over it, and to decide how men and money could be used to the very best advantage and to the avoidance of many of the evils of denominationalism.[12]

Thus, the early preparations for the Protestant missionary work in the Philippines were guided by the principles of comity and cooperation. The tensions and disputes that would arise from the modernist-fundamentalist controversy in North America had not yet affected these missionary boards so that they were able to readily agree on cooperative efforts for the work that was ahead of them.

The Evangelical Union (1901)

After Manila was secured, the North American forces began the process of transforming this old Spanish city to a "foothold" in their efforts to colonize the entire country. When the American colonial government finally gave the

---
11. Brown, *New Era*, 179–180.
12. Brown, 194.

permission for missionary work to begin, Rev and Mrs James B. Rodgers of the Presbyterian Church became the first permanently assigned Protestant missionaries to arrive in the Philippines by April 1899.[13]

By December 1899, Rev Rogers was able to conduct regular worship services – his very first sermon was on the first Sunday of May 1899 – for the American community and was able to organize a native church with nine members inside the city of Manila.[14] By March 1900, the Presbyterians, the Methodists and the Baptists had begun their missionary efforts.[15] However, the missionary work among the different denominations was still limited to Manila and its immediate surroundings as the Philippine-American War was still being waged outside the city.[16]

In time, the hostilities between the *Katipuneros* and the American forces slowly receded and finally ended by 1902, which opened the whole

---

13. This claim has been contested by some as Bishop James M. Thoburn of the Methodist-Episcopalians arrived in February 1899 (two months ahead of Rev Rodgers) to open their work and to add the Philippines under his Episcopality (Gerald H. Anderson, "Thoburn, James Mills," in *Biographical Dictionary of Christian Missions*, ed. Gerald H. Anderson [Grand Rapids: Eerdmans, 1999], 665). Although he baptized hundreds, his stay was brief and limited since he had to eventually return to his Episcopal seat. Thus, while Bishop Thoburn arrived two months earlier, it was Rev Rodgers who had been the first "permanently assigned" missionary to the Philippines.

14. Brown, *New Era*, 181–182.

15. Rev and Mrs James B. Rodgers arrived in Manila on 21 April 1899 and were immediately joined by Rev and Mrs David S. Hibbard (Brown, *New Era*, 181). The first permanent missionary for the Methodist-Episcopalians was Rev T. H. Martin who arrived in March 1900 to take over a fledgling mission point held by a layman named Mr A. W. Prautch (Brown, *New Era*, 182–183). On 2 May 1900, the first Baptist missionary began work at Jaro, Panay. Rev Eric Lund was accompanied by Rev Braulio Manikan (a Filipino convert who traveled to Spain to become a priest and was converted when he met Rev Lund). Rev Manikan was instrumental in the "translation of the Bible and some religious tracts into Hiligaynon language" (Francis Neil Gico Jalando-on, *A History of Philippine Baptist Pastors, 1898-2002*, IATS Series, vol. 2 [Iloilo City, Philippines: Religion, Ecumenics, Mission and Society, 2003], 77).

16. The Philippine-American War (1899–1902) was a continuation of the Filipinos' bid for independence. When the Americans took over from the Spaniards, Gen Emilio Aguinaldo declared created the Malolos congress in January 1899 and declared himself as the president of the new Philippine Republic. However, the Americans rejected their claims and thus the conflict continued. For details, see Mariano C. Apilado, *Revolutionary Spirituality: A Study of the Protestant Role in the American Colonial Rule of the Philippines, 1898-1928* (Quezon City, Philippines: New Day, 1999); Reuben F. Trinidad, *A Monument to Religious Nationalism* (Quezon City, Philippines: Evangelical Methodist Church in the Philippines, 1999); and José S. Arcilla, *Recent Philippine History 1898-1960* (Manila: Office of Research and Publications, Manila University, 1990).

archipelago for American missionary work. As new territories were being secured, missionaries began to spread into these new areas. The first few years proved to be fruitful as missionary accounts and reports of the period indicate that thousands of Filipinos converted from Roman Catholicism to Protestantism, despite the condemnation of the Roman Catholic clergy and the sporadic persecutions against the missionaries and their early converts.[17] Among the contributing factors for this surge in growth were the initial gap in spiritual leadership left behind by the withdrawal of the Spanish Roman Catholic orders[18] and the assumption of some Filipinos that they would be required to embrace this new faith.[19] Regardless, several new Protestant missionary stations and congregations were established throughout the Philippine Archipelago.[20] As Brown recalls, "There are over two thousand adult Protestant Christians in the Philippine Islands within five years after the landing of the first Protestant missionary, and the number is increasing so rapidly that the Philippine Mission gives every promise of becoming one of the most fruitful fields in the history of Protestant missions in Asia."[21] Due to the overwhelming response of the Filipinos, enthusiastic Protestant missionaries began moving into areas without consultation or coordination with other missionary organizations that were currently operating within the same area.

---

17. As Osias and Lorenzana explain, "so strongly entrenched in the hearts of the masses was the old religion to which they had been accustomed for centuries that many of the early converts suffered not only social ostracism but persecution" (Camilo Osias and Avelina Lorenzana, *Evangelical Christianity in the Philippines* [Dayton, OH: United Brethren Publishing House, 1931], 98). Apilado also gives several accounts of persecution of the new converts that were supposedly instigated by the Roman Catholic priest. For details see Apilado, *Revolutionary Spirituality*, 112.

18. For details on the anti-clerical movement and the decrease number of Spanish clergy during this period, see Gerald H. Anderson, ed., *Studies in Philppine Church History* (Ithaca, NY: Cornell University Press, 1969), 152–202.

19. Brown, *New Era*, 117.

20. According to Anne Kwantes, "a 'mission station' referred to any area in which there was at least one appointed missionary; this indicated an emphasis on the foreign missionary, as he or she went about the work of missions. A 'congregation' denoted an organized body of Christian believers, belonging to a wider organization with its own government and support" (Anne C. Kwantes, *Presbyterian Missionaries in the Philippines: Conduits of Social Change (1899-1910)* [Quezon City, Philippines: New Day, 1989], 43–44).

21. Brown, *New Era*, 209.

Despite the Missionary Board Conference agreement in New York City (1898) and the newly formed Missionary Alliance,[22] the spirit of cooperation and order was broken when these denominations failed to restrain their missionaries from crossing the "boundaries" of other missionary stations in Manila and the other provinces. For example, the Presbyterians and the Methodists were both claiming Manila and San Fernando, Pampanga, while the Presbyterians and Baptists were duplicating each others effort in Iloilo.[23] Adding to the tension were the complaints that the Presbyterians had "lost" several of their baptized members to the efforts of a Methodist-Episcopal lay-preacher named Mr Arthur W. Prautch; his actions were considered "sheep-stealing."[24] There was a growing concern that the situation would lead to potential conflicts among missionaries in the field, confusion among their Filipino converts, and the ineffective use of resources. Thus, the current condition in the mission field required a formal agreement which would bind these churches and missionary organizations to the spirit of comity.

It was Rev Rodgers who took the initiative to call for a consultation among the missionary organizations in the country. Recounting this situation, he writes, "we were already receiving members in all the missions and there was danger of stepping on one another's toes, an irritating process even if done with the best of intentions and for the glory of God."[25] Beginning with an initial conference held among the Presbyterian missionaries on 13–19 December 1900, a proposal was drafted that laid out the principles and guidelines of a comity agreement. Some of the more salient points of the proposed resolutions were as follows:

> 1. That all Protestant Filipino churches be designated "Iglesias Evangelicas" without further distinction than marks their location.

---

22. The Missionary Alliance was formed by the newly arrived American missionary groups on 11 June 1900 to avoid such conflict and foster cooperation. However, many considered it as simply a "fellowship" or an informal organization composed of missionaries from several Christian and mission bodies; with the expressed purpose for fellowship, for mutual support, and for other social gatherings (Sitoy, *Comity and Unity*, 8).

23. Sitoy, *Comity and Unity*, 8.

24. Sitoy, 9.

25. James B. Rodgers, *Forty Years in the Philippines: A History of the Philippine Mission of the Presbyterian Church in the United States of America, 1899-1939* (New York: Board of Foreign Missions of the Presbyterian Church in the USA, 1940), 163.

2. That one mission station is sufficient for one town or district of a city.

3. That we shall respect the prior claims of a mission where positive and definite steps have been taken to occupy towns or districts and shall not establish preaching places in such places.

4. That where people from another district attend our services and wish us to open in their district already occupied by another mission, we refer them to the mission already in their district as being the branch of our church doing work there.

5. That an effort be made to form an agreement with the other missions doing work in the islands to divide the territory in such a way that our different spheres of labor may not overlap.

6. That a copy of these resolutions be sent to each mission doing work in the islands, requesting their cooperation in carrying out these plans.[26]

In order to resolve the ministry concerns and to vote on the Presbyterian proposal, a conference for all Protestant missionary organizations working in the country was held at the Young Men's Christian Association center (YMCA) in Manila on 24–26 April 1901. The conference was supported by representatives from the Methodists-Episcopalians, Presbyterians, United Brethren, Christian and Missionary Alliance, British and Foreign Bible Society, the American Bible Society and a representative of the YMCA. Although the Baptists were unable to join since they were not notified in time, they later agreed to details laid out in the conference.[27]

By the end of the conference, the proposal was unanimously accepted by all participants resulting in the formation of an organization that would ensure comity among current and future mission groups working in the Philippines; thus on 25 April 1901, the Evangelical Union of the Philippine Islands (Evangelical Union) was formed, with a commitment to

---

26. Rodgers, *Forty Years*, 163.
27. Sitoy, *Comity and Unity*, 11.

meet annually where conflicts would be resolved and lessons learned would be shared among them.[28] The following are some the key resolutions of the agreement:

Dividing the Philippines into Denominational Districts

In order to avoid duplication and conflict, the council members of the Evangelical Union decided to divide the Philippines into several denominational territories with each missionary board being assigned to a specific area and those who were in these territories should yield their claims.[29]

The distribution of the territory was as follows: the Methodists-Episcopalians had the non-Ilocano provinces which are in Luzon, north of Manila. The Disciples and the United Brethren received the Ilocano provinces, Laguna and Tayabas were also given to the Disciples. The Presbyterians received the remaining provinces of Luzon which were south of Manila, including Palawan and the Cebuano-speaking provinces of the Eastern Visayas. The Baptists held all the Ilonggo-speaking provinces of the Western Visayas, including Negros Occidental and Romblon. The Congregationalists took Mindanao except for the provinces given to Christian and Missionary Alliance. The Christian and Missionary Alliance took responsibility for Sulu, Basilan, southern Zamboanga and Cotobato. It was further agreed that Manila was established as a neutral zone where no particular denomination could claim it; however, they were still allowed to develop the churches that they had already planted and establish new congregations within the city.

Part of implementing this distribution required the Evangelical Union to intervene and adjudicate between counter claims. Some of the resolutions required a particular church to abandon its claim to a particular area while others required a creative way of dividing the mission field. An example was the Presbyterian and the Baptist rivalry in Iloilo. While both churches had legitimate reasons for their claim, the Evangelical Union divided the

---

28. Apilado, *Revolutionary Spirituality*, 82.

29. It is not clear whether these missionaries were aware that they had adopted a similar strategy employed by the Roman Catholic Orders where the Philippines was previously divided into territories so that the religious orders would "try to excel one another without the work of one hindering or overlapping that of the others" (John N. Schumacher, *Readings in Philippine Church History*, 2nd ed. [Quezon City, Philippines: Ateneo de Manila University, 1987], 17).

territory based on the local dialect—with the Ilonggo-speaking areas given to the Baptist and the Cebuano-speaking areas given to the Presbyterians.[30]

A Unified Name, "Iglesia Evangelica"

In their desire to avoid the misconception among their Filipino converts that the different churches represented different religions, the board of the Evangelical Union agreed that all churches planted by these Evangelical Union members would have a common name *Iglesia Evangelica* (the Evangelical Church) with their particular church or denomination in parenthesis.[31] Article IV of their constitution states, "The name 'Iglesia Evangelica' shall be used for the Filipino Churches which shall be raised up, and when necessary the denominational name shall be added in parentheses, e.g., 'Iglesia Evangelical de Malibay (Mision Metodista Ep.).'"[32]

Establishment of Cooperative Seminaries

In the spirit of cooperation and mutual support, the members of the Evangelical Union decided to merge existing schools and establish several common seminaries where the next generation of Filipino pastors and leaders for the newly established Protestant churches would be trained. For example, instead of establishing separate denominational seminaries, the Siliman University and the Union Theological Seminary were jointly established by different denominations to develop and train the future pastors and religious leaders of the country.[33]

---

30. For details on this and other conflicts and readjustments, see Sitoy, *Comity and Unity*, 23–36.

31. According to Kwantes, it was "Jacob Gould Schurman, secretary of the Schurman commission [that convinced Rev. Rodgers] that American Protestantism must come as one church, rather than with many denomination voices, each representing a facet of the American Protestant churches" (Kwantes, *Presbyterian Missionaries*, 22).

32. Brown, *New Era*, 189.

33. The Siliman Institute in Dumaguete, Negros Oriental was established by the Presbyterians in 1901 whose very "first class of college graduates" were given "government-recognized" degrees (Kwantes, *Presbyterian Missionaries*, 8). The Union Theological Seminary was started when the Ellinwood Bible School and Seminary (Presbyterian, founded in 1905) and a Methodists seminary merged in 1907; renamed as the Ellinwood Bible Seminary (Kwantes, *Presbyterian Missionaries*, 62). Later other denominations merged with the seminary, namely the "the United Brethren (1911), the Disciples (1916), and in 1919 the Congregationalists" (Deats, *Story of Methodism*, 61).

As these newly established Filipino churches have similar names and their leaders trained from the same schools, it was hoped that the process of creating a unified church would come easily and naturally.[34] By 1920, Filipino church leaders trained from these seminaries became members of the Evangelical Union and in the following year, Dr Jorge Bocobo was elected as the Evangelical Union's first Filipino president.[35]

Dissent and Unwillingness

Although the Evangelical Union was able to form a cooperative council among the majority of these Protestant churches and missionary groups, they were unable to find a common ground to include all the churches that were not part of the Roman Catholic Church. This included the *Iglesia Ni Cristo* (INC), the Seventh-Day Adventist, Philippine Independent Church (*Iglesia Filipina Independiente*) (IFI) and other independent churches.

While there was a strong call for unity under the Evangelical Union, there were differences that proved too difficult to resolve. For example, there were some initial efforts and discussions on the possibility of including the nationalist Philippine Independent Church (*Iglesia Filipina Independiente*) (IFI) under the leadership of Bishop Gregorio Aglipay.[36] In August 1902, representatives of the Evangelical Union and Bishop Aglipay met to discuss the possibility of a cooperative union.[37] However, due to their disagreement on theological and leadership issues, Bishop Aglipay chose to remain independent. According to Osias and Lorenzana, the differences between the American Protestant churches and the IFI was far from superficial since the theological stance of the Aglipayan church at that time was as follows,

> It has chosen the Bible and science, love and liberty as its supporting pillars. It has stood for "the unity of God in Jesus" (*La unidad de Dios en Jesus*) thus inclining toward Unitarianism. It

---

34. Apilado, *Revolutionary Spirituality*, 84.

35. Dr Jorge Bocobo did not only serve as a key leader in Philippine Protestantism; he was also an active leader within Philippine society, becoming the fifth president of the University of the Philippines (Sitoy, *Comity and Unity*, 63).

36. For details, see Mary Dorita Clifford, "Iglesia Filipina Independiente: The Revolutionary Church," in *Studies in Philippine Church History*, ed. Gerald H. Anderson (Ithaca, NY: Cornell University Press, 1969), 223–255.

37. Deats, *Story of Methodism*, 12.

has enthroned reason as the guide in religious interpretation. It has sought to harmonize and unify the "authentic parts of the four Gospels" and evolve a Filipino Gospel simplified and coordinated.[38]

Early Proclamation and Reform Efforts

With the early conflicts and divisions resolved for the moment, as early as June 1901 when a civil government was established and especially when the Philippine-American War ended in 1902, the Protestant missionary effort began to expand from Manila to the provinces that were assigned to the different missionary groups by the comity agreement.[39] Their missionary strategies included both elements of gospel proclamation and social reforms.

Proclamation Efforts

These missionaries were enthusiastic in spreading the gospel message to those who would listen to them. Some were engaged in street preaching and other evangelistic ministries such as tent-meetings and open-air debates. For example, American missionaries would engage Roman Catholic priests in public debates to present their views and to win Filipino converts.[40] These early American and Filipino preachers took advantage of every opportunity as they preached in the "open fields or under trees and in tents."[41] In time, the task of preaching was also taken up by their Filipino converts who were sometimes more effective and persuasive than their American contemporaries.[42]

---

38. Osias and Lorenzana, *Evangelical Christianity*, 129.

39. Arcilla, *Recent Philippine History*, 36.

40. An example of this is Felix Manalo (founder of Iglesia ni Cristo) who "witnessed a debate on the use of images in worship in which a Roman Catholic priest was pitted against a Methodist pastor" resulting in Manalo's conversion to Methodism (Anne C. Harper, "A Filipino Church at Eighty Years: The Iglesia ni Cristo at the Turn of the Century," in *Chapters in Philippine Church History*, ed. Anne C. Kwantes [Manila: OMF Literature, 2001], 431).

41. This was part of the experience of Rev Melecio Melquiades de Armas, who was ordained as a minister of the Methodist church in 1914 (Gamaliel T. de Armas, Jr, "My Grandfathers Were Both Pastors," in *A Century of Bible Christians in the Philippines*, ed. Anne C. Kwantes [Manila: OMF Literature, 1998], 50).

42. Among these was Braulio Manikan, considered by many as the first Filipino Baptist pastor, who was indefatigable in his efforts to preach and communicate his new found faith (Jalando-on, *Philippine Baptist Pastors*, 77–79). Another example was father and son Paulino and Nicolas Zamora, who were related to Jacinto Zamora, one of the martyred priests

These early missionaries also distributed Bibles and Christian literature to help with their evangelistic efforts which had the added benefit of alleviating the problem of illiteracy. Many Filipinos were curious about the Bible since "the very possession of a Bible was considered seditious, and punishable by law" during the Spanish colonial period.[43] It soon became a bestseller, and everyone was asking for a copy. Converts would bring their Bibles to their relatives; reading portions and sharing the truths that they had learned from the Bible and the missionaries. As a result, the British and Foreign Bible Society and the American Bible Society accompanied the missionary efforts in the country; Bible translations and distributions became part of the proclamation ministry of these early missionaries.[44]

Aside from direct proclamation and Bible distribution, other strategies were employed by these missionaries such as public shows, picnics, concerts, reading programs, etc. so that the Christians not only presented the gospel, but also helped assuage the condition of Philippine society. For example, the Presbyterian missionary wives gathered mothers to teach "hygiene, child care, nutrition, and sometimes sewing . . . together with such lessons, or later, they would then teach Bible lessons."[45] Because Filipinos love music, the missionaries also taught music and the use of musical instruments, using Christian songs so that their Christian messages could be brought home by these students. Through these creative methods, the gospel began to spread among the Filipinos.

Social Reform Efforts

These early missionaries were also engaged in addressing public issues and concerns. They were involved with social reforms as they boldly engaged and

---

GomBurZa who was executed in connection with the Cavite Mutiny of 1872. Both father and son had initially served as interpreters for the American missionaries but eventually took the task of preaching the gospel to their own countrymen (Trinidad, *Monument to Religious Nationalism*, 65–66).

43. Kwantes, *Presbyterian Missionaries*, 37. Part of the reason for the ban on the Bible was to stem the influx of "political and religious concepts from overseas . . . [which] might result in uprisings against the Spanish regime . . . [thus, reading and owning a] Bible . . . gradually came to be seen as a symbol of liberty and democracy" (Anne C. Kwantes, "The Bible Comes to the Philippines," in *A Century of Bible Christians in the Philippines*, ed. Anne C. Kwantes [Manila: OMF Literature, 1998], 23).

44. Kwantes, "Bible Comes," 13–27; also Kwantes, *Presbyterian Missionaries*, 37–40.

45. Kwantes, *Presbyterian Missionaries*, 34.

challenged the moral and societal problems in the country. The Evangelical Union took advantage of their contacts to influence the law-makers of the land. Similar to the social gospel movements in America, these missionaries launched moral crusades against prostitution in the red-light district of Manila, campaigning against gambling and public dance halls, banning drunkenness, and opposing the Opium Bill of 1903.[46]

Aside from these, missionaries connected with the Evangelical Union were also involved in establishing institutions that addressed poverty, poor health, illiteracy, and other issues. These early missionaries and other laymen offered their particular strengths, abilities, and resources to institutions that would not only help the cause of the gospel but would help to create a growing and capable nation with its necessary infrastructures.

In terms of healthcare, several hospitals were established as union members shared their resources and manpower to operate them. One of the hospitals established by the Methodists was the Mary Johnston Hospital in Tondo that was built in 1908; established under the direction of the missionary doctor Dr Rebecca Parish. "Soon after the hospital was built the Mary Johnston Hospital School of Nursing was established."[47] Other medical facilities and hospitals were established both in Manila and key provinces of the country.

As for the area of literacy, the cooperative efforts of union members enabled them to reach more children and young adults through evangelistic classes and to help in the incipient educational system of the country. Aside from the impact of the Bible literacy program, other missionaries started educational programs and schools for the Filipinos. For example, the Methodists were able to establish the St. Paul Kindergarten School in Tondo on 1906 which offered education to the Filipino children.[48] Joint inter-denominational Sunday schools and other trainings were offered to the Filipinos. For example, Rev Dr Elmer K. Higdon championed the "plight

---

46. For a short summary of details, see Sitoy, *Comity and Unity*, 41; also Kwantes, *Presbyterian Missionaries*, 55–56.

47. de Armas, "My Grandfathers," 50

48. de Armas, 51.

of the rural people" and Dr Frank C. Laubach who strongly campaigned for the cause of education and literacy.[49]

Thus, in the first two decades of Philippine Protestantism, the Americans were the primary source of manpower and leadership with Filipinos supporting, as the latter was being prepared for leadership. It was a period of growth and expansion. As Deats summarizes this period by referring to the success of the Evangelical Union, "As a result of the comity agreement and further evidences of good will on the part of the groups concerned, Protestant work was able to advance rapidly with little effort being wasted upon denominational rivalry and doctrinal quarrels. A united front against a decadent veneer of Christianity and widespread paganism was thus made."[50] This serene outlook would soon change as schisms and mergers took place among these churches, and as the Filipinos began to assert themselves.

Mergers and Schisms Among Pre-War Protestant Churches (1910–1920s)

The second and the third decade of Philippine Protestantism could be described as years of "growing pains." While the Americans were primarily focused on establishing Protestantism as the main religion,[51] the emerging Filipino leaders were beginning to aspire for autonomy and independence as they longed to lead these growing Filipino churches.[52] While these two goals would often coincide with each other, there were times that they did not. It was the latter that caused a growing dissatisfaction and unrest among these nationals. Among the sources of this growing resentment were "the bitter debates in the United States Congress on the issue of Philippine independence, where derogatory speeches were leveled against the Filipino people,

---

49. For details, see Sitoy, *Comity and Unity*, 45–55.

50. Deats, *Story of Methodism*, 11.

51. Among their strategies, Apilado mentions the printing of "unusually large number of written literature expressing reiteration of the goal of Protestantism in the Philippines to counteract the errors of Roman Catholicism" (Apilado, *Revolutionary Spirituality*, 108–109).

52. According to Achútegui and Bernad, the motivations of the Katipuneros were not religious rather their goal was to be free from "the political domination of Spain and the socio-political ascendancy of the friars" (Pedro S. de Achútegui and Miguel A. Bernad, *Religious Revolution in the Philippines: The Life and Church of Gregorio Aglipay 1860-1960*, vol. 1, *From Aglipay's Birth to His Death: 1860-1940* [Manila: Ateneo de Manila, 1960], 235).

continued to reach the Philippines and to stir the people's emotions against the colonial status to which they were being relegated."[53] This reverberated within the churches as some of these Filipino leaders grew impatient as they waited for the time that they would be given autonomy. It is therefore unfortunate that the Americans who sought to liberate the Filipinos from the Spaniards and were preparing them for independence were seen as replacements of their former colonial masters.[54] The following are some of the key events during this period.

The IEMELIF (1909)

As mentioned, prior to the arrival of Protestantism, Spanish authorities outlawed the ownership and reading of the Bible where violators were "severely punished."[55] Despite the ban, copies of the Bible continued to enter the country as intrepid individuals smuggled the Bible into the Philippines. One of these "contraband" Bibles was eventually bought and read secretly by Paulino Zamora, the nephew of the martyred priest Jacinto Zamora. This defiance to Spanish authority may have been caused by Don Paulino's dissatisfaction with Roman Catholicism beginning with the "unjust execution of his priest-uncle . . . [he] started questioning the Church restrictions on the individual's right to exercise his own judgment on any pronouncement of the Church or to blind conformity to the arbitrary actions of the friars."[56] Unfortunately, Don Paulino was caught, arrested, and sent into exile in the Cueta Penal Colony of Spain in the Mediterranean.[57] During his time of exile, his son Nicolas followed his example and read the Bible for himself whereupon he secretly embraced this new faith too. After Don Paulino Zamora was finally released from Spanish incarceration and returned to the Philippines; he and his son, Nicolas became supporters and passionate preachers of the gospel even before the Protestant missionaries arrived.

---

53. Trinidad, *Monument to Religious Nationalism*, 116

54. Apilado, *Revolutionary Spirituality*, 257–260

55. Anne C. Kwantes, "The Bible Society in the Philippines: The Story of Bibles Society Work," in *Chapters in Philippine Church History*, ed. Anne C. Kwantes (Manila: OMF Literature, 2001), 464.

56. Trinidad, *Monument to Religious Nationalism*, 49.

57. Ruben F. Trinidad, "Nicolas Zamora and the IEMELIF Church," in *Chapters in Philippine Church History*, ed. Anne C. Kwantes (Manila, Philippines: OMF Literature, 2001), 206.

Thus, when the American missionaries arrived, the Zamora family was among the very first converts, offering their house as a venue for the first Filipino Presbyterian meeting in Manila.[58] The whole family was committed to the work; in particular, Don Paulino and his son Nicholas were both active in the propagation of Protestantism and served as interpreters for the Americans as they helped established a Filipino congregation in Tondo, Manila. Don Paulino continued to serve under the Presbyterians until his death in 1907.

Initially affiliated with the Presbyterians, Nicolas Zamora transferred to the Methodists after he was asked to help the ministry efforts of Arthur W. Prautch.[59] By March 1900 he was ordained as a deacon of the Methodist-Episcopal Church which earned him the title as the "first Filipino ever ordained as a minister of the Gospel."[60] In 1903, he was installed as the first Filipino pastor of the Methodist Church in Cervantes, now known as the Knox Memorial Church. In the same year, he was given the title "presbyter" during the annual gathering of American Methodist Missions. Admired and respected by both Americans and Filipinos alike, he was a gifted speaker and a nationalist who dreamt of an autonomous Filipino church which was self-governing and self-sustaining.

As more Filipinos were trained and began serving alongside the American missionaries, dissatisfaction grew among these local church leaders who felt that they weren't given more authority to lead and to decide for these congregation. As a result, some groups began to exercise their freedom to choose for themselves and eventually broke away from American leadership.[61] One such group that was considered as a threat of schism was the *Ang Kapisanang Katotohanan* (The Society of Truth) in the Methodist church in Tondo,

---

58. Carlos Quirino, "Nicolas V. Zamora," in *Who's Who in Philippine History* (Manila: Tahanan Book, 1995), accessed 3 October 2009, http://www.nhi.gov.ph/downloads/rel0017.pdf.

59. While there were some tensions regarding the denominational affiliation of the Zamoras, the resolution came as the senior Zamora stayed with the Presbyterians while Nicolas joined the Methodist where he served as a regular lay evangelist/preacher. For details, see Trinidad, *Monument to Religious Nationalism*, 63–67.

60. Trinidad, "Nicolas Zamora," 208.

61. There were several incidents of schisms. For example, Manuel Aurora formed the *Cristianos Vivos* in Baliwag, Bulacan which separated from the Methodist church in 1906 (Sitoy, *Comity and Unity*, 57).

which was initially started to help the spread of the gospel. Suspicions began with some of the initiatives of these Filipinos who felt that there were better ways in preaching the gospel that they felt were "more attuned to the temper of the Filipinos."[62] Sadly, instead of encouraging the initiative of the society, the Americans tried to control their efforts. This resulted in increased tensions and some resentment with a growing desire for autonomy.

In an effort to resolve the situation; Zamora, who had been instrumental in establishing the Methodist work in Tondo, was reassigned to the troubled church in 1906 to deal with the "dissenters" who were on the verge of breaking away to form their own political-religious organization.[63] When Zamora met the leaders of the society, some had challenged him to consider becoming the head of a breakaway group. However, Zamora declined the offer and calls for secession were suppressed, eventually bringing growth to this Methodist church in Tondo. By 1907, Zamora reported to the Methodist leadership that the issue of the society was finally resolved.[64]

However, in 1909, Zamora began to seriously reconsider the call for autonomy as he was provoked by two major issues. The first was on matters pertaining to the control of the Methodist Church in America of their churches in the Philippines where the Filipino leaders felt that they were given a very "small voice" in the church which they had labored to build.[65] The second reason was on a more personal matter as it stemmed from "frictions" that Zamora had with certain American missionaries. For example, District Superintendent Harry Farmer accused Zamora of charging higher fees for solemnizing weddings and that he (Zamora) had solemnized the marriage of minors without parental consent. In his defense, Zamora felt that the issue of wedding fees and decisions to solemnize weddings was

---

62. Trinidad, *Religious Nationalism*, 113.

63. Deats, *Story of Methodism*, 39–40.

64. Trinidad explains that Zamora diverted their energies to "more meaningful activities" such as "conducting an intensive nightly evangelistic campaign for three and a half months" where "more than one hundred members accepted the Lord and joined the Church" (Trinidad, *Religious Nationalism*, 115).

65. Deats, *Story of Methodism*, 42. During the Methodist General Conference of 1908, the proposal to change the status of the Philippine Methodist church from a "home field status" (which meant that they would continue to be under the Americans control) to a "foreign field status" (which meant that the Philippine Church could have an autonomous church government) was rejected (Trinidad, *Monument to Religious Nationalism*, 117).

already within the pastor's personal discretion. Thus, this unjust treatment and false accusation finally drove Zamora to seriously consider separating from the Americans as he felt that this was another example where Filipinos were "exploited" by the American missionaries and were not given "proper recognition in the Church hierarchy."[66]

Realizing that their hope for autonomy could only be gained through the establishment of their own church, Zamora and the lay preachers of Tondo established the *La Iglesia Evangelica Metodista en las Islas Filipinas* (IEMELIF) during the Philippine Islands Annual Conference in 1909. His dissent caused a rift among the Filipinos of the Methodist Church. Those who had been trained under the American schools disagreed with Zamora, while he was strongly supported and followed by "a movement of the older Tagalogs, who had been nurtured on a fervent nationalism that a more moderate younger generation did not share."[67] Zamora inaugurated the IEMELIF in Moriones, Tondo, Manila on the morning of 28 February 1909, and became its first bishop and General Superintendent, severing all ties with their American counterpart. Thus the IEMELIF became one of the first autonomous Protestant churches in the Philippines, prompted by their leader's desire for independence and self governance.

The Evangelical Church of the Philippines (Independent Presbyterian) (1914)

The Presbyterians were also experiencing similar tensions within their Filipino churches. While these American missionaries were committed to see that these "indigenous churches should press forward . . . to be self-propagating, self-governing, and self-supporting;"[68] the majority of the American leaders were not convinced that it was time for a transition in leadership despite the growing number of capable Filipino leaders. As Kwantes describes the perspectives of these American leaders, "most Protestant missionaries thought that the fledgling young churches were not yet mature enough to

---

66. Trinidad, *Monument to Religious Nationalism*, 118.
67. Deats, *Story of Methodism*, 43.
68. Rodgers, *Forty Years*, 181.

gain independence, and that pastors' periods of education and experience were as yet too brief."[69]

Sadly, due to the prevailing political atmosphere, this was not taken well and the delay was interpreted as a continuation of American domination upon the Filipino church. As a result, four Presbyterian congregations in Cavite and several groups in Rizal and Laguna formed the breakaway, *Iglesia de los Cristianos Filipinos* in 1912. This created a ripple effect as other Presbyterian congregations began to voice their desire for independence. This resulted in a re-evaluation of the current status of the American Presbyterian missionary efforts in the Philippines. Fearing that more schisms would follow and that all their efforts would be lost, it was decided by the General Assembly and the Synod of California that the Presbyterian congregations in the Philippines be withdrawn from the "jurisdiction of the Presbyterian Church in the United States of America" and an autonomous Filipino church – Evangelical Church of the Philippines (Independent Presbyterian) – with "three Presbyteries" in Manila, Iloilo and Dumaguete be formed.[70] Although the Evangelical Church of the Philippines (Independent Presbyterian) (ECP-IP) was established in 1914, the full reality of the transition was still in the future as the American missionaries continued to work and lead in some of the churches while some of the property titles were still under the Americans especially with those "land and buildings" where "more than half of the cost had been provided by Christians overseas."[71]

The Union Church of Manila (1914)

While the IEMELIF and the ECP-IP were formed as new denominations, the first successful merger on a local church level was the formation of the Union Church of Manila (UCM) which was the "fusion" of the American members of the Presbyterian and Methodists churches and several members from the Disciples in Manila on 11 October 1914. While such a union had always been discussed on a hypothetical level by union members, the matter never progressed from the apparent lack of enthusiasm among these churches and denominations.

---

69. Kwantes, *Presbyterian Missionaries*, 65.
70. Rodgers, *Forty Years*, 172.
71. Kwantes, *Presbyterian Missionaries*, 66.

However, the situation changed when Bishop William F. Oldham of the Methodist Board of Foreign Missions and Arthur J. Brown of the Presbyterian Missionary Board informed their respective local churches in Manila that a merger should be seriously considered in light of the current financial constraints. Hence, negotiations were held between the Presbyterians and the Methodists for the terms of union between their local churches in Manila. As their differences and concerns were settled, these two local groups became one local church; due to the excitement generated by the merger, twenty-five members from the congregation of the Disciples joined as individuals. Rogers reports that for their part, "the Presbyterian Church contributed the original lot . . . and the building as it was in 1914 . . . [while] the Methodist Church contributed its organ and $26,000."[72] UCM was a truly unified organic church with one pastor leading one flock.

Nevertheless, there was not enough momentum for their mother denominations to consider a merger; the differences were still insurmountable at that time. While the impetus for the merger was due to financial difficulties, nevertheless UCM was a milestone in setting an example of how churches could set aside their differences to form one local body.

The Evangelical Christian Church of the Philippine Islands (1915)

Encouraged by the successful inauguration of the Union Church of Manila, several members of the Evangelical Union came up with an ambitious attempt to merge all existing Protestant churches into the *La Iglesia Cristiana Evangelica de las Islas Filipinas* (The Evangelical Christian Church of the Philippine Islands) in 1915. The proposal suggested the formation of a unified national church that broke down the denominational divisions among the American-established churches with four major divisions or districts, namely "the Ilocano District, the Tagalog District, the Western Visayas District and the Eastern Visayas District" (the whole of Mindanao included in the last district).[73]

---

72. Rodgers, *Forty Years*, 131.
73. Sitoy, *Comity and Unity*, 58.

When the proposal was brought to the different churches for confirmation, the merger was opposed by the Baptist and the Disciples, the problem was on a specific issue:

> The clause concerning the powers of the General Advisory Council of the United Church proved to be a serious stumbling block to the Baptists and the Disciples. . . . both jealously guarded their congregationalist polity and their strong sense of congregational independence, feared that in the future the majority might invest the General Advisory Council with powers which both groups believed should properly reside only in the individual congregations and not in any centralized ecclesiastical body.[74]

Although both churches were a minority among the merging bodies, the negotiations failed since the other churches would not continue without the presence of the two.

The United Church of Manila (1924)

On 24 February 1924, the United Church of Manila was formed by several churches that longed for independence and were frustrated with the slowness of the negotiations to form a unified Filipino church. The initial members were from the United Brethren Student Church in Manila and a number from the Congregationalists and the Baptists. Led by Rev Juan Abellera,[75] several Filipino leaders and their missionary advisers established this Filipino church which was not directly under the Evangelical Union.[76] With the vigor and enthusiasm of the youth, the leaders of this unified Filipino church were

---

74. T. Valentino Sitoy, Jr, *Several Springs, One Stream: The United Church of Christ in the Philippines*, vol. 1, *Heritage and Origins (1898-1948)* (Quezon City, Philippines: United Church of Christ in the Philippines, 1992), 215–216.

75. Rev Juan Abellera was the "first Filipino United Brethren minister to graduate from the Union Theological Seminary" in 1912 where he had the privilege of giving the graduation address (Apilado, *Revolutionary Spirituality*, 110).

76. Sitoy gives the name of several of these Filipino leaders who negotiated for the formation of the United Church of Manila, these are: Dr Camilo Osias, Mr Leoncio Dacanay, Mr Isaac Barza, Mrs Josefa Jara Martinez, Dr Mauro Baradi, Dr Gumersindo Garcia, Atty Mateo Occeña, the Rev Juan A. Abellera, and the "three missionaries, namely, Dr. Frank C. Laubach, of the American Board, and two United Brethren missionaries, Dr. Clayton C. Witmer and Dr. Howard W. Widdoes" (Sitoy, *Comity and Unity*, 67).

motivated by their desire to show their elders that unification was possible. This merger would provide the pattern and encouragement for future mergers among the Protestant churches as they sought for independence through the establishment of an independent Filipino church.

When Rev Abellera resigned due to ill health; Dr Laubach served as interim until he was "succeeded by a dynamic and energetic young United Brethren minister," named Enrique C. Sobrepeña.[77] Through his efforts, Rev Sobrepeña was able to increase the church's membership until it reached the two-thousand-member mark when he finally left the church in 1953.[78] This was another important achievement for the cause of ecumenism as the church became the motivation for the formation of a new denomination through the merger of several churches.

The United Evangelical Church in the Philippines Islands (1929)

In the atmosphere of cooperation and unity that were taking place among the Filipino churches, the Presbyterians and the Congregationalists initiated talks on the possibility of a merger among the churches that were planted by these two missionary groups. Meeting in Marawi City in April 1921, leaders from these two denominations "adopted resolutions . . . [to] consider the possibility of union, together with any other churches which might be interested."[79]

This vision was taken up by the new generation of Filipino Protestants. In November 1926, Rev Sobrepeña inaugurated and served as the first president of the Filipino Christian Youth Movement; a student movement that called upon their fellow Christian youth to live morally upright lives.[80] Its main contribution to the unity of the church was the fifth article of the *Decalogue of the Filipino Youth* where it affirmed the call for the Protestant Filipino

---

77. Sitoy, *Several Springs, One Stream*, 228.

78. Otilio R. Gorospe, "Church Builder and Pastor," in *Enrique C. Sobrepeña: His Life and Work,* eds. Fern Babcock Grant, Domini Torrevillas-Suarez, and Leon O. Ty (Quezon City: Sponsorship Committee, 1975), 34.

79. Norwood B. Tye, *Journeying with the United Church of Christ in the Philippines: A History* (Quezon City, Philippines: United Church of Christ in the Philippines, 1994), 12.

80. Mauro O. Baradi, "Youth Leader," in *Enrique C. Sobrepeña: His Life and Work*, eds. Fern Babcock Grant, Domini Torrevillas-Suarez, and Leon O. Ty (Quezon City: Sponsorship Committee, 1975), 19.

youth to support the formation of a unified national church. Osias gives an abbreviated form of the said article, "We believe the Christian church to be God's chosen instrument for the founding of His kingdom on earth. We shall therefore endeavor to establish a self-supporting, self-propagating, Filipino-led, evangelical church."[81] As one of its principal authors, Rev Sobrepeña continued this call for a unified national church through a series of sermons that he delivered in the United Church of Manila during the mid-1920s. His main theme was a challenge for all Filipino Protestants to unite and form an indigenous church.[82]

Thus on 15 March 1929, the plans to form a unified national church finally came true when the "Presbyterians, the Congregationalists, the United Brethren, and the independent United Church of Manila" merged to form the United Evangelical Church in the Philippines Islands (UECPI).[83] One key development was the growing number of Filipinos that were involved in the committee that was directly involved in the decision making of the Protestant churches in the mid-1920s.[84] This new denomination was the first to "cross the boundaries" set by the Evangelical Union as its churches were located throughout the entire country.

The National Christian Council (1929)

With the shift from American to Filipino leadership and the growth in the number of Filipino churches, the function and role of the Evangelical Union was re-evaluated by its member churches. It became apparent that there was a need to acknowledge and expand the role of Filipino pastors. This desire had reached its fullness in 1929, when Dr John R. Mott of the International Missionary Council went to the Philippines to confer with "60 selected

---

81. Osias and Lorenzana, *Evangelical Christianity*, 119–120.

82. Cornelio M. Ferrer, "Apostle of Church Union," in *Enrique C. Sobrepeña: His Life and Work*, eds. Fern Babcock Grant, Domini Torrevillas-Suarez, and Leon O. Ty (Quezon City: Sponsorship Committee, 1975), 101.

83. Sitoy, *Comity and Unity*, 68–69

84. "The committee was composed of the following: Rev. Irving M. Channon and Rev. Proculo A. Rodriguez, representing the Congregational Church; Rev. J. L. Hooper, Rev. Marciano Evangelista, Rev. John Dunlop, and Rev. Dr. Charles R. Hamilton, representing the Presbyterian Church; and Rev. Howard W. Widdoes, Rev. Cecilio P. Lorenzana, and Rev. Enrique C. Sobrepeña, representing the United Brethren" (Apilado, *Revolutionary Spirituality*, 253).

missionaries and Filipino church leaders" which led to the decision to replace the aging Evangelical Union with the National Christian Council (NCC).[85]

While the NCC continued the goals and the functions of the Evangelical Union, there were several key changes that were instituted. First, the leadership of the council was no longer dominated by the Americans as it was composed of a majority of Filipino church leaders. Dr Jorge Bocobo served as its president while Rev Enrique C. Sobrepeña and Rev Elmer K. Higdon functioned as the vice president and the executive secretary, respectively. In fact, by 1936 all leadership positions within the council were held by nationals, securing the Filipino church leaders' role in Philippine Protestantism. Second, instead of being a collective group of American missionary organizations, the council became a collection of local churches, religious agencies and mission groups. And, unlike the Evangelical Union where the Americans dominated the council, the Filipino churches were more influential than the mission groups. In addition, the Christian and Missionary Alliance and the newly established Philippine-Borneo Faith Mission became part of the NCC. The council continued the work that the American-led Evangelical Union had done in the past. For example, in 1932 the council was involved in the adjudication of a conflict between the Christian and Missionary Alliance and the United Evangelical Church regarding the territorial division in Cotobato.

The UNIDA (1932)

By November 1929, encouraged by the formation of the United Church of Manila and the establishment of the UECPI, Rev Sobrepeña invited several independent Filipino churches that had broken off from the Presbyterians and the Methodists to consider joining the UECPI. While some were willing to talk about the possibility of a merger, several remained reluctant for various reasons. Sitoy offers two reasons: first, these churches still saw the prominent presence of Americans in the UECPI – Rev Dr George W. Wright (general secretary) and Rev Dr S. L. Hooper (general treasurer) – second, that these independent churches had decided to stay within their close-knit fellowship.[86]

---

85. Sitoy, *Comity and Unity*, 72.
86. Sitoy, 75.

Through the influence and leadership of Don Toribio Teodoro, a key lay leader of the *La Iglesia Evangelica de los Cristianos Filipinos*, representatives of thirteen autonomous, indigenous Protestant churches came together to consider the possibility of forming their own united church. Of the original thirteen churches, only six were willing to enter into negotiations for a possible union at that time; namely, the *La Iglesia Evangelica de los Cristianos Filipinos*, the Reformed Methodist Evangelical Church, the Trinitarian Church, *La Iglesia de Jesucristo, Jerusalem Nueva, La Iglesia de Dios*, and the *Iglesia Evangelica de Atlag*.[87] In October of 1931, a committee was formed from among the leaders of these churches to finalize the terms of union and to determine a name for this unified church; thus the United Evangelical Church of the Philippines (*La Iglesia Evangelica Unida de Filipinas*), more commonly known as the UNIDA, was formed and publicly proclaimed on 3 January 1932.

The Philippine Methodist Church (1933)

Another schism took place within the Methodist Church when several ordained Filipino ministers, American missionaries and church leaders disagreed with the Church leaderships' decision resulting in the formation of the Philippine Methodist Church (PMC) in 1933.[88] The "rupture" stemmed from discord among the Methodist leaders when the decision of the Appellant Committee of the General Conference of the Methodist Church of America (GCMCA) reversed the judgment of local leaders who expelled Melecio de Armas from the ministry on the charge of adultery. The reversal was seen as another tangible example of American domination over the Filipinos and GCMCA's disregard of the local leadership's perspective and judgment.

The break started during the Philippine annual conference of the Methodist church when Rev Cipriano Navarro raised the question of the authority of the GCMCA to overrule the decision given by the local leadership. The resulting discussion soon became a heated debate with both parties unwilling to yield so that a break in the proceedings was called to ease the tensions. However, when compelled to return to the discussion, Rev Samuel

---

87. Sitoy, *Several Springs, One Stream*, 250.
88. Deats, *Story of Methodism*, 72.

W. Stagg, Rev Cipriano Navarro, five American missionaries, and twenty-seven Filipino ministers walked out of the conference and resigned from the Methodist Church; thus, the independent Philippine Methodist Church was formed with Rev Navarro as its bishop. It became self-supporting as the new church took care of financial needs of these American missionaries that joined the schism.

The Philippine Federation of Evangelical Churches (1938)

By 1938, the Filipino Protestant horizon had changed considerably with more local churches, denominations and religious organizations being led by Filipinos. The leaders of the National Christian Council, which replaced the Evangelical Union in 1929, decided to encourage churches to enter into a conciliar union. Thus in February 1938, the National Christian Council was replaced by the Philippine Federation of Evangelical Churches (PFEC) with two goals; first, to continue the spirit of comity, cooperation and effectiveness, and second, to search out the "possible bases for organic union with the view to bringing the churches to such union in due time."[89]

The transition was more than just a name change as there were several key differences between the NCC and the PFEC. First, all the top officers of the federation were now Filipinos with Dr Jorge Bocobo serving as president. Second, the federation was organized around local churches and denominations, and no longer around American mission organizations. Unlike in the early stages of Protestantism where the missionaries were in charge, many of these American missionaries were now working alongside or under the leadership of Filipino churches – the United Evangelical Church of the Philippine Islands, the Methodist church, the Church of Christ (Disciples) and the Convention of Philippine Baptist Churches. Third, there were two categories of membership; "full membership" which was open to all churches and "associate membership" which was offered to "agencies of interdenominational or non-denominational character."[90] Although the federation had

---

89. Estanislao Q. Abainza, "Leader in Two Movements: Cooperation of National Churches in Federations or Councils Organic Union of Churches," in *Enrique C. Sobrepeña: His Life and Work*, eds. Fern Babcock Grant, Domini Torrevillas-Suarez, and Leon O. Ty (Quezon City, Philippines: Sponsorship Committee, 1975), 104.

90. Sitoy, *Comity and Unity*, 83.

begun to function in place of the council, their plans and functions were suddenly interrupted by the outbreak of war.

Thus, the formation of the IEMELIF, the ECP-IP, and the PMC were examples of the aggressive efforts of the emerging Filipino leaders to seek autonomy and independence as they wrested control of their churches. It was also a time for mergers and unions as independent churches and other denominations combined to form new congregations and denominations as seen in the formation of the Union Church of Manila, United Church of Manila, UECPI, UNIDA. This period also marked the shift from American to Filipino leadership, as in the transformation of the American controlled Evangelical Union to the National Christian Council where both Americans and Filipinos were sharing the leadership role, and to the pre-war Philippine Federation of Evangelical Churches where Filipino leaders took full control of these councils.

Fundamentalism in the Philippines

Before moving into the World War II period, it is important to discuss the arrival of the modernist-fundamentalist controversy and the rise of fundamentalist churches in the pre-World War II era. It is through these churches that the fundamentalist/evangelical council would emerge in the post-war era.

Schisms Caused by Modernist-Fundamentalist Controversy (1920s)

After a brief hiatus during World War I, the modernist/liberal-fundamentalist controversy erupted once again among the churches and missionary organizations in the United States of America. While the Philippines was previously exempted from the "dispute," in the late 1920s and the early 1930s the controversy became an issue among the American missionaries and was carried on by their Filipino followers.

Schism within the Disciples of Christ (1926)

In the late 1920s, a dispute between liberals and conservatives erupted within the Disciples' Foreign Christian Missionary Society as a result of a conflict between missionaries on the issue of open membership.[91] The conflict began from an inquiry from Rev Leslie Wolfe on the Disciples' policy regarding new members who transferred from other churches.[92] Due to the fact that the Disciples had become a part of the United Christian Missionary Society which had "agreements to work in federation with several denominational boards in the Orient in order to present a more unified witness in preaching the gospel," it became a common practice to simply accept new members without requiring adult rebaptism.[93] Unfortunately, the discussion on the issue evolved into an argument that escalated into the issues of the modernist-fundamentalist controversy. Eventually, the two sides found it impossible to reconcile; Rev Wolfe led the conservatives who agreed with him on the issue of re-baptism to form the Churches of Christ – "Wolfe Group."[94]

The Formation of ABEO (1927)

Another missionary group that was affected by the controversy was the American Baptist Foreign Mission Society (ABFMS). Being given the Ilonggo-speaking provinces by the Evangelical Union, the Northern Baptist Convention missionaries were actively involved in evangelism and social work. In 1924, Miss Ellen Martien started a one-year Bible Institute course in the Baptist Student Center in Iloilo which was supported by Dr Raphael C. Thomas, Baptist missionary and director of the Iloilo Mission Hospital. In the past, the practice of medicine and the ministry of proclamation were considered as complementary.[95]

Tensions began when the Baptist Missions Board, which was committed to the establishment of "educational institutions" during this period, asked Dr Thomas to discontinue his involvement with the Bible Institute classes

---

91. The issue of open membership centers on whether new members needed to be baptized with with their confession of faith. For details, see David Filbeck and Robert S. Bates, "Asia, Missions in," in *The Encyclopedia of the Stone-Campbell Movement*, eds. Douglas A. Foster, Paul M. Blowers, Anthony L. Dunnavant, and D. Newell Williams (Grand Rapids: Eerdmans, 2004), 34–35.

92. For details of the conflict, see Apilado, *Revolutionary Spirituality*, 208–213.

93. Filbeck and Bates, "Asia," 35.

94. Sitoy, *Comity and Unity*, 49.

95. For example, Kwantes recounts the attitude of the Presbyterians when it came to the practice of medicine during this period, "medical missions and evangelism were closely linked . . . follow the example of Jesus Christ, who preached and taught but—who also healed" (Kwantes, *Presbyterian Missionaries*, 78–79).

and evangelistic trips, and instead limit his work to teaching and to the practice of medicine.[96] Disagreeing with the new Baptist policy and having a greater burden for missions and evangelism; Dr Thomas, Miss Martien, and a handful of staff who shared the same passion resigned and returned to America to reconsider their alternatives in 1925.[97] Back in the United States, through several consultations and meetings with key financial supporters who shared their theological convictions and commitment to missions, the Association of Baptists for the Evangelization of the Orient (ABEO) was established in Rhode Island with Dr Thomas as the leader of this newly established fundamentalist substitute for the ABFMS.[98]

The Arrival of Fundamentalist/Conservative Churches

While the mainline Protestant churches were establishing mergers, conciliar unions, and breakaways; several fundamentalist and conservative denominations began to operate in the Philippines during the late 1920s and the early 1930s. The following describes the beginnings of the three denominations that played an important role in the foundation and growth of PCEC.

The Assemblies of God (1926)

By the early 1920s, the Assemblies of God (AG) in the United States began sending out missionaries to help spread their Pentecostal teachings both in America and in other countries. The first AG missionary couple, Mr and Mrs Benjamin H. Caudle arrived in the Philippines in 1926.[99] They began their work in Pasay where they distributed gospel tracts, preached in public places

---

96. Arthur L. Tuggy and Ralph Toliver, *Seeing the Church in the Philippines* (Manila: OMF, 1972), 46.

97. Elaine Kennedy describes this conflict,
   the fundamentalist struggle concerned major doctrines and philosophy of ministry. The liberals emphasized social work ("social gospel") over evangelistic work. At this same time, Dr. Thomas, who loved "outreach work" in order to evangelize the people and start churches, was told by his fellow missionaries and by the Board in the States that he was to remain in the hospital as staff doctor and to stop his outreach evangelistic ministries. This command was a direct result of the "social gospel" and "institutional" philosophy of the Liberals.
   Kennedy, *Baptist Centennial History*, 52.

98. For details, see Association of Baptists for World Evangelism, "Our History," accessed 28 April 2010, https://www.abwe.org/our-history; and Doane Rest, "About Us: ABWE-Philippines," accessed 28 April 2010, http://doanerest.com/abwe-philippines/.

99. Tuggy and Toliver, *Seeing the Church*, 79.

(e.g. public markets, city streets, etc.), "conducted Sunday school classes for children in their backyard and a weekly Bible class for high schoolers and students of the University of the Philippines."[100] However, the summer heat and the ministry workload overwhelmed and affected Mrs Caudle's health, ending their missionary efforts as the couple returned to America.

In the 1930s, the AG missionary effort in the Philippines was continued by returning Filipino migrant workers who were exposed to the teachings of the AG while they worked in the United States.[101] As a result of the Great Depression where many lost their jobs and the conviction that they needed to bring the gospel to their home land, several Filipinos returned as "missionaries" to the Philippines. For example, Cris Carsulao was trained in Glad Tidings Bible Institute in California and eventually returned to his province in Sibalong, Antique in 1930.[102] Other AG pioneers such as Benito Acena, Rosendo Alcantara, Eugenio Suede, and Rodrigo C. Esperanza reached out to their families and neighbors, where small informal congregations were formed.[103]

When Leland E. Johnson and other American AG missionaries finally returned to the Philippines in 1939, they found these AG congregations were able to continue the work in the country. By 1941, the Bethel Bible Institute was opened in Baguio City.[104] Although they were beginning to experience some growth, their efforts were suspended by the Japanese occupation. Despite the absence of American workers and foreign aid, it was the Filipinos who continued the work and helped prepare them for the time when they would lead the ministry on their own. By 1953, the Philippine General Council of the Assemblies of God was established with Rev Rodrigo C. Esperanza as its first general superintendent.

---

100. Eleazer E. Javier, "The Pentecostal Legacy," in *Supplement to Chapters in Philippine Church History*, ed. Anne C. Kwantes (Manila: OMF Literature, 2002), 63.

101. As a result of World War I, Asia became a source for America's manpower needs. As Javier writes, "it is estimated that from 1920 to 1929 more than 80,000 Filipinos migrated to the mainland Unite States and to Hawaii" (Javier, "Pentecostal Legacy," 64).

102. Joseph Suico, "History," *Philippine General Council of the Assemblies of God*, accessed 27 May 2010, http://pgcag.wordpress.com/about/.

103. Javier, "Pentecostal Legacy," 64.

104. For details, see Trinidad E. Seleky, "The Organization of the Philippine Assemblies of God and the Role of Early Missionaries," *Asian Journal of Pentecostal Studies* 8, no. 2 (2005): 271–287.

The Wesleyan Church (1930s)

During the 1920s Filipino migrant workers were exposed to the Pilgrim Holiness Churches during their time in America. It was Rev Will Chambers of Pomona, California who began working among the Filipino fruit pickers in Alta Loma, California where he did not only establish a church among them but began training Filipinos who had the ability and the burden to preach.[105] And like the experience of the AG, these migrant workers returned to the Philippines in the 1930s when the Great Depression hit America.

Among the first Filipinos from this group was Miguel Zambrano, a former sailor in the US Navy who had joined and was trained at the Alta Loma Church. In 1932, he returned to the Philippines to share the gospel with his family in Balaoan, La Union; this resulted in a revival among his town-mates.[106] Although Zambrano abandoned the work that he had started, he was replaced by Rev Cornelio T. Bolayog and Antonio Campos who were instrumental in regathering the congregation which became the Pilgrim Holiness Church in the Philippines.[107]

Soon other Filipinos followed his example, returning to their families who were mainly farmers and low-income workers; thus, the Wesleyan Church began initially in the Ilocano area in the pre-World War II era. By 1937, Rev and Mrs R. K. Storey established a Pilgrim Holiness church "and a Bible school in Cabanatuan, Nueva Ecija."[108] In 1968, the Pilgrim Holiness Church and the Wesleyan Methodist Church merged and formed what is now known as the Wesleyan Church.[109]

ABEO and the Fundamental Baptist Efforts (1930s)

As for the Association of Baptists for the Evangelism in the Orient (ABEO), Dr and Mrs Raphael C. Thomas with four other women (i.e. Ellen Martien, Bessie Traber, Miss Drake, and Helen Hinkley) returned to the Philippines

---

105. Robert A. Bickert, "Perception and Response to Receptivity: The History and Growth of the Wesleyan Church in the Philippines 1932-1994" (Dmiss. diss., Asbury Theological Seminary, Wilmore, Kentucky, 1996), 184–185).

106. Floyd T. Cunningham, "Diversities within Post-War Philippine Protestantism," *Mediator* 5, no. 1 (October 2003): 65.

107. Bickert, "Perception and Response to Receptivity," 188.

108. Cunningham, "Diversities," 65.

109. Mead and Hill, *Handbook of Denominations*, 248.

to begin the missionary effort of their newly established missionary organization. It was initially dismissed by their fellow American missionaries as a "flash in the pan, [with] a handful of malcontents . . . a little family affair, just one man and a group of women on the field with the man's mother-in-law running things at the home end."[110] Despite this critique, this fundamentalist non-ecumenical mission organization that aimed to reach the entire Philippines and beyond began their work on two fronts – Iloilo and Manila.[111]

By 1928, ABEO's work in Iloilo was focused on reorganizing the "makeshift" Bible Institute which had previously operated from the Student Center in front of the Iloilo National High School in La Paz, Iloilo City.[112] The Student Center and the Bible Institute were established by Ellen Martien in 1923, where she and Dr Thomas conducted trainings among Filipinos for evangelism and church planting during their time with the ABFMS. Under ABEO's reorganization in 1928, the original "one-year Bible and evangelistic training course for Christian workers" was transformed into a "two-year training program with Miss Helen Hinckley as the first Director" and the Bible Institute was transferred to Ledesma Street in the middle of Iloilo city.[113] Its main objective was to train Filipino pastors and church workers who would labor alongside the American missionaries in planting churches throughout the country. Thus, Iloilo became a key city in the early efforts of the Fundamental Baptist churches in the pre-war period. The Bible school in Iloilo was named the Doane Evangelistic Institute (DEI) which was later renamed Doane Baptist Bible Institute (DBBI). The name Doane comes from William Howard Doane who was the father-in-law of Mrs George W. Doane – Dr Thomas's major financial contributor who used her inheritance to finance the work in the Philippines (DEI).[114]

---

110. Harold T. Commons, *Heritage and Harvest: the History of the Association of Baptists for World Evangelism* (Cherry Hill, NJ: Association of Baptists for World Evangelism, 1981), 29.

111. Nacita, *Celebrating God's Mercy*, 10.

112. n.a., "Historical Sketch of Doane Baptist Seminary," in *Advancing the Gospel Towards 2000*, Souvenir Program at the 23rd AFBCP Biennial Conference, Malaybalay, Bukidnon, Philippines, 5–8 May 1997.

113. n.a., "Historical Sketch of Doane Baptist Seminary."

114. Commons, *Heritage and Harvest*, 7.

The second ABEO effort was in Manila. As soon as the efforts to re-establish DEI were secure, Dr Thomas immediately turned over the responsibilities to his female coworkers and began work in the country's capital within that same year. In Manila, he sought out the Baptist students from Iloilo who had transferred to the capital for further studies and for a better future. Aside from this, Dr Thomas employed creative approaches to spread the gospel. At one point, he had put up "a booth selling Bibles" and invited people to attend gospel meetings in the midst of Manila's carnival where dancing and gambling were the norm. It was a huge success where "180 or more wrote down that they would like to join an evangelical church."[115] Through his creative efforts, Dr Thomas was able to establish ABEO's ministry in the city of Manila. Within the same year, he was able to establish the Manila Evangelistic Institute (MEI) which offered a Bible institute that had a similar curriculum and objectives to the DEI in Iloilo.[116] By late 1928, Dr Thomas founded and led the First Baptist Church of Manila (FBCM)[117] from an initial group of thirty-two members who were from the "church families he had known for years in the Visayas."[118] Initially, the Bible school and the church shared a rented property next to the University of the Philippines campus in Taft Avenue; however, seeing a need for a more permanent location, they purchased a property which was located on Pennsylvania and Oregon Avenues (now known as Leon Guinto Sr. St. and Padre Faura St. in Ermita, Manila). With Dr Thomas as the main preacher, pastor, and teacher; the membership of the FBCM continued to grow and the MEI was able to train new workers for the ministry. Around the early 1930s, Dr Thomas transferred leadership of the FBCM to Dr Paul Culley "so that he could put more time and energy into trips to Iloilo."[119]

---

115. Kennedy, *Baptist Centennial History*, 67–68.

116. Commons, *Heritage and Harvest*, 13.

117. The title "First Baptist" refers to the very first Baptist church that was established in that particular city irrespective of denominational affiliation. In this case, the First Baptist Church was affiliated with the Fundamental Baptist denomination (Nacita, *Celebrating God's Mercy*, 10).

118. Commons, *Heritage and Harvest*, 13.

119. Kennedy, *Baptist Centennial History*, 68.

Baptist Separation Issues in Iloilo (1930s)

Prior to the arrival of ABEO in the late 1920s, the Baptist churches that were established in the Visayas were all connected with the Northern Baptist Convention; hence, these churches referred to themselves as "Convention Baptist" or simply "Convention." However, by the late 1920s and early 1930s, a growing number of churches were planted by fundamentalist Baptist pastors and missionaries trained by ABEO. These churches referred to themselves as "Fundamentalist Fellowship Baptist" or simply "Fellowship."

Unfortunately, this resulted in antagonism between these two Baptist groups as they competed with each other in the Western Visayan region.[120] Some questioned the need for existence of these two separate Baptist churches. First, there seemed to be no apparent difference between the churches since they were both called Baptist and were both led by American missionaries and Filipino pastors. Second, to a degree, the two groups held similar practices and doctrines, and both were engaged in evangelistic efforts despite the growing emphasis by some of the Convention Baptist churches on the "social gospel."[121] Third, some Filipino families were becoming "divided and separated" as a result of their affiliation with either of the two Baptist churches, causing undue friction and difficulties especially when some family members would insist on their separation from each other during family events and other occasions.[122] Finally, in these early years, some of the DEI graduates served as pastors and church leaders in some of the Convention Baptist churches, fostering the impression that there were really no differences between the two Baptist churches after all. In fact, some of these

---

120. Kennedy, 70.

121. Although some of the more liberal-leaning Convention Baptist churches were becoming more focused on social work in lieu of evangelism, at this time, it was more of the exception than the rule and was due to the conviction of the local leadership of that particular church or of the missionaries who established the church. This is due to the inclusivist stance of ABFMS which allowed for both modernists/liberals and fundamentalist to serve under them. In fact, the author has met and known several pastors and members from the Convention Baptist Church who are equally zealous in evangelism and are committed to conservative and fundamentalist theology, thus to generalize that all Protestants from the Convention Baptist group are liberals is quite erroneous. In fact, one can argue that there are "liberals" and "fundamentalists" in every religious group.

122. Bishop Fred Magbanua had a similar experience where he was unable to speak in his hometown church – a Fellowship Church, since he was ordained in the Conservative Baptist Church. See Appendix D: "Interview with Fred Magbanua Jr," particularly the responses to questions 19–23.

Convention Baptist Churches were conservative and even fundamentalist in their practice and doctrines.[123] Unfortunately, both groups had become critical of each other; where the Convention churches were accused of being liberals by the Fellowship, and the Fellowship churches were accused of "being deserters" by the Convention Baptists. Thus, it was suggested that the two Baptist churches should merge to amend the situation.

However, the leadership of the Fundamental Baptists was set against any form of merger. Kennedy gives the following reasons for their decision to remain separate:

> 1. Such a union would require "compromise between modernists of various shades" and these Fundamental Baptists "cannot compromise" their theology;
>
> 2. The fundamentalists could not "approve of the undue proportion given to secular education" by the ABFMS;
>
> 3. They could not "accept the control and domination of a Convention which requires 36% of contributions for home expenses in an un-Baptistic organization";
>
> 4. They could not "accept the merger of churches" under the United Evangelical Church of the Philippines, which were not Fundamental Baptist;
>
> 5. The accusation of compromise of those "so-called fundamentalists who remained on the Foreign Mission Board are in reality endorsing the *majority* who advocate modernism teaching or an inclusive policy for harmony."[124]

Thus, the two Baptist churches continued to compete with each other which resulted in confusion and tensions in both parties.

---

123. These churches were either conservative or liberal "depending upon the position of the founding missionary and the training of the Filipino pastor" (Kennedy, *Baptist Centennial History*, 69).

124. Kennedy, *Baptist Centennial History*, 71.

Fundamental Baptist Churches Growth and Expansion (late 1930s to 1940s)

Despite their tensions with the other Protestant churches in the country, the pre-war period saw the expansion of the Fundamental Baptist work as newly trained Filipino pastors and evangelists from the MEI and DEI labored alongside the newly-arrived American missionaries from ABEO. Within the next few years, two provinces – Palawan and Bukidnon where added to ABEO's missionary field.

Fundamental Baptist Efforts in Palawan.

Although Palawan was initially assigned to the Presbyterians by the Evangelical Union, the province remained virtually untouched except for the work of a Dr Jansen in a leper colony and three small churches. In the later part of the 1920s, negotiations began on the possibility of transferring the missionary territory of Palawan from the Presbyterian church to the missionaries of ABEO. This "unexpected gift" was given after reports of ABFMS' efforts to prevent the ABEO from expanding their work in other areas of Panay became known among the American missionary groups in the Philippines.[125] Sympathetic to their troubles, some of the "old-time Presbyterian missionaries" (who had "admired his courageous stand" and shared similar convictions with Dr Thomas) agreed to the transfer of Palawan from the Presbyterians to the ABEO as their missionary field in 1930.[126] Thus, the territory was officially handed over to ABEO through a letter sent by the Presbyterians to Dr Thomas on 17 October 1930. Since Palawan was not part of the inter-island shipping route at that time, ABEO acquired a ship and a captain to facilitate the work in the islands of Palawan. ABEO missionaries chose to establish their home base in Cuyo and soon several churches were formed in the different islands within the province. Among those who were commissioned to work: "1. Mr. Catano (the first graduate of DEI) was sent to Cuyo. 2. Mr. Hibala was sent to Coron. 3. Mr. Alejandro Caspe was sent to Aborlan."[127]

---

125. Kennedy, 68.
126. Commons, *Heritage and Harvest*, 16.
127. Kennedy, *Baptist Centennial History*, 68–69.

Fundamental Baptist Efforts in Bukidnon.

The vision to start work in Bukidnon began as a result of a Missionary survey done by Rev Henry De Vries in 1925. After his furlough, Rev De Vries began his efforts in Malaybalay in 1929. As the work progressed, a nurse named Rhoda Little and a Bible woman named Beatrice Kuer joined in expanding the missionary effort. Miss Kuer, who was a "graduate from Moody Bible Institute in Chicago . . . started the Bukidnon Bible Institute to train National Workers."[128] Soon the medical clinics and the Bible classes brought converts. The Bible school training was intense with a required "jungle ministry for one week in itinerary preaching . . . [where] students came home worn out and fatigued [where some] walked sometimes on trails with knee-deep mud"; it was difficult and very few were able to complete their four-year study.[129] Due to financial difficulties, Rev De Vries joined ABEO in 1937. Afterwards, financial support and missionary manpower from ABEO came to continue the work in the province. When war came to Bukidnon, the ministry was continued by intrepid and indefatigable Filipinos who labored until the end of the war and beyond.

Thus, as a result of their aggressiveness and unwillingness to be restricted by the comity agreement, several "infant churches were established throughout the Visayas, on the islands of Panay, Guimaras and Negros . . . the work spread from Manila to towns and barrios in the province of Rizal . . . [and] in the province of Palawan" and Bukidnon.[130] By 1939, ABEO was renamed the Association of Baptists for World Evangelism (ABWE) as new missionary efforts were started in South America and other fields.

Wartime Union and Activities (1942–1946)

All these church and missionary efforts were put on hold at the onset of World War II. On the morning of 7 December 1941, Japan declared war on the United States when it attacked the American Naval Base in Pearl Harbor and four hours later, the Japanese airplanes bombed Clark Field,

---

128. n.a., "The Concise History of the Bukidnon Association of Fundamental Baptist Churches," in *Advancing the Gospel Towards 2000*, Souvenir Program at the 23rd AFBCP Biennial Conference, Malaybalay, Bukidnon, Philippines, 5–8 May 19970, n.p.

129. "Concise History."

130. Commons, *Heritage and Harvest*, 26.

Nichols Field, and other American military installations in the Philippines. By January 1942, Japan had secured most of the key places in the country except for Bataan and Corregidor.[131]

And even before the two strongholds fell, the Japanese had already ordered American and British citizens to be confined by 4 January 1942 at the University of Santo Tomas in Manila. Hartendorp describes their situation,

> within 10 days, there were over 3,000 people in the camp, some 2,000 of whom were lodged in the main building, 700 in the gymnasium, and 400 in the annex. From 30 to 50 people were jammed in each of the rooms in the main building an annex, and the average floor space per person was only around 22 square feet; in some rooms it was at one time as low as 16 square feet. . . . They were thrown into the camp stripped of virtually all their possessions, without the commonest necessities and conveniences; many of them without other clothing than they had on, without bedding, without food, without money.[132]

With the victory of the Imperial Japanese Army and the arrest of all westerners, American leadership in the Protestant church in the Philippines finally came to an abrupt end. As part of their strategic plan, the Japanese sought to win the hearts of the Filipinos and convince them to take part in the Japanese vision of a "Greater East Asia Co-Prosperity Sphere." The Japanese were familiar with the Filipinos desire to gain independence from the American control.

In their effort to undo all traces of American influence, the Japanese were careful with how they dealt with the religious convictions of the Filipinos. Thus, the Imperial Japanese Army studied the religious situation in the Philippines and sought for a way to subvert the Filipinos over to the Japanese side. In line with this, the Japanese formed the Religious Section of the Japanese Imperial Army with the goal of supplanting the religious influence of the westerners in Asia. According to Wakai,

---

131. Despite heroic efforts of the United States Army Forces in the Far East (USAFFE), Bataan fell into Japanese hands by April and Corregidor fell a month later.

132. A. V. H. Hartendorp, *The Japanese Occupation of the Philippines* (Manila: Bookmark, 1967), 11–12.

the need to establish an organization to win the hearts of Asians was anticipated within the Japanese military government several years before the war began. The first propaganda force was organized in 1938, under the supervision of the Bureau of Military Affairs of the Department of the Military. This unit was to engage in information gathering and propaganda activities.[133]

Religious Section of the Japanese Imperial Army

On 24 December 1941, the Religious Section of the Japanese Army landed with the rest of the Japanese forces at Lingayen Gulf. By 1 January 1942, the Religious Section, with twenty-six members – fourteen Roman Catholics and twelve Protestants – under the leadership of Lt. Col. Narusawa Tomonori, began their work in Manila and Baguio.[134] The Japanese had three specific goals according to Wakai,

> In the space of one year the members of the Religious Section were to accomplish three miracles: 1) to win the hearts and minds of Filipino Christians within this limited time; 2) to eradicate decades of American influence from the Protestant churches in the Philippines; and 3) to establish a church union in the country.[135]

On 4 January 1942, the Religious Section had entered Manila and set up their headquarters within the Ateneo Grade School building in Intramuros.[136] The Japanese started their propaganda efforts by showing their desire to become friends and that there were Japanese Roman Catholics and Protestants who shared the same faith and religious practices. For example, Japanese Roman Catholic priests "officiated at 'friendship masses' in Manila on the second Sunday following the occupation" to convince the Filipinos that

---

133. Kazuo Wakai, "Protestants in the Japanese Imperial Army in the Philippines, December 1941 to December 1942," in *Chapters in Philippine Church History*, ed. Anne C. Kwantes (Manila, Philippines: OMF Literature, 2001), 293.

134. Wakai, "Japanese Imperial Army," 295–297.

135. Wakai, 298.

136. Wakai, 298–299.

they have nothing to fear from the Japanese and that religious freedom was assured by the Imperial Army.[137]

However, there was a disparity in the way that the Japanese treated the Roman Catholics and the Protestants under their control. For the former, they maintained friendly relations with Archbishop Michael J. O'Doherty, who was given "a special personal passport . . . and the Japanese promised that priests, brothers and sisters would not be placed in concentration camps."[138] Sadly, the Japanese were not similarly inclined with the Protestants as they realized that "they were not so strongly organized as the Catholics, they treated them with much less ceremony."[139]

Forced Agreement at the Manila Hotel

As part of their effort to fully control these churches, the Japanese pressured the Filipino Protestant leaders to form a union that would sever all ties with the Americans. Thus, on 27 January 1942, the Japanese met with several Protestant leaders from the major denominations in the country; in the meeting were twelve American, one British, and twenty-six Filipinos.[140] During the gathering, these leaders were asked to sign a pledge declaring the following:

> We, the Protestant missionaries and those who are connected with Christian works, will gladly cooperate with the Japanese as it proclaims the military administration in the Philippines, and do hereby pledge ourselves to take the duties of the restoration and maintenance of peace by observing the following items;
>
> (1) Although we are granted the freedom of faith, we will gladly offer our buildings and their equipment whenever they are needed for military strategy.

---

137. Hartendorp, *Japanese Occupation*, 226.

138. Hartendorp, 227. For a summarized detail of the initial attempts of the Religious Section to coerce the Roman Catholic Church, see Sitoy, *Comity and Unity*, 90–91.

139. Hartendorp, *Japanese Occupation*, 230.

140. At the time of the Internment at the University of Santo Tomas, around one hundred fifty ministers and missionaries with members of their families were imprisoned in the camp. However, in a show of goodwill, Japanese allowed some of these missionaries and their family to be released.

(2) We would never hold meetings primarily held for the people of the hostile nations (worship services included).

(3) We would not hold, for the time being, any other meetings than religious services.

(4) We would lead and instruct our church members, trusting in the Japanese Army, understanding that the great ideal of the Greater East Asia Co-Prosperity Sphere is on the road to its realization, and believing that the very fulfillment of that great ideal is in line with the will of God.

(5) We would positively cooperate with the Japanese Army and would not fail its generous consideration toward us.[141]

While the rest of the participants signed the declaration under strong intimidation, four American ministers resisted and were immediately sent back to the interment camp. The Japanese wanted full cooperation and obedience from these churches so that "the Religious Section of the Japanese Army made them sign a pledge offering the mission and church properties to the Japanese Army when needed and requested."[142]

Federation of Evangelical Churches in the Philippines and the Evangelical Church of the Philippines

Because of the "fragmented" state of the Filipino Protestant churches, the Japanese wanted to establish an organic union among all Protestant churches so that the new government could easily control them.[143] Thus, the Japanese called for another meeting in Manila Hotel on 20 May 1942 and ordered the participants to begin immediate negotiations to form an organic union

---

141. Hartendorp, *Japanese Occupation*, 230.
142. Enrique A. Sobrepeña Jr, "Court Martial," in *Enrique C. Sobrepeña: His Life and Work,* eds. Fern Babcock Grant, Domini Torrevillas-Suarez, and Leon O. Ty (Quezon City: Sponsorship Committee, 1975), 58.
143. Deats explains,
> there was the overt pressure from the Japanese, who sought to Filipinize [sic] the churches, in order to separate them from dependence upon American churches. The Japanese not only wanted Filipino leadership, they also wanted the Protestants organically united so as to make for easier surveillance and control of the denominations.

Deats, *Story of Methodism*, 94.

of all the Protestant churches in the country. While there was ambivalence, regardless of their perspective or convictions, everyone agreed to this "forced" union.[144]

As a result, the Federation of Evangelical Churches in the Philippines (FECP) was established on 10 October 1942 at the United Church of Manila. In this Federation, all current members of the Philippine Federation of Evangelical Churches were merged with the Philippine Methodist, the IEMELIF, the UNIDA, and other smaller churches. As part of its goals, Article III of the FECP constitution states, "to effect comity and cooperation among the various Evangelical Churches in the Philippines, to promote Christian movement, to lead the people spiritually, and to serve for establishment of peace in the Great East Asia."[145]

While Rev Dr Sobrepeña was chosen to serve as its president, he maintained that this was against his will. In a post-war General Court Martial, he was accused of being a Japanese collaborator for his acceptance of this post.[146] In his defense, Rev Sobrepeña explained that he only accepted the position because resisting the Japanese would only bring pain and suffering to the Filipino Protestant churches. Witnesses agreed and defended Rev Sobrepeña by stating that, "No one could say 'No' to a Japanese at that time. There are many living witnesses here to testify to that fact. To do otherwise would be to face the alternative; there is Fort Santiago, there is the bayonet, or the torture chamber; and the accused was one of those who thus suffered."[147] Rev Sobrepeña added that he really wanted to assuage the Japanese and eventually supplant the Japanese sponsored Federation with his newly established Evangelical Church of the Philippines (ECP). In his testimony before the court, Rev Francisco Galvez testified that it was Rev Sobrepeña who led in the formation of the ECP and "within a year or so

---

144. Those who had longed for full autonomy from the Americans "hailed this as a welcome event" while others were perturbed and hesitant (Sitoy, *Comity and Unity,* 99).

145. Sobrepeña, Jr, "Court Martial," 56.

146. The three major accusations against Rev Sobrepeña were the following: first, that he had delivered sermons favoring Japanese war efforts and that he cooperated with Japanese Propaganda Corps; second, that he accepted the presidency of the Federation of Evangelical Churches of the Philippines which was controlled by the Japanese; and third, that he sought to transfer mission properties to FECP (Sobrepeña, Jr, "Court Martial," 53–54).

147. Sobrepeña, Jr, "Court Martial," 63.

following the inauguration of the Union, the Federation of Evangelical Churches ceased to function, but there was no formal action to dissolve it."[148] Thus the court martial which began 19 July 1945 and ended on 3 August 1945 gave its final verdict and pronounced the verdict of "not guilty" and acquitted Rev Sobrepeña of all charges filed against him.

As for the FECP and the ECP, by late 1943 the Japanese had lost interest in forcing the Filipino Protestant churches to merge with each other since by this time the tides of war were going against them. Thus, both churches only lasted during the duration of the war and were immediately dissolved with churches returning to their pre-war affiliation as soon the Philippines was liberated. However, the formation of these two denominations and the actions of the Filipino leaders' during the war caused alienation and resentment among the survivors, which "became a source of confusion and bitterness" during the period that followed immediately after the war.[149]

Wartime Fundamentalist Efforts

As the Japanese forces took control of the cities, a majority of the population had gone into hiding – staying in the forest, hiding in caves, etc. – to avoid persecution. Many of the church leaders of the different churches found themselves among these refugees. And in the midst of the leadership vacuum the took place when the American missionaries and leaders were confined in the Japanese prison camps, the Filipinos continued the work of ministering and caring for those who were afraid and spiritually hungry. This resulted in makeshift congregations for those in hiding.

It was during this time that the Fundamental Baptist churches grew as the MEI and DEI seminary students and graduates took the initiative and aggressively spread the Word of God, their urban ministries were replaced by jungle ministries so that "souls were saved and Christian congregations gathered . . . [even] under the cover of the jungle."[150] The territorial division laid by the Evangelical Union was set aside and it was a time of great harvest. As Nacita describes,

---

148. Sobrepeña, Jr, 59.
149. Sitoy, *Comity and Unity*, 106.
150. "Concise History."

The Baptist pastors fled to the different provinces during the war, they began to minister to these areas. After the war, these converts acknowledged these pastors and formed the Baptist churches all over the country. Wherever you "landed" during the war that is where you served as a pastor. After the war, with the help of ABWE missionaries, the Baptists began to enter territories that were formerly assigned to other denominations and groups by the Comity Agreement. As part of their tradition, the Baptist pastors were aggressive in evangelism and church planting.[151]

When the war in the Pacific had finally ended, the Fundamental Baptist pastors were among those who were actively involved in the process of reconstruction and rebuilding their congregations and their church facilities. Like the rest of the churches, they gathered their surviving members and the majority of their wartime converts joined their churches resulting in the growth of the number of churches and in the expansion of their territories as they were able to preserve the fruit of their wartime efforts.

Immediate Post-War Period (1946–1948)

The immediate post-war era was a challenge for all; the death and devastation left behind by the Japanese had brought chaos and disruption for all sectors of society including the church. The decision of the remaining Japanese forces to make a "last stand" and make Manila into an "open city" resulted in many needless deaths and the majority of the infrastructure was reduced to rubble as the Americans wrested control of the Manila from the hands of the Japanese.[152] Thus, this period was a time to search for those who survived the conflict and to rebuild what had been destroyed.

---

151. Appendix H: "Interview with Ebenezer Nacita," response to question 4.

152. Petillo describes the last battle of the Japanese forces in Manila, "Rear Admiral Sanji Iwabuchi, had elected to make a final stand in the city . . . these [Japanese] forces waged an urban guerilla and block by-block defense of terrifying proportion. . . . The Japanese decision resulted in a month-long fierce battle. . . . The outcome was predictable in that the superior American forces ultimately achieved their goal, but for everyone involved . . . the price was overwhelming . . . more than 100,000 Filipino civilians had been killed, and a major portion of their city laid waste. . . . Nothing remained of the sturdy government

Mergers and Unions among Mainline Protestant Churches

During the late 1940s, several Filipino Protestant church leaders initiated efforts to resolve wartime conflicts and bitterness among them, especially those that were accused of collaborating with the Japanese. Among those who intervened was Dr Melquiades Q. Gamboa, assistant secretary of President Sergio Osmeña, who called a meeting for a select number of church leaders on 18 July 1945 to initiate steps for "reunion" and "heal the postwar disintegration of unity" among these mainline Filipino Protestant churches.[153] This was followed by several other meetings which began to open communications and restore relationships among these leaders and their churches.

Philippine Federation of Evangelical Churches (1946)

As a result of renewed goodwill, the post-war Filipino leaders initiated several moves to revive the pre-war Philippine Federation of Evangelical Churches (PFEC) and possibly expand its membership to include the IEMELIF and the Philippine Methodist Church who could not join previously due to the resistance of the American-led Methodist-Episcopal Church. Thus by 1946, the pre-war PFEC was revived and its members were from the United Evangelical Church (1929), the Methodist church, the Convention of Philippine Baptists, the Disciples, the Evangelical Church of the Philippines (1943), the IEMELIF, the UNIDA, and the Philippine Methodist Church (1933). Bishop Cipriano Navarro of the Philippine Methodist Church was elected Executive Secretary of the revived PFEC. It is important to note that the modernist-fundamentalist controversy had begun to polarize the Filipino churches as seen from the members of the Federation who were mostly from mainline Protestant churches in America – Presbyterians, Congregationalist, Northern Baptist, etc. – which were affiliated with the Federal Council of Churches, while those who aligned themselves with the fundamentalists remained outside of the PFEC.

---

structures but piles of rubble" (Carol Morris Petillo, *Douglas MacArthur: The Philippine Years* [Bloomington, IN: Indiana University Press, 1981], 223–224).

153. Sitoy, *Comity and Unity*, 114.

The United Church of Christ in the Philippines (1948)

With the dissolution of American control, discussions about establishing a united organic Filipino Church were resumed by November 1947 as several Protestant churches entered into negotiations. Thus, in May 1948, the United Church of Christ in the Philippines (UCCP) was inaugurated at the Ellinwood Malate Church in Manila.[154] This new denomination was the merger of the United Evangelical Church (1929), the Philippine Methodist Church (1933), and the remnants of the wartime Evangelical Church of the Philippines (1943).[155] The UCCP elected "Bishops Enrique C. Sobrepeña, Cipriano Navarro, Leonardo C. Dia, and Proculo A. Rodriguez, as jurisdictional bishops for Northern Luzon, Southern Luzon, Visayas, and Mindanao, respectively."[156]

This was the nearest that could be managed in achieving the goal of a united Filipino Church. However, several major Protestant denominations remained separated.[157] Their doctrinal and ecclesiastical differences were too wide for a union to take place. Thus, another strategy was needed to see unity among these churches.

Philippine Federation of Christian Churches (1949)

One of Rev Sobrepeña's constant aspirations was to see the unity of all the non-Roman Catholic churches in the country into one indigenous Protestant Church. Hence, when Rev Sobrepeña learned of the possibility that the

---

154. Sitoy, 116.
155. World Council of Churches, "United Church of Christ in the Philippines," accessed 10 July 2018, https://www.oikoumene.org/en/member-churches/united-church-of-christ-in-the-philippines.
156. Sitoy, *Comity and Unity*, 116.
157. According to von Oeyen,
    of a number of churches which profess to be non-Roman but Catholic there are two which are of considerable importance in Philippine church history: the Philippine Independent Church (Iglesia Filipina Independiente) and the Philippine Episcopal Church. The former is important in secular Philippine history as the most lasting institution to come out of the Revolution and the Philippine-American War, and the second is important for its mission to religious minorities and its present close association with the Philippine Independent Church.

    Robert R. von Oeyen, Jr, *Philippine Evangelical Protestant and Independent Catholic Churches: An Historical Bibliography of Church Records, Publications and Source Material Located in the Greater Manila Area*, Bibliography Series no.1 (Quezon City, Philippines: Asian Center, University of the Philippines, 1970), 58.

Philippine Independent Church (IFI) and the Philippine Episcopal Church (PEC) were willing to consider a merger except for the IFI's objection to the term "evangelical," it was suggested that the PFEC "give way" to accommodate other groups within the union. Thus, in May 1949, believing that the replacement of the word "Evangelical" with "Christian" could entice the two churches to join, the Philippine Federation of Christian Churches was formed. Despite the change, these two non-Roman Catholic churches remained unwilling to join the reconstituted council because they would rather "cooperate . . . but it did not wish to merge with them."[158] As Sitoy explains,

> Because of divergences in theological understanding, religious attitudes, liturgical life and historical experiences, such a union was too remote a possibility between the two Churches of catholic tradition and the Evangelicals. Hence, a mere change in name, without a corresponding change in constitutional objectives, could not in all integrity be accepted by either the Episcopal or the Philippine Independent Church.[159]

Mergers and Arrival among Fundamentalist/Conservative Churches

The immediate post-war period was also a time for growth among the pre-war fundamentalist and conservative churches and the arrival of other evangelical missionary groups. However, the modernist-fundamentalist schism had began to manifest itself as these fundamentalist and conservative churches chose to remain separate from the mainline Protestant churches. The mainline Protestant churches also did not attempt to recruit these fundamentalist/evangelical churches into their unions.[160] The latter were unwelcome as they were perceive to be a continuation of previous American control and intervention.[161]

---

158. Abainza, "Leader in Two Movements," 104.

159. Sitoy, *Comity and Unity*, 119.

160. Magbanua recalls, "they know where we stand in terms of liberal and conservative theology . . . I do not recall any attempt on their part to recruit us" (Appendix D, "Interview with Fred Magbanua, Jr," response to question 16).

161. As Apilado describes some of the suspicions that these "Protestant missionaries were agents of colonialism and instruments of a foreign power demanding that Filipinos

Thus, the gap that began in America continued. Nevertheless, these churches and missionary efforts grew. The following are some of the post-war growth and mergers by these fundamentalist and conservative churches.

CAMACOP (1947)

Like many of the churches that were caught in the Philippines during World War II, the work of the American Christian Missionary Alliance (CMA) missionaries was put on hold during the Japanese occupation with several experiencing martyrdom and most suffering incarceration. In their absence, the Filipino CMA pastors and laymen continued the work. Despite the hardship and the dangers, these faithful Filipino pastors and laymen, ministered even in the jungles and remote areas where they laid the foundation for the resurgence and growth of CMA in the post-war period. After the conflict ended, work among the Muslims in Mindanao was resumed and displaced churches were reestablished by CMA missionaries and these Filipino pastors.[162]

Seeing the need to empower and equip these Filipino CMA ministers, in February 1947 Rev Ralph E. Bressler conducted the first National Workers Conference where thirteen local churches and their pastors were organized to form the Christian and Missionary Alliance Churches of the Philippines (CAMACOP). This new church was autonomous and Filipino-led with Rev Jeremias Dulaca serving as its first President (1947–1957) followed by Florentino de Jesus, Sr (1957–1960).[163] As the CMA missionaries continued their work, the churches that were established were led by the Filipino CAMACOP workers and pastors. Due to the hard work and initiative of these laborers, CAMACOP membership grew by "112 per cent" during this post-war era (1949 to 1958)."[164] This autonomous national church remained true to its fundamentalist heritage; it was conservative in its theology and evangelistic in its emphasis and efforts, choosing to stay out of the Federations.[165]

---

surrender and become subservient to its rule," (Apilado, *Revolutionary Spirituality*, 264).

162. For other details, see Frank C. Pardue, "The Philippines' Last Frontier" (DMin. diss., Columbia Biblical Seminary and Graduate School of Missions, 2001).

163. Toril Capital Alliance Church, "About Us: CAMACOP," accessed 27 February 2019, http:// http://www.torilcapitalalliancechurch.org/about-us/camacop.

164. Tuggy and Toliver, *Seeing the Church*, 74.

165. For details, see Cunningham, "Diversities," 97–99.

The Far East Gospel Crusade (1947)

During the immediate post-war period, a new missionary agency was formed as a result of the work of the American Gis in the Philippines. In 1947, the Far East Gospel Crusade (FEGC) was established; while it was non-denominational, its doctrinal emphasis was more closely connected with the Fundamentalists.

After the Americans secured Manila, Chaplain Hixson and several dedicated Christian soldiers took the initiative to establish a prayer and fellowship meeting for their fellow soldiers who were longing for spiritual comfort and interaction while on "shore leave."[166] They wanted to give a Christian alternative for the military men, instead of the sordid pleasures offered in the streets of Manila. As these Gis sought for a place to conduct a regular fellowship, they met Edward and Marion Bomm, an ABWE missionary couple who chose to remain to rebuild their ministry and secure their missions property while waiting for the return of their missionaries from the West.[167] After their release from the Japanese prison, the Bomms resided in the refugee camp since their property was destroyed in the war, and were financially unable to rent a home because the financial help from ABWE had not yet arrived. Working together, Mr Bomm found a house where his family could stay and which served as a place of fellowship and prayer for these lonely Gis. It was an ideal setup as the Bomms became the foster parents for many of these young military personnel and their residence became the Christian Service Center. The center, as the Gis casually called the Bomms' house, met a great need as shown by the growing number of

---

166. Chaplain Hixson met several Christian soldiers while stationed in Hollandia, New Guinea and began having a regular time of prayer and fellowship with them. As they were being shipped to the Philippines, they began a plan of conducting similar meetings to the ones that they had held in Hollandia. These eight men prayed and made a commitment to start a weekly prayer time in Manila (SEND International, "History," accessed 10 July 2018, http://www.send.org/about/history/).

167. Commons recalls the condition of the ministry after the war ended,
>The city of Manila was a shambles. All our properties had been destroyed. Property deeds and official records were gone. It was necessary to file claims to our prewar real estate and to reestablish our ownership with the Bureau of Lands lest others make claims which would have to be disproved. It was also important to reestablish contact with our former Filipino leaders and pastors and to encourage them in every way possible. The Bible institute was gone. The First Baptist Church was gone. Doane Dormitory was gone.

Commons, *Heritage and Harvest*, 75.

soldiers and servicemen who came to their weekly meetings. According to Commons, "that first Saturday night over fifty of them crowded into the sala for evening fellowship. On Sundays the first boys appeared by eight o'clock in the morning. They kept coming all day long."[168]

Eventually, the Bomm's *sala* proved to be too small as more soldiers joined the fellowship; thus they decided to transfer. Unable to find a place, they utilized a mortuary that was owned by Mr Antonio Quiogue after their first request to use a church was denied. It was in this mortuary that the GI Gospel Hour was born on 6 May 1945. Their ministry soon expanded, as Chaplain Russell Honeywell describes, "Those GIs were really turned on for Christ. In addition to the Saturday night Gospel Hour, our weekly schedule included a Radio Broadcast, Youth for Christ meetings at Ellinwood Malate Church, Bible studies at the Christian Service Center and a lot of personal evangelism. This went on for a number of months."[169]

As their numbers grew, the Christian Service Center needed a bigger location.[170] It was through their continued partnership with ABWE that a suggestion was made to occupy the old FBCM property whose pre-war building was flattened by bombs during the conflict. With military surplus materials donated by an American camp, a tabernacle was erected on the old FBCM site in November 1945; the makeshift church served five to six hundred people in their Saturday night fellowship and evangelistic outreaches. While their efforts were primarily focused on US personnel; eventually Filipinos began to join their weekly gathering. In time, a growing number of Filipinos were involved in the GIs' ministry efforts.

As these military men saw the growing need in the Philippines, several had decided to return as missionaries when their time in the military was over. They realized that there was a need for an organization that would not only send missionaries but continue the work that had been started by these American chaplains. Realizing the "resistance within the older

---

168. Commons, 78.

169. Russell Honeywell and Betty Honeywell, *Faith under Fire* (Manila, Philippines: self-published, 1974), 56.

170. Although they were able to use the mortuary for a while, they were eventually forced out of it. According to the Honeywells, it was rumored "that the President's wife, Mrs. Aurora Quezon . . . [who] began to pull strings behind the scenes to get us out" (Honeywell and Honeywell, *Faith under Fire*, 56).

denominations to their efforts" these military men decided to organize the Far Eastern Gospel Crusade (FEGC) in Minnesota in February 1947.[171] The FEGC was the merger of the GI Gospel Hour in the Philippines and Japan and the Far Eastern Bible Institute and Seminary (FEBIAS). The FEGC chose to be an "interdenominational mission organization," a perspective that they had probably inherited from their founders who had once served in the US Chaplaincy Service. In the 1950s, FEGC focused their missionary efforts in Mindoro. By 1981, FEGC was renamed SEND International which continued to reach out to the different nations around the globe.[172]

ABWE and FEGC Part Ways (1948)

As World War II ended with the Japanese surrender on 2 September 1945 and as the end of their military service drew near, the question of what could be done for their local contacts who had expressed a desire to be trained as pastors and evangelists became a major issue among these servicemen.[173] Because the Philippines was still in its early stages of recovery, these military men and women felt the call to personally provide the help that was needed. Thus, the vision of building a Bible school where Filipinos could be trained to plant and pastor local churches began to germinate in the minds of these American servicemen; they dreamt of putting up a Bible school that was similar to the Moody Bible Institute.[174]

---

171. Cunningham, "Diversities," 127.
172. SEND International, "History."
173. Chaplain Honeywell (ret.) remembers this longing from a Filipino member, "I wish there was a school where we could go and study God's Word," a young Filipino said plaintively in the hearing of Roger Johnson . . . a nineteen-year-old GI from South Carolina, stationed near Imus, Cavite. Another Filipino said to the chaplain, "you fellows can go back and study at any number of schools, but here we have none"
Honeywell and Honeywell, *Faith under Fire*, 69.
174. This burden to help the Philippines was not limited to FEGC. Around the same time, a navy personnel who was on an aircraft carrier began to plan and dream of starting a Christian radio station that would be located in Asia and whose target are the millions of people in this part of the world. When John Broger retired from the navy, he approached Robert Bowman, Christian radio broadcaster, with plans of starting his dream. Having problems with Shanghai, they decided to establish the Far East Broadcasting Company (FEBC) in the Philippines instead (Gleason H. Ledyard, *Sky Waves: The Incredible Far East Broadcasting Company Story* [Chicago, IL: Moody Press; Mandaluyong, Philippines: OMF, 2008], 36–39).

On 21 September 1945, during a prayer meeting, forty servicemen and women prayed and decided to put up a local seminary with seed-money of $6,000. By 5 July 1948, the Far Eastern Bible Institute and Seminary (FEBIAS) opened its doors with an initial twenty students.[175] This inter-denominational seminary would be managed and supervised by ex-servicemen who were now connected with the newly established organization – FEGC. For that reason, Russell Honeywell, Carl Urspringer, and their families became the first missionaries of FEGC in the Philippines, and FEBIAS's first offices and training schools were made of army surplus Quonset huts. In time, FEBIAS became one of the leading Bible schools for conservative evangelicals. Their alumni have occupied many of the key positions in the evangelical church. In fact, many of the leaders who were connected with the formation of PCEC were either alumni or had connections with FEBIAS. Gadiel Isidro, Faustino Ruivivar, Jr, Eustaquio Ramientos, and Rogelio Baldemor were graduates of FEBIAS and Fred Magbanua, Jr, had studied for a year in FEBIAS. Antonio Ormeo, Sr, had also sent one of his sons to study in FEBIAS to be trained as a pastor.

Going back to the time when the establishment of FEBIAS was still being considered, one of the ideas offered was to build the proposed Bible school on the previous MEI location since they already had a building on the site. They negotiated with the leaders of ABWE to see if the old MEI could be transformed into FEBIAS as an inter-denominational Bible school "patterned after the Moody Bible Institute in Chicago" and students who did not agree with its inter-denominational attitude could simply choose to study in DEI in Iloilo.[176] And to protect their Baptist heritage Edward Bomm (ABWE) could serve as its first president and Russell Honeywell (FEGC) would be the vice chairman.[177]

This was a good idea at that time since many of the ex-GIs who founded the FEGC and FEBIAS were also fundamental Baptists who shared the same theological values and convictions; thus it was just logical for both groups

---

175. Febias College of Bible, "History," accessed 10 July 2018, http://www.febias.edu.ph/index.php/about-fcb/history.

176. Commons, *Heritage and Harvest*, 82.

177. Honeywell and Honeywell, *Faith under Fire*, 70.

to merge in their efforts.¹⁷⁸ However, the leaders of ABWE had misgivings about these ex-Gis inter-denominational approach to ministry and the absence of a strong stand against liberalism as they were willing to work with churches connected with the WCC.¹⁷⁹ Thus, ABWE declined this merger with the FEGC. According to Commons:

> The ABWE administration saw problems ahead. We would be involved in something of a nondescript character over which we would have no control. There would be a doctrinal mixture with some of which we could not agree. Arminian elements were already in evidence. Some members of the Far Eastern Gospel Crusade came from mainline denominational churches with World Council affiliations. Our strong Baptist and separatist convictions would be unwelcome and probably outnumbered.¹⁸⁰

In time, the MEI was rebuilt in its original location and FEBIAS purchased a property in the north of the Manila. While both school would serve the growing fundamentalist-evangelical community, the former was non-denominational while the latter was open to all.

AFBCP (1948)

During the post-war years, the number of Fellowship Baptist churches grew as a result of aggressive evangelism and spiritual revivals throughout the country. Hence, the need for mutual support and assistance felt by these Filipino leaders brought about the formation of several regional associations among these Fundamentalist Baptist churches. For example, a year before the arrival of manpower and financial help from America, the Bukidnon Association of Baptist Churches (BABC) was created in 1946 through the efforts and initiative of Filipino pastors who reorganized and rebuilt

---

178. Appendix G: "Interview with Pio Tica," response to question 4.

179. As Leones explains their difference with FEBIAS, "I think that there was no question about their being fundamentalist in their doctrine, only that there is no specific stand on separation from modernists. Their philosophy was to work inside [the liberal churches] hoping to remedy and rescue. But penetration does not work" (Appendix E: "Interview with Mariano Leones," response to question 23).

180. Commons, *Heritage and Harvest*, 82–83.

their churches in Northern Mindanao.[181] In Western Visayas, the Visayas Fellowship of Fundamental Baptist Churches (VFFBC) was formed after "no less than twenty-two Fundamental Baptist Churches from the Island of Panay and Negros" to "help facilitate the activities and plan the programs of the new organization, such as to evangelize more towns and cities, and build-up the spiritual life of believers in the churches."[182] It was a period of growth and spiritual revival among the Fundamental Baptist churches, and as a result three other regional associations – the Association of Baptist Churches in Palawan, the Davao Fellowship of Fundamental Baptist Churches, and Association of Baptist Church in Luzon (ABCL) – were formed from the 1940s to the 1950s.[183]

By the late 1940's, there were seven key regional associations that were established: Association of Baptist Churches in Northern Luzon, Association of Baptist Churches in Central Luzon, Association of Baptist Churches in Southern Tagalog, Palawan Association of Baptist Churches, Visayan Fellowship of Fundamental Baptist Churches, Bukidnon Association of Baptist Churches, and Davao Association of Fundamental Baptist Churches.[184] As their number grew, their leaders – ABWE missionaries and the Filipino pastors – realized that there was a need to unify these Fundamental Baptist churches into a national council. By 1948, the leaders of the seven regional associations formed the Association of Fundamental Baptist Churches in the Philippines (AFBCP) which was formally recognized in December of 1951 in a conference held at the FBCM.[185] According to its Articles of Incorporation with the SEC, the purposes of the AFBCP were as follows:

(1) To provide fellowship for Baptist churches which subscribe to these By-laws and Articles of Faith;

---

181. "Concise History."

182. "History of the Western Visayas Fellowship of Fundamental Baptist Churches, Inc.," in *Advancing the Gospel Towards 2000*, Souvenir Program at the 23rd AFBCP Biennial Conference, Malaybalay, Bukidnon, Philippines, 5–8 May, 1997.

183. Appendix E: "Interview with Mariano Leones," response to question 2.

184. Nacita, *Celebrating God's Mercy*, 12–13.

185. "The Association of Fundamental Baptist Churches in the Philippines," in *The Light, 1956* (Doane Evangelistic Institute Year Book for 1956, Iloilo City, Philippines, 1956), 6–7.

(2) To encourage and promote evangelism and to assist in the establishing and organizing of indigenous Baptist churches;

(3) To advance Baptist Missionary enterprises throughout the world;

(4) In accord with the historic Baptist principles of the independence and sovereignty of the local Baptist church, it is not the purpose of this Association to legislate for the local church, dictate its policies, or attempt to interfere with its internal affairs. When invited to do so, the Association may advise and counsel any local Baptist church or may recommend action in relation to any problem which a local church may bring before it, in consultation with the regional association in which the local church is in fellowship.[186]

The founding leaders of the AFBCP saw that apart from drawing strength from each other through their conciliar union, their unity could help strengthen each other in their calling to uphold the fundamentals of the faith and to ensure that it is defended from any compromise or dilution.

By 1957, the leaders of AFBCP decided to form the Philippine Association of Baptist for World Evangelization (PABWE) as part of their effort to become autonomous. Dr Ormeo served as its interim president and became the Regional Representative of Luzon when PABWE was established with its own set of leaders in March 1957.[187]

Conclusion

The history of Philippine Protestantism reveals the journey of self-discovery as schisms and mergers among these churches became the "stepping stones" in their quest for identity and autonomy. While these Filipino leaders continued to struggle with the challenges and influences inherited from the

---

186. Republic of the Philippines, Securities and Exchange Commission, *Articles of Incorporation of Association of Fundamental Baptist Churches in the Philippines, Inc.* (Mandaluyong City, Philippines: SEC, 2007), 3.

187. n.a., "Philippine Association of Baptist for World Evangelism," in *Advancing the Gospel Towards 2000*, Souvenir Program at the 23rd AFBCP Biennial Conference, Malaybalay, Bukidnon, Philippines, 5–8 May 1997), n.p.

controversies and denominationalism in the West, there were "moments" of growth when they chose their own destiny as seen in the merger to form new churches, in the conciliar unions, and even in the schisms brought about by calls for independence and the differences among these churches both prior to and immediately after the war. As the Philippines finally gained its freedom at the end of the war in the Pacific, so did Philippine Protestantism gain the opportunity to finally determine its future. However, the actions and the choices of these churches, both the pre-war mainline denominations and the newly-arrived fundamentalist/evangelical churches and organizations, reveal that they continued to be influenced by past prejudices and inclinations as these two groups failed to find a common ground. It is these traditions and perspectives that would continue to influence the leaders of Philippine Protestantism in the next few decades.

CHAPTER 4

The Formation of the Philippine Council of Evangelical Churches (1960s)

The post-World War II era brought changes within Philippine Protestantism. Among these was the reorganization of the older mainline Protestants which resulted in mergers, cooperation, and conciliar unions. As the pre-war fundamentalist-evangelical churches were occupied with rebuilding and re-establishing themselves, several new American churches and organizations with similar conservative values and theological affirmations arrived and began their church-planting efforts within the country. While there had been mergers and cooperation within each camp, the older pre-war Protestants and the fundamentalist-evangelicals were independent from each other. Their varied polity, theology, and praxes, which were further complicated by the modernist/liberal-fundamentalist controversy in North America, kept these groups apart.[1]

At the same time, there was a growing alienation among the fundamentalist churches in America (e.g. Bob Jones Sr was opposing Billy Graham's evangelistic approach, McIntire's American Council of Christian Churches was in disagreement with the National Association of Evangelicals, etc.).[2]

---

1. The divergence caused by the modernist/liberal-fundamentalist controversy among these churches in America was directly affecting the relationships and attitudes of their Filipino progeny. As a result, any offer of conciliar union had been rejected and dismissed (See Appendix D: "Interview with Fred Magbanua, Jr," response to question 19–23).

2. For details, see Cairns, *Christianity Through the Centuries*, 485–488.

This was also affecting relationships among these fundamentalist-evangelical churches in the 1940's both in America and in the Philippines.

Thus, the formation of a fundamentalist-evangelical council in the 1960s was a major accomplishment by these Filipino leaders. This chapter examines the inclinations of each group in the 1950s and the process by which these fundamentalist-evangelical leaders were able to successfully cooperate with each other to form a council of churches in the 1960s and the ensuing schism that broke the council apart in the 1970s.

Transitions and Changes (1950s)

When the Philippines gained its independence on 4 July 1946, transitions began to take place within all sectors of society. This included changes within Philippine Protestantism as seen in the following developments.

The Arrival of New Fundamentalist/Evangelical Churches in the Post-War Period

While the pre-war fundamentalist/evangelical churches (e.g. the fundamental Baptists, Wesleyan Church, etc.) were still in the process of rebuilding their congregations and their chapels, the spiritual resurgence among several fundamentalist churches in North America launched a new wave of missionary efforts in the Philippines.[3] As mentioned above, the pre-war fundamentalist/evangelical missionary groups, such as the Association of Baptists for World Evangelization (ABWE) and the Christian and Missionary Alliance (CMA) were joined by churches and organizations with similar values and doctrines. In particular, several fundamentalist/evangelical missionary organizations and churches were "diverted" to the Philippines when the newly created People's Republic of China demanded the closure of all foreign missionary efforts and their religious institutions.[4] The following were some of these "diverted" churches and organizations that arrived and established themselves in the Philippines.

---

3. For details, see Ahlstrom, *Religious History*, 956–960.

4. As Pierson summarizes the situation, "Christian institutions were seized, church leaders persecuted and imprisoned, missionaries expelled, and eventually, all churches closed" (Pierson, *Dynamics of Christian Mission*, 317). For a brief description, see Leung KaLun, "China," in *A Dictionary of Asian Christianity*, ed. Scott W. Sunquist, [Grand Rapids; Cambridge, UK: Eerdmans, 2001], 145).

The Conservative Baptist Association of the Philippines

In May 1943, fifty concerned members of the Northern Baptist Convention met to discuss and pray about what they perceived as growing liberalism in their midst.[5] On 9 September 1943, in an effort to pressure the leaders of the ABFMS to take a more decisive fundamentalist stance, the conservatives "presented a statement of irrevocable principles" as a condition for their further participation in the missionary organization.[6] Sadly, this offer was rejected as the ABFMS maintained its inclusive policy; as a result the Conservative Baptist Foreign Mission Society (CBFMS) was formed. While the two groups attempted to work together; eventually, the widening gap proved too extensive and this steered the conservative leaders and their churches to finally separate and form the Conservative Baptist Association on 17 May 1947 in Atlantic City, New Jersey.[7]

The following year, CBFMS sent its missionaries to the Philippines, initially "loaned" to other missionary organizations. For example, Beulah Heaton taught in FEBIAS,[8] while Mr and Mrs Homer Kreps, and Mr and Mrs Howard Erikson helped with the Far East Broadcasting Company (FEBC).[9] In 1951, William Simons and his family were forced to abandon their ministry in China after the Chinese communists closed its doors to American missionaries.[10] As a result, they were diverted to the Philippines where they helped the American missionaries who were supervising the

---

5. Worldventure, "History," accessed 10 July 2018, https://www.worldventure.com/about/history/.

6. Bruce L. Shelley, *A History of Conservative Baptists* (Wheaton, IL: Conservative Baptist Press, 1981), 26–29, 32.

7. Mead, *Handbook of Denominations*, 45.

8. According to Kennedy, Beulah Heaton was previously connected with ABWE (Kennedy, *Baptist Centennial History*, 166).

9. Tuggy and Toliver, *Seeing the Church*, 88.

10. As Dr Spahr was a close friend and the minister who officiated their wedding, the Simons chose to work with him in reaching the Chinese expatriates in Manila (Jim Davis, *From Carryall Beginnings to Crossing Borders: A 50-Year Journey of Conservative Baptist Ministries in the Philippines* [Manila, Philippines: LifeChange, 2006], 7).

Grace Christian High School,[11] a school for Chinese expatriates which was led by Dr Edwin Spahr.[12]

After being exposed to the religious condition of the country, Rev Simons saw the potential for a church planting ministry in the Philippines. In a survey that he conducted in 1954 to determine the feasibility of missionary work, Rev Simons observed that Laguna was one of the areas that had been overlooked in the past by the pre-war Protestant churches and mission groups.[13] Receiving approval from CBFMS, Simons began his efforts to plant a church in this region of the Philippines.

The Simons' ministry began in the Tagalog-speaking Laguna province after they were able to connect with five Filipinos who were previously trained by ABWE.[14] Although Rev Simons was initially bed-ridden and had to relearn how to walk as a result of being stricken by polio, the work in Laguna prospered as he was assisted by these Filipino pastors.[15] In May 1955, their efforts bore fruit as the Santa Maria Evangelical Baptist Church became the very first Conservative Baptist church in the Philippines.[16]

By 1958, five more churches and several mission points were planted within Laguna and nearby areas through the help of other American missionaries and Filipinos from FEBIAS. Experiencing success, more CBFMS missionaries started to arrive and began work in other regions of the country. As their numbers grew, it was decided on 29 December 1961 that the Conservative Baptist Association of the Philippines (CBAP) should be

---

11. Started by Dr and Mrs Edwin G. Spahr and Mrs Julia L. Tan on 5 July 1950 "this church-school duality was based on the founder's desire for the school to have a spiritual 'church-home' for its students, parents and community—in a seven-day-a-week Christian education-filled environment" (Paul Lee Tan, "Official History of GCC," in *Grace Christian Church, 40 Years of God's Grace: Onto Greater Heights*, Souvenir Program at the 40th Anniversary [Quezon City, Philippines, 27 April, 2009], 19).

12. Dr Spahr arrived in 1946 as a missionary of ABWE and had served as the senior pastor of the First Baptist Church of Manila. However, due to a disagreement with ABWE's separation doctrine and policy, Dr Spahr resigned from his post. For details, see Commons, *Heritage and Harvest*, 84–86.

13. Davis, *From Carryall Beginnings*, 11.

14. The five Filipinos who started the work were Jose Galuego, Castro Quimba, Felonito Sacapaño, Esteban Salcedo, and Luis Pantoja, Sr (Kennedy, *Baptist Centennial History*, 11).

15. Rev Simons had been stricken with polio while his wife was recovering from dengue (Davis, *From Carryall Beginnings*, 12).

16. James Montgomery and Donald McGavran, *The Discipling of a Nation* (Santa Clara, CA: Global Church Growth Bulletin, 1980), 82.

established to unify these churches that were planted by both the nationals and the CBFMS missionaries. Rev Fred Magbanua, who had been converted through the ministry of FEBC, served as CBAP's first president.[17]

The Overseas Missionary Fellowship and the Alliance of Bible Christian Communities of the Philippines

The Overseas Missionary Fellowship (OMF) which was formerly known as the China Inland Mission (CIM) was a missionary group that was organized in mainland China by Hudson Taylor in 1854.[18] Their inter-denominational efforts were able to penetrate and establish churches throughout China.[19] Despite its origins, OMF had to close its headquarters in China as it was among those that were expelled in the early 1950s by communist China. As Chinese refugees scattered throughout Asia, OMF missionaries followed their disciples resulting in the arrival of their missionaries in the Philippines.

By 1951, these newly-arrived OMF missionaries began focusing their efforts among the Chinese with several "loaned" to work in other Christian organizations and schools such as the Grace Christian High School where they served as teachers and ministers. However, within the same year, their missionary efforts expanded to include work among the "tribal people of Mindoro" and six years later they "began their evangelistic and

---

17. Federico "Fred" M. Magbanua, Jr (1932–2013), a native of Negros Occidental, came to know the Lord when he was seventeen years-old through "listening to Sheryl Brook's Bible School on the air" in 1949 (See Appendix D: "Interview with Fred Magbanua, Jr," response to question 13). While his home church was a Fundamental Baptist church, Magbanua was ordained under the Conservative Baptists (Appendix D, response to question 19, 20). After serving in the ministry for two years, he went to FEBIAS to study in 1959. Being a convert through the FEBC ministry and since he was an engineer by profession, he was hired by FEBC where he initially served in the engineering department, being promoted until he became its managing director in the 1960s (Appendix D, response to question 24).

18. For details on Hudson Taylor, see Alfred James Broomhall, *Hudson Taylor and China's Open Century*, 7 vols. (Kent, UK: Hodder & Stoughton, 1981–1990), John C. Pollock, *Hudson Tyalor and Maria: Pioneers in China* (New York: McGraw-Hill, 1962); Howard Taylor and Mary Geraldine Taylor, *Hudson Taylor and the China Inland Mission* (London, UK: Morgan and Scott, 1920).

19. The organization continued to grow so that by 1915, "CIM had 1,063 workers working at 227 stations" and missionary funds were raised through prayer and without any request or campaign for funds (OMF International, "Resources: CIM/OMF History," accessed 4 May 2010, http://www.omf. org/omf/us/ resources__1/omf_archives/china_inland_mission_stories/cim_omf_history).

church-planting work in Bauan, Batangas" among the lowlanders.[20] By 1953, it was apparent that OMF missionary work was no longer limited to the Chinese and to the tribal areas as they began expanding their efforts among the Filipinos – planting churches in the different provinces, helping teach in Bible Schools such as FEBIAS, and supporting mission organizations like FEBC.[21]

As a mission organization, they were willing to work with any church or group; thus, several of these churches were either assumed by other denominations or continued to remain as independent churches. By the 1970s, several of these independent churches that were planted by missionaries of the FEGC, OMF, and workers from FEBIAS decided to form an association of churches called the Alliance of Bible Churches of the Philippines (ABCOP).[22] This new denomination was established when several "independent, indigenous evangelical churches," decided to form an association whose primary purposes were "fellowship in the ministry and continuance of the mission."[23]

Southern Baptist Convention

The Southern Baptist Convention (SBC) was formed in May 1845 when the American Baptists broke apart into the Northern and the Southern conventions due to their political and ecclesiastical disagreements stemming from the issue of slavery and other resentments between the two parties. The dispute started with the issue of the new policy on recruitment of missionaries and on missionary funding. At that time, the headquarters of the Baptist Board of Foreign Mission was located in Boston where the anti-slavery movement was quite popular. The growing tensions came to a head when the "Home Board declined . . . James E. Reeves, who was stated to be a slaveholder."[24] Old "wounds" and resentments between these two

---

20. Arthur Tuggy, *The Philippine Church: Growth in a Changing Society* (Grand Rapids: Eerdmans, 1971), 151.

21. Tuggy and Toliver, *Seeing the Church*, 111.

22. In 1989, the name was change to Alliance of Bible Christian Communities of the Philippines (ABCCOP).

23. Alliance of Bible Christian Communities of the Philippines, "About Us: History," accessed 27 May 2010, http://www.abccop.org/newbegining.html.

24. Ahlstrom, *Religious History*, 664.

The Formation of the Philippine Council of Evangelical Churches 119

camps were rehashed until the gap between the two became unbridgeable. Thus, the Southern Baptists took the final step by breaking fellowship and establishing their own convention with its own mission board in 1845.[25]

While the SBC had an active foreign missionary effort, it was only in the 1950s that they started their ministry efforts in the Philippines. Due to the growing tensions in China, SBC missionaries began arriving in 1948 where their first efforts were focused on the Chinese immigrants in Baguio. By 1950, Dr J. Winston Crawley helped organize the Baguio Chinese Baptist Church which was SBC's very first church in the country.[26] By the following year, work in Manila and Mindanao began which resulted in the planting of several more churches.

Although SBC's efforts in the Philippines were initially intended as a temporary substitute while they waited on Chinese authorities to lift the ban on foreign missionaries, work among the Filipinos eventually began after an evangelistic crusade was held in Dagupan City in August, 1951.[27] Thus, the Dagupan Baptist Church became the first SBC Filipino church planted in 1952. In time, the Philippine Baptist Theological Seminary (PBTS) was started in Baguio City in 1952. While PBTS's first six students were all Chinese, by the following year, over half of the students enrolled were Filipino.[28] Soon, SBC churches were started in different parts of the country.[29]

Thus, both the recovering pre-war fundamentalist/evangelical churches (e.g. Christian and Missionary Alliance, Assemblies of God, etc.) and these "newly arrived" missionary groups (e.g. OMF, SBC, etc.) were energetic and committed to the evangelization of the Philippines. Although these churches and mission organizations were relatively few in the beginning, they eventually surpassed the pre-war mainline Protestant churches. As Sitoy states, "their coming changed the complexion of Philippine Protestantism. . . . By

---

25. Mead and Hill, *Handbook of Denominations*, 54.
26. Kennedy, *Baptist Centennial History*, 162.
27. Montgomery and McGavran, *Discipling of a Nation*, 72–73.
28. Kennedy, *Baptist Centennial History*, 163.
29. Montgomery and McGavran, *Discipling of a Nation*, 72–73.

the 1990s the total membership of these postwar groups had exceeded that of all the earlier arrived Protestant missions combined."[30]

Developments within the Pre-War Mainline Protestant Churches

While the fundamentalist/evangelical churches were engaged in establishing themselves through their expansion efforts, the older pre-war mainline Protestant churches (e.g. Convention Baptist, UNIDA, UCCP, United Methodist Church, etc.) were also focused on reorganizing themselves by "breaking away" from their colonial past and by working to form a unified Filipino church. The following gives an overview of a few of their efforts during the 1950s and the early 1960s.

The Dissolution of the Comity Agreement (1950)

As the revival of the pre-war Philippine Federation of Evangelical Churches in the post-war era was considered a triumph; the dissolution of the Comity Agreement was seen as a final break of these mainline Protestant churches from their colonial past. There were several factors that rendered the Comity Agreement as inadequate. First was the influx of fundamental and evangelical Christian groups and the rise of indigenous sects (e.g. *Iglesia ni Kristo*) that did not acknowledge the Comity Agreement and its territorial divisions. Second, the post-war shift and migration of Filipinos from one region to another had muddled the ethnic and tribal boundaries that once formed the basis of the territorial divisions of the agreement. Third, those who migrated did not merge with existing churches in the area and instead had started their own churches which caused confusion on the demarcation of the territories guaranteed by the comity.[31] Fourth, the merger of Filipino churches

---

30. T. Valentino Sitoy, Jr, "Philippines," in *A Dictionary of Asian Christianity*, ed. Scott W. Sunquist (Grand Rapids; Cambridge, UK: Eerdmans, 2001), 656.

31. In his summary, Leiffer points to the problem of migration of Protestants from the provinces and the lack of integration with the churches located within Manila. "There seems to be little organized effort to seek out the hundreds and perhaps thousands of Protestants who come to Manila each year from the provinces but most of whom do not relate themselves to a city church—or, if they do attend, do not transfer their membership" (Murray H. Leiffer, *An Introductory Study of Methodist and Other Protestant Churches: Greater Manila 1965 with Notes on Self-Study Program For a Local Congregation* [Manila, Philippines: Methodist headquarters, 1965], 41).

resulted in the formation of the United Church of Christ in the Philippines (UCCP) whose scope encompassed the entire country.

The incident that caused the actual dissolution of the comity was the territorial dispute between the Methodist Church and the UCCP. The main complaint of the Methodists was that the UCCP had entered Northern Luzon which was their "territory" under the terms of the old comity agreement, while the UCCP complained that the Methodists were taking the UCCP congregations in Mindanao that formed from "Tagalog or Ilocano settlers who were formerly Methodists in Luzon."[32] Both churches were working throughout the entire country; the UCCP had divided the entire Philippines into four Episcopal jurisdictions (i.e. Northern Luzon, Southern Luzon, Visayas, and Mindanao), while the Methodists were also establishing congregations in Southern Luzon, Visayas, and Mindanao as they followed their former members who had migrated to these other regions in the postwar era. It also did not help that the relationship between the leaders of the Methodists and the UCCP was not amicable due to previous schisms and tensions that took place in the 1930s; it was Bishop Cipriano Navarro of the UCCP who had instigated the breakaway from the Methodist Church in 1933.[33]

While the Philippine Federation of Christian Churches (the council that succeeded the Philippine Federation of Evangelical Churches in 1949) attempted to restore the peace and settle the dispute between the two churches; the Methodist Church unilaterally declared the dissolution of the Comity Agreement on 3 March 1950 after being frustrated with the inaction and the delays in the negotiations.[34]

While some were saddened by the dissolution, one of the positive outcomes was that the restrictions previously imposed by the Comity Agreement on territorial boundaries ended. Each ecclesiastical body was free to determine in which area they would like to work, it allowed for cooperative ventures among churches/denominations in reaching a particular region, and it unburdened a particular church from doing all the work. Thus, the

---

32. Sitoy, *Comity and Unity*, 121.
33. Deats, *Story of Methodism*, 72.
34. Deats, 109–111.

demise of the Comity Agreement helped accelerate the spread and growth of these churches.

The Commission on Philippine Chinese Mission (1963)

The fall of China to communism affected the rest of Asia in the late 1940s. Fearing the expected persecution, Chinese Christians and ministers were forced to flee from the mainland and settle in the surrounding Asian nations. Aside from the fundamentalist/evangelical churches' help and accommodations, the mainline Protestant churches also helped in facilitating the entry of these refugees into the country. For example, the UCCP formed a sub-committee so that these Chinese citizens who were encountering problems with Philippine Immigration laws could have a sponsor to enable them to stay in the country. According to Uayan,

> The Philippines was a prime destination for the exodus of missionaries, but the emigration policy set by the government limited the entry of Chinese Christians. The UCCP was quick to respond to the situation. It formed a sub-committee on Chinese work that was placed under the Philippine Board of Missions, composed of three Chinese, two Filipinos and two Americans.[35]

Moreover, in their effort to win and integrate these Chinese Christian Churches within their ranks, the UCCP created the Commission on Philippine Chinese Mission (CPCM) in 1963. While the initial outlook seemed positive with several Chinese Churches joining the Commission, the CPCM's life was brief.[36]

It was the UCCP's increasing ecumenical efforts with the Roman Catholic Church that had an adverse effect on several conservative churches in the Philippines.[37] Along with the fundamentalist/evangelical churches, several conservative Chinese churches became increasingly uncomfortable resulting

---

35. Jean Uy Uayan, "A Study on the Emergence and Early Development of Selected Protestant Chinese Churches in the Philippines" (PhD diss., Asia Graduate School of Theology, 2007), 326.

36. Uayan, "Study on the Emergence," 330–331.

37. According to Tuggy and Toliver, many among the UCCP considered the Roman Catholic Church as a "sister communion" and thus, "the U.C.C.P. is establishing ecumenical relationships with the Roman Catholic Church on a functional basis, that is, for specific projects" (Tuggy and Toliver, *Seeing the Church*, 31).

in the withdrawal of their membership from the CPCM.[38] Although the Chinese churches continued to maintain friendly relationships with the UCCP, they chose to remain separate despite efforts to invite them back to form mergers and cooperative unions. The CPCM was finally dissolved after the UCCP decided to restructure itself in 1972. Uayan describes the resulting relationship: "the relationship between the Chinese churches and the UCCP deteriorated as well, with the negative perception of the UCCP, because of its ecumenical stance, lasting in the minds of the Protestant Chinese until the present time."[39]

The Formation of the National Council of Churches in the Philippines (1963)

The pre-war mainline Protestant churches were experiencing developments and growth among their ranks as their churches spanned the entire Philippine archipelago. For example, according to Tuggy and Toliver's research on church growth in the Philippines, the UCCP became the fastest growing church in the late 1940s and early 1950s. However, this remarkable growth was "not due to conversion growth and biological increase . . . [as much] as it is to the merger of its constituent bodies into one homogenous whole."[40] Aside from their efforts to draw other evangelical churches like the Chinese churches to become part of the UCCP, the leaders of the UCCP continued their efforts to find common ground with the other Philippine churches.

Due to the influence and efforts of Filipino leaders like Bishop Sobrepeña, the Philippine Federation of Christian Churches (PFCC) sought to establish ecumenical ties with other churches in the Philippines. Since the pre-war era, Bishop Sobrepeña had always maintained an "open door" towards unity and had strong desires to establish communion and cooperation with other churches and religious bodies including the Philippine Independent Church

---

38. For example, Sitoy reports "on the campus of Silliman University . . . in December, 1964 . . . the very first time that a Filipino Bishop of the Catholic Church, who happened to have come fresh from the third session of the Second Vatican Council, would address a huge Protestant assembly of youth" (Sitoy, *Several Springs, One Stream*, 141).

39. Uayan, "Study on the Emergence," 333.

40. Tuggy and Toliver, *Seeing the Church*, 29.

(IFI), the Philippine Episcopalian Church (PEC), and the Roman Catholic Church (RCC).[41]

Although the initial effort to include the IFI and PEC into PFCC failed, it did not deter Bishop Sobrepeña from continuing to explore other possibilities for an eventual union. Since the foremost objection of the IFI was the final objective of the PFCC, which was to form a unified national church, on 4 April 1961 Bishop Sobrepeña organized an informal consultation to discuss the possibilities of uniting all the non-Roman Catholic churches in the Philippines into one conciliar body.[42] It was concluded that there was a greater "need for a conciliar organization which would be more inclusive than the existing federation."[43] Thus, the outcome of this informal meeting provided the opportunity for the PFCC to officially revive the discussion regarding the process of seeking unity with other ecclesiastical bodies through the formation of a cooperative council whose constitution and objectives could include a wider scope of churches and religious organizations.

After a constitutional convention within the PFCC in November 1963, the Federation gave way to the establishment of the National Council of Churches in the Philippines; where the Philippine Episcopal Church and the Philippine Independent Church joined the mainline Protestant churches in this new council.[44] The NCCP "possessed a looser structure" and there were no indications within its constitution of the "hope for eventual church

---

41. The doctrines that once kept the Evangelical Union from considering the IFI had now changed. According to von Oeyen, "the Philippine Independent Church has gone through a recent reformation which brought about a return to the catholic faith from a past Unitarian profession and finally its present close association with the Episcopal Church. Dissenting elements have withdrawn or have been forced to form a separate church" (von Oeyen, *Philippine Evangelical*, 58–59).

42. IFI and the PEC were ready for a closer cooperation; however, they favored a looser cooperation of a council rather than a Federation, due to their unwillingness to give up their distinctiveness (Abainza, "Leader in Two Movements," 104–105).

43. Sitoy, *Comity and Unity*, 125.

44. Today, the NCCP is composed of the following member churches: The Apostolic Catholic Church, Convention of the Philippine Baptist Churches, Episcopal Church in the Philippines, *Iglesia Evangelica Metodista En Las Islas Filipinas* (IEMELIF), *Iglesia Filipina Independiente*, *Iglesia Unida Ekyumenical* (UNIDA), Lutheran Church in the Philippines, The Salvation Army, The United Methodist Church, and the United Church of Christ in the Philippines (National Council of Churches in the Philippines, "About Us: Our Member Churches," accessed 30 August 2013, http://nccphilippines.org/about-us/our-member-churches/).

union."⁴⁵ However, like its predecessor, the new council continued the task of interchurch cooperation and fellowship. And due to its unity, the NCCP did not only address the spiritual needs of its constituents; it also gained a "united witness and common action on concerns affecting the religious, moral, social and civic life of the country."⁴⁶

Thus the dream that was shared by many of these pre-war mainline Protestants to form a united ecclesiastical body had finally come to fruition. It was a major step which helped Philippine Protestantism gain a united voice to speak and influence the Filipino people.

Differences Between the Pre-War Mainline Protestants and the Fundamentalist/Evangelical Churches

While the atmosphere of cooperative unions and councils seemed to be the trend during the 1950s and the 1960s, the pre-war mainline Protestant churches and the fundamentalist/evangelical churches continued to remain separated. The following were some of the issues and difficulties that continued to separate the two camps.

The Issue of Ecumenism

Unity among the churches and mission groups was one of the critical issues that confronted the delegates of the World Missionary Conference in Edinburgh in 1910.⁴⁷ As a result, modern ecumenism or inter-church cooperation was born out of the resolution of this conference. Among the pre-war mainline Protestant churches, almost all of its leaders were open and supportive of the ecumenical movement. In fact, the formation of the NCCP was their greatest accomplishment in bringing about unity and cooperation among the non-Roman Catholic churches in the Philippines. By the mid-1960s, efforts had been made to try and reach out to the Roman Catholic Church by NCCP member churches. For example, on 26 January 1968, an article entitled "Ecumenism" was reported by the Silliman University's *Weekly Calendar* that describes a joint candlelight procession of Roman Catholics and Protestants where two thousand individuals marched through the rain

---

45. Sitoy, *Comity and Unity*, 129.
46. Sitoy, 130.
47. Erickson, *Christian Theology*, 1138.

singing both Protestant and Catholic hymns, and offering prayers. Then on 31 December 1968, an "Ecumenical Rally for Peace" was held where both Roman Catholic Priests and Protestant ministers of the UCCP concluded the gathering with a celebration of the Roman Catholic mass.[48]

On the other hand, the fundamentalist/evangelical churches restricted their fellowship to churches and organizations that shared similar Christian values and theological convictions. This was the pattern that they adopted from the American churches that struggled with the modernist/liberal-fundamentalist controversy.[49] These churches and organizations do practice cooperative efforts in such matters such as evangelism and social efforts (e.g. providing relief during disasters, medical missions, etc.). However, for the most part, they reject any form of partnership with those that they consider to be erroneous in their theology or those that they consider non-Christians.[50] Instead, most of these churches employ what is often termed as "levels of fellowship" where one's relationship with another is determined by the other person's spiritual status.[51] Thus, interchurch cooperation and relationship must be guided by certain standards.[52]

---

48. Tuggy and Toliver, *Seeing the Church*, 30. Sadly, the actions of the UCCP which promoted cooperative efforts in the late 1960s had been taken as a representative of these older protestant churches thus bringing further separation to both camps (Uayan, "Study on the Emergence," 332).

49. It must be noted that the previous efforts of the early revivalists of the Awakenings in America and in England were ecumenical in nature since the revivals were "breaking out" across the different churches (Pierson, *Dynamics of Christian Mission*, 214).

50. For example, among the fundamental Baptist such as ABWE, Commons explains, "As individuals and as a mission, we seek and enjoy personal fellowship with all members of the body of Christ. . . . We can have no such fellowship with unbelievers, even though we make friends with them and try to win them to Christ. Many of them are lovely and likeable people" (Commons, *Heritage and Harvest*, 87).

51. As Weber observes,
> the conservative evangelicals are the last group to remain outside the ecumenical movement. . . . This reticence to become actively involved in the ecumenical movement does not necessarily mean that evangelicals are against all collective action. . . . The cooperative model of conservative evangelicals sought to restore evangelism to primary place in the church's mission in the hope that more visible kinds of unity would follow

Timothy P. Weber, "Ecumenism," in *Evangelical Dictionary of Theology*, 2nd ed., Baker Reference Library, ed. Walter A. Elwell (Grand Rapids: Baker, 2001), 364–365.

52. For the fundamental Baptists, in keeping with their efforts to remain distinct from the world, they employ a stricter categorization for the levels of fellowship. For example, Nacita explains that in their church, their members are guided to observe five levels of

The Issue of the Role of American Missionaries

As the Second World War effectively ended American and foreign control over the pre-war mainline Protestant churches, the number of foreign missionaries and ministers also decreased in the post-war period. While many of the UCCP churches continued to welcome the American missionaries in their churches, there was a growing sentiment that these foreign missionaries were no longer needed and this attitude was being noticed by these foreign missionary sending nations. Hence, several American churches began to lessen the number of missionaries that were sent to the Philippines and "some introduced policies focused on short-term specialists and discontinued 'career' missionary appointments."[53] Another reason was the missionary trend among these mainline churches to support nationalism and indigenization. For example, the Commission on World Mission and Evangelism of the World Council of Churches (WCC) announced that "from now on mission was each church in its own place proclaiming the gospel and carrying on mission" since there is a church in every nation.[54] Thus, as the national churches were expected to carry on the effort of evangelizing their own country, the call for American or foreign missionary efforts went on a decline.[55]

On the other hand, while some of the pre-war Protestant churches were declining foreign help, a new breed of missionaries and churches that were from the fundamentalist/evangelical movement in America began to arrive in the Philippines. Some were from the pre-war fundamentalist/evangelical churches (ABEO, AG, etc.), others came from the newly established conservative churches (e.g. CBFMS, FEGC, etc.) and there were those that were "diverted" from China (e.g. OMF, SBC, etc.). The "newcomers" were

---

fellowship with other churches/groups and individuals. For details, see Nacita, *Celebrating God's Mercy*, 56–57.

53. Tye, *Journeying with the United Church*, 242.

54. Donald A. McGavran, *Understanding Church Growth*, 3rd ed., rev. and ed. Peter C. Wagner (Grand Rapids: Eerdmans, 1970), 44.

55. By the 1990s this trend was observed by Kane,
> there is reason to believe that the rapid decline in missionary interest and activity on the part of the main-line denominations will continue in the days to come . . . the total number of missionaries in six large denominations dropped from 3,160 in 1971 to 1,494 in 1985 . . . no indication that steps are being taken to reverse the downward trend

J. Herbert Kane, *Understanding Christian Missions*, 4th ed., Reprint (Grand Rapids: Baker, 1991), 402.

more aggressive and they started to win new converts and establish their own churches within the country. Within these churches and mission groups, the American missionaries and pastors played an active role as they either lead or vigorously worked alongside the Filipinos.

The Issue on Evangelism vs. Dialogue

As mentioned above, the UCCP and the other churches within the NCCP began to change in their evangelistic efforts and emphasis. Due to their conviction that the Roman Catholic Church was a sister communion, many of their churches (e.g. the Episcopal Church of the Philippines) discontinued or decreased their evangelistic programs among Roman Catholics. As Tye states, "the Church's task was increasingly no longer seen as winning all Catholics to the 'true' Evangelical faith."[56] Instead of evangelization, many among these older Protestants felt that the efforts of their churches should be shifted towards "social action" where they envisioned the "church building will be used only for special occasions" instead of preaching the gospel.[57]

In contrast, the fundamentalist/evangelical churches were energetic and aggressively committed to the evangelization of the Philippines. Most of these churches and organizations were openly reaching out to anyone and everyone regardless of their religious backgrounds. Similar to the early American missionaries in the early 1900s, they saw the Philippines as a missionary field.[58] As one church growth study observes, "with the mainline denominations for the most part turning to more benign ecumenical pursuits, God used these evangelical missions to rekindle the dampened fires of fervent evangelism."[59] As a result, the majority of these churches were experiencing numerical growth. For example, CAMACOP showed "remarkable growth in the 1950s, jumping from 6,874 members in 1949 to 14,556 in 1958, or more than doubling in ten years!"[60]

---

56. Tye, *Journeying with the United Church*, 261.

57. Tuggy and Toliver, *Seeing the Church*, 32.

58. Augustin B. Vencer, "The Evangelicals in the Philippines: A Brief History of the Philippine Council of Evangelical Churches," *Evangelicals Today and Asia Ministry Digest* 21, no. 10 (October 1994): 27.

59. Montgomery and McGavran, *Discipling of a Nation*, 48.

60. Tuggy and Toliver, *Seeing the Church*, 74.

Summary

Thus, by the 1960s, the pre-war mainline Protestant churches and the fundamentalist/evangelical churches continued to remain apart due to their different emphases. Through its cooperative efforts and unions, the former became recognized as an established united ecclesiastical institution while the latter continued to remain a collection of independent and autonomous churches and mission organizations that were considered newcomers. Although both groups continued to expand in the post-war era, the ecumenical efforts of the older mainline Protestant churches slowed their growth, while the aggressive fundamentalist/evangelical churches experienced an upsurge in the number of churches planted.

The Formation of PCEC (1960s)

In the early 1960s, a group of Fundamental Baptist pastors and church leaders were having one of their regular meetings inside the First Baptist Church of Manila (FBCM).[61] Most recall that it was just another regular business meeting among the officers of the Association of Baptist Churches in Luzon (ABCL) which was a regional representative of the Association of Fundamental Baptist Churches in the Philippines (AFBCP).[62] In attendance were Rev Gavino Tica, Rev Leo Calica, Rev Manuel Alesna, Rev Apolinario Apoong, a church secretary, and ABCL's chairman, Dr Antonio Ormeo.[63]

---

61. The following is a reconstruction based on recollections and interviews of several individuals on the events described in the narrative. Some details like names and dates are unknown and some of the sequence of events as presented within this narrative may not be fully accurate. It is unfortunate that there are no written reports or papers and many of the details have been forgotten.

62. The ABCL was one of the associations of Fundamental Baptist churches that were formed during the immediate post-World War II era. For further details, see Kennedy, *Baptist Centennial History*, 176–235.

63. Appendix G: "Interview with Pio Tica," response to question 8–10, 17. Rev Antonio Ormeo completed his religious training in the Doane Evangelistic Institute in 1930. During the war, he actively ministered to those in the jungle and was also involved in the Guerrilla Movement (Appendix H: "Interview with Ebenezer Nacita," response to question 4). After the war, he was heavily involved in evangelistic and church-planting efforts. For example, in 1952 he led a team that conducted several revival meetings among the Ilonggos that migrated to Mindanao which strengthened the churches in Bukidnon and helped start the Davao Fellowship of Fundamental Baptist Churches ("Davao Fellowship of Fundamental Baptist Churches, A Brief History of Davao Fellowship of Fundamental Baptist Churches, Inc.," in *Advancing the Gospel Towards 2000*, Souvenir Program at the

Among the topics that were discussed were some of the religious trends that they had been noticing in the Philippines, such as the growing number of Filipino Protestant churches that were leaning towards liberalism and the ecumenical movement. They were particularly concerned with the effort to form a conciliar union among several Filipino mainline Protestant churches who were connected with the WCC.[64]

Being part of the fundamentalist International Council of Christian Churches (ICCC) which was the rival council of the WCC, Dr Ormeo and his group felt that the time had come to form their own fundamentalist council. This council would not only include the AFBCP but the other independent conservative Baptist churches and fundamentalist organizations that were ministering in the Philippines. Dr Ormeo had been instrumental in convening and establishing partnerships and mergers such as the formation of the Philippine Association of Baptists for World Evangelism (PABWE) and in the establishment of the Far Eastern Council of Christian Churches (FECCC) in 1951.[65] It was in the formation of the FECCC that Dr Ormeo became friends with Dr Carl McIntire, the founder of the ICCC.[66] Together, these two Christian leaders would champion the cause of fundamentalism in the Philippines and beyond.

23rd AFBCP Biennial Conference, Malaybalay, Bukidnon, Philippines, 5–8 May 1997). Rev Ormeo was also instrumental in establishing the "Mindanao Baptist Bible Institute (MBBI) now called the Mindanao Fundamental Baptist Seminary" ("Davao Fellowship"). When Rev Richard Durham retired in 1956, Rev Ormeo was installed as the very first Filipino Senior pastor of the FBCM.

64. Appendix G: "Pio Tica," response to question 10.

65. The FECCC was attended by one hundred and fifty one delegates from nine countries in Asia, including Australia. Dr Ormeo served as its first president, Dr Timothy Tow as vice president, Rev K. C. Quek as Secretary, and Rev Epifanio de la Pena as Treasurer (Nacita, *Celebrating God's Mercy*, 13–14). FECCC was the ICCC's response to the formation of the East Asia Christian Conference that was sponsored by the WCC (ICCC.Org, "A Short History of FECCC").

66. Carl McIntire (1906–2002) was considered one of the foremost advocates and champions of fundamentalism in his time. He was one of the students who left Princeton Seminary and transferred to Westminster Seminary, a fundamentalist seminary established by J. Gresham Machen as a counterpart to Princeton. He was among those who saw the need to respond to the growing liberalism in America. "Ruthlessly insistent on doctrinal purity, McIntire formed the American Council of Christian Churches in 1941 and the International Council of Christian Churches in 1948 to oppose and offer an alternative to the ecumenical positions of the National Council of Churches and the World Council of Churches" (David K. Larsen, "McIntire, Carl," in *Biographical Dictionary of Evangelicals*, ed. Timothy Larsen [Downers Grove, IL: InterVarsity Press, 2003], 394).

The Philippine Council of Fundamental Churches (1964)

It is unclear when and who initiated the first contact between the evangelicals and the fundamentalist leaders, but sometime around 1964 a meeting took place between Dr Ormeo, Faustino Ruivivar, Jr[67] and several individuals[68] in the First Baptist Church of Manila.[69] The goal of the meeting was to discuss the possibility of a merger in response to the newly established NCCP. It was reported that NCCP was recognized by the Philippine Government as the council that represented all the Protestants in the Philippines. However, these fundamentalist/evangelical leaders did not agree with this pronouncement since they strongly disagreed with "pronouncements and positions" made by the NCCP.[70] Bishop Fred Magbanua, Jr[71] recalls their struggle and concerns at that time,

> Because the main reason we gathered together at that time was the fact that the National Council of Churches [of the Philippines—NCCP] was representing all the non-Catholic groups, the Protestant groups. And many times their pronouncements were not exactly what we believe. [For example] at the height of liberal theology when at that time they would even consider . . . you know Mao Zedong as savior and all those kinds of liberal views that [infiltrated the older Protestant churches].[72]

---

67. Faustino Ruivivar, Jr, an alumni of FEBIAS served as a missionary among the Mangyan people in Mindoro when he was connected with the New Tribes Mission. He served as the Director of Every Home Crusade (EHC) in the Philippines where "under his direction they twice covered the entire Philippines with Christian Literature" and became "EHC's Director for all of Southeast Asia . . . in addition, for a number of years he served as editor of the *Evangelical Thrust*, a magazine he founded to disseminate the Gospel and build up Christians throughout the Philippines" (Honeywell and Honeywell, *Faith under Fire*, 162).

68. Although the names of these individuals have been forgotten, there is a possibility that one of these was Russell Honeywell – one of the founders of FEBIAS, and/or Charles Hufstetler – President of FEBIAS at that time (Appendix G: "Pio Tica," response to question 4).

69. Vencer, "Evangelicals in the Philippines," no. 8, 16.

70. Appendix D: "Fred Magbanua, Jr," response to question 8.

71. Bishop Magbanua had also served as the first Filipino pastor of Capital City Baptist Church. His position in FEBC and his connection with FEBIAS enabled him to establish credibility among the leaders of the evangelical movement.

72. Appenidx D: "Fred Magbanua, Jr," response to question 7.

These fundamental and evangelical leaders agreed that there was a great need to form their own counterpart council, one that would represent and voice out their concerns and one that broadcast their conservative theological perspectives. It was this commitment to the fundamentals of the faith that banded these fundamentalist and evangelical leaders together as they rejected these modernist/liberal views in the first place.[73] For example, the evangelicals and the fundamentalists affirmed the inspiration of the Bible, the trinity, the deity of Christ, and several other doctrines which they reckoned were no longer held by some of the leaders and theologians that represented the NCCP.[74] Thus, these leaders decided that they would proceed with their plans to establish an alternative national council.

The meeting in FBCM was soon followed by several other meetings, one of which was held in FEBIAS. The meeting in FEBIAS was among a bigger number of individuals who represented several fundamental and evangelical groups: the fundamentalists were led by Dr Ormeo (President of ABCL) with Rev Leo Calica and Rev Gavino Tica in attendance, while the evangelicals were represented by Rev Magbanua (President of CBAP; Administrative officer of FEBC) with Charles Hufstetler (President of FEBIAS), Franklin W. Allen (FEGC), Valmike Apuzen (CAMACOP), Gadiel Isidro (Caloocan Bible Church), and Donald McGregor (Foursquare Church). Dr Ruivivar (President of Every Home Crusade) was also present in the meeting where he served as the "bridge" between the two groups.[75] After discussing their common concerns and values, everyone agreed that there was a need to lay aside their differences and establish a council which would serve as the conservative counterpart to the NCCP. Thus, the participants gave their full support and commitment to become part of a national council which would represent the fundamentalist/evangelical Christians in the country.

In his article, Dr Vencer gives the following as the major reasons that motivated the leaders to finally lay aside their differences and work together.[76]

---

73. Tica explains that American missionaries who served as faculty members of FEBIAS were "diehard fundamentalists" who didn't join the ecumenical movement; this encouraged Dr Ormeo to motivate these churches and organizations in forming a fundamentalist council (Appendix G: "Pio Tica," response to question 4).

74. Appendix G: "Pio Tica," response to questions 57–59.

75. Appendix D: "Fred Magbanua, Jr," response to question 10.

76. Vencer, "Evangelicals in the Philippines," no. 10, 26–27.

First was "the defense of the fundamentals of the faith;" while there are conservative churches within the NCCP, some of these churches and their theologians were branded as "too 'modernist' or 'liberal' or 'humanist' in their theological orientation."[77] Second was "the need to evangelize the Philippines;" there had been some disagreement as to who should be "evangelized" as these fundamentalist/evangelical churches disagreed with some of NCCP members' perspective which no longer saw the need to "evangelize the Roman Catholics."[78] Third was "the necessity for holistic ministry;" these fundamentalist/evangelical leaders were convinced of the need to maintain a balance between proclamation and social work.[79] Fourth was "the need for a distinct public witness;" the fundamentalist/evangelical leaders wanted to spread their conservative spiritual values and beliefs. For example, the leaders of Council wanted to have a chance to influence and work with the Philippine government such as the armed forces of the Philippines, which up to the writing of this chapter allows only NCCP-recognized ministers to serve as military chaplains.[80] And their final reason was the importance

---

77. Aragon, "Philippine Council," 372. For example, Tica mentions Bishop Nacpil from the NCCP who held a liberal view on the Bible (Appendix G: "Pio Tica," response to question 57).

78. Jun Vencer explains this major disagreement regarding the need to evangelize the Roman Catholics,
> some major denominations within the NCCP would not consider Roman Catholics as constituting part of their evangelistic field. The Aglipayan Church, historically, was an attempt at the indigenization of Roman Catholicism, and the Episcopalian Church held that the Roman Catholic Church was a sister body and therefore they should work only among the non-Catholics. In contrast, the Protestant bodies that came during and after World War II were evangelicals. . . . These groups, along with the ABWE-rooted denominations, the Pentecostals, and other Evangelicals carried on intense evangelistic work all throughout the Philippines. To them the Philippines was, and still is, a mission field.

Vencer, "Evangelicals in the Philippines," no. 10, 26–27.

79. It is unfortunate that at this point, the ministry of proclamation was closely associated with the fundamentalists and the evangelicals while the ministry of social transformation became the sole purview of the modernist-liberals. This false dichotomy was a creation of the fundamentalist-modernist/liberal controversy in the US which had been "imported" to the Philippines.

80. Vencer explains that "the NCCP, being an older Protestant organic body, became the recognized voice of Protestantism in the Philippines" (Vencer, "Evangelicals in the Philippines," no. 10, 27). Since the evangelicals no longer saw the pre-war Protestants as being a consistent representative of their faith, they longed for their own "public witness." Thus, PCEC has tried to establish itself as a recognized organization by the Philippine government.

of unity; "growing together . . . by God's grace" so that the synergy among these churches could help in the increase of membership and resources.[81]

As a result, an agreement was made between the two camps to form the Philippine Council of Fundamental Churches (PCFC). One of their immediate actions was to promote the PCFC to the different fundamentalist and evangelical leaders, churches, and mission organizations throughout the country. Among those who went out to promote the PCFC were Rev Magbanua and Dr Hufstetler who met with key evangelical leaders.[82] The idea of the council was warmly welcomed by all and thus it gained support from several churches and organizations throughout the archipelago. One can describe this period as the "honeymoon period" of the council as everyone was willing to turn a "blind eye" to their apprehensions and differences.

Thus, the PCFC was formed with high hopes that the council would "express their 'oneness' in Christ."[83] Several churches and organizations immediately joined the council. However, there were some limitations as to who could be invited to become part of the council; its initial members came primarily from the Fundamental Baptist churches and the evangelicals who were connected with FEBIAS; these churches were neither liberal nor Pentecostal.[84] This membership limitation would later change as the council continued to redefine its nature and purpose.

Philippine Council of Fundamental-Evangelical Churches (1964)

During the preparation period for the first National Assembly of PCFC, Dr Ormeo served as its interim President of the board while Dr Gadiel Isidro was appointed to convene a Constitutional Convention at the Fellowship Center Church in Sampaloc, Manila on 23 November 1964. The task of this

---

81. It was a sad truth that while the fundamentalist and evangelical churches shared a common passion for conservative theology, their distinction and passion for purity often resulted in schism and further fragmentation caused by denominationalism. It was hoped that a conciliar unification could help "bridge" the gap between these churches.

82. Appendix D: "Fred Magbanua, Jr," response to question 3.

83. Vencer, "Evangelicals in the Philippines," no. 8, 16.

84. Although the role and the contribution of the Pentecostals to PCEC have been invaluable, Ruivivar and Tica assert that there were no Pentecostals in the very first or early meetings (Appendix I: "Correspondence with Faustino Ruivivar, Jr (6 June 2010)" and Appendix G: "Pio Tica," response to question 44–47).

committee was to draft the constitution and by-laws of PCFC in preparation for the first assembly and the council's incorporation with the Securities and Exchange Commission (SEC).

During the deliberations held at the Constitutional Convention, the tenuous unity was immediately threatened as heated arguments and discussions erupted among the committee members in their deliberations especially when it came upon the issue of what should be included within PCFC's doctrinal statement. Their varied denominational and theological backgrounds soon divided the committee members into factions. For example, one specific issue that almost "split" the newly formed council pertained to the doctrine of the second coming. The committee had a long and heated debate which almost ended in a schism had not Rev Magbanua stood up and suggested that the issue be set aside for a later date and that they simply affirm the fact that all of the members agree with the basic details of the doctrine of the second coming of Christ; they agreed to simply write this affirmation without any further explanation or categorizations.[85] As a result, the members of the committee were able to maintain a tenuous unity by merely avoiding their theological and traditional differences. While apprehensions and tensions continued, they all agreed to momentarily set aside these topics and simply "explored areas that would unite the group."[86]

However, the tension between the two camps that manifested itself during their deliberations at the convention did not abate; in fact the antagonism between the fundamentalists and the evangelicals was only just beginning. An issue that caused another round of debate came from the choice of the name for the council. While the omission of the word "evangelical" was initially accepted by the non-fundamental Baptist members in their haste to form a council and to avoid any tension and further debate; by this time, several committee members began to question its absence and the choice of the word "fundamental" to describe the churches that were connected with the council. Some argued that the word did not truly represent their tradition and that it should be noted that the council was not solely made up

---

85. Appendix G: "Pio Tica," response to question 42.

86. Vencer explains that despite their differences in their theological interpretations "they prudently avoided the issues that would have divided them, and explored the areas that would unite the group" (Vencer, "Evangelicals in the Philippines," no. 8, 16).

of fundamentalists or Fundamental Baptist churches.[87] It became apparent that the fundamentalist and evangelical factions were beginning to pull the council in two different directions as seen in their different goals and purposes. For the fundamental Baptists represented by Dr Ormeo, it was quite evident that their purpose was to form a council which would champion the fundamentalist ideals of McIntire and the ICCC.[88] However, the evangelicals wanted a non-extremist council that would unite them so that they could have a stronger and more effective witness. As Ruivivar remembers,

> It's true that Rev. Antonio Ormeo was the initiator of the first meetings of the council that would eventually become PCEC. But most of us from the non-Ormeo group would not be willing to be involved with Carl McIntire's international council. We accepted Ormeo's invitation to join the early committee because we *were* interested in seeing the evangelicals united in concrete ways.[89]

These evangelicals had envisioned a council which would follow the ideals and emphases of the "National Association of the Evangelicals in the US which is more or less the umbrella organization of most of these Evangelical churches."[90] Therefore, as a compromise, a new name was given, the Philippine Council of Fundamentalist and Evangelical Churches (PCFEC). It was meant to settle their disagreement by affirming both traditions; sadly, the name became the demarcation line between the members of the council as the tensions and the differences grew stronger.

---

87. There were several evangelical churches who did not consider themselves as separatists but as centrists, following the pattern of their mother organizations and churches in the United States that were affiliated with the NAE. As Magbanua states, "what we were trying to veer away from is becoming a separatist group" (Appendix D: "Fred Magbanua, Jr," response to question 7).

88. Appendix J: "Correspondence with Faustino Ruivivar, Jr (7 June 2010)."

89. Appendix O: "Correspondence with Faustino Ruivivar, Jr (16 August 2010)," epmhasis in original.

90. Appendix D: "Fred Magbanua, Jr," response to question 5.

Association of Baptist Churches in Luzon, Visayas, and Mindanao (ABCLVM)

While Dr Ormeo's decision to cooperate with the evangelicals helped paved the way in the formation of the council, his actions were not appreciated by everyone. There were several in the AFBCP who considered his relationship with the evangelical and Pentecostals as a breach in their stand against liberalism. These fundamental Baptist churches held to a well-defined relationship with other churches; those who held to similar doctrines and convictions were openly welcomed while those who did not were treated with antipathy. This predisposition was born out of the modernist/liberal-fundamentalist controversy in America where liberalism eventually overwhelmed those churches that accommodated the liberal beliefs of these groups. Thus, to avoid such a recurrence and the danger of compromising their beliefs, they strictly separated from the liberals and from those who related and tolerate them. As Nacita describes their understanding on the doctrine of separation,

> Biblical Separation is the principle which forbids Biblical Christians either individually or as a group, from cooperating ecclesiastically or personally with another person, or group of persons, who are not of like faith, in activities which will water down, distort or undermine the standards of Scriptures for right and wrong doctrines, ethics, methods and practices (2 Cor. 6:14).[91]

The list of those that were to be "unwelcomed" included almost all the non-fundamental Baptists with the addition of those who may have similar doctrines but were not willing to separate from the rest. The latter were branded as "compromisers" since their attitude and actions had potentially "compromised" the fundamentals of the faith; they may have the right theological beliefs but they have failed to correctly sever ties with these groups. It was this stance that the AFBCP adopted from their very beginning; as Rev Mariano Leones, one of their former leaders states, "separation was part of our doctrinal statement. And separation from disobedient [Christians and

---

91. Nacita, *Celebrating God's Mercy*, 57.

churches], that is, those evangelicals who worked together with liberals, with modernists, and with neo-evangelicals."[92]

Whether there had been some confrontations or discussions leading up to AFBCP'S Biennial Conference is unknown; however, it became apparent that actions of Dr Ormeo and the others who joined him were no longer acceptable. Thus, one of the sad outcomes of the formation of PCFEC was the removal of Dr Ormeo's group (i.e. First Baptist Church of Manila under the leadership of Dr Ormeo, Fellowship Center Church under Rev Calica, and the Mandaluyong Baptist Church under Rev Tica) from the membership of the AFBCP during its Biennial Conference in Kabankalan, Negros Occidental in June 1965. The main issue was their involvement with evangelicals which was considered as a form of compromise on the doctrine of separation.[93] The decision by the leaders of AFBCP to oust the three pastors and their church members resulted in a "three-day debate during the business meetings which centered on the interpretation and application of Biblical Separation . . . [which] ended in an overwhelming majority vote to dismiss them and their respective churches."[94] Whether from sympathy and/or agreement with the three leaders, more than forty other pastors and their churches left the AFBCP to form the Association of the Baptist Churches in Luzon, Visayas and Mindanao (ABCLVM) which became a separate independent fundamentalist Baptist movement headed by Dr Ormeo as its president.[95]

The schism that formed the ABCLVM took place a month before the First National Assembly of the newly formed fundamentalist/evangelical council. It was a difficult time for Dr Ormeo and those that followed him as their former collegues had turned their backs on them.

---

92. Appendix E: "Mariano Leones," response to question 16.

93. Appendix E, response to question 1.

94. Nacita, *Celebrating God's Mercy*, 17.

95. While the antagonism among these Fundamental Baptist churches continued for several decades; in time, these churches were reconciled back into the AFBCP. In 1997, Dr Ormeo and the others were welcomed back in another conference in Malaybalay, Bukidnon (Appendix E: "Mariano Leones," response to question 11).

The First National Assembly (July 1965)

Despite the difficulties and the tensions experienced by those who were involved in the process, the Constitutional Committee was able to produce a working constitution and by-laws which included the council's purpose and statement of faith. According to Dr Vencer's article, the council's purposes for PCFEC were as follows:

(1) To provide fellowship among Evangelical Christians;

(2) To provide a means of united action in the furtherance of the Gospel of Christ;

(3) To maintain the purity of the Gospel and to defend its truth;

(4) To provide a representative evangelical voice before the government and public; and

(5) To encourage all member bodies in aggressive and effective evangelism, church planting and church growth.[96]

On 9–10 July 1965, the PCFEC held its first national assembly in Capital City Alliance Church with seventy-three delegates from twenty-three founding bodies. Among those in attendance were the evangelical leaders such as Bishop Magbanua, Dr Ruivivar, and Dr Isidro while the fundamental Baptists were represented by Dr Ormeo and the leaders of his newly established Association of Baptist Churches in Luzon, Visayas, and Mindanao (ABCLVM), a separate fundamental Baptist group that broke away from the AFBCP in June 1965. As PCFEC's interim Executive Committee Chairman, Dr Ormeo "gave the keynote address" after which the "constitution and by laws were approved with minor amendments" with recommendations that the council be incorporated with the SEC.[97] Another item that was approved was the creation of the "15-man Executive Committee (EXCOM)" which was the "governing body" of PCFEC and the election of Rev Magbanua as the EXCOM Chairman and President of the council.[98] Dr Ormeo continued to serve as vice-chairman of the EXCOM during the early years of the council.

---

96. Vencer, "Evangelicals in the Philippines," no. 10, 25.
97. Vencer, "Evangelicals in the Philippines," no. 8, 17.
98. Vencer, 17.

PCFEC's beginnings were quite modest, its office was initially located in the basement of the Capitol City Baptist Church (a CBAP church), with hardly any funding and any office equipment available.[99] Nevertheless, its members rejoiced at this momentous occasion as the two camps had successfully merged to form a united council.

Continued Fundamentalist-Evangelical Tensions

However, the debate on the name of the council returned as soon as the First Assembly was over. Dr Vencer perceived that the controversy over the name was really rooted in the future direction of the newly established council: would it identify with the ICCC or with the NAE? Would it be fundamentalist or evangelical?[100] Thus, between the first and the second national assemblies, several meetings and arguments occurred among the council members that further increased the "fissure" within the council and among its leaders. With the successful launch of the council, several new evangelical churches and organizations joined the council. Since these new groups identified themselves as more evangelical than fundamental, the number of those who preferred the word "evangelical" over "fundamental" increased. In fact, Constancio Amen made a logical argument that the word "fundamental" is a subclass of the word "evangelical," thus having both words in the council's name was redundant. He further argued that using the word evangelical would be sufficient since it would encompass all the founding members of the council.[101]

Changes were also taking place within the council; one of these was the inclusion of Pentecostal churches and organizations as members of PCFEC.[102] Previously, some of the more conservative leaders who had a different theological tradition or understanding were unwilling to include the Pentecostals

---

99. Agustin B. Vencer and John Allan, *Poor Is No Excuse: The Story of Jun Vencer* (Dagupan City, Philippines: Alpha Printing Press, 2011), 57–58.

100. Vencer, "Evangelicals in the Philippines," no. 8, 17.

101. Rodrigo Tano, interview with author, Timog, Quezon City, 11 June 2010.

102. Although Donald McGregor of the Foursquare Church was able to attend several of the earlier meetings, his acceptance to the group was not readily assumed. He remembers that "he was first interviewed to qualify as an initiator by a panel of four: Florentino de Jesus, William Simons and Arthus Beals (Conservative Baptist missionaries), and Antonio Ormeo" (Appendix P: "Correspondence with Felipe Ferrez, Jr [11 June 2013]").

into the council.¹⁰³ However, the council's opinion about the Pentecostals began to change as they perceived that these Pentecostals shared a common passion for evangelism and sound doctrine. Except for their doctrines and practices that were focused on the "grace gifts" of the Holy Spirit, they were as conservative in their theology and praxis as the rest of the fundamentalist/evangelical churches.¹⁰⁴ As Ruivivar recalls,

> I'm **positive** there were no Pentecostals involved with PCEC in the beginning. As I told you, I was the one who advised the PCEC board to invite the Pentecostals. I told them I had been blessed listening to Rev. Paul Pipkin's messages at my home church, Kalimbas Evangelical Church in Manila. Pipkin was an Assemblies of God missionary. We did invite him to speak at a PCEC assembly. After that we invited the Assemblies of God and the Foursquare people to join PCEC. Later, a few more Pentecostal groups became involved.¹⁰⁵

However, these changes and new directions within the Council were beginning to disturb the Fundamental Baptist members as these were perceived as precursors to liberalism as evidenced by the Council's desire to join an "evangelical fellowship which is ecumenical."¹⁰⁶ As tensions reached a breaking point, Dr Ormeo resigned as vice-chairman of the EXCOM sometime before the second national assembly. This position was assumed by Dr Ruivivar. Although Dr Ormeo did not officially withdraw his membership

---

103. During this period, opinions over the Pentecostals were divided – from fully accepting them to outright condemnation. Suffice to say, the majority of the early leaders of the council were unfavorable to them.

104. For further discussion, see Donald W. Burdick, *Tongues: To Speak or Not to Speak* (Chicago: Moody, 1969); Wayne A. Grudem, ed., *Are Miraculous Gifts for Today?*, Counterpoints (Grand Rapids: Zondervan, 1996); Harold Horton, *The Gifts of the Spirit* (Springfield, MO: Gospel Publishing House, 1934); Leslie B. Flynn, *19 Gifts of the Spirit: Which Do You Have? Are You Using Them?* (Colorado Springs, CO: Chariot Victor Publishing, 1974); Robert L. Thomas, *Understanding Spiritual Gifts: An Exegetical Study of 1 Corinthians 12-14* (Chicago: Moody, 1978); Chuck Smith, *Charisma vs. Charismania* (Eugene, OR: Harvest House, 1983); Jack Deere, *Surprised by the Power of the Holy Spirit* (Grand Rapids: Zondervan, 1993).

105. Appendix L: "Correspondence with Faustino Ruivivar, Jr (9 June 2010)." Bold print in the original.

106. Appenidx G: "Pio Tica," response to question 54.

from the board of PCFEC, he was no longer active and withdrew from Council meetings and deliberations.

The Philippine Council of Evangelical Churches (1969)

Despite the enlistment of other conservative and pentecostal churches, PCFEC's future was again a major issue due to the continued tensions among its leaders and the waning involvement of the Fundamental Baptists.[107] Questions on whether there was a need for another name change were debated by several of the Council's members even before the second national assembly actually began.

The Second National Assembly (1968)

On 1 May 1968, the second national assembly of PCFEC was held at the Capitol City Baptist Church. Unlike the previous assembly in 1965, where everyone was exultant and excited by the union of the two camps, the second conference was beset by heated debates among the delegates, especially regarding the question of whether the council would drop either the word "fundamental" or "evangelical" from its name.[108] Another incident which further heightened tensions was the disagreement of whether a Pentecostal pastor would be allowed to speak.[109]

Tensions reached their breaking point when Bishop Magbanua asked this critical question, "Will PCFEC be a fundamental separatist council or an evangelical fellowship?"[110] The question was like an ultimatum which forced the council members to finally choose the path that they would take. Rev Magbanua answered his own question by affirming that the council's unity was not simply for the sake of "oneness" but a unity based on a shared purpose of "proclamation" and "social ministries."[111] Thus, it was decided by the majority vote that the word "evangelical" be retained and there was a motion from the floor which suggested the removal of the word "fundamental" from the council's name. However, the motion could not enacted

---

107. Appenidx D: "Fred Magbanua, Jr," response to question 11.
108. Vencer, "Evangelicals in the Philippines," no. 8, 17.
109. Appendix G: "Pio Tica," response to question 46.
110. Vencer, "Evangelicals in the Philippines," no. 8, 17.
111. Vencer, 17.

immediately due to the constraints of PCFEC constitution and by-laws.[112] Nevertheless, it was clear that this was the direction of the council and it was resolved by the council members that Rev Magbanua remain as President of the board of PCFEC.

The Third National Assembly (1969)

On 20–21 November 1969, the council held its third national assembly where the main agenda was the rectification of "the procedural defect in the amendment to change the official name."[113] The previous motion to remove the word "fundamental" was put to a vote, and with a majority decision, the name of the council was changed to Philippine Council of Evangelical Churches. While the evangelicals hailed the decision as a step forward, the fundamental Baptist pastors felt betrayed and offended, and realizing that PCEC would no longer be pursuing the fundamentalist agenda, they began to pull out of the council and the partnership between the two camps finally ended.[114] Although Dr Ormeo no longer actively participated in PCEC, he did not officially resign from the board of PCEC. On their part, the council leaders did not strike out Dr Ormeo's name and continued to retain ABCLVM's membership in PCEC; probably hoping for a future reconciliation.[115] However, it was clear that Dr Ormeo and his group had left the council since they perceived that the council, was no longer a "pure" fundamentalist group. Thus, the evangelicals were left to rebuild the council.

---

112. Appendix O: "Correspondence with Faustino Ruivivar, Jr (16 August 2010)."

113. Vencer, "Evangelicals in the Philippines," no. 8, 17.

114. It was this decision that finally divided the council, soon after the Fundamental Baptists withdrew themselves from the council (Appendix F: "Interview with Eliseo Capile," response to question 6). According to Tica, many were hurt and offended by the decision of the Assembly (Appendix G: "Pio Tica," response to question 52). See also Appendix D: "Fred Magbanua, Jr." response to question 5.

115. In July 1974, Dr Ormeo finally resigned from the PCEC Board and the ABCLVM withdrew its membership from the council as a protest against what happened in in Lausanne Congress on Evangelism that same year. According to Rev Tica, McIntire, who joined other protesters in a picket line outside the Congress, had sought for an audience with Billy Graham; however, when that didn't happened, the Fundamentalist took it as an insult. (Appendix G: "Pio Tica," response to question 12). As Ruivivar recalls, "after the Lausanne Congress on Evangelism in 1974, at a meeting of the PCEC board, Rev. Ormeo said he was withdrawing from PCEC in protest against the Lausanne Congress's 'shabby treatment' of Carl McIntire" (Appendix J: "Faustino Ruivivar, Jr [7 June 2010]"). Thus ended Dr Ormeo's relationship with the evangelicals.

Fundamentalist Schisms

As mentioned, one of the repercussions of their involvement with the evangelicals in the formation of PCEC, Dr Ormeo and the other Fundamental Baptists that joined him were "expelled" from the AFBCP in 1965. Immediately following this dismissal, ABWE and the AFBCP reclaimed the property on which the FBCM was currently located in Padre Faura. This resulted in a seven-year legal battle (1965–1972), referred to by Nacita as the "Tribulation Period" of the FBCM, where the Philippine Supreme Court ordered the eviction of FBCM and the property "was turned over to the Manila Baptist Church."[116]

When Dr Ormeo left PCEC in the 1970s, he was heavily involved in the process of relocating and restoring their ministry efforts after being evicted from Padre Faura.[117] As a result of their involvement with the evangelicals, among these efforts were the "construction of [a] temporary chapel . . . in Project 6, Q.C." and the relocation of their Bible Institute "at Fellowship Center Church in Sampaloc, Manila."[118] Another decision was to "divide" the current members of FBCM into smaller congregations; namely, Onyx which was located in Paco, Manila, Pildera in Pasay City, Sikatuna which was in Quezon City, and Project 6 which served as the mother church of these churches.[119]

Sadly, due to their commitment to doctrinal purity and their stand against what they perceived as ecumenism, several schisms within these fundamentalist churches took place. According to Nacita, there were three major "separations" that took place within the ABCLVM.[120] In 1972, after his return from the US, Rev Gavino Tica formed the Baptist International Missions, Inc. or BIMI, which drew several ABCLVM churches located in the Eastern Rizal area.[121] The second schism took place in 1989 when several churches withdrew from the ABCLVM and formed the Hilltop

---

116. Nacita, *Celebrating God's Mercy*, 18.
117. Appendix H: "Ebenezer Nacita," response to question 23.
118. Nacita, *Celebrating God's Mercy*, 21.
119. Nacita, 21.
120. The following are from Nacita, *Celebrating God's Mercy*, 28–31.
121. The incident caused some bitter exchanges between Dr Ormeo and Rev Gavino Tica (Appendix G: "Pio Tica," response to question 53).

Ministries and the Center for Biblical Studies led by Rev Dan Ebert III, a former New Tribes Missions missionary. The third schism took place in 2000 when Rev Rocky Diaz and Rev Gideon Romero formed the Filipino Baptist Fundamental Fellowship International.

While there have been efforts to reconcile and unify these fundamentalist churches and several successful partnerships in some conferences, the fundamentalists continue to be separated and fragmented as a result of their insistence on the doctrine of separation.[122]

PCEC Regains Stability (1970s–1980s)

After the fundamentalists left the council, the remaining churches struggled to keep the organization secure and to remain true to its objectives. It is the commitment and determination of these evangelical leaders that established PCEC as a strong council. By 1970, PCEC was incorporated with the Securities and Exchange Commission with forty member bodies.[123] The *PCEC Bulletin* was published as the council's official organ. By 1 August 1970, Florentino de Jesus was installed as the first Executive Director of PCEC and Magbanua remained as president of the board until he was replaced by Ruivivar in 1973.[124] Rev de Jesus provided the leadership and prestige necessary to restore and rebuild the council after the fundamentalists had left.[125] And it was the CAMACOP's involvement in the council that truly made it a nation-wide body. On 22 November 1974, the sixth national assembly of PCEC voted to join the World Evangelical Fellowship (WEF).

---

122. Appendix G, response to question 64.

123. According to Vencer, "on December 20, 1970, the PCEC Articles of Incorporation were filed with the Securities and Exchange Commission. The Certificate of Incorporation was issued on March 3, 1971. It was followed by the Certificate of Filing of By-Laws on January 11, 1973" (Vencer, "Evangelicals in the Philippines," no. 8, 17).

124. The new title Executive Director of PCEC (later given the title "Bishop") was a new leadership position created to facilitate and free up the Executive Director of PCEC while the management of the Board was under the President of the board (Appendix D: "Fred Magbanua, Jr," response to question 33–36).

125. Dr Florentino de Jesus's background as a pastor in Mindanao and the support and involvement of the CAMACOP made PCEC a truly nationwide group with member churches from Luzon, Visayas, and Mindanao. His reputation and statesmanship were able to bridge the gap among council members, enabling the group to heal and continue on (Felipe Ferrez, Jr, interview with author, Capitol City Foursquare Church, Quezon City, 17 May 2013).

PCEC's Directions and Emphasis (Late 1970s–1990s)

In 1975, having reached the mandatory retirement age of sixty-five, Rev de Jesus stepped down as Executive Director after having kept the council afloat through its turbulent early years. While the board of Directors of PCEC sought for a suitable replacement, Dr Ruivivar served as interim Executive Director while keeping his office as president of PCEC.[126] In 1977, after serving as the office administrator of the Billy Graham Crusade in Manila, Augustin (Jun) B. Vencer, Jr was asked by the PCEC Board to consider serving as its new Executive Director.[127] After much prayer and deliberation, Vencer was installed as PCEC's second Executive Director on 25 February 1978.[128] In his sixteen years as General Secreatry, he brought several innovations within the council which propelled PCEC to its current place.

Proclamation Ministry Efforts

One of PCEC's major involvements in evangelism and church planting was the Discipling A Whole Nation Movement (commonly known as the DAWN 2000 movement). This was a nation-wide, inter-church cooperation where "representatives from 81 evangelical denominations and Christian organizations committed themselves to the common vision of discipling the nation by planting a local church in each of the 42,000 barangays (communities or villages) by the year 2000" which produced the "document known as the Congress '80 Covenant."[129] DAWN 2000 finds its beginnings in 1966

---

126. Appendix Q: "Interview with Agustin B. Vencer," response to question 56.

127. In 1977, Rev Dr Augustin (Jun) B. Vencer, Jr who was an attorney by profession and a member of the CAMACOP became PCEC's General Secretary which he held for sixteen years. His knowledge of the conditions of the member churches and organizations of PCEC was due to the fact that he often served as their legal consultant/adviser. For details, see Vencer and Allan, *Poor Is No Excuse*, 51–55.

128. He recalls his beginnings in PCEC in this way, "during his installation as Executive Director, Jun commented wryly in his inaugural speech, 'I am glad we cannot go down anymore for we are already at the basement. We can only rise higher by His grace.' And this proved to be a prophetic statement" (Vencer and Allan, *Poor Is No Excuse*, 58). And it was true since PCEC's offices were indeed located at the basement of the Capitol City Baptist Church, their "total budget came to only 35,000 pesos, barely enough to allow one secretary, and Jun himself on a part-time basis" (Vencer and Allan, 58). In fact, he had to continue working as a lawyer to help with his financial obligations. He mentions in an interview that he was not excited about the appointment, but his wife Annabella was the first to respond and motivated him to take the responsibility (Appendix Q: "Agustin B. Vencer," response to question 21).

129. Efraim M. Tendero "The Philippines Model-Efraim M. Tendero," http://www.ad2000.org/ gcowe95/tend.html (accessed 28 February 2019).

The Formation of the Philippine Council of Evangelical Churches

where several Filipino leaders from five missions groups (Baptist General Conference, Evangelical Free Church, CBFMS, Far Eastern Gospel Crusade, and OMF) "attended a Church Growth Workshop in Winona Lake, Indiana" which resulted in sending a team of researchers (Gordon Swanson, Ralph Toliver, and Leonard Tuggy) "to research the growth of the churches in the Philippines under a project called Church Growth Research in the Philippines (C-GRIP)."[130] This was followed by two other congresses on evangelism; namely, the first World Congress on Evangelism held in Berlin in 1966, and the Asia-South Pacific Congress on Evangelism in Singapore in 1968. In 1969, Filipino delegates from these two international congresses formed the National Fellowship for Evangelism which "sponsored a ten-day All-Philippine Congress on Evangelism" where the Christ the Only Way Movement (COWN) was established whose goal was "to organize 10,000 Lay Evangelistic Group Studies (LEGS) to reach unbelievers, and 10,000 CORE (Christian Organized for Renewal and Evangelism)."[131] However, its coordinators realized that there was a greater challenge than merely starting 20,000 Bible studies throughout the country. During the National Church Growth Workshop that was co-sponsored by COWN, PCEC, C-GRIP, and Philippine Crusades held in Angono Rizal in October 1974, "church leaders representing about 85 groups united their hearts in earnest prayer in seeking God's mind and direction so that the work of the evangelicals in the Philippines would be delivered from long years of dormancy and stagnation."[132] In 1980, DAWN 2000 was launched in Cebu City on 3–7 November and in Baguio City on 10–14 November. Thus, DAWN 2000 was adopted by PCEC as its main strategy on evangelism and church planting.

In 1983, Dr Greg Tingson[133] and Bishop George Castro founded the Bayanihan Fellowship of Philippine evangelists (BAFPE) when several

---

130. Jun Balayo, "Historical Sketch of the DAWN 2000 Movement in the Philippines," in *Making Missions Practical: A Compendium of the Regional Consultation on Missions*, ed. Averell U. Aragon (Davao City, Philippines: Mindanao Challenge, 1990), 3.

131. Balayo, "Historical Sketch," 4.

132. Balayo, 4.

133. Connected with the Convention Baptist in Iloilo, Greg Tingson became involved with Torrey Johnson's Youth for Christ (YFC) while he was studying in America in 1946. During his involvement with the YFC, he gained a reputation of being a passionate and articulate preacher. During his lifetime of ministry, Dr Tingson helped establish "several indigenous ministries, which reached multitudes for Christ within the Philippines . . . in

Filipino delegates attended a ten-day conference for itinerant evangelists in Amsterdam sponsored by the Billy Graham Evangelist Association.[134] Realizing their common goals, PCEC invited BAFPE to consider merging itself with the DAWN 2000 strategy. Thus, BAFPE was renamed League of Philippine Evangelists and became a part of PCEC.[135]

In 1985, PCEC and Philippine Crusades jointly sponsored the National Church Growth Strategy Congress in Baguio City where "one hundred sixty-seven delegates representing 67 Evangelical groups from all over the nation attended the 4-day congress" where the goals of DAWN 2000 were reaffirmed by Dr Vencer.[136]

According to the National Director's Report during PCEC's 25th National Assembly in July 2003, the numerical goal of seeing fifty-thousand churches was surpassed "based on the final report, there were already 51,625 churches nationwide and 9.1% of the country is Evangelical/Full Gospel by the end of 2000."[137] However, in terms of planting a church in every baranggay, the efforts had only reached less than half of the 41,500 baranggays in the country. In response, PCEC launched "the Baranggay Church Planting

---

other Asian countries . . . [he founded the] Asian Christian Outreach . . . in 1973 to conduct evangelistic campaigns in numerous East Asian countries, as well as the Philippines" (Christian Aid Mission, "Greg Tingson Goes Home to Glory," accessed 15 August 2013, http://www.christianaid.org/News/2010/mir20100430.aspx).

134. Philippine Council of Evangelical Churches, "Commissions: League of Philippine Evangelism," accessed 15 August 2013, http://pceconline.org/commissions/lpe.htm.

135. The League of Philippine Evangelists was launched during the time of Bishop Tendero. As the new General Secretary reports,
> The **League of Philippine Evangelists** was formally launched on May 13, 1994. Its first project was the ***Congress of Itinerant Evangelism*** held on May 31 to June 3, 1994 with 287 delegates. The League aims to recruit and train 2,000 evangelists by year 2000 and to conduct evangelistic campaigns in 1,570 towns and cities. LPE Congress was echoed in Bacolod City with 120 delegates and then in Dumaguete City with 221 potential evangelists. Membership has grown to 336 nationwide

Efraim Tendero, "PCEC Accomplishment Report, June 1993 – May 1995," in *Philippine Council of Evangelical Churches, 21st General Assembly: That the World May Believe*, Souvenir Program at the 21st General Assembly, (Brokenshire Resource Center, Davao City, 20–23 June 1995), 10. Bold and bold-italic in the original.

136. Augustin B. Vencer, "PCEC Update," *Evangelical Thrust* 12, no. 4 (April 1985): 24.

137. Efraim Tendero, "National Director's Report (July 2001-June 2003)," in *Philippine Council of Evangelical Churches, 25th National Assembly: Developing Healthy Churches for National Transformation*, Souvenir Program at the 25th National Assembly (Christian Development Centre, Tagaytay City, 8–11 July 2003), 22.

The Formation of the Philippine Council of Evangelical Churches 149

Commission . . . so we can reach far-flung and un-churched areas where the gospel has never been heard, until every baranggay will have a church—and every Filipino will be discipled for Jesus Christ."[138]

Aside from the DAWN 2000, PCEC also helped mobilize evangelical churches and Christian organizations to present the gospel. For example, the council was able to mobilize 1,256 churches and eight missions organizations for the Rev Mike Evan's *Manila for Christ '95* (24–25 February 1995) where attendance drew "10,000, 15,000 and 150,000 people to the Quirino Grandstand on its three campaign nights. On the first night, 1,500 responded to the altar call; there were 2,000 on the second night and about 10,000 on the third night!"[139]

Social Involvement and Transformation

Dr Vencer had always had a passion to be involved in helping the poor and the powerless in society. Before his time in PCEC, he had served as the Associate Director for Church Relations of World Vision Philippines.[140] When he led the council, one of his earliest proposals was to start a relief program that was similar to World Vision. However, realizing that the social needs of the country were far greater with the constant and almost regular visitation of natural disasters such as fires, famine, and typhoons; Dr Vencer proposed the creation of the Philippine Relief and Development Services (PHILRADS). While there had been efforts to help those in crisis, Vencer had envisioned a more organized and systematic approach in caring for the needy. While all the leaders of PCEC were in agreement, the proposal was shelved due to two major concerns: financial and calling.[141]

---

138. "PCEC Commissions & Networks: Baranggay Church Planting Commission," in *Philippine Council of Evangelical Churches, 29th National Assembly: Churches Transforming Communities: Working Together Toward National Transformation*, Souvenir Program at the 29th National Assembly (Christian Development Centre, Tagaytay City, 12–15 July 2011), 16.

139. Tendero, "Accomplishment Report," 11.

140. World Vision is an "international Christian relief and development organization" which was started in China by Bob Pierce in 1947 (John McCoy, "World Vision," in *A Dictionary of Asian Christianity*, ed. Scott W. Sunquist [Grand Rapids; Cambridge, UK: Eerdmans, 2001], 901). World Vision began its work in the Philippines when it helped provide "musical instruments and textbooks for the children" of a local orphanage in Guimaras in 1957 and operated its own orphanage in South Cotobato in 1960 (World Vision, "Who We Are: Our History," accessed 20 May 2011, http://www.worldvision.org.ph/who-we-are/our-history).

141. Appendix Q: "Agustin Vencer," response to question 2.

In terms of their financial constraints; when Dr Vencer assumed the leadership of PCEC, the council had barely enough money to finance its own operations. The main question was, "how could they help others when they were barely surviving?" Instead of being powerless, the new head of the council took the initiative by conducting a series of networking and fund development strategies where several international and local organizations helped in raising the funds. Since then, PCEC had made financial stability as one of its core values, "PCEC ensures financial viability by trusting God to provide and through an effective generation of resources. It observes prudent use of resources and efficient financial control."[142] Dr Vencer recalls that by the late 1980s and early 1990s, PHILRADS was "helping 35,000 families a year" and had become a "multi-million organization."[143]

The second concern stemmed from the apprehension that PHILRADS might potentially distract or redirect PCEC from its goals and begin prioritizing relief operations over proclamations of the gospel. The council was still determining how to balance these two major tasks of the church – evangelism and social involvement. Part of the confusion lies in the modernist/liberal-fundamentalist controversy that had created a perspective that social work was the sole domain of the liberals.[144] In addition, there was a danger that the strength and resources of the council would be drained by PHILRADS efforts in relief and social engagement. However, "the necessity for holistic ministry" was one of the major reason for the formation of the council.[145] Thus, the council leaders voted on pushing forward in establishing PHILRADS in 1980. The only requirement that was asked by the PCEC board was that Dr Vencer would hold both positions "to ensure that the balance will be there."[146] Within five years, the PHILRADS was in

---

142. Philippine Council of Evangelical Churches, "About Us: Core Values," accessed 11 May 2010, http://www.pceconline.org/about/corevalues.htm.

143. Appendix Q: "Agustin Vencer," response to question 4.

144. For further details, see Ahlstrom, *Religious History*, 785–804.

145. It was the third reason given as a justification for the formation of the council (Vencer, "Evangelicals in the Philippines," no. 10, 26–27).

146. Appendix Q: "Agustin Vencer," response to question 2.

the forefront of the council's efforts to help provide relief for those who had experienced natural and man-made disasters such as fires.[147]

Aside from these humanitarian efforts, the council through its publications and public declarations attempted to faithfully address the current societal issues that confronted the evangelicals in the country. For example, Dr Ruivivar wrote an article regarding the issue of the Christian's involvement in war,[148] divorce in the Philippines, and human rights[149] among other issues.[150] This passion to engage the societal concerns was continued by Bishop Efraim M. Tendero, the next General Secretary, as efforts were made to mobilize churches and organizations to formulate and declare their views on the matter.[151]

Engaging National Leaders

Another innovation that was introduced during this period was PCEC's relationship with the religious and national leaders of the country. Dr Vencer realized that it was important for the evangelical church to engage the "other Christians" – the NCCP. Unfortunately, animosity and prejudice had risen between these two groups of churches. Part of the problem was an inherited suspicion between them which had been formed during the height of the modernist/liberal-fundamentalist controversy in America.[152] To break out

---

147. To keep this balance, every PCEC Update would include reports on evangelistic efforts and social engagement. For example of such relief efforts, see Augustin B. Vencer, "PCEC Update," *Evangelical Thrust* 12, no. 1 (January 1985): 26.

148. For details, see Faustino Ruivivar Jr, "Do You Have a Question? Can a Christian Become a Soldier?" *Evangelical Thrust* 12, no. 1 (January 1985): 21.

149. Both issues were addressed in *Evangelical Thrust* 12, May 1985 issue.

150. Dr Vencer was also involved in the anti-pornography campaign. In an article where he challenges his evangelical readers to get involved in the issue, he writes "Mayor Bagatsing and other groups are fighting pornography and smut literature. What is the Evangelical church doing? Can it be that we care less for the morals of our young and society? God forbid!" (Augustin B. Vencer, "What Kind of Christian Workers Should We Prepare in Times of Crisis," *Evangelical Thrust* 12, no. 1 [January 1985]: 7).

151. In its core values, PCEC affirms its role "as a credible and prominent moral guardian of the nation . . . for the issues affecting the cultural, social, political and economic life of our nation. It presents a distinctly evangelical voice and presence to our government and other publics as a witness to the lordship of Christ in all things" (Philippine Council of Evangelical Churches, "About Us: Core Values.")

152. According to Bishop Magbanua, some of these attitudes against the mainline protestant churches were passed on to them by the America missionaries that had experience the impact of the controversy in the West (Appendix D: "Fred Magbanua, Jr," response to question 11).

of this mold, Dr Vencer decided to meet with Bishop Laverne Mercado over lunch. Fondly recalling the luncheon meeting, Dr Vencer challenged Bishop Mercado by saying, "I want to find out how liberal you are and I want you to find out how narrow I am."[153] Thus began a close relationship between the two leaders that had been separated by past prejudices inherited by their generation.

This relationship of trust and partnership continued to grow; in fact, the leaders of the NCCP had made the recommendation that PCEC would become part of the Church-Military Liaison Committee. It was during the height of the Martial Law period when several individuals who were suspected of allegiance either to the government or to the communists led National People's Army (NPA) were abducted and summarily executed. It was unfortunate that several pastors became targets of harassment and some were even killed. This became a major concern for the leaders of PCEC. As a result, they supported Dr Vencer's involvement in the committee which helped in identifying genuine pastors to protect them from being abducted and murdered by extremist groups.[154]

When the Marcos regime fell, the new Cory Aquino government decided to form a national consultative body of religious leaders who could aid in the task of reuniting and leading the country. Thus, members of the former Church-Military Liaison were invited to form a committee of religious leaders. Dr Vencer accepted the opportunity for PCEC to become part of this committee. As the group was initially being formed, there was some confusion and difficulties as the Muslims, *Iglesia ni Kristo*, the Roman Catholic Church, the NCCP, and the PCEC struggled with their working relationships. Taking the lead, Dr Vencer argued that while they may come from different religions with their different agendas, he said "wait a minute, we are citizens who are here who happen to be religious with different persuasions," he then asked if he could be allowed to draft proposal on the nature of the committee; after two weeks, he presented the draft proposal and after two hours of deliberations, it was approved.[155] Thus, they were inducted into the National Ecumenical Consultative Committee (NECCOM) where the

---

153. Appendix Q: "Agustin Vencer," response to question 4.
154. Appendix Q, response to question 33.
155. Appendix Q, response to question 4.

group could "meet with the President for every three or four months and we can request any cabinet member or anyone in the government to meet with us and discuss issues."[156] During the Presidency of Fidel V. Ramos, PCEC continued its involvement and Bishop Tendero served as NECCOM chairman for a time. He saw this as an opportunity to place "PCEC in a strategic position where it can help in charting the religious destiny of the nation."[157]

This relationship between the two councils also produced some coordination and partnerships in ministry. For example, as PCEC prepared for the launching of DAWN 2000, a dialogue took place between the leaders of the NCCP and PCEC which resulted in the support and participation of several NCCP churches. Thus, DAWN 2000 became a successful cooperative effort where "over five hundred participants representing 81 denominations and other agencies (affiliated with both the NCCP and the PCEC) signed a covenant committing themselves to participate in the cooperative strategy."[158]

Transforming PCEC's Structure

Another crucial area of development took place within PCEC itself. Appropriate changes were introduced so as to "ensure that there is a structure for growth" as Dr Vencer had envisioned that PCEC would be transformed from merely a ministerial fellowship to an effective organization that serves the body of Christ.[159] The following were some of the changes that he introduced.

---

156. Appendix Q, response to question 4.

157. "GS Report," in *Philippine Council of Evangelical Churches, 22nd National Assembly: Empowering the Churches*, Souvenir Program at the 22nd National Assembly (Christian Development Center, Tagaytay City, 15–18 July 1997), 14.

158. Averell U. Aragon, "A Study on the History and Development of the Philippine Council of Evangelical Churches and Its Contribution to the Growth of Protestantism in the Philippines" (ThM thesis, Asia Graduate School of Theology, 1999), 48.

159. In a recent publication, PCEC defines its role in the evangelical church, "we seek to connect the evangelical churches in the Philippines to strengthen the impact of the Christian community in society, for them to be effective in the transformation of the state" ("Philippine Council of Evangelical Churches," in *Philippine Council of Evangelical Churches, 29th National Assembly: Churches Transforming Communities: Working Together Toward National Transformation*, Souvenir Program at the 29th National Assembly [Christian Development Centre, Tagaytay City, 12–15 July 2011], 12).

Changed the title of Executive Director to General Secretary
Initially, the position of Executive Director was not a career position since there was a required "yearly election" from the national assembly which could potentially lead to politicking as the person would try to gain sufficient votes to maintain their position.[160] Realizing the need for stability, the new title – General Secretary (GS) was given a defined tenure as follows:

> the General Secretary shall be the Chief Executive Officer of the Council and shall, under the direction of the Board of Directors, provide general supervision, administration and oversight of the entire work of the Council . . . the General Secretary shall be appointed by the Board of Directors. He shall serve until he is incapacitated due to death, physical and mental incapacity, resignation or terminated for cause by the Board of Directors.[161]

It was this amendment that freed the GS from being pressured by certain factions within the council. The pressure of winning the votes had been removed.

Integration of System Management within PCEC
One of the difficulties of working among church leaders was that smooth interpersonal relationship was more important that the goals. While keeping an atmosphere of love and grace, Dr Vencer introduced system management and organizational restructuring within the council to ensure efficiency in the delivery of service and to provide the necessary platform that could allow for the organization to grow. As a result, the council achieved its goals, "training our leaders, allowing delegations and putting standards of performance in their entire action plan . . . at one point we were managing the works of about 17 organizations in the country."[162]

---

160. Vencer, "Evangelicals in the Philippines," no. 10, 32.

161. "Amended By-Laws of the PCEC," in *Philippine Council of Evangelical Churches, 22d National Assembly: Empowering The Churches*, Souvenir Program at the 22nd National Assembly (Christian Development Centre, Tagaytay City, 15–18 July 1997), 42.

162. Appendix Q: "Agustin Vencer," response to question 4.

The Formation of the Philippine Council of Evangelical Churches

Funds and Resources Development

As mentioned earlier, PCEC was struggling financially in its early years.[163] In his effort to bring in the necessary funding, Dr Vencer initiated a fundraising campaign. However, his efforts were met with some resistance where some had asked, "why are we to help you? What are you doing to help us? . . . if salvation is free then why is PCEC expensive?"[164] These responses revealed that PCEC must be seen as an organization that effectively serves the evangelical body. In addition, several of their member churches were also in the same financial situation; for this reason, there was a need to seek out international and local partner agencies to help provide the funding that they needed. For example, PCEC was able to contact World Relief and Tearfund, an organization who shared their passion to help the poor. It was this organization that help in the purchase of a property so that the Evangelical Center could be built by 1990.

Changes in the Purposes of PCEC

Finally, one important amendment was the council's purposes. Dr Vencer clarified and defined the calling of the council. The new objectives of PCEC are as follows:

> (1) Promote unity and encourage cooperative ministries among Evangelicals in the Philippines;
>
> (2) Develop effective evangelism strategies and a strong missions program for the evangelization of the Philippines and the world;
>
> (3) Present a distinctively evangelical voice and presence to our government and other publics as a witness to the lordship of Christ in all things; and

---

163. Vencer and Allan, *Poor is No Excuse*, 57–58. According to Vencer, "while the national Evangelical leaders understood the purpose of PCEC, the common Evangelical Christian and their churches were ignorant on the need and value of PCEC's existence" (Vencer, "Evangelicals in the Philippines," no. 10, 32).

164. Appendix Q: "Agustin Vencer," response to question 4.

(4) Engage in ministries by helping the needy and poor in the Philippines to become economically self-reliant and rightly related with God in Christ Jesus.[165]

From the above, it is clear that the council was living up to the ideals of evangelicalism – a balance between proclamation and social transformation so that they could have a credible voice in society.

As a result of all these efforts, PCEC is considered one of the fastest growing networks or councils of churches in the country. Its webpage reports that its current membership is "20,000 denominations, para-church organizations and local churches nationwide" after more than forty years of existence.[166] Through its concerted efforts and interactions with other religious bodies and government entities, PCEC has steadily gained recognition and a "voice" in the nation's concerns and issues.[167]

Conclusion

While the journey towards achieving this particular conciliar union was beset with difficulties and conflicts, PCEC propelled itself from its fundamentalist foundation to become an evangelical council that is committed to Christ through the ministry of proclamation and social work. The loss of their Fundamental Baptist brethren was a big setback for the purpose and goals of PCEC; nevertheless, this gave the council the freedom to connect itself with other churches both locally and internationally. In time, the council's cooperative unity helped gain for itself a credible and distinct evangelical voice that speaks not only to the Philippines but to the world as well.

---

165. "Amended By-Laws of the PCEC," 37.

166. Philippine Council of Evangelical Churches, "Commissions: Commissions and Networks," accessed 11 May 2010, http://www.pceconline.org/commissions/index.htm.

167. A local popular news agency states that "the PCEC is the largest network of evangelical denominations, local churches, and parachurch and mission organizations in the Philippines" and wrote a full article on PCEC's call for peace (GMA NewsTV, "Council of Churches Urges Filipinos to Become 'Instruments of Peace,'" *GMA NewsTV*, 24 December 2007, accessed 31 May 2010, http://www.gmanews.tv/story/ 74056/ council-of-churches-urges-filipinos-to-become-39instruments-of-peace39).

CHAPTER 5

Analysis and Synthesis of the Formation and Developments within PCEC Using Hiebert's Bounded versus Centered Set Categories

Since its arrival in the Philippines in 1899, Protestantism has grown so that it now constitutes roughly eleven percent of the Philippine population.[1] While early American missionaries of the Evangelical Union attempted to present a united front (e.g. a common name – *Iglesia Evangelica*, joint seminaries, etc.), churches within Philippine Protestantism continued to remain autonomous; this situation continued even with the arrival of several fundamentalist and evangelical churches in the late 1930s and in the post-World War II era.[2] However, as a result of the determination and the initiative of key Filipino leaders, a conciliar union was formed – the National Council of Churches

---

1. According to one newspaper report,
   The Philippines remains to be the bastion of Christianity in Asia with 86.8 million Filipinos—or 93 percent of a total population of 93.3 million—adhering to the teachings of Jesus Christ, a recent study by the US-based Pew Research Center has found. . . . Of the Filipino Christians, 81 percent are Catholic, 11 percent Protestant and one percent belong to other Christian groups. The remaining seven percent of the Philippine population are non-Christian
   Lawrence De Guzman, "Philippines Still Top Christian Country in Asia, 5th in World," *Philippine Daily Inquirer*, 21 December 2011, accessed 4 September 2012, http://globalnation.inquirer.net/21233/philippines-still-top-christian-country-in-asia-5th-in-world.
2. This spirit of independence and autonomy or denominationalism is common in North America from which Philippine Protestantism gets its origin. For example, Mead in, *Handbook of Denominations in the United States*, shows that the name "Church of God" refers to at least nine different groups that are distinct from each other (Mead and Hill, *Handbook of Denominations*, 81–87).

in the Philippines (NCCP) in 1963. Among their goals was to establish a united ecclesiastical body so that the Filipino Church could fulfill its role as a prophetic voice – "united witness and common action on concerns affecting the religious, moral, social and civic life of the country."[3] And even with the changing times, this calling was reiterated in 1971, where NCCP called upon its member churches to evaluate their current direction and emphasis in the changing times,

> Therefore, it becomes the churches' role to be prophetic by exposing those existing oppressive systems and structures in order to bring about fundamental changes for a more humane society. In Philippine society, the task of the institutional churches should be to emphasize those activities which will enhance human development and liberation, such as organizing people for action to effect the necessary change. There is now open to the people of God an opportunity to respond responsibly for their liberation in any given political, social and economic system or structure.[4]

As a result of this united voice, the NCCP was recognized by the Philippine Government as the representative of all the non-Roman Catholic churches in the country.[5] However, several independent and conservative churches did not accept NCCP's representation and pronouncements; as a result, they decided to form their own fundamentalist/evangelical council – the Philippine Council of Evangelical Churches (PCEC).

In order to understand the preference and actions taken by these church leaders; one can consider the question, "why did they choose one church or organization over another?" There is a host of possible answers such as a passion for theological purity, western influence through denominationalism, tribal and regional loyalties, etc. Since Dr Vencer mentioned that he was inspired by Paul Hiebert's "bounded versus centered set theory" when

---

3. Sitoy, *Comity and Unity*, 130.

4. "Statement of Concern on Development and the Churches' Role in the 70s," in *A Public Faith, A Social Witness: Statements and Resolutions of the National Council of Churches in the Philippines*, vol. 1 (Quezon City, Philippines: National Council of Churches in the Philippines, 1995), 114.

5. Appendix D: "Interview with Fred Magbanua, Jr," response to question 7.

he began to implement the changes that took place within PCEC, this chapter would attempt to employ this model to discern some patterns in these conciliar unions.[6]

Bounded versus Centered Set Unions

In his book, *Anthropological Reflections on Missiological Issues*, Hiebert describes several models by which Christians are identified and grouped.[7] Using the two main categories that he presented – bounded set and centered set) – the following is a brief explanation of the two categories as applied in understanding the behavior of these churches and their conciliar unions.

The "bounded set" union is a merger wherein participating churches and organizations have a perceived "intrinsic uniformity" in their theology, praxis, ecclesiology, etc. In other words, these churches and organizations share a common "boundary" based on a well-defined theology, missiology and liturgy, a "theological border, a doctrinal fence."[8] And it is these accepted "boundaries" that regulate the membership within this union.[9] Since the bond that they share is based on their intrinsic nature, their relationship draws similar-minded churches while deterring those that do not uphold these intrinsic characteristics.

On the other hand, the "centered set" union among churches is "created by defining a center or reference point and the relationship of things to that center."[10] There are no "gatekeepers" or demarcation lines that distinguish a member from one that is not. While these churches and organizations may

---

6. Appendix Q: "Interview with Agustin B. Vencer," response to question 17. For more details on bounded versus centered set theory, see Paul G. Hiebert, *Anthropological Reflections on Missiological Issues* (Grand Rapids: Baker, 1994), 107–136; Michael L. Yoder, Michael G. Lee, Jonathan Ro, and Robert J. Priest, "Understanding Christian Identity in Terms of Bounded and Centered Set Theory in the Writings of Paul G. Hiebert," *Trinity Journal* 30, no. 2 (Fall 2009): 177–188.

7. Hiebert, *Anthropological Reflections*, 110.

8. Jeremy Myers, "Bounded Sets vs. Centered Sets" *Redeeming God*, accessed 10 July 2018, https://redeeminggod.com/ bounded-sets-centered-sets/.

9. Hiebert, *Anthropological Reflections*, 116. In a bounded set view, a person is considered as a Christian if they "affirm right beliefs, and practice right behaviors" (Tim Harmon, "Who's In and Who's Out? Christianity and Bounded Sets vs. Centered Sets," *Transformed*, 17 January 2014, accessed 10 July 2018, https://www.westernseminary.edu/transformedblog /2014/01/17/whos-in-and-whos-out-christianity-and-bounded-sets-vs-centered-sets/).

10. Hiebert, *Anthropological Reflections*, 123.

not necessarily share the same set of doctrines and behavior; their solidarity is based on each member's relationship to that defined "center" or common goal. Hence, the membership is no longer based on uniformity but on their relationship to the "center," whether they are drawing near or withdrawing from it.

Applying Hiebert's Categorization to the Post-War Councils in the Philippines

The following section is an attempt to evaluate two particular councils which existed during the post-war period using Hiebert's bounded set versus centered set models. The evaluation can help provide categories to help understand the differences between the two models of unification.

Two Councils in Contrast

As a context to the formation of PCEC, there were two major unions that took place within Philippine Protestantism during the post-World War II era that help show the differences between the bounded set and centered set unions.[11] These are the AFBCP and the NCCP, both of which were part of the history of PCEC.

AFBCP – Bounded Set Union

The AFBCP had a significant role in PCEC's history since several of its founders (i.e. Dr Ormeo, Rev Tica, and Rev Calica) were from the former council. In 1948, the Fundamental Baptist churches which were the fruit of the efforts of the fundamentalist ABWE, the Baptist Bible Seminary and Institute (Manila), Mindanao Baptist Bible Institute, and the Doane Baptist Bible Institute established the AFBCP in their efforts to create an autonomous Filipino council which would unite these churches and provide "an appropriate response to the developing ecumenical and charismatic climate in the international Christian community."[12] The following is a brief overview of the council which includes its stated purposes, followed by a

---

11. It must be noted that there are no completely bounded set or completely centered set church unions. It appears that these conciliar unions tend to adopt an "almost" rather than a "complete" form of unity.

12. Nacita, *Celebrating God's Mercy*, 45.

brief assessment of the council and its characteristics employing Hiebert's description of a bounded set.[13]

The stated purposes of the AFBCP as written in their Articles of Incorporation with the Philippine Securities and Exchange Commission, states:

> (1) To provide fellowship for Baptist churches which subscribe to these By-laws and Articles of Faith;
>
> (2) To encourage and promote evangelism and to assist in the establishing and organizing of indigenous Baptist churches;
>
> (3) To advance Baptist Missionary enterprises throughout the world;
>
> (4) In accord with the historic Baptist principles of the independence and sovereignty of the local Baptist church, it is not the purpose of this Association to legislate for the local church, dictate its policies, or attempt to interfere with its internal affairs. When invited to do so, the Association may advise and counsel any local Baptist church or may recommend action in relation to any problem which a local church may bring before it, in consultation with the regional association in which the local church is in fellowship.[14]

Emphasis on Becoming a Uniform, Homogenous Group

According to Hiebert, one characteristic of a bounded set church is its emphasis on having the "same doctrines . . . observer[ing] the same behavior. Its unity would be based on uniformity," and it is in this manner that other churches are evaluated so that churches with a different set of doctrines and behavior are considered "*other* sets."[15] This specific set of doctrines and particular behaviors are the basis for determining whether one should be in union with another group. Evaluating the AFBCP, one observes that this

---

13. Hiebert, *Anthropological Reflections*, 116–117.

14. Republic of the Philippines, Securities and Exchange Commission, *Articles of Incorporation*, 3. It is must be noted that Mariano B. Leones appears to be one of the key individuals in drafting their constitution and by-laws as his name appears as the author of this official document.

15. Hiebert, *Anthropological Reflections*, 116.

expectation was characteristic of their council. For example, in examining their requirements for membership, under Article 1, Section 2 entitled "Fellowshipping Churches" of their constitution and by-laws, it states that "Baptist churches . . . are automatically considered fellowshipping churches, provided . . . their agreement and subscription to the By-Laws and Articles of Faith."[16] And anyone who wishes to join their fellowship/church must also abide with this standard – one's commitment to AFBCP's Articles of Faith. It is this commitment that has been a trademark for these fundamental churches since the beginning of the modernist/liberal-fundamentalist controversy in America.[17]

Commitment in Maintaining Clear Boundaries
Another characteristic of a bounded set church is its clear distinction between those that they relate to and those that they don't; one's life and words are seen as a way to verify one's faith.[18] This means that their relationships are clearly defined based on the categories by which a person is gauged as Christian or not, based on their adherence to a common doctrine and behavior. In the case of the AFBCP, this characteristic is seen in their commitment to the doctrine of separation.[19] Their commitment to this standard is seen in what is referred to as "Levels of Fellowship" of their church where the highest degree is

> Level 5: Fellowship involving financial and administrative partnership among Fundamental Baptist Churches that agree on the Fundamental Doctrines, Conservative Ethics, Non-Ecumenical/Non-Charismatic Methods . . . [while] Level 1: Evangelistic and missionary attitude . . . openness and a cordial relationship with all unbelievers with the desire to bring them to the Lord for Salvation."[20]

While these boundaries may seen stern and intolerant of others, they see them as guides in their association with individuals, groups, and churches.

---

16. Securities and Exchange Commission, *Articles of Incorporation*, 8.
17. Dollar, *History of Fundamentalism*, 72.
18. Hiebert, *Anthropological Reflections*, 116.
19. Appendix E: "Interview with Mariano Leones," response to question 16 and 31.
20. Nacita, *Celebrating God's Mercy*, 57.

Equality Among its Members With Clearly Defined Relationships and Roles
While the relationship between the members of these bounded set churches are democratic in nature where "all votes would be of equal value," they function like a "corporation" where its members have "clearly defined roles, explicit rules, well-planned programs."[21] Since the correct doctrine and behavior have confirmed them as bonafide Christians, these members have the freedom to choose and guide the policies of their churches; yet once the policies have been laid down, its members are expected to follow this directive as dutiful members. In the AFBCP, this is seen in the right of their member churches to vote under Article 1, Section 6 under "Fellowshipping Churches," which states "fellowshipping churches may send up to six (6) of their church members as voting messengers . . . to the biennial conference."[22] It is in these biennial conferences where members vote to decide on matters of policy. It was in such a conference where Dr Ormeo and several pastors along with their churches were expelled from the AFBCP due to their participation in activities which the AFBCP had declared as ecumenical.[23]

Evangelism – Bringing People Within the Boundary
Hiebert explains that once the definition of who is a *Christian* had been clarified (i.e. those who are within the boundary), then the task is to bring others into the church through "conversion . . . by which people enter the church."[24] This perspective is seen in the AFBCP's purpose 2 where it states, "to encourage and promote evangelism and to assist in . . . organizing of indigenous Baptist churches." Their evangelistic efforts are aimed at the establishment of mission outreaches which would eventually become a church. And in these new churches, it is expected that their members would subscribe to the same fundamental doctrines and prescribed behavior.

Maintain Uniformity among Member Churches
Finally, the main effort is to maintain their common intrinsic nature to safeguard their church and/or organization. Hiebert explains that the efforts of these bounded set churches are focused on "maintaining the identity of

---

21. Hiebert, *Anthropological Reflections*, 117.
22. Securities and Exchange Commission, *Articles of Incorporation*, 8.
23. Appendix E: "Mariano Leones," response to question 1.
24. Hiebert, *Anthropological Reflections*, 117.

the church and its organization."²⁵ As an outcome of their commitment to uniformity, their efforts are in developing and planting churches that are identical with the mother church. This value is seen in AFBCP's purpose 1 and 4 where the council was formed to strengthen and to maintain their distinct Fundamental Baptist heritage. This commitment is seen in their passion to enforce the Doctrine of Separation which is stated in their Articles of Incorporation with the Philippine Government's Securities and Exchange Commission (SEC),

> Separation of God's people from all unbelief and corruption (Eph. 5:11; 2 Cor. 6:14-18), as it is the duty of all true churches of the Lord Jesus Christ to make a clear testimony of their faith in Him, especially in these darkening days of apostasy in many professing churches, by which apostasy, whole denominations in their official capacity, as well as individual churches, have been swept into a paganism stream of modernism under various names and varying degree. A. Separation from sin and worldliness (I John 2:15-17). B. Separation from groups or churches that have departed from the fundamental doctrines of the faith once for all delivered to the saints. C. Separation from groups or churches, though fundamental in doctrines, yet are connected with apostate organizations, like the United Church of Christ in the Philippines (UCC) and the World Council of Churches (WCC).²⁶

The founders of the AFBCP believed that part of their primary calling was the preservation of the fundamentals of the faith and to ensure that it is defended from any compromise or dilution. This is seen in Nacita's appreciation of AFBCP's formation and role, as "an appropriate response to the developing ecumenical and charismatic climate in the international Christian community. . . . Polarization to either side became the order of the day."²⁷

Thus, it appears that the AFBCP follows the pattern of a bounded set union. These characteristics had been inherited from churches that founded

---

25. Hiebert, 117.
26. Securities and Exchange Commission, *Articles of Incorporation*, 15.
27. Nacita, *Celebrating God's Mercy*, 13.

the council which were from conservative American churches that struggled when their values and theology were threatened by the encroaching modernist values. As Hiebert explains the rationale, "maintaining boundaries is essential in a bounded set world, otherwise categories begin to disintegrate and chaos sets in."[28]

NCCP – Centered Set Union

Another council which was a part of PCEC's history was the NCCP which was formed in 1963 when several pre-war mainline Protestant churches came together to form their own council. It was the formation of the NCCP that compelled the founders of the PCEC to form their own council since they felt that the NCCP did not represent their values and perspective.[29] The following attempts to explain their emphasis and direction through a brief overview presenting the council's stated objectives followed by a brief assessment of its characteristics using the framework of Hiebert's centered set model.[30]

The NCCP's objectives, reproduced in Oscar Suarez's *Protestantism and Authoritarian Politics*, states the following:

> (1) To promote the growth of ecumenical interests in the study of Christian unity and cooperation among churches and their members.
>
> (2) To serve as a channel for united witness and common action on matters affecting moral, social, and civic life of the nation.
>
> (3) To safeguard fundamental human rights and uphold the principle of the separation of church and state.
>
> (4) To foster closer relationships with Christian bodies in all lands.
>
> (5) To support cooperative work among churches and Christian organizations as such may be agreed upon.

---

28. Hiebert, *Anthropological Reflections*, 114.
29. Appendix D: "Fred Magbanua, Jr," response to question 10.
30. Hiebert, *Anthropological Reflections*, 123–124.

(6) To undertake other work which may be referred to it by any of the member bodies.[31]

Union is Founded on an External Center
Hiebert explains that a centered set church/council finds oneness among its members from a defined "center or reference point and the relationship of things to that center" which is Christ in the Christian church's case.[32] In addition, the focus is "not on knowledge or behavior . . . [but] communion with Christ would be the central focus. . . . Instruction in doctrine and behavior would follow."[33] As a Filipino council, the NCCP affirms its union with Christ and with their fellow believers in its commitment to ecumenism. This can be seen in a statement given in November 1977 entitled "Promotion of Christian Unity"; the NCCP declares "as a confessing Church, it is our task to restore the unity we once had."[34] This perspective is further seen in the NCCP's Executive Committee official statement in 1972, "since the Church is the whole people of God, the laws of God in the six continents, the mission inevitably assumes an ecumenical character."[35] To facilitate this unity, the NCCP made provisions to define the relationships of these member churches so that the problems that had troubled their union would abate.[36] It is their commitment to that common center which enables these churches from varied polity, tradition, doctrine, and praxis to work together in unity.

---

31. Oscar S. Suarez, *Protestantism and Authoritarian Politics: The Politics of Repression and the Future of Ecumenical Witness in the Philippines* (Quezon City, Philippines: New Day, 1999), 45.

32. Hiebert, *Anthropological Reflections*, 123.

33. Hiebert, 127.

34. "Promotion of Christian Unity," in *A Public Faith, A Social Witness: Statements and Resolutions of the National Council of Churches in the Philippines*, vol. 1 (Quezon City, Philippines: National Council of Churches in the Philippines, 1995), 2.

35. "Statement on the Ecumenical Sharing of Personnel and Funds," in *A Public Faith, A Social Witness: Statements and Resolutions of the National Council of Churches in the Philippines*, vol. 1 (Quezon City, Philippines: National Council of Churches in the Philippines, 1995), 67.

36. For an example, see "Code of Ethics Among Christian Churches in the Philippines," in *A Public Faith, A Social Witness: Statements and Resolutions of the National Council of Churches in the Philippines*, vol. 1 (Quezon City, Philippines: National Council of Churches in the Philippines, 1995), 22–26.

Their Boundary is Defined by Their Relationship to this Common Center
Hiebert explains that affiliation to the centered set church is not vague; in fact it is based on their relationship to this common center – Christ. The union is among followers of Christ and not to all religions as "there are tenets we believe mature Christians hold and immature Christians should learn."[37] This is seen in the council's efforts to reach out and find commonality among churches belonging to their union,[38] with the evangelicals,[39] and seeking closer ties with the Roman Catholic Church[40] which are all related to Christ. However, it does make a distinction between itself and other religions. For example, while the NCCP seeks to find reconciliation and peace with Filipino Muslims through "dialogue," their goal is "remove prejudice and negative images" so that these two religions could co-exist with their distinctions and uniqueness intact.[41] Although the NCCP had accommodated varied groups, they made a stand against the Maharishi Technology (MT) in 1984 when they declared that "the Maharishi Technology is a contradiction

---

37. Hiebert, *Anthropological Reflections*, 128.

38. The NCCP prescribed the following as part of the proper decorum of their members towards other Christian groups,
    1. Churches must refrain from speaking disparagingly about the work or the workers of other groups. 2. Never embarrass co-workers or other churches by meddling in their affairs. 3. Hold in sincere respect any minister or church worker whose work is well done, regardless of the size or the nature of the field served. 4. Consider all church workers co-laborers and all churches part of One Body, respecting their Christian earnestness and sincerity though they may differ from one another. 5. When a minister of another church is called to perform a funeral, wedding or the Sacraments, he should request the permission and the participation of the resident minister of the church
"Code of Ethics," 22–26.

39. "Statement on Christian Unity," in *A Public Faith, A Social Witness: Statements and Resolutions of the National Council of Churches in the Philippines*, vol. 1 (Quezon City, Philippines: National Council of Churches in the Philippines, 1995), 4.

40. In November 1975 during their 7th General Convention, this recommendation was made in answering the question "how do we achieve this kind of unity? . . . By strengthening the program for ecumenical action with the Roman Catholic Church" ("Statement on the Unity We Seek," in *A Public Faith, A Social Witness: Statements and Resolutions of the National Council of Churches in the Philippines*, vol. 1 [Quezon City, Philippines: National Council of Churches in the Philippines, 1995], 1).

41. "A Statement of Intent: Framework for the NCCP Thrust in Muslim-Christian Reconciliation," in *A Public Faith, A Social Witness: Statements and Resolutions of the National Council of Churches in the Philippines*, vol. 1 (Quezon City, Philippines: National Council of Churches in the Philippines, 1995), 228.

of the Christian faith" and goes on further to distinguish authentic Christian belief with the claims of the MT.[42]

Evangelism as a Means of Calling Others to Follow Christ

Hiebert explains that in centered set churches, the emphasis of evangelism is "calling people to turn and follow Christ . . . not simply . . . giving mental assent to the truths of the gospel."[43] As a council, the NCCP recognizes that the "primary task of the Church is to proclaim God's redemptive love. All forms of witness are signs of the commitment to proclaim the Gospel to all people."[44] It further admonishes that evangelism should be done in the spirit of cooperation and unity while "refraining from proselytizing members of other denominations."[45] As Filipino Christians, the council further admonishes that certain emphases be added in their member churches' efforts in proclaiming the gospel. For example, dialogue is an important tool as the council admonishes that "this may involve more listening than what we have been used to, and a willingness to start from what we know, proceeding on to the less known or unknown."[46] In being sensitive to their target audience, it is further admonished that "fresh emphasis be given to singing the Gospel in a medium understandable to the people (e.g., adopting the Gospel to secular and tribal music). . . . Fresh emphasis be given to Gospel communication through dance and drama forms."[47] However, in its goal of seeking ecumenical relationships, the council does not require rebaptism and seeks to work alongside the Roman Catholic Church (e.g. does not seek to

---

42. "The Maharishi Technology: An Antithesis to the Christian Faith," in *A Public Faith, A Social Witness: Statements and Resolutions of the National Council of Churches in the Philippines*, vol. 1 (Quezon City, Philippines: National Council of Churches in the Philippines, 1995), 38.

43. Hiebert, *Anthropological Reflections*, 129.

44. "Code on Evangelism," in *A Public Faith, A Social Witness: Statements and Resolutions of the National Council of Churches in the Philippines*, vol. 1 (Quezon City, Philippines: National Council of Churches in the Philippines, 1995), 16.

45. "Code on Evangelism," 17.

46. "Communicating the Gospel," in *A Public Faith, A Social Witness: Statements and Resolutions of the National Council of Churches in the Philippines*, vol. 1 (Quezon City, Philippines: National Council of Churches in the Philippines, 1995), 20.

47. "Communicating the Gospel," 20–21.

convert its members).⁴⁸ As for its methods in witnessing, the council states, "We shall witness in evangelism and development – through concrete social action programs, proclaiming and doing the work of the Lord."⁴⁹

The Church as an Outpost of God's Kingdom
As Christ is the main focus and center, the church's main focus is to draw people to Christ, build their relationship with Him, and draw the rest of the world to Christ.⁵⁰ To accomplish this, the NCCP has been involved in engaging what it perceives as the social ills of the country. In 1972, the NCCP Executive Committee states, "In the Philippine reality, we believe the mission of the Church today is man's liberation and development. . . . The Philippine churches and the National Council of Churches in the Philippines are called upon to examine themselves and their role in the light of the demand for change and renewal."⁵¹ In an earlier declaration, the NCCP saw its evolving role in the Philippine church as becoming more engaged in serving the country where "theological education and training must be girded for human development and liberation."⁵² Thus the NCCP has repeatedly issued its stands and perspectives challenging the current issues and problems of the Philippines. For example, the NCCP issued calls for reform and re-election during the Martial Law Period.⁵³ While during the

---

48. "Churches should refrain from proselytizing members of other denominations" ("Code of Evangelism," 17); and also, "strengthening the program for ecumenical action with the Roman Catholic Church" ("Statement on the Unity We Seek," 1).

49. "Statement on Evangelism and Development," in *A Public Faith, A Social Witness: Statements and Resolutions of the National Council of Churches in the Philippines*, vol. 1 (Quezon City, Philippines: National Council of Churches in the Philippines, 1995), 11.

50. Hiebert, *Anthropological Reflections*, 129.

51. "Statement on the Ecumenical Sharing," 67.

52. "Churches' Role in the 70's," 114.

53. For example, in 1971, the NCCP asked for the restoration of the privilege of Writ of Habeas Corpus. For details, see "Resolution on the Writ of Habeas Corpus," in *A Public Faith, A Social Witness: Statements and Resolutions of the National Council of Churches in the Philippines*, vol. 1 (Quezon City, Philippines: National Council of Churches in the Philippines, 1995), 328. From 1973 to 1975, the NCCP repeatedly urged the President Marcos to lift the martial law. For details, see "Resolution on the Lifting of Martial Law," in *A Public Faith, A Social Witness: Statements and Resolutions of the National Council of Churches in the Philippines*, vol. 1 (Quezon City, Philippines: National Council of Churches in the Philippines, 1995), 328–331. In 1975, the Council called on the president to restore the Filipino's right to vote. For details, see "Resolution Calling for Elections," in *A Public Faith, A Social Witness: Statements and Resolutions of the National Council of Churches in the Philippines*, vol. 1 (Quezon City, Philippines: National Council of Churches in the Philippines, 1995), 88.

time of President Corazon Aquino, the NCCP supported the decision of the Philippine Senate and urged the president to support the senate's decision which called for the withdrawal of the US bases from the Philippines.[54]

Thus, NCCP follows the pattern of a centered set union. It is because of this desire to work with others that NCCP sees their role as a voice for reforms and justice in the Philippines. More than just addressing the spiritual needs of its constituents, the NCCP sees itself as the guardian of society whose responsibility is to protect the rights of the Filipino people. As the 6th General Convention declared the role of the Church,

> The Church must always be the guardian of man's dignity and freedom. We recall our history as a people. Our heroes died for the independence of our nation, as well as for the dignity and freedom of each man. The rights of man must never be denied by anyone, not by the government even as it seeks to promote the progress and welfare of all.[55]

Summary

Therefore, it is clear that the AFBCP (fundamentalist council) and the NCCP (pre-war mainline Protestant council) had different emphases and directions. The former's commitment to maintaining a homogeneous council which is motivated by its goal of preserving the fundamentals of the faith is in contrast with the latter's commitment to ecumenism which is driven by their shared passion to address what they consider as societal ills and problem. This explains why the AFBCP, and later on the initial founders of PCEC (Dr Ormeo and the other fundamentalist leaders) could not foresee any possible partnership with any group that it considers intrinsically different from them. On the other hand, the NCCP's commitment to becoming a voice that represents these pre-war churches allowed for a wider acceptance of divergent groups all working together for the common good.

---

54. For details, see "Resolution on the US Bases Withdrawal," in *A Public Faith, A Social Witness: Statements and Resolutions of the National Council of Churches in the Philippines*, vol. 1 (Quezon City, Philippines: National Council of Churches in the Philippines, 1995), 155–156.

55. "Statement on Evangelism and Development," 10.

PCEC in the Lens of Hiebert's Model

In the last fifty years, changes have taken place within PCEC's goals and functions as it went through its changing context. The following examines these transitions in light of Hiebert's bounded versus centered sets theory to appreciate these developments and innovations.

PCEC's Early Years – Bounded Set (1964–1966)

Evaluating the behavior and the characteristics of PCEC in the early years, it appears that the council was more inclined towards a bounded set union. This is probably due to the strong influence of Dr Ormeo's group who were the first to envision the formation of a fundamentalist council.[56] The following is a brief overview of the council which includes its stated purpose followed by a brief assessment of the council and its members' characteristics which showed its inclination towards a bounded set union.

The following are the stated purposes of PCEC reproduced from Dr Vencer's article:

(1) To provide fellowship among Evangelical Christians;

(2) To provide a means of united action in the furtherance of the Gospel of Christ;

(3) To maintain the purity of the Gospel and to defend its truth;

(4) To provide a representative evangelical voice before the government and public; and

(5) To encourage all member bodies in aggressive and effective evangelism, church planting and church growth.[57]

Emphasis on Becoming a Uniform, Homogenous Group

As seen in the above discussion, a bounded set union emphasizes uniformity in its beliefs and practices. This is often seen in the organization's emphasis in having the correct doctrine and behavior. As for the early years of PCEC, it does appear that this was an important value that the council upheld. For example, one of the earliest recorded conflicts among the council members

---

56. Appendix G: "Interview with Pio Tica," response to questions 8–10, 17.
57. Vencer, "Evangelicals in the Philippines," no. 10, 25.

occurred during its Constitutional Convention presided by Gadiel Isidro in Fellowship Center Church in November 1964. While there were several points of doctrinal arguments that took place, the one that almost wrecked the council was the pre-tribulationist or post-tribulationist debate on the second coming of Christ.[58] It is this kind of theological dispute that clearly points to how much clearly defined and homogeneous doctrines were valued in the early years of the council.

Commitment to Maintaining Clear Boundaries

Another characteristic of a bounded set union is its emphasis on making a clear distinction between itself and others through a defined boundary. The organization's main basis for forming a union is in their intrinsic characteristics, and those that are deemed "different" are unwelcomed by the group. This characteristic was evident in the early years of PCEC; as Dr Ruivivar recalls that there was an unwillingness to accept those who were considered Pentecostals and liberals.[59] This intentionality in limiting its membership can be seen in the fact that the earliest members of the council were chosen from churches and organizations which were either from fundamentalist or conservative Baptist denominations or from churches and organizations connected with the Far Eastern Gospel Crusade (FEGC) and the Far Eastern Bible Institute and Seminary (FEBIAS).[60]

Evangelism as a Primary Responsibility

Another key characteristic of a bounded set union is its desire to bring others into their "fold." Hence, evangelism becomes one of the main activities of the group. This emphasis can seen in the PCEC's purpose statements 2 and 5 where there is a call for its members to engage in evangelism. In fact, the early activities of the council were characterized by its participation in evangelistic efforts and its reluctance to engage in social issues.[61] This is seen

---

58. Appendix G: "Pio Tica," response to question 42.

59. Dr Ruivivar distinctly remembers that there were no Pentecostals during the early years of PCEC (Appendix L: "Correspondence with Faustino Ruivivar, Jr [9 June 2010]").

60. Appendix I: "Correspondence with Faustino Ruivivar, Jr (6 June 2010)" and Appendix G: "Pio Tica," response to question 44–47.

61. This was one of the perspectives that Dr Vencer had seen that was prevalent among the evangelicals of his time. As a result, one of his earliest efforts was to undo this isolationist attitude. For example, Dr Vencer writes an article in the *Evangelical Thrust* where he calls

in the council's hesitation when Dr Vencer proposed the establishment of PHILRADS to address the physical needs of the Filipinos. The proposal was postponed due to their concern that this new emphasis might dilute the message of the gospel or sidetrack the council from its task of evangelization.[62]

Reproducing Themselves through Church Planting
Finally, the main effort is to build a copy of themselves in the churches that they plant. One of the characteristics of a bounded set union is that its goal is to continue the "church" and to reproduce it in the new churches that they were establishing. Dr Ormeo and the other fundamentalist leaders of PCEC were clearly passionate in keeping the council as a continuation of their fundamentalist values. As seen in their choice of members and the council's purpose, it was evident that PCEC was initially intended to become an extension of the fundamentalist ICCC that was founded by Carl McIntire, as its initial name suggests, the Philippine Council of Fundamentalist Churches.

Thus, it is appears that PCEC was more of a bounded set council in its early years which explains why they did not merge with the NCCP. However, several of its evangelical leaders were unwilling and uncomfortable with this fundamentalist direction. By 1966, tensions began to appear within the council as some began to question the title "fundamental" to describe the council.[63] This marked the beginning of the transition period where the council began to define its true identity and its role in Philippine society.

PCEC's Transitional Period (1966–1980s)
Beginning in 1966 until the early years of Dr Vencer's time as General Secretary, the council was beginning to "shift" in its emphasis and direction.

---

upon evangelicals to be involved with the issues of their day as they should not fail to be concerned with "the morals of our young and society" (Vencer, "What Kind of Christian," 7).

62. Appendix Q: "Agustin Vencer," response to question 56.

63. According to Bishop Magbanua, the controversy among the leaders of PCEC was related to the issue of the name of the Council, whether it would be fundamental or evangelical was based on the reality that they "were trying to veer away from is becoming a separatist group" (Appendix D: "Fred Magbanua, Jr," response to question 7).

The following were some of the events and perspectives that influenced and redirected the perspectives of the council's leaders.[64]

Wheaton Declaration (1966)

The Congress on the Church's Worldwide Mission (CCWM) was a conference among evangelical missionary organizations held at Wheaton College (Illinois) in 1966. It was sponsored by the Interdenominational Foreign Mission Association (IFMA) and the Evangelical Foreign Missions Association (EFMA), and where 938 delegates from seventy-one countries gathered together to address the growing concerns among missionaries throughout the world.[65] Prepared papers were presented on ten mission-related problems, which were "syncretism, neo-universalism, proselytism, neoRomanism, church growth, foreign missions, evangelical unity, evaluating methods, social concern, and a hostile world."[66] After the presentations and their attendant discussions, a final drafting committee worked together to prepare a summary of the delegates' affirmation entitled the *Wheaton Declaration*. It was this document that was brought to the different churches and missionary organizations connected with IFMA, EFMA, and other evangelical bodies. The following are some of its affirmations.

On the issue of evangelical unity, the CCWM delegates confessed that it was the evangelicals' denominational disunity that had hindered "missionary advance and the fulfillment of the Great Commission."[67] They affirmed that unity among the different churches and organizations was possible since it is a "unity of belief, centered in the person and work of Jesus Christ."[68]

---

64. While there might be other factors that have influenced the choices and actions of PCEC's leadership, the following were some of the main issues based on Dr Vencer's recollection of the period.

65. According to the Wheaton Declaration, "Protestantism is afflicted with doctrinal uncertainty, theological novelties, and outright apostasy. . . . The Church needs the courage to implement the New Testament disciplinary process to guard its purity, its peace, and its unity . . . calling for a separation from sin and error" ("Wheaton Declaration," Wheaton, IL, 9–16 April 1966, *Billy Graham Centre Archives*, accessed 20 September 2013, https://www2.wheaton.edu/bgc/archives/docs/wd66/b01.html, 6).

66. "Wheaton Declaration," *Biblical Training*, accessed 21 September 2013, https://www.biblicaltraining.org/library/ wheatondeclaration.

67. "Wheaton Declaration," *Billy Graham Centre Archives*, http://www2.wheaton.edu/bgc/archives/docs/wd66/b20.html, 20.

68. "Wheaton Declaration," *Billy Graham Centre Archives*, 20.

Thus they made this declaration, "THAT we will encourage and assist in the organization of evangelical fellowships among churches and missionary societies at national, regional, and international levels."[69]

As for the issue of social involvement, the congress observed that evangelicals during the eighteenth and nineteenth centuries were at the forefront of social engagement. However "in the twentieth century many have lost the biblical perspective and limited themselves only to preaching a gospel of individual salvation without sufficient involvement in their social and community responsibilities."[70] Sadly, the theological discussions and debates among the churches that do not address the current issues and the "felt needs" of society have made the evangelicals appear to be "detached" from the world and rendered them irrelevant to the world. Hence, to uphold their commitment to both evangelism and social engagement, the congress makes this declaration,

> THAT we reaffirm unreservedly the primacy of preaching the gospel . . . and we will demonstrate anew God's concern for social justice and human welfare. THAT evangelical social action will include, whenever possible, a verbal witness to Jesus Christ. THAT evangelical social action must avoid wasteful and unnecessary competition. . . . THAT we urge all evangelicals to stand openly and firmly for racial equality, human freedom, and all forms of social justice throughout the world.[71]

Thus, the Wheaton Declaration helped stir a renewed passion for the ideals of evangelicalism among churches and mission organizations throughout the world. It is possible that the Filipino leaders who had been influenced by the Wheaton Declaration began to change the direction of the council.[72]

---

69. "Wheaton Declaration," *Billy Graham Centre Archives*, http://www2.wheaton.edu/bgc/archives/docs/wd66/b21.html, 21.

70. "Wheaton Declaration," *Billy Graham Centre Archives*, http://www2.wheaton.edu/bgc/archives/docs/wd66/b23.html, 23.

71. "Wheaton Declaration," *Billy Graham Centre Archives*, http://www2.wheaton.edu/bgc/archives/docs/wd66/b24.html, 24.

72. It is possible that the redirection influenced by the *Wheaton Declaration* began a direction and emphasis that was not acceptable among the fundamentalists since Dr Ormeo resigned from the Board of PCEC the same year as the CCWM took place. Regardless, it appears that the affirmations made by the delegates of CCWM began to influence the evangelicals in the council so that during the Second National Assembly in 1968, the main

As Dr Vencer observes, "It could be that the 1966 Wheaton Congress of the Church's Worldwide Mission influenced the outcome. Many of the delegates were related to the denominations and mission organizations that met in Wheaton."[73]

Although a "rift" had appeared between the fundamental Baptists and the evangelicals, there were still efforts to try and reconcile the two parties; as Rev Nacita recalls a meeting between members of PCEC and some fundamental Baptist leaders in the Fellowship Center Church sometime in 1971.[74] However, this fragile relationship was finally severed by the events that took place at the Lausanne Congress in 1974.

Lausanne Congress on World Evangelism (1974)

Lausanne I: The International Congress on World Evangelism (LICWE) was started through the initiative of Billy Graham.[75] In 1972, Billy Graham gathered 120 church and mission organizations leaders to announce his intent to sponsor an international congress which would tackle the task of evangelization; it was not to be another training congress on evangelism but rather a conclave which would tackle the major theological and philosophical issues of evangelization.[76] The LICWE's organizers were prompted by the World Council of Churches' (WCC) call for "a moratorium on all forms of evangelization."[77] During the LICWE, the delegates reaffirmed evangelism as the primary task of the church; as the Lausanne Covenant declares,

> Our Christian presence in the world is indispensable to evangelism, and so is that kind of dialogue whose purpose is to listen sensitively in order to understand. But evangelism itself is the proclamation of the historical, biblical Christ as Savior

---

discussions centered on the issue of unity and social engagement based on the definitions outlined during the Wheaton conference.

73. Vencer, "Evangelicals in the Philippines," no. 8, 17.

74. Appendix H: "Interview with Ebenezer Nacita," response to question 23.

75. John R. Reid, "Lausanne Congress on World Evangelism," in *A Dictionary of Asian Christianity*, ed. Scott W. Sunquist, (Grand Rapids; Cambridge, UK: Eerdmans, 2001), 471.

76. John Pollock, *Billy Graham Evangelist to the World: An Authorized Biography of the Decisive Years* (San Francisco, CA: Harper & Row, 1979), 191.

77. Reid, "Lausanne Congress," 471.

and Lord, with a view to persuading people to come to him personally and so be reconciled to God.[78]

Prepared Papers were presented that discussed the issues, problems, and concerns that evangelicals encountered in the efforts to evangelize. Once more, the issue of social engagement became a major issue within the congress after two papers were presented on the topic which resulted in a heavy discussion among the delegates.[79] As affirmed in the Wheaton Declaration, evangelicalism's lack of social engagement was seen as the major reason for the loss of its "prophetic role in society."[80] As a result, the Lausanne Covenant once more reiterated the earlier affirmation of the Wheaton Declaration,

> We affirm that God is both the Creator and the Judge of all people. We therefore should share his concern for justice and reconciliation throughout human society and for the liberation of men and women from every kind of oppression. Because men and women are made in the image of God, every person, regardless of race, religion, color, culture, class, sex or age, has an intrinsic dignity because of which he or she should be respected and served, not exploited. Here too we express penitence both for our neglect and for having sometimes regarded evangelism and social concern as mutually exclusive. Although reconciliation with other people is not reconciliation with God, nor is social action evangelism, nor is political liberation salvation, nevertheless we affirm that evangelism and socio-political involvement are both part of our Christian duty. For both are necessary expressions of our doctrines of God and man, our love for our neighbor and our obedience to Jesus Christ. The message of salvation implies also a message of judgment upon every form of alienation, oppression and discrimination, and we should not be afraid to denounce evil and injustice

---

78. "The Lausanne Covenant," *The Lausanne Movement*, accessed 21 September 2013, http://www.lausanne.org/en/documents/lausanne-covenant.html.

79. Namely, the "Evangelization and the Word," by Rene Padilla from Argentina and "Evangelization and Man's Search for Freedom, Justice and Fulfillment," by Samuel Escobar who was South American residing in Canada (Reid, "Lausanne Congress," 471).

80. Reid, "Lausanne Congress," 471.

wherever they exist. When people receive Christ they are born again into his kingdom and must seek not only to exhibit but also to spread its righteousness in the midst of an unrighteous world. The salvation we claim should be transforming us in the totality of our personal and social responsibilities. Faith without works is dead.[81]

Once more, PCEC delegates to the Lausanne Congress returned with a renewed passion to implement the affirmations of the LICWE. Sadly, it was also in this congress that the fundamentalists finally severed their ties with the evangelicals as they irrevocably withdrew their membership from the council as a response to what they considered Billy Graham's "shabby" treatment of Carl McIntire.[82] While this schism was a major blow to the progress of the council, it afforded the evangelicals the freedom to change PCEC's future.

Changing Emphasis, the Martial Law Era

Aside from these two international congresses (CCWM and LICWE) that made an impact among the evangelicals in the Philippines, the country's changing political and social context called for some re-evaluation of the council's directions and goals. As Dr Vencer describes the 1970s when he took over as General Secretary,

> In the beginning the whole issue was unity . . . the issue was survival where we wanted to affirm that we are a distinct religious Christian community and at that time preservation of our values . . . I think those were necessary beginnings but in due time as they began to feel their unity and began to grow together, the context around them changed as well and the evolutionary process of PCEC took place quite naturally.[83]

The following were some of the needs and issues that called for a "different" council, one that was able to respond to the changing Philippine society.

---

81. "The Lausanne Covenant."
82. Appendix G: "Pio Tica," response to question 64.
83. Appendix Q: "Agustin Vencer," response to question" 13.

Analysis and Synthesis of the Formation and Developments within PCEC

The Need for a Cooperative Approach to Social Involvement
When Dr Vencer became the leader of PCEC, one of his major concerns was the way the evangelical churches were responding to the problems created by natural and man-made disasters that regularly visited the country (e.g. typhoons during the rainy seasons, droughts and fires during the summer months, and occasional earthquakes, to name a few). Although the evangelicals were involved in providing relief when these crises occurred, Dr Vencer felt that there was no "systematic" approach and lasting impact.[84] To correct this, he established PHILRADS which would help bring together the resources of the different evangelical churches and organizations so that their help would be effective. This new direction was not meant to replace evangelism; rather through their social involvement, the evangelical church would gain the necessary recognition needed to help bring the gospel to the Filipino people and its leaders. Thus, there was a need to "realign" the council's perspective so that it could seek out and develop partnerships with churches and organizations who share a common concern and vision; to help those in need by working with those who had the capacity and resources to accomplish the task.

The Need to Build the Next Generation of Spiritual and Nationalistic Evangelical Leaders
Another need that Dr Vencer saw was the lack of training to produce Christians who would be able to engage and provide leadership in Philippine society. During this period, most fundamentalists and evangelicals saw a sharp distinction between the spiritual and the temporal, between the sacred and the secular. As a result, most churches and seminaries did not have a specific goal to engage government and the business sector as these were secular "realms" where the spiritual had no place to be. As Dr Vencer describes the situation, "our leaders were not really encouraging the young men to move into politics and business because they were the domains of compromises and the domains of evil . . . we were trying to prepare a generation of employees rather than employers."[85] In his effort to change this situation, PCEC began a campaign to encourage the Bible Schools and Seminaries to be in the

---

84. Appendix Q: "Agustin Vencer," response to question 4.
85. Appendix Q, response to question 4.

forefront of community development. As a result, by 1983 he reports that they "have laid down the foundation for a long term effective involvement of our churches by helping integrate a course on Community Development in 14 of our Bible Colleges and Seminaries."[86] But more than just passing on a series of knowledge and information, he wanted these centers of Christian education to examine their "curricula and make them respond to the needs of the times and to prepare men and women who can effectively synthesize the dynamic interaction of the daily news and the Bible."[87]

The Need to Establish the Kingdom of God on Earth
One of the questions that often bothered Dr Vencer was the whole issue of the Kingdom of God as it related to the efforts of the evangelicals. During the interview, he related his perspective on the issue,

> We believe that if the Kingdom is present in the Church then the church should be concerned with the economic sufficiency for the people. It must deal with social things not just peace with God but peace with your neighbor. It must deal with the issue of labor, racial harmonies, ethnicities, and civility. It must deal with things with the environment.[88]

Thus, it was a question of impact and influence; does the presence of an evangelical church affect society at all? This was a very controversial issue since evangelical leaders were divided when it comes to politics – non-participation or active involvement.[89]

The council struggled with these matters, especially in the last few years of the Martial Law period. As a result of the growing political unrest caused by the assassination of Senator Benigno Aguino, there were calls for an armed uprising among the populace and Christians were asking whether they should participate or not. As a stand, Dr Vencer did not support a violent

---

86. Vencer, *Biblical Framework*, 4.
87. Vencer, 24.
88. Appendix Q: "Agustin Vencer," response to question 7.
89. An example of this is found in Gadiel Isidro's article in the *Evangelical Thrust* in January 1986 where this leader of PCEC states, "Yes, I agree that we need men and women who are truly born again by the Holy Spirit to occupy positions of administrative leadership" (Gadiel T. Isidro, "Participation? Yes! Political Party? No!," *Evangelical Thrust*, 13, no. 1 [January 1986]: 10).

uprising as he had affirmed, "I do not believe that the desired government of peace and justice can be ushered in by the blood of Filipinos in a violent revolution."[90] Instead, the council issued a response that was written by Dr Vencer where he issued a series of "clear-headed" responses and called on its members to pray.[91] During the EDSA (People Power) Revolution in 1986, the council leaders were struggling with the proper response as its members were seeking for guidance. The council and its members were divided, some were calling for calmness and prayer while others were calling for an active participation.[92] In the end, the leaders of PCEC joined those who were in EDSA.[93] Dr Vencer and the leaders of PCEC had taken a risk by joining with other groups both secular and religious. They believed that it was their duty to join those who shared a common purpose – to see peace and justice to return to the Philippines.

It was clear that the actions and the changes that took place within PCEC were due to the growing needs of the Philippines. Dr Vencer led the council through its evolution from a bounded set to a centered set union – preserving the purity of the fundamentals while cooperating with those who were engaged in transforming Philippine society.

PCEC as a Centered Set Union (1978–1990s)

As the PCEC slowly transitioned into a centered set union, a series of changes could be observed, most of which were during Dr Vencer's time as its General Secretary.

Changes in PCEC's Purposes

One of the major changes that manifested this transition from a bounded set union (i.e. PCFC and PCFEC era) into a centered set union (PCEC)

---

90. Vencer, *Biblical Framework*, 12.

91. PCEC had always called upon its members to pray. For an example of a call for prayer during a political crisis, see Agustin B. Vencer Jr, "Guest Editorial: As the Election Draws Near . . . Participate . . . and Pray (Condensed from an appeal by the PCEC General Secretary)," *Evangelical Thrust* 13, no. 1 (January 1986): 2.

92. Dr Vencer relates his struggle as he tried to maintain the unity of the council during this crucial moment in Philippine history. For details of his statement, see Appendix Q: "Agustin Vencer," response to question 24.

93. Appendix Q: "Agustin Vencer," response to question 29.

was the amendment of PCEC's purposes. The earlier version of PCEC's purposes are as follows:

(1) To provide fellowship among Evangelical Christians;

(2) To provide a means of united action in the furtherance of the Gospel of Christ;

(3) To maintain the purity of the Gospel and to defend its truth;

(4) To provide a representative evangelical voice before the government and public; and

(5) To encourage all member bodies in aggressive and effective evangelism, church planting and church growth.[94]

The amended version reproduced in a facsimile of the by-laws of PCEC found in the souvenir program are as follows:

(1) Promote unity and encourage cooperative ministries among Evangelicals in the Philippines;

(2) Develop effective evangelism strategies and a strong missions program for the evangelization of the Philippines and the world;

(3) Present a distinctively evangelical voice and presence to our government and other publics as a witness to the lordship of Christ in all things; and

(4) Engage in ministries by helping the needy and poor in the Philippines to become economically self-reliant and rightly related with God in Christ Jesus.[95]

---

94. Vencer, "Evangelicals in the Philippines," no. 10, 25.

95. The purposes of PCEC, which were reproduced by Dr Vencer in an article published in 1994, was probably written earlier as the editor explains that "Dr. Vencer wrote this piece (an earlier version came out in 1979) over a year ago before he turned over his post to Rev. Ef Tendero" (Editor's Note, in Vencer, "Evangelicals in the Philippines," no. 8, 16). While the souvenir program clearly states that the facsimile of the By-Laws was "amended as of November 21, 1980" ("Amended By-Laws of the PCEC" in *Empowering The Churches* [Souvenir Program at the PCEC 22nd National Assembly, Tagaytay, Philippines, 15–18 July 1997], 36). Thus, one can posit that the version reproduced by Dr Vencer 1994 article was based on the pre-amended version of the By-Laws of PCEC written on or before 1979.

Comparing the two versions of the purposes of PCEC, one can see the following changes: First, the original purposes 1 and 2 are combined into the amended objective 1. Second, the original purpose 3 was discarded from the amended version. Third, the original purpose 4 had an additional phrase "as a witness to the Lordship of Christ in all things." Fourth, the original purpose 5 was modified where the phrase "church planting and church growth" was deleted and replaced with "strong missions program for the evangelization of the Philippines and the world." Fifth, the addition of objective no. 4 in the amended version which was focused on social work.

From these changes, one can make several conjectures as to the "redirection" that took place during the leadership of Dr Jun Vencer.[96] First, the deletion of purpose 2 which is focused on "purity of the gospel" was probably done to allow for a wider acceptance of different doctrinal traditions among its members.[97] Second, the addition of the phrase "as a witness to the lordship of Christ in all things" was added so that the "evangelical voice" would not be an ideology or a church tradition, instead it would be in accordance with God's will. Third, the replacement of the phrase "church planting and church growth" with the phrase "a strong missions program for the evangelization of the Philippines and the world" is an adjustment to the scope and the actual goal of evangelism.[98] Finally, the addition of objective 4 of the amended by-laws, which is focused on social transformation, was added to help the evangelicals return to the original purpose of the church which is proclamation and transformation of society.[99]

---

96. The amendment took place on 21 November 1980, two years after Dr Vencer was installed as the General Secretary of PCEC (i.e. Executive Director) which was on 25 February 1978. It is clear that this was part of the new General Secretary's vision and the changes within its constitution and by laws reflected Vencer's perspectives and values.

97. One remembers the debates that took place within the Constitutional Committee when they attempted to write a narrow definition for their doctrinal beliefs (Appendix G: "Pio Tica," response to question 42). In addition, the phrase "purity of the gospel" would have probably been deleted since attempts at its definition may cause tensions or even schisms to take place within the council members.

98. It could also be that the "church planting" goal was removed so that other organizations, para-churches, and institutions who may not have "church planting" as their specified primary goal could still become members of the council (e.g. Bible schools, Bible society, Radio stations, etc.). It was consistent with the command of Christ in Mark 16:15.

99. As Dr Vencer states,
   PCEC refused to be caught on the horns of the dilemma, either to preach the Gospel or to engage in social ministries. Full obedience to the Word of God has

Thus, the council had become a centered set union as the focus was no longer based on a required uniformity of belief and praxis (e.g. "purity of the Gospel) but on a common center or purpose which is the proclamation of the gospel (i.e. objective 2) and the transformation of society (i.e. objective 4).[100] Unity is sought for a greater purpose than mere oneness, the goal is a "distinctively evangelical voice . . . as a witness to the lordship of Christ in all things."[101] The leaders of PCEC had achieved unity and cooperation with their fellow evangelicals both locally and internationally; gaining for themselves a voice and a unique identity in Philippine society.

Unlike the NCCP whose emphasis had become primarily involved with the social needs and calls for social justice, PCEC was desiring to help establish the Kingdom of God on earth; saving the souls through gospel proclamation while being engaged in societal transformation to provide the necessary environment for God's people to live and grow. In fact, Dr Vencer himself states that he saw the need to shift from a bounded set to a centered set since the former was imposing pressures that was really beyond what is considered as the fundamentals of the faith. He states,

> Even again in my early years with PCEC, the one that helped me was basically Paul Hiebert. His concept of bounded and centered set. Centered set: it does not matter how far we are from the center as long as our direction is Christ. So as long as the focus of our hearts is Christ, then we should be one. You maybe near but if your focus is not on Christ then you are really off. But the bounded set was really fascinating because we tend to take western categories and define ourselves in that

---

no room for such polarization. . . . The Council believes in the preaching of the Gospel as indispensable to salvation. It also believes in the social implications of the Gospel to touch needy people and communities in Christ's name
Vencer, "Evangelicals in the Philippines," no. 10, 27.

100. An example of this is seen in their acceptance of each other's theological differences. As Dr Ruivivar testifies, "one thing I appreciated about the PCEC leaders was their willingness to overlook doctrinal differences. I considered all of them—Pentecostals and non-Pentecostals—as true brothers and sisters in Christ. For my part, I purposely avoided discussing doctrinal matters—except our differences with liberal theology" (Appendix N: "Correspondence with Faustino Ruivivar, Jr [19 June 2010]").

101. "Amended By-Laws of the PCEC," 37.

category and many times those categories are way beyond the fundamentals of the Gospel.[102]

PCEC as a Centrist Organization

The leaders of the PCEC had finally achieved unity and cooperation with their fellow evangelicals both locally and internationally; gaining for themselves a voice and a unique identity in Philippine society. This is seen in their answer to the question, "Who are the Evangelicals?"

> The **Evangelical Christians** belong to a centrist movement with diverse streams but they are united in the following: **EVANGEL**—Zeal for Gospel, or the evangel, the good news of salvation by grace through faith alone; **JESUS**—Devotion to Jesus, the God-Man who came to serve the world by dying on the cross, who rose from the grave, and will come again as LORD of all; **BIBLE**—Loyalty to the Bible as the Word of God, the final authority in all matters of faith and conduct; **TRINITY**—Evangelicals uphold the doctrine of the Trinity: God is One, but He exists in Three Persons—Father, Son, and Holy Spirit; **NEW BIRTH**—Conviction on the need for the new birth, being born again by the Holy Spirit; the Spirit is the power for the new life and for Christian service; **CHURCH**—Evangelicals recognize and respect the diversity of churches in their forms of worship, in their patterns of organization and leadership; **SOCIAL JUSTICE**—Concern for social justice, as the fruit of love for neighbor, because "faith without works is dead." [103]

Summary

Therefore, it is clear that the choices of the leaders of PCEC were consistent with their assessment of what the proper response should be in the midst of the challenges that confronted these churches. In its early years, their main

---

102. Appendix Q: "Agustin Vencer," response to question 17.
103. Typewritten note handed to the author by Dr Jun Ferrez on 17 May 2013 which he attributes to Dr Isabelo Magalit but had not been verified at the time of this writing. Bold print in the original.

concern was on the issue of threat of liberalism which they perceived to be a major concern for their conservative values and doctrines; with NCCP's association with the WCC and its liberal declarations, the leaders of PCEC saw that the NCCP did not represent their conservative theology and values. Thus, they chose to form an alternate council which would not only represent their values but "protect" the purity of the gospel.[104] However, during Dr Vencer's leadership in the late 1970s, PCEC began to change and evolved as it realized that becoming irrelevant was the new threat to Christianity in light of the changing needs and context of their time. The main purpose was still the issue of knowing and making Jesus known and thus, proclamation required social engagement so that the former could be validated by the latter.

Conclusion

As a council of churches, PCEC has seen tremendous growth as more churches and organizations have joined and helped with the growth of evangelicalism. While it had begun as a bounded set council, the changing needs of Philippine society required a change in the council's nature and function. Thus, as a centered set council, PCEC has been able to effectively work alongside different churches and organizations as it seeks not only to see growth in the number of evangelical churches planted but in seeing the evangelical church gain the trust and confidence of the Filipino people as the evangelicals became active and crucial contributors to the health and needs of the Filipino people. As a centrist council, PCEC has helped provide a balance between proclamation and social engagement which has helped gain a voice to help in the Philippines' growth and direction. Their changes and emphasis were guided by the challenges and concerns of their time.

---

104. As seen in the third purpose of the council as stated in the original version of their constitution and by laws, "To maintain the purity of the Gospel and to defend its truth" (Vencer, "Evangelicals in the Philippines," no. 10, 25).

CHAPTER 6

Recommendations and Conclusion

Introduction

Although PCEC owes its origins and influences to the West, it has become a truly Filipino council of churches which aims to serve the interests and concerns of the Filipino people. Beginning as a bounded set union which restricted its functions and relationships by its definition as a fundamentalist council, it moved to become a centered set union where knowing and making Jesus known became its center. The proclamation of the gospel and social engagement and transformation became its tools so that it could work with other councils and religious groups in its efforts to gain a platform by which it could speak to the Filipino people and the world.

A Summary of Findings

The first chapter provided the main question of the study which is, "What caused a group of post-World War II churches to refrain from uniting with the newly established National Council of Churches in the Philippines (NCCP) and instead to form their own parallel council, the Philippine Council of Evangelical Churches (PCEC)?" It also provided the outline of the study, its scope and limitations, and a brief analysis of related literature on the topic.

Chapter 2 provided the historical context of the beginnings of the modernist/liberal-fundamentalist controversy which divided the church in North America. It examined the key events that led to the widening gap between the mainline Protestant churches, which had aligned themselves with the modernist/liberal movement, and the fundamentalist/conservative churches. It also presented the historical development within the fundamentalist/conservative churches, which led to the formation of the evangelical movement during the post-World War II era, and the resulting conflict between the fundamentalists and the evangelicals as their divergent emphases broke their fellowship apart. These controversies and tensions among the modernist/liberals, the fundamentalists, and the evangelicals in North America greatly influenced the Filipino churches in their relationships and outlook towards the other churches. As their attitudes towards each other were passed on to the churches and organizations that they planted in the country, their Filipino counterparts continued these theological "battles" in the Philippines.

Chapter 3 provided the historical context of Protestantism in the Philippines from its inception leading up to the post-World War II era. It introduced the efforts of the early American missionaries to form a united Filipino church and their early efforts to replace Roman Catholicism as the main religion of the country. It recounted the mergers, schisms, and conciliar unions among the mainline Protestant churches and the arrival of fundamentalist-conservative churches during the pre-World War II period. The next part gave a brief summary of the experiences and the efforts of these Protestant churches during World War II and their growth in the post-war era. The post-war era can be described as a time for autonomy and independence among these Filipino churches as the Philippines gained its independence from America in 1948. As a result, the mainline Protestant churches were engaged in establishing their own identity and autonomy from their American leaders. Thus, the new American evangelical missionaries were not as warmly welcomed among these pre-war mainline churches as they were among the independent fundamentalist and Pentecostal groups. Aside from this, there was further separation as seen by divergent trends among the two groups where the mainline churches where drawn to ecumenism while the fundamentalists and the evangelicals were focused on evangelism and separation.

Chapter 4 gave the historical developments which led to the formation of PCEC, its internal struggles, its eventual break-up, and its restoration. The first portion of the chapter elaborated on the diverging paths and emphases of the mainline Protestant churches and the fundamentalist churches, which pushed the two camps further apart. The second portion was dedicated to narrating the events related to the formation of PCEC in the 1960s until the 1980s when changes took place within the council during the leadership of Dr Agustin B. Vencer, Jr.

Chapter 5 was an analysis and synthesis of the historical data that had been presented regarding the formation and development of PCEC. Using Paul Hiebert's bounded set versus centered set categorization, the actions and emphases of three councils (i.e. AFBCP, NCCP, and the PCEC) were evaluated. The first was a comparison between the AFBCP which represented the bounded set union and the NCCP which represented the centered set union. The next section revealed the evolution that took place within PCEC where it had begun as a bounded set and eventually transformed itself to become a centered set union during the leadership of Dr Vencer. It explained briefly the influences that led to this transition and the resulting changes within the council. Hiebert's bounded set and centered set model provided the categories that were helpful in shedding light on the actions and inclinations of these churches and in understanding the rationale behind their choices and preferences.

Recommendations

As a result of the study conducted about the history of the formation of PCEC and the employment of Hiebert's model, there are several recommendations that can be made.

First, the bounded set and the centered set have their own strengths and weaknesses. Both approaches offer their own set of opportunities and limitations which must be evaluated by its implementers. While the bounded set can offer a sense of security, since the well-defined "boundaries" can help keep those who belong to this group to remain and effectively serve within the body, it is this boundary which becomes a "wall" that limits those who can become part of this group. As a result, growth can be hampered. On the other hand, the centered set can help foster growth since the defined center or common purpose can act as a "magnet"; however, due to the flexibility of its membership, there is a danger that values and traditions can be diluted and lost as part of maintaining the unity of all. Thus, it is important that those who wish to assess which model is best suited for the changing times should recognize that both models have their own strengths and limitations.

Second, it is important and necessary to know the changing needs of the time and to be able to act accordingly. Although some programs and methodologies can be helpful and effective in a particular time and place, the effective leader is one who can see the emerging trends and needs of the time. During the 1960s, Dr Ormeo saw that for the fundamentalists and the evangelicals to gain their own voice in society, it was important that they lay aside their differences and unite as a council. This is also seen in Dr Vencer's decision to "abandon" the traditions of the past and to enact changes which were not acceptable to all of his constituents but were necessary if PCEC was to be an effective ecclesiastical body in the late 1970s and the 1980s. While there is comfort in holding onto traditions and the past, the changing needs of one's ministry context demands that one must abandon these so as to remain effective and to avoid becoming obsolescent.

Recommendations for Further Study

This study followed the specific historical developments related to the formation of the Philippine Council of Evangelical Churches. Several lines of inquiry were not pursued due to the limitations set by the scope of this study but can be considered in a future study to provide a more comprehensive understanding of the history of Philippine Protestantism. Recommendations for further studies are listed below.

The Adjustments Taken by the Roman Catholic Church

With the arrival of these Protestant churches and organizations, what strategies and changes were employed which enabled Roman Catholicism to remain as the main religion of the Filipino people despite the efforts of the early American missionaries to replace this with Protestantism?

Historical Developments within the Mainline Protestant Churches

As the pre-war mainline Protestant churches unified themselves under the NCCP, it is important to study the developments and the changes that took place with their objectives and emphases. What have been their growth and adjustments as they took a more active role in the post-Marcos era?

The Present Condition of the Fundamentalist Churches
While there is a brief mention of the growth and schisms experienced among these churches, it is important to see what has been the result of their continued emphasis on doctrinal purity and separation.

The Current Trends and Developments within the Mega-Churches
Within the last few decades, several churches have achieved mega-church status as a result of their new approaches and strategies. One can ask whether the paradigm shift from a bounded set to a centered set among the evangelical leaders in the early 1980's had any bearing or impact on this mega-church phenomenon.

Dialogue between the Evangelicals and the Roman Catholic Churches
There has been a growing openness to dialogue between the evangelicals and the Roman Catholic Church. Although the Evangelicals and Catholics Together ecumenical document signed in 1994 by evangelicals (e.g. Charles Colson and Richard Neuhaus, Bill Bright, etc.) and Catholics (e.g. Bishop Francis George, Bishop William Murphy, etc.) was coolly accepted by some and heavily criticized by other Filipino leaders, the religious horizon today is totally different because of it. At the present time, cooperation and partnerships between evangelicals and Catholics are fast becoming a common sight. Thus, one may ask whether the initial attitude of Dr Vencer and the leaders of PCEC helped "break down" the barriers between these two ecclesiastical bodies. What are the current statuses and developments within ecumenism in the Philippines?

The Possibility of a Future Unification among the Religious Leaders of the Country
Will there be a future reunification between the evangelicals and fundamentalists? Will there be a united Christian church someday? What are the remaining impediments for a future reconciliation and reunification among these Christian churches?

The Future for PCEC and Its Constituents

As the PCEC enters its sixth decade of existence, what are the challenges that confront the council's leadership? Are there any efforts to study the changing trends and their implication for evangelicalism? Is the council prepared for these new challenges and opportunities for growth?

Conclusion

It is clear that the formation of and the developments within the PCEC were guided by its leaders' assessment and response to the needs and challenges of their time. They initially rejected the idea of cooperating with the NCCP since they perceived that this council could not fully represent their theological convictions and values. Thus, PCEC was formed in reaction to the formation of NCCP and due to their concern for protecting what they perceived as the "fundamentals of the faith" which limited their membership to a certain "kind" of Christian. However, several of its evangelical leaders saw that having a united voice among all the evangelicals and conservatives was a greater need. It was their choice to shift the council's focus from maintaining a particular form of Christianity (i.e. fundamentalism) to a broader and inclusive membership which was based on a common center – "knowing and making Jesus known." This brought a schism which ended the fundamentalist participation within the council. In time, the need and the context changed specifically during the 1970s. Due to the rise of militancy brought about by the dissatisfaction with the Marcos Regime, Dr Vencer saw the new challenge was the issue of the gospel's irrelevancy, as calls for rebellion and liberation theology were being discussed among the religious leaders of their time. Thus, PCEC "evolved" to respond to the new context. The main purpose was still the issue of knowing and making Jesus known, but now proclamation required social involvement and engagement so that the former could be validated by the latter.

This inquiry has shown there is a need for leaders to evaluate the changing needs and context of their ministry. While a bounded set union, which requires adherence to a certain form, may help in the continuity of one's church, its difficulty lies in its apparent lack of flexibility, which may or may not be beneficial to face the changing needs of the time. On the other hand, while a centered set union can offer flexibility as it allows for cooperative efforts with like-minded bodies to face the changing context and need, its "flexibility" could potentially "dilute" its message. Thus the challenge truly lies in the leader's ability to gauge what form is more beneficial in their specific context. As the Scripture gives an example, the men of Issachar were men "who understood the times and knew what Israel should do" (1 Chr 12:32).

This study will help shed light on the rationale of certain churches and Christian organizations in choosing which council to join. It can also provide an additional factor to consider when evaluating issues of unity and cooperation.

APPENDIX A

PCEC Timeline

1948 **May**: United Church of Christ in the Philippines was inaugurated. Inauguration held at the Ellinwood Malate Church. Association of Fundamental Baptist Churches in the Philippines (AFBCP) was formed with seven regional associations.

1961 International Missionary Council merges into the World Council of Churches.

1963 **November 7–9:** National Council of Churches in the Philippines (NCCP) is formed; a conciliar union among the seven mainline protestant denominations in the Philippines. Meeting was held at the Episcopal Church's Cathedral Hall of the Church of St. Mary and St. John in Quezon City.
Early discussions among Dr Ormeo and other pastors of AFBCP on the formation of NCCP and the probable need to form a separate Fundamentalist council. Meeting held in First Baptist Church of Manila.

1964 First meeting to discuss possible union to form the a council among Fundamental Baptist and other conservative evangelicals. Meeting held in First Baptist Church of Manila.
Philippine Council of Fundamental Churches (PCFC) is formed with Dr Ormeo as Interim Executive Committee Chairman prior to the First National Assembly. Meeting held in FEBIAS.[1]

---

1. Some of the interviewed sources were unsure whether First Baptist Church of Manila was the site of the first meeting. The same is true for the PCFC meeting in FEBIAS.

November 23: PCFC's Constitutional Convention; Drafting of constitution and by-laws of PCFC, discussions on the historical and theological differences between fundamentalism and evangelicalism, sought unity by avoiding differences and explored areas that would unite them, and a new name was given to the council – Philippine Council of Fundamental Evangelical Churches (PCFEC). Meeting held in Fellowship Center Church in Sampaloc, Manila.

1965 Purposes and Statement of Faith finalized.

June: Dr Ormeo, Rev Calica, Rev Tica were expelled from the AFBCP for their involvement with non-separatist groups (i.e. Back to the Bible, etc.) during Biennial Conference at Kabankalan, Negros Occidental. This resulted in the formation of the Association of Baptist Churches in Luzon Visayas and Mindanao (ABCLVM) when the expelled pastors were joined by several delegates of the conference (around forty pastors and their churches). Meeting was held in Caingin Beach, Pontevedra, Negros Occidental. ABCLVM joins PCFEC.

July 9 / 10: First National Assembly – seventy-three delegates from twenty-three founding member bodies. Discussion was focused on the concern over NCCP being the only voice of evangelicalism. The following were approved by the delegates: a) Constitution and By-Laws were approved with minor amendments; b) fifteen-man Executive Committee formed; c) Magbanua voted as Executive Committee Chairman and President of PCFEC's board, Dr Ormeo serves as vice-chairman of PCFEC; d) vote to incorporate PCFEC passed; and e) PCFEC's first office was in Capitol City Baptist Church. Assembly Meeting was held in Capital City Alliance Church. Heated argument on the name of PCFEC as some did not agree with the title "fundamental." Meeting at the Caloocan Bible Church (Source: Dr Magalit, phone interview with author, 8 June 2010).

1966	**April 9:** Congress on the Church's Worldwide Mission – co-sponsored by Evangelical Fellowship of Mission Agencies (EFMA) and Interdenominational Foreign Mission Association (IFMA). 938 delegates from seventy-one countries (although majority were from North America). Congress was held in Wheaton College Campus in Wheaton, Illinois. According to Dr Vencer, these conferences may have influenced the evangelical Filipino delegates – denominations and mission agencies – in the way they voted in the Second National Assembly. Dr Ormeo steps down as Vice-Chairman and from PCFEC's Board, Bishop Magbanua assumes the vacated positions (source: Dr Ruivivar). Dr Ormeo resigns over perceived new directions of PCFEC sometime before the Second National Assembly.
1968	**May 1:** Second National Assembly – discussion is on the Fundamentalist-evangelical debate; major schism among delegates dividing into two camps, fundamental Baptist versus evangelicals; key question asked by Magbanua, "Will PCEFC be a fundamental separatist Council or an evangelical fellowship?" The following were reaffirmed and approved: a) unity for the purpose of evangelism and social ministries; b) call for confessional cooperation; c) commitment to evangelism and mission; d) recognition of social concerns as a biblical ministry; e) the word "evangelical" was not removed from the Council's name but reaffirmed with a vote; f) despite calls to remove the word "fundamental" from Council's name, the name PCFEC was retained due to the Council's constitutional provisions and conditions; and g) Bishop Magbanua remains as President of PCFEC. Meeting held in Capitol City Baptist Church.
1969	**November 20–21:** Third National Assembly – PCFEC is renamed Philippine Council of Evangelical Churches (PCEC) by majority vote which results in the withdrawal of many of the fundamental Baptists from the Council.

1970	**August 1**: Florentino de Jesus becomes first Executive Director of PCEC (a new position formed after some reorganization within PCEC). Bishop Magbanua remains President of the Board.
	PCEC Bulletin published as the Council's official organ.
	December 20: PCEC files Articles of Incorporation with the Philippine's Securities and Exchange Commission (SEC). There were forty member bodies.
1971	**March 3:** PCEC is officially registered with SEC.
1973	**January 11:** PCEC files By-Laws with SEC.
	Magbanua steps down as President of PCEC's Board and Dr Ruivivar, Jr assumes the position.
1974	**April**: *Evangelical Thrust* replaces *PCEC Bulletin,* Dr Ruivivar serves as its editor.
	July 16–25: International Congress on World Evangelization (ICWE); PCEC delegates attended. McIntire holds rally against congress; Rift between evangelicals and fundamentalist widens as McIntire disagrees with Billy Graham. International Congress held at Lausanne, Switzerland.
	July: Antonio Ormeo officially resigns from PCEC Board as a result of Billy Graham's "shabby" treatment of McIntire at ICWE in Lausanne; ABCLVM officially withdraws its membership from PCEC (source: Dr Pio Tica).
	Church Growth Congress – co-sponsored by PCEC, Church Growth Research in the Philippines, and Philippine Crusades; this was a pre-cursor to the formation of DAWN 2000 Philippines. Congress held in Baguio City.
	November 22: Sixth National Assembly; PCEC votes to join the World Evangelical Fellowship (WEF)
1975	Rev de Jesus retires and steps down as Executive Director of PCEC. PCEC's Board takes leadership of the Council.

PCEC Timeline

1978   **February 25:** Atty. Agustin B. Vencer, Jr becomes General Secretary (this is the same position as Executive Director) of PCEC (fifty-seven member bodies). Installation as General Secretary held at Capitol City Baptist Church.

1980   Dr Ruivivar steps down as PCEC President of the Board and Ernie Lagasca (Foursquare) takes his position, the title President of the Board is replaced with Chairman of the Board.
July: PCEC moves to its current headquarters at Project 3, Quezon City (after moving from several locations; namely, CCBC, CCAC, Every Home Crusade, and the Vencer residence).
October: PCEC and PHILRADS offices were officially dedicated.
November: PHILRADS was established and DAWN 2000 is launched.

1985   Ernie Lagasca steps down as Chairman of the Board. PCEC becomes charter member of the Evangelical Fellowship of Asia.

1986   *Evangelical Thrust* is renamed *Evangelicals Today*.
February 25: PCEC leaders decide to support EDSA People Power Revolution; in their joint declaration they justified their decision with two reasons: a) to support the People Power Movement to avoid bloodshed, and b) to demonstrate their disappointment with the conduct of the national elections. Official position: civil disobedience through peaceful means. Meeting held in Capital City Alliance Church.

1990   Evangelical Center was dedicated (the old four-bedroom house which served as PCEC's office was torn down and in its place the new center was built).

1993   **June 11:** Dr Vencer steps down and Ptr. Ef Tendero becomes CEO (same title as General Secretary and Executive Director). National Ecumenical Consultative Committee (NECCOM) was established by Pres. Cory Aquino; PCEC was asked to take leadership.

December: Christian Development Centre officially turned over to PCEC, five-storey dormitory type retreat center in Tagaytay City.

1994 **September 5:** Investiture of Bishop Tendero, Bishop Magbanua changes the title of CEO to Bishop; eight-hundred Christian leaders in attendance. Investiture held in Greenhills Christian Fellowship.

PCEC is composed of foty-seven denominations, eighty independent local churches, sixty-four mission groups and parachurch organizations, Bible schools, seminaries, and other church-related service agencies. Estimated constituency of over 9,000 local churches, groups, and fellowships.

May 13: League of Philippine Evangelists (LPE) was formally launched. LPE aims to recruit and train Filipino evangelists who will conduct evangelistic campaigns throughout the Philippines.

1995 **June 20–23:** PCEC 21st General Assembly. Bishop Tendero reports on the accomplishments of PCEC in accomplishing its purposes: a) promoting unity and encouraging cooperative ministries among the evangelicals in the Philippines; b) developing effective strategies in evangelism and a strong missions program for the evangelization of the Philippines and the world; c) presenting a distinctively evangelical voice and presence to our government and other publics as a witness to the Lordship of Christ in all things; and d) engaging in ministries by helping the needy and poor in the Philippines to become economically self-reliant and rightly related with God in Christ Jesus. Assembly held in Brokenshire Resource Center, Davao city.

1997 **May:** Dr Ormeo and ABCLVM is reconciled with AFBCP. Reconciliation was held at Bethel Baptist Church in Bukidnon.

1999 Felipe Ferrez Jr becomes Chairman of the Board of PCEC.

APPENDIX B

PCEC Constitution and By-Laws

Article I – Name and Office

Section 1. **Name.** The name of the organization shall be the *PHILIPIPINE COUNCIL OF EVANGELICAL CHURCHES* and hereinafter referred to as PCEC.

Section 2. **Office.** The principal office of the Philippine Council of Evangelical Churches, Inc. shall be in Metro Manila.

Article II – Statement of Faith and Objectives (As amended Nov. 21, 1980)

Section 1. **Statement of Faith.** Among other equally biblical truths, the members of PCEC believe in:

    1.1 The Bible, the Word of God, its divine, verbal, plenary inspiration and its inerrancy and infallibility as originally written; and its supreme and final authority in faith and life (2 Tim. 3:16; 2 Pet. 1:20-21);

    1.2 One God eternally existing in three distinct persons: Father, Son, Holy Spirit (Deut. 6:4; Matt. 28:19; 2 Cor.13:14);

    1.3 The Lord Jesus Christ
        His essential, absolute and eternal deity (Phil. 2:6; Jn. l:1, 14; Heb. l:8)
        His true and sinless humanity (1 Pet. 2:22; 1 Jn 3:5)
        His virgin birth (Isa. 7:14; Matt. 1:20)
        His substitutionary, propitiatory death (Mk. 10:45; 1 Tim. 2:16)
        His bodily resurrection (Acts 1:11)
        His ascension to the right hand of the Father (Mk. 16: 19; Acts l:20)

His coming again with power and great glory (Rev. l0:11-16)

1.4 The Holy Spirit who shows the redeeming purpose of God to the World by convicting the world of sin, of righteousness and judgment and by regenerating, uniting to Christ, indwelling, sanctifying, illuminating and empowering for service all who place complete faith in the Lord Jesus Christ;

1.5 The total depravity of man because of the Fall. (Gen. 3:10-24);

1.6 Salvation by grace through faith in Jesus Christ apart from works (Eph. 2:8);

1.7 The everlasting bliss of the saved and the eternal suffering of the lost (Dan. 12:2; Jn. 5:25; Rev. 20: 14; Lk. 16:24-26);

1.8 The real spiritual unity in Christ of all redeemed by His previous blood (I Cor. 12:13; Eph. 1:4-6; 4: 11-15, 5:25-26); and

1.9 The necessity of maintaining, according to the Word of God, the purity of the church in doctrine and life (1 Cor. 6: 19-20; 1 Thess. 4:3).

Section 2. **Objectives of PCEC.** In accordance with its Articles of Incorporation, PCEC shall:

1.1 Promote unity and encourage cooperative ministries among Evangelicals in the Philippines;

1.2 Develop effective evangelism strategies and a strong missions program for the evangelization of the Philippines and the world;

1.3 Present a distinctively evangelical voice and presence to our government and other publics as a witness to the lordship of Christ in all things; and

1.4 Engage in ministries by helping the needy and poor in the Philippines to become economically self-reliant and rightly related with God in Christ Jesus.

Article III – Official Organ

Section 1. PCEC shall establish an official organ which shall be the voice of the council.

Article IV – Membership

Section 1. **Types of Membership.** PCEC shall have the following types of membership:

1.1 Regular Membership, which are open to the following, provided they are duly registered with the government;

1.1.1 Individual churches with at least twenty-five (25) adults (voting members) and a written constitution (the Board of Directors may waive registration with the government);

1.1.2 Fellowship or association of independent churches;

1.1.3 Denominations;

1.2 Associate Membership, which shall be open to the following, provided they are duly registered with the government;

1.2.1 Missionary societies;

1.2.2 Bible schools, seminaries and other evangelical institutions of learning;

1.2.3 Church-related service agencies or establishments.

1.3 Special Membership, which may be granted to any group which falls under one of the above categories but whose constitution or practices limit their cooperation with PCEC only to certain areas of its objectives.

1.4 Individuals may apply to become affiliated members of PCEC provided that they subscribe unreservedly to PCEC's Statement of Faith, support its objectives, programs and budget, and comply with such requirements and pay such membership fee as may be required by the Board of Directors, and provided further that they cannot vote in the National Assembly and cannot be voted into office except when they attend as delegates of voting PCEC member (As amended Nov.21, 1980.)

Section 2. **Qualifications for Membership.** Any of the above types of membership that subscribes to PCEC's Articles of Incorporation, By-laws, policies and procedures and Statement of Faith may apply for membership.

Section 3. **Admission of New Members.** New members may be accepted by a three fourths (3/4) votes of the Board of Directors, subject to ratification by two-thirds (2/3) votes of the National Assembly.

Section 4. **Withdrawal of Membership.** A member may withdraw its membership from PCEC by serving to the Board of Directors a written notice of withdrawal of membership, or PCEC membership may be withdrawn from any member for any of the following reasons upon the recommendation of the Board of Directors and two-thirds (2/3) votes of the National Assembly:

    1.1 If it is proven to the satisfaction of the Board of Directors that the member has officially deviated from the doctrinal position of PCEC; and;

    1.2 If the Board of Directors is convinced that the member has been guilty of acts inimical to the objectives of PCEC.

Article V – The National Assembly

Section 1. **Composition.** The National Assembly shall be composed of the voting and non-voting delegates in accordance with this By-laws as well as the guests that may be invited by the Board of Directors.

Section 2. **Voting Power.** The voting power of the National Assembly shall be in accordance with the following voting proportions:

    1.1 Individual Church Members. Each individual church member shall have two (2) voting delegates;

    1.2 Denominations or associations of churches are entitled to two (2) voting delegates for every member church, provided that the total number of delegates does not exceed fifty (50) or twenty-five percent (25%) of the total votes in the Assembly, and provided the denominations, associations or independent churches shall make sure their delegate are in accord with PCEC objectives.

(The term "church" as used in these By-laws shall be a group of believers meeting regularly in a given place with duly elected or appointed officers and leaders. It must have a written constitution duly approved by the congregation. In the case of denomination with a common constitution, there must be a congregational vote adopting the said constitution)

(The votes of regular independent church, associate and special members that belong to the same denomination or association shall be included in the limitation with respect to the twenty-five percent (25%) of the total

Assembly votes provided that their votes shall have priority). (As amended Nov. 21, 1980)

    1.3 Associate Members shall be entitled to one (l) voting delegate each.

    1.4 The members of the Board of Directors shall be entitled to one (l) vote each and may or may not be included in the total number of voting delegates of their respective groups, provided they remain members of good standing with their denominations, associations or groups.

    1.5 Individual members and observers shall have no vote. They must have their proper credentials, officially registered and paying the same fees as delegates. They may participate in the discussion, but only when the Chairman gives them the floor. Observers will be seated in a special section, apart from the delegates and guests.

    1.6 Guests are registered visitors who may not participate in either discussion or voting.

Section 3.   **Credentials of Delegates.** The proper credentials of delegates shall come from the responsible officials of member bodies and shall be registered with the Council secretary before the meeting of the Assembly. Authorized delegates must be present to vote.

Section 4.   **Officers of the National Assembly.** The officers of the Board of Directors shall be the officers of the National Assembly, namely, chairman, vice chairman, secretary and treasurer.

Section 5.   Meetings of the National Assembly. (As amended July 7, 1999)

    1.1 The regular National Assembly shall convene on the first two weeks of July every 2 years. Special assemblies may be called by the Board of Directors, provided that notice thereof is sent to all member bodies at least 60 days beforehand.

    1.2 Venue. The Assembly may convene in any place in the Philippines to be determined by the Board of Directors.

    1.3 Whenever possible the National Director shall send to the member bodies the agenda of the National Assembly as least thirty (30) days before the Assembly.

(As Amended Feb. 7, 1985)

Section 6. **Authority of the National Assembly.** The Council recognizes that the full and final authority belongs to the Holy Spirit as revealed in the Holy Scriptures. The Council, unless especially authorized, shall not act for any member body on any matter whatsoever. It may, however, offer counsel and suggestion for united action in matters of common interest. The Council does not seek organic union of its member bodies, nor may it trespass their autonomy.

Section 7. **Functions.** The Council when in Assembly shall:
- 1.1 Elect the appropriate number of Board of Directors and transact business in matters within its jurisdiction;
- 1.2 Decide to join an international body or organization by a two-thirds (2/3) vote of the National Assembly, provided at least fifty percent (50%) of the voting member groups are represented; and
- 1.3 Initiate, on its own or when requested by any two regular members, the investigation of charges preferred against any member body and by a two-thirds (2/3) vote of the Assembly remove any member from PCEC membership for sufficient cause.

Article VI – The Board of Directors (As amended Nov. 21, 1980)

Section 1. **Functions.** The Board of Directors, who are elected by the National Assembly, shall have charge of the policy-making functions, direction and discipline of the entire work of the Council. It shall fulfil its responsibilities as a body and no member shall commit the Council on any matter except under proper instruction and authority by the Board of Directors. Furthermore, it shall;
- 1.1 Appoint the National Director and at his recommendation appoint Associate Directors.
- 1.2 Call for special National Assemblies;
- 1.3 Approve membership applications for Assembly ratification and the PCEC budget;
- 1.4 Call for regional conferences whenever necessary at the request of the region or at its own instance; and

1.5 Create commissions and committees and appoint their members upon recommendation of the National Director.

Section 2. **Composition.** The Board of Directors shall be composed of eleven (11) members, ten (10) of whom shall be elected by the National Assembly subject to the following provisions:

1.1 Two (2) each must come from Mindanao, Visayas and Luzon and four (4) may be elected at-large

1.2 No denominational body shall have more than two (2) of its members in the Board of Directors, and no individual church or associate member shall have more than one (l) of its members in the Board; and

1.3 Not more than three (3) members of the Board of Directors may come from the total associate membership.

1.4 To ensure maximum support of PCEC programs only the Chief Executive Officers, or their equivalent position, of member bodies, which have been members of PCEC for a least two (2) years, may be elected in absentia through their official delegate provided there is a written acceptance of nomination, if nominated, duly submitted to the National Director, before the election.

Should a member of the Board of Directors cease to be the chief executive officer of the member body which he represented at the time of election during his term of office, his position shall be considered vacant, and the Board shall appoint another qualified person to fill in the vacant seat only for the unexpired term. This provision shall not apply when the said member body of PCEC within (30) days from the date of separations from his previous organization or before the next meeting of the Board of Directors whichever comes from first, provided that the provisions of Articles VI Section 2.3 are met. (As Amended Feb. 7, 1985)

Section 3. **Tenure of Office.** Initially, five (5) directors shall be elected for four (4) years and five (5) for two years. Thereafter, the regular term for Board members will be four (4) years. Vacancies in the Board caused by incapacity, resignation or termination for cause may be filled by the Board for the unexpired term in accordance with the provisions of these By-laws.

    1.1 A Board can only serve for one (1) full term of four (4) years after which shall be ineligible for election as such. He shall qualify for the office after a rest period of (2) years. This provision applies to the elections in 1980. (As Amended Feb. 7, 1985)

Section 4.   **Officers.** The Board of Directors shall organize themselves immediately after their election and elect their officers from among themselves which shall be: chairman, vice-chairman, secretary and treasurer. These officers, together with the National Director, shall constitute the Executive Committee.

Section 5.   **Tenure of the Officers.** The officers of the Board of Directors shall serve for a term of two (2) years to coincide with the regular corporate election provided that no officer can hold the same office for more than two (2) consecutive terms: The chairmanship shall be rotated among the denominations, associations and groups represented in the Board of Directors.

Section 6.   **Duties of the Officers.** The officers of the Board of Directors shall have the following duties and responsibilities:

    1.1 The Chairman shall preside at the meetings of the Board of Directors and of the National Assembly during their business sessions. He shall call, through the National Director, special meetings of the Board of Directors and Executive Committee.

    1.2 The Vice Chairman shall act in the absence or inability of the chairman, and shall exercise the same powers and duties while so acting.

    1.3 The Secretary who is a Filipino citizen and resident, shall record and file the minutes of the meetings of the Board of Directors, the National Assembly and the Executive Committee, and through the National Director, distribute the minutes to the members of the Board and each PCEC member. He shall supervise the work of two recording secretaries at each National Assembly.

    1.4 The Treasurer or his designated representative as duly approved by the Board of Directors shall receive and disburse funds and keep an account of all financial matters of the Council. He shall solicit and/or expend funds of the Council as authorized by the Board. He shall prepare regular financial reports for the Board and annual reports for all members of the Council. He shall post a bond to be approved by the Board of Directors to insure the faithful performance of his accountabilities. (As Amended Nov. 2l, 1980)

Article VII. The National Director (As amended during the 23rd National Assembly, July 7, 1999)

The National Director shall be the Chief Executive Officer of the Council and shall, under the direction of the Board of Directors, provide general supervision, administration and oversight of the entire work of the Council. He shall promote the work of the Council and represent the Organization wherever and whenever it is needed. He shall render reports to the Executive Committee, the Board of Directors, and the National Assembly. He shall serve as a regular member of the Board of Directors and the Executive Committee and shall be ex-officio member of the commissions and committees. He may be appointed as Corporate Secretary.

Section 1. **Tenure.** The National Director shall be appointed by the Board of Directors and shall serve for (4) years with reappointment. (As amended, July 7, 1999);

Article VIII – Commissions and Committees

Section 1. **Commissions.** Their Functions: (As Amended Nov. 2l, l980);

    1.1 **Commission on Theology,** to reflect on theological issues, define biblical evangelism especially in the Philippine setting, prepare theological papers for PCEC and conduct theological consultations with evangelical Christian workers and scholars;

    1.2 **Commission on Christian Education,** to define the scope of Christian Education, prepare an effective program for Filipino Evangelicals, assist PCEC members in Christian Education and training through publications and seminars;

1.3 **Commission on Mass Media,** to define the extent of evangelical involvement in mass media, develop standards based on Scriptures and existing laws and assist PCEC members in establishing effective mass media programs in communicating the Gospel in the Philippines; and

1.4 **Commission on Laity,** to enable evangelical laymen and women to exercise their priesthood as believers by preparing effective programs on lay involvement in evangelism and mission and to prepare a directory of evangelical professionals in the Philippines.

Section 2. **Committees.** Their Functions: (As Amended Nov.21, 1980)

1.1 **Finance Committee,** to prepare a self-reliant financial program for PCEC within a period of six (6) years, standards in fund raising from and for PCEC members and other publics, and assist the administration in the preparation of budgets;

1.2 **Committee on Membership,** to prepare an effective membership outreach, identify all Evangelicals in the Philippines, process and screen applications for membership to PCEC before endorsement to the Board and standards in membership for the consideration of the Board of Directors;

1.3 **Committee on Easter Sunrise Service,** to plan and prepare an annual Easter Sunrise service which will be participative of all evangelical groups in the area and financially self-liquidating and encourage evangelical involvement in the service to promote visible unity and for a witness;

1.4 **Committee on Chaplaincy,** to prepare a standard in the endorsement of evangelical applicants to the chaplaincy, a program in the recruitment, screening and endorsement of applicants and a directory of evangelical military personnel in active service; and

1.5 **Committee on Election,** to have charge of the election during the Assembly, determine qualifications of candidates, conduct the balloting, canvass the votes and proclaim the winners.

Section 3. **Relation to the National director.** The commissions and committees will assist the Board of Directors in the formulation of policies and programs through the National Director who shall be responsible for the implementation and execution of such policies and programs. (As amended Nov. 21, 1980)

Article IX – Finance

Section 1. **Sources of Income.** The Council shall have the following sources of income;

    1.1 Annual membership fees as determined by the National Assembly;
    1.2 Donations from members and friends here and abroad;
    1.3 Grants or aids on PCEC approved projects;
    1.4 Grants for special ministries and for services rendered and from publications; and
    1.5 PCEC Sunday special offerings to be taken by all member churches for PCEC once a year on a Sunday as may be specified by the Board of Directors.

Section 2. **Fiscal Year.** The fiscal year shall be from January 1 to December 31 of the same year. (As amended Nov. 21, 1980)

Article X – Quorum

Section 1. **National Assembly.** The presence of fifty percent (50%) plus one of the total number of registered voting delegates shall constitute a quorum in the National Assembly, provided that at least one half (1/2) of the total number of voting member bodies during the Assembly are represented; save in those cases where the affirmative vote of a greater proportion is required by law

Section 2. **Board of Directors.** The presence of six (6) members of the Board shall constitute a quorum, except when membership applications are taken up which shall require two-thirds (2/3) majority.

Section 3. **Executive Committee.** The presence of a simple majority shall be a quorum to transact business in accordance with law, (As Emended Feb. 7, 1985).

Article XI – Amendments of the By-Laws

Section 1. **Regular Assembly.** These By-laws may be repealed altered or amended by a majority vote of the members present at a regular meeting of duly called assembly of the Council.

Section 2. **Special Assemblies.** Amendments to the By-laws may be made during a special meeting duly held for the purpose.

APPENDIX C

Aragon's List of Attendees Who Initiated the Formation of PCEC[1]

1. Gadiel T. Isidro, pastor of the Caloocan Bible Church;
2. Faustino Ruivivar, Jr., of the Every Home Crusade;
3. Florentino de Jesus, Sr., of the Christian and Missionary Alliance Churches of the Philippines (CAMACOP);
4. Eleazar (Eli) Javier of the Assemblies of God;
5. Eustaquio (Nene) Ramientos, pastor of Faith Bible Church (UCCP);
6. Greg Tingson, founder and honorary pastor of Faith (Convention) Baptist Church;
7. Frederico (Fred) Magbanua of Far East Broadcasting Corp. and Capitol City Baptist Church;
8. Franklin W. Allen of the Far East Gospel Crusade;
9. Rogelio (Roger) C. Baldemor of the Fellowship of Baptist Churches in Southern Luzon (Conservative Baptist);
10. Donald McGregor of the International Church of the Foursquare Gospel;
11. Edwin Spahr, pastor of the Grace Bible Church;
12. Rudolfo P. Parreño of the Inter-Varsity Christian Fellowship; and
13. Antonio F. Ormeo Sr., who had convened the meeting at the First Baptist Church of Manila.

---

1. Averell U. Aragon, "The Philippine Council of Evangelical Churches" in *Chapters in Philippine Church History,* ed. Anne C. Kwantes (Manila, Philippines: OMF Literature, 2001), 372.

APPENDIX D

Interview with Fred Magbanua, Jr

(Interview took place at Jesus Our Life Center, Makati City, 8 June 2010.)

1. **Question:** *So bali po ang first question ko po* (So my first question is), "when did you become part of PCEC?" *Na e-mail ko po si* (I emailed) Dr Faustino Ruivivar, Jr and *sabi niya* (he said that) there was a first meeting and I am just checking *kung tama yung names* (if the names are correct): Dr Ormeo, Pastor Gadiel Isidro, Pastor Ruivivar, Pastor Tingson. *Ito po yung mga names* (these are the names), *tama po ba* (is the list accurate)?
   Response: I don't remember that Greg was there. Frank Allen was there. Chuck Hufstetler was there, I know. Gavino Tica, Pastor then of Fellowship Center, who is now in San Francisco. Calica, Leo Calica was there.

2. **Question:** Leo Calica?
   Response: Yes. And Ptr. Gavino Tica was there. *Sila yung mga* (They were the) leaders *ng* (of the) Fundamentalist group. Ormeo, Tica, Leo . . . that I could remember *sa* (in the) organizing meeting.

3. **Question:** The very first one *po* (sir)? You said another name after you said Frank Allen?
   Response: Chuck Hufstetler. In fact, Chuck was the one who traveled with me to other regions to talk with the leaders about the organizations. I can still remember that because we stayed in the hotel together.

4. **Question:** *ano po* spelling of the name [how do you spell his name]?
   Response: Chuck, Charles Hufstetler, H-U-F-S-T-E-T-L-E-R. Used to be . . . He was president at one time in FEBIAS College of Bible.

215

5. **Question:** So I can just check that with FEBIAS *po* (sir).
   Response: So those are the people that I remember very well. I was then a Pastor of Capitol City Baptist Church, I was President of Conservative Baptist Association of the Philippines and I was the Administrative officer *ng* (of) FEBC. That's the reason why I was involved in this meeting. Of course they . . . I was elected as the first chairman, founding chairman of the Philippine Council. But of course the Ormeo group insisted that we will link up with the separatist group of McIntire in the US. And the majority of us did not feel like that is where we want to be. We were more or less on the side the National Association of the Evangelicals in the US which is more or less the umbrella organization of the most of the evangelicals. And some of those in the group of course like the Assemblies of God, Foursquare were Pentecostal and they of course did not want to join the Fundamentalist group. So we tried to make a compromise by naming the organization Philippine Council of Fundamental Evangelical Churches. But the ensuing discussion when the fundamentalist group were not able to push with their agenda, they withdrew. So, *ang naiwan yung* (what remained was the) evangelical group. So that is why eventually we decided to call it Philippine Council of Evangelical Churches. *Drinop* (we dropped) out *yung* (the) [name] "fundamental."

6. **Question:** *Yun pong* (what about the) very first meeting, do you recall was it in '63 or '64?
   Response: I could not recall the year. I was already pastor at Capitol City [Baptist Church] and administrative director *ng* (of) FEBC. So it must have been '64. But the initial meeting [that I attended] was held in FEBIAS College of Bible.

7. **Question:** The very first [meeting] *po* (sir)? I see. So, was it more of a meeting of those who were considered Baptist or not so much?
   Response: Well, I think the . . . you know when you think of the group represented by Frank Allen and Hufstetler they are ABCCOP [Alliance of Bible Christian Communities of the Philippines]. So it's OMF [Overseas Missionary Fellowship] churches and SEND [formerly Far Eastern Gospel Crusade-FEGC] churches. And then of course Conservative Baptist leaders who were there and Foursquare, Alliance,

Assemblies of God were the main people there. So that would be Baptist and Pentecostals under the umbrella of the evangelicals but they were not fundamental – Separatist. Now what we were trying to veer away from is becoming a separatist group. Because the main reason we gathered together at that time was the fact that the National Council of Churches [of the Philippines – NCCP] was representing all the non-Catholic groups, the Protestant groups. And many time their pronouncements were not exactly what we believe at the height of liberal theology when at that time they would even consider . . . you know Mao Zedong as savior and all those kinds of liberal views that [infiltrated the older Protestant churches].

8. **Question:** [They were teaching and representing] liberal theology *po* (sir)?
   Response: *Oo* (yes). So that comes out in many of their pronouncements and positions and we could not accept it. That is why we said we need to have an evangelical voice. And that's when it started. To provide an evangelical voice to the churches that we represent that did not agree with the liberal views of the NCCP.

9. **Question:** Who initiated the very first gathering [that] you said [took place] in FEBC or FEBIAS. So who initiated it?
   Response: Basically, the Ormeo group and our group that I led, which of course I was with Conservative Baptist then.

10. **Question:** So they approached you or [did] you approach them?
    Response: I could not remember exactly how it happened. I think there were telephone calls, conversations about the problems that we commonly face, that is, the liberal statements that we could not accept which is [was taken to be representative of all protestants], which includes us as at that time, [since the NCCP] being the only recognized national group. So we felt there was a need for another council to represent our side: Conservative theology. I guess [that's how] the conversation [went] and eventually, we met together. I think Faustino Ruivivar who was then the editor of what is now *Evangelicals Today*, it was then . . . what was the name of the magazine that time? *Evangelical Thrust* that was the name of the magazine. Being you know the only evangelical magazine,

he was writing and some of these problems of course were written by him and I think that caused others to call and then eventually we met to discuss what we will do.

11. **Question:** Was it more because of the thing [referring to the National Association of Evangelicals – NAE] in the US or was it really something *na talagang* (that really was), even in the grassroots among the Filipino pastors, a concern.
    Response: Well, I think foremost I think was the concern of the [American] missionaries who were here. And of course those of us who were working with them cannot help *masagap namin yung kanilang mga* (absorbing the issues that were their) concern. So, while PCEC grew out of the local leadership, you cannot deny that there was an influence of [the American] missionaries that mentored us. At that time, *magkasama yun* (they were connected). *Siyempre sa* (of course in the) US, *clear cut yung stand ng* (it is clear what the [doctrinal] stand of the) evangelicals *at ng* (of the) liberal groups. So *nadadala dito ng mga* (these issues were brought here by the) missionaries that represented these groups. So *kung paano nanduon din yun grupo ni* (as it was there [in America] where the group of) McIntyre *yung* (that was a) separatist-fundamentalist group, separate from the evangelicals in the US. That is why you have Ormeo's group and then our group. So that was the scenario at that time and of course we are thankful that out of that the PCEC developed and while we had the difficulties at the beginning trying to get off the ground, we thank the Lord that now PCEC is very clearly recognized and functioning as an evangelical body.

12. **Question:** In fact many have written that PCEC has already surpassed the NCCP in many ways.
    Response: Oh yes, that is true.

13. **Question:** Going back to the 50s and 60s, were you a pastor at that time?
    Response: I was a pastor at Capitol City. I started in the ministry in 1957. I was pastor-pioneer church planter in Laguna with the concept of the Baptist. Then in 1959, I went to study in FEBIAS and while studying, I had a family to support, I worked part time in Far East

Broadcasting Company. They knew me because I came to know the Lord through listening to the [FEBC] DZAS in 1949. So, *kilala nila ako* (they knew me). So it was that easy for them to . . . It was not difficult for them to accept me. So being a Civil Engineer, I started working in the Engineering Department. I was seventeen years old when I accepted Christ through listening to Sheryl Brook's Bible School on the air [in 1949]. [In 1957] We did pioneering church planting in Victoria, Laguna but after 2 years I decided that I need to get some theological training so I went to FEBIAS. [At that time] I had a wife and a little girl. So I had scholarship from the Yangco foundation but our food, I have to find ways to support my family so I worked part time.

14. **Question:** What was the atmosphere of Christianity or even people in terms of their faith in the 50s and 60s

    Response: Well, of course in the 50s and 60s when we started, the Vatican II has not taken place, the Catholics were still prohibited from reading the Bible. So during those days when we hold evangelistic meetings in Laguna, the atmosphere was still very antagonistic and they would stone us in the plaza where we have a tent. When we go out and give tracts they will accept it and tear it in front of you and throw it to the ground. That's the attitude then. Of course, it has changed a lot since that time with the Word of God going out through mass media: through radio, television and the new spread. Of course the Vatican II has changed the attitude of the Catholics when they were now allowed to read the Bible. So, those were difficult days. As you will recall in 1975, after seventy-five years of missionary work there were only total of 5,000 [Protestant] churches all over the country.

15. **Question:** [Does] That include the pre-war churches?

    Response: Yes, all the non-Catholic churches. But of course you know how it has grown from that time until now. They say that now . . . at least there are several estimates . . . it ranges from fifty to seventy thousand [Protestant] churches now. So there is tremendous growth and we thank the Lord for that.

16. **Question:** With regards [to] the relationships of the evangelicals and the NCCP, were the NCCP trying to recruit the evangelicals like the Conservative Baptist because they (i.e. the NCCP) are into ecumenism?
    Response: I do not recall any attempt to that effect. They know, I think, that from our mother organization from the US that they know where we stand in terms of liberal and conservative theology. So they know that they have no hope of getting us. I do not recall any attempt on their part to recruit us.

17. **Question:** *Talagang in the beginning meron na talagang distinction* (So there was really a distinction from the very beginning)?
    Response: There were some attempts on the part of some to join the NCCP. But there has been no actual [evangelical who joined them]. I think that the only Baptist group that NCCP was able to recruit was the Convention of Philippine Baptist in the Visayas, which until now they are members of the NCCP.

18. **Question:** Someone told me that you are from the Visayan area?
    Response: Yes, [I am] from Negros Occidental.

19. **Question:** The Negros area has a very deep Christian heritage with the ABWE.
    Response: In fact, my home church is [an] ABWE [church].

20. **Question:** But you were not trained with the Doane training institute?
    Response: No, I did not. I sent many of my cousins [who] studied there because [of] my home church, the young people, you know they go to Doane for studies . . . But Doane is you know the Fundamental Baptist group they are quite separatist. I cannot even speak in my own home church. Because I was not ordained under them, I was ordained under the Conservative Baptist. So I cannot speak in my own home church.

21. **Question:** Even now?
    Response: Yes. So in fact what they would do, because all the leaders in that church are my relatives, but the pastor there is afraid that if he allows me to speak he will be replaced or reprimanded or something. So what we do, adjacent to the church is my Uncle's house with a big yard. So what they will do when I come, they would bring all the chairs and the benches outside.

22. **Question:** [Chairs] from the church?
    Response: Yes. And I will speak there so the pastor will not be in trouble. But now the church has split. So there is now the issue about this church which became CBAP and the Grace New Testament Church which is the fundamental. So I cannot speak there now but I can speak here now.

23. **Question:** So these are some of your relatives?
    Response: Yes, both sides. In fact the pastor in the other side is my relative too.

24. **Question:** It's quite amazing. I talked to Pastor Eli Javier, he is still doing well but he is now undergoing dialysis. He mentioned that in the beginning, the relationship between FEBIAS and the more evangelical churches and the Pentecostal churches were not as harmonious. And they would even be labelled as demonic. Maybe he is referring to the fundamentalist. I am not sure. How did the process of bringing them together took place within PCEC?
    Response: Well I think being the founding chairman and being becoming the managing director of FEBC that gave me a very strong influence in bringing together all the Assemblies of God, because they were broadcasting, supporting FEBC, Foursquare and the other groups. So I became close with them. And as we begun to meet together and fellowship I think it was not difficult for them to become part and it was not difficult for the more "Baptistic" group to accept the Pentecostals. I think that played a very important part.

25. **Question:** So FEBC and indirectly FEBIAS became the bridge, *parang ganon* (is it something like that)?
    Response: Well I think probably FEBC more because FEBIAS is [more cautious]. If you are going to divide the evangelicals into Pentecostals and the non-Pentecostals, FEBIAS would be in the non-Pentecostal side. But you know, Eli Javier and Fausto Ruivivar and Jun Vencer, we became very good friends. So it was not difficult to convince their own denominations to become part of PCEC.

26. **Question:** So it was the friendship then that facilitated the merger. Just another question, looking at the history, I am a little confused *kasi* (because) you became the President of PCEC from the article [that] I

was reading. First of all *sabi nila dito* (they said here that) Ormeo became the President of PCFC.

Response: Yah, Philippine Council of Fundamental Churches.

27. **Question:** But then [what happened to the Fundamentalist]?
    Response: They separated from us. They were already out of PCEC.

28. **Question:** And then in 1968, in the second national assembly that was somewhere in May. The tension between the Fundamentalist and the evangelical issue became pronounced issue that is why the PCFC became the PCFEC. And that's when, according to the article, you became the president of the organization the PCFEC?
    Response: No. I have never was.

29. **Question:** You were never was the president of the . . .
    Response: PCFEC. No. That was the Fundamental side. I was never there.

30. **Question:** So, [during the PCFC and PCFEC] it was still Ptr. Ormeo?
    Response: Ormeo. That's Ormeo's group.

31. **Question:** So in the third national assembly, PCFEC became the PCEC. That's when you became the president . . .
    Response: What year was that?

32. **Question:** 1969 *po* (sir)?
    Response: It should be before that.

33. **Question:** 1968 *po* (sir)?
    Response: Yes. The title then was chairman . . . Chairman of PCEC. Then we have an executive director, Ptr. Florentino de Jesus was our first executive director.

34. **Question:** According to this article, that took place in 1970 when Florentino de Jesus became the first executive director of PCEC.
    Response: Yes.

35. **Question:** So you have the executive director but then there is the board then there is a president within the board?
    Response: Chairman [not president].

36. **Question:** Ah so you were the chairman of the board. I see. So in '73 Ruivivar . . .
    Response: became chairman.
37. **Question:** After you *po* (sir)?
    Response: That's right.
38. **Question:** You had left at that time until 1980. Ok so this was more of the chairman of the board? Separate from the general secretary?
    Response: Yes.
39. **Question:** What was the relationship between the . . . I am just a little confused with the organizational chart with the general secretary and the . . .
    Response: Board.
40. **Question:** Chairman of the board?
    Response: Well, of course the chairman preside the board meeting. We were the one who appointed the general secretary, Florentino de Jesus. He is the fulltime national director like what Ephraim Tendero is now. The national director, he is the executive officer of the organization.
41. **Question:** I see. *Kasi* (Because), it says in the article: between '75 when de Jesus stepped down, until '78 when Dr Vencer became the General Secretary, there were no General Secretary or Executive Secretary *ng* (of) PCEC. *Wala daw po yung* (there was no one for the) position *ni* (of) Bishop Tendero, that was empty. At least that is what the article says.
    Response: No. That is not true because from Florentino de Jesus, Jun Vencer then Tendero.
42. **Question:** I see. So there was no gap?
    Response: There was no gap.
43. **Question:** *Kasi* (Because) I was wondering was that the period when the chairman of the board sort of assumed authority.
    Response: No. Never. I never did that.
44. **Question:** I see. Then there was a . . . *pasensya na po kasi* (my apologies, because) I am referring to this article *kasi* (because) this is the only one that talks about the history of the PCEC. There was supposed to be a controversy that happened within PCEC in 1980 with the change in the

title president of the board to chairman of the board, what controversy is this?

Response: I don't even recall about that particular controversy. But to me whether you are president or chairman, my recollection is that if I was the one then, I would always function as a presiding officer of the board separate with the General Secretary or the Executive Director who is the executive office of the organization. So I think I do not know what controversy they are talking about. It could be that when Nonoy Ruivivar took over, he assumed that name, "president." But I think it was . . . I would not consider that as a controversy. It was just a play of words. Maybe they wanted a more prestigious title rather than chairman / president.

45. **Question:** Actually, I emailed Dr Ruivivar and he was saying that he had jokingly told Lagasca that he doesn't want the position because the title "president" has became a chairman. But it was a joke he said. So it's just the way it is. Just a clarification *lang po* (only, sir) Bishop, there was a time when meeting took place in FEBIAS. Do you recall the year of that meeting. Was it '64?

    Response: Sorry I do not know if they have records in PCEC of maybe we don't have those. I don't even remember who the secretary was. I would have no recollection but the fact that I was already in FEBC at that time, and the reason I assume, or I was recognized, the fact that I was president of CBAP, a pastor of Capitol City and a position in FEBC, I think that would be sometime in '64. Somewhere there.

46. **Question:** Just to clarify *lang po* (only, sir): There was a meeting that supposedly had taken place in the First Baptist Church in Manila in Padre Faura. There was one meeting there then Dr Ruivivar said there were two other meetings that took place before that meeting in . . .
    Response: FEBIAS?

47. **Question:** No. First Baptist Church. So there was a meeting in First Baptist Church where Eli Javier and the Pentecostals were there already. But he was saying there was one more meeting or two more meetings prior to that that do not include the Pentecostals. *Kasi* (because) he said that he was the one who invited them later on si Ruivivar. So, could it

be the first or the second that was held in FEBIAS or FEBC. You said FEBIAS pala.
Response: I think the one in FEBIAS . . .

48. **Question:** Was that the first one?
Response: [This meeting] was the time when the organization really took place when the Fundamental groups pulled out.

49. **Question:** Ah ok. That would already be in '68 or '69
Response: Yes, could be. Somewhere there. In fact I was not in the other preliminary meetings.

50. **Question:** So you became part of it (i.e. the meetings) in '68?
Response: Maybe I attended one meeting prior to the FEBIAS meeting.

51. **Question:** *Kasi* (Because) there was one meeting supposedly that had taken place in a Fellowship Center Church in Sampaloc Manila.
Response: That is Leo Calica's Church.

52. **Question:** And that was to draft the PCEC constitution and by-laws that was in 1964.
Response: I think I was there.

53. **Question:** Ah Ok. And then there was another meeting supposedly earlier *pero* (but) the names according to Ruivivar are wrong. *Kasi sabi nya* (because he said), "these things were never there." But supposedly this took place in the First Baptist Church of Manila convened by Ormeo.
Response: I think that is true. Those early meetings, I was not there. But Ruvivar would be there.

54. **Question:** I see. So you were there and you said Greg Tingson were also not there.
Response: In the organization meeting, I did not see Greg there.

55. **Question:** I see.
Response: He maybe in the earlier meetings.

56. **Question:** Yes, I emailed is Dr Ruivivar to clarify *kasi* (because) he said that some of the names I mentioned he does not recall. But he recalls Frank Allen was there. Which is with SEND International.
Response: SEND International. In fact, I think Frank I think was vice president of FEBIAS then and Chuck Hufstetler was, I think, president at that time.

57. **Question:** And they were the ones helping facilitate the merging itself?
Response: Yes.

58. **Question:** So it is quite unfortunate that there are no records. Would you have any records lying around?
Response: In 1970, we went to Indonesia as missionaries. I put all my files in a drum and left it at the warehouse of FEBC. When we came back, we cannot find it.

59. **Question:** *Oh sayang* (what a loss).
Response: I lose a lot. In fact our wedding picture and many other things were lost.

60. **Question:** So sad. *Yun nga po ang ginagawa ko ngayon eh* (that's what I am trying to do now). I am trying to piece together the history. I am looking at the list of names, is there anyone that I can talk to? I've already talked to Ptr. Javier, I am in contact with Ruivivar.
Response: Did you talk to Lagasaca?

61. **Question:** Not yet *po* (sir). How could I talk to . . .?
Response: through Foursquare office, I guess they will link you to him.

62. **Question:** There is another name with the Foursquare *si* (a certain) Ferrez.
Response: Yes, Jun Ferrez. I think you should talk to Jun because he has been with PCEC in fact several times he presided as Chairman of PCEC during the time of Jun Vencer. So he would probably have a good recollection of some the meetings in the early years. Other than that, the Ormeo's group, Ormeo is gone, Gavino Tica is comatose.

63. **Question:** Really?
    Response: Yes. I guess he is conscious but in wheelchair but I think *wala na siya sigurong ma-re-recollect* (he wont be able to recollect the story). Other than that, Jun Vencer would be another person you should email.

64. **Question:** But he (i.e. Jun Vencer) was not there in the early meetings?
    Response: No. But he is a very good reader and I am sure he read all the past records. Being the head there for a number of years I am sure he got it into his mind recalling some of the past events. Because every now and then every anniversary you would retell the story. So he would have a better recollection.

65. **Question:** *Yung sa* (What about the one from) Philippine Crusade *po kasi* (because) Ptr. Javier was mentioning someone from Philippine Crusade.
    Response: It would have been Nene Ramientos.

66. **Question:** Ok. Nene, his name is here. He is the pastor of Faith Bible Church?
    Response: Yes.

67. **Question:** But that is a UCCP church?
    Response: Yes that is correct but Nene was the founding pastor there. And Nene being a graduate of FEBIAS although, mingling with UCCP, more or less the church did not become a member of UCCP. I think it was not until later. In fact the church has split but it was there for a long time.

68. **Question:** But in the recollection by Dr Magalit he mentions them (i.e. Eli Javier of Assemblies of God, Nene Ramientos of Faith Bible Church-UCCP, and Greg Tingson of Faith Baptist Church-Convention Baptist) as part of I think the convening meeting with the other Pentecostal groups. Why would they be in that meeting? Because you said previously UCCP and or NCCP and people in PCEC were not in that meeting.
    Response: Yes but Faith Bible was not really identified with UCCP. Because Nene Ramientos being the founding pastor, although many of the people there were UCCP that started it, he being a FEBIAS graduate, I think did not have a strong link with UCCP.

[the rest of the conversation is about trying to find other contacts and exchanges of phone and contact details]

END

APPENDIX E

Interview with Mariano Leones

(Interview took place at Antipolo, Rizal, 24 April 2013.)

1. **Question:** Can you give some details to the expulsion of the three pastors (i.e. Rev Ormeo, Rev Calica, and Rev Tica) from the AFBCP (Association of Fundamentalist Baptist Churches of the Philippines.
   Response: It was discussed in the biennial conference and the assembly decided to terminate their [membership] on account of compromise. That was an action of the assembly of the biennial conference in Kabankalan. So on account of that, because they are part of the ABCL (Association of Baptist Churches of Luzon) so they decided to have the ABCL separate from the AFBCP. And they formed the ABCLVM instead of just the ABCL, they included Visayas and Mindanao as part of their national organization.

2. **Question:** So even when they were part of the AFBCP, they had their own group which were composed of Baptist churches in Luzon?
   Response: Yes, that is why it is called ABCL. These were churches from Batanes, Ilocos Region, Mountain Province, and Southern Tagalog. This was the composition of the ABCL. And when they (i.e. Rev Ormeo's group) had separated and formed their own ABCLVM, those in Tagalog area that did not join them formed the Samahan ng Iglesya Baptista Fundamental sa Katagalugan (SIBFK). *Yan ang* (That is the) progress of division and the organization of the regional association. The ABCP is composed of churches in Palawan, the Association of Baptist Churches in Palawan. Then in the Visayas, the Visayan Fellowship of Fundamental Churches. Then in Mindanao, we have the Bukidnon Association of

Baptist Churches. Then in Davao, we have the Davao Fellowship of Fundamental Baptist Churches of the AFBCP.

3. **Question:** Would you remember the issues why they were expelled.
   Response: *Hindi ko na naaalala* (I could no longer recall) the specific issues.

4. **Question:** Pastor Nacita wrote "the controversy stems with their involvement with the Billy Graham crusade and others groups such as the FEBC . . ."
   Response: No, I don't think that they were involved with Billy Graham.

5. **Question:** So this incident with Billy Graham came later?
   Response: No, they were not involved in [the Billy Graham crusade] because they believed that Billy Graham was a compromiser. And so the issue was not with Billy Graham. The issue was more like this one [gesturing to the article written by Pastor Nacita] with the Far Eastern [Broadcasting Company] (FEBC). Because the Far Eastern [Broadcasting Company] does not have a separation stand. And because they [i.e. Rev Ormeo's group] participated with the Far Eastern [Broadcasting Company].

6. **Question:** Is this connected to the fact that FEBC would allow some churches like the UCCP to use their radio?
   Response: yes.

7. **Question:** How about the other groups such as Back to the Bible, Overseas Missionary Fellowship, and New Tribes Missions.
   Response: Yes, because these organizations do not have separation stand. This is the main issue.

8. **Question:** So this [issue of separation stand] became the demarcation line?
   Response: Because these groups would work with all kinds of protestants. So that's why the AFBCP does not have any working relations with these Back to the Bible, Campus Crusade [for Christ]. I know those [groups had worked with other protestants]. Although we do not question their [faith], the fact that they are just compromising with liberals and neo-evangelicals.

9. **Question:** And these three pastors [Rev Ormeo, Rev Calica, and Rev Tica] were accused of having connections with these groups?
   Response: Those were the allegations against them at that time.

10. **Question:** And the vote [went] against them?
    Response: And that's what the findings was that they sort of violated the [separation stand] and have compromised on account that they've been participating in some of these neo-evangelicals. So [these is what happened] in Kabankalan.

11. **Question:** But there was a later time in 1997, in Malaybalay, Bukidnon when they had the reconciliation [between Rev Ormeo's groups and the AFBCP]?
    Response: yes, there was the reconciliation during the biennial conference in Malaybalay, Bukidnon.

12. **Question:** Where you there at that time, Pastor?
    Response: Yes, I was there [in the reconciliation in Bukidnon] and I was there in Kabankalan [when the three pastors were expelled].

13. **Question:** So how was the proceedings? What was the atmosphere in Malaybalay, Bukidnon?
    Response: It was a different atmosphere. We truly welcomed them back.

14. **Question:** Did they rejoin the council [AFBCP]?
    Response: They maintained the ABCLVM. So it was not an issue of them dissolving the ABCLVM. Although they are not part of the AFBCP, yet that atmosphere of separation and that atmosphere of termination of fellowship [no longer existed]. So there was a working relationship between the two.

15. **Question:** Do you remember who took the initiative to reconcile the two groups?
    Response: I wasn't chairman of the AFBCP at the time of the negations. There were preliminary talks with Pastor Ebenezer Nacita. I can't recall all the details, all I remember was that there were preliminary talks that worked out and then during that time in the biennial conference, in Malaybalay, we welcomed them back.

16. **Question:** When I talked with Pastor Pio Tica, the brother of Rev Gavino Tica, he mentioned that there were a lot of schisms or separations that took place in the 1960's among the fundamentalist Baptist churches. Would you know why these churches separated from each other? Aside from issues of compromise and separation?
    Response: The Association of Fundamental Baptist have already taken that stand from the very beginning, [the doctrine] of separation was part of our doctrinal statement. And separation from disobedient [Christians and churches], that is, those evangelicals who worked together with liberals, with modernists, and with neoevangelicals. There are several Baptist groups in the Philippines; for example the Conservative Baptist but then they have their own national organization, then we have the Bible Baptist who had their own separate organization.

17. **Question:** So beyond that, the schisms that resulted with Pastor Ormeo's group was the result of their involvement with some of these groups with FEBC, with these other organizations which were disobedient and did not have a strong separation stand.
    Response: Although Pastor Ormeo and this ABCLVM are part of the International Council of Christian Churches (ICCC) which have taken a strong stand against the World Council of Churches (WCC).

18. **Question:** It has been mentioned in [Dr Aragon's] thesis that Pastor Ormeo had helped found the Philippine Council of Fundamentalist Churches (PCFC) which eventually became the Philippine Council of Evangelical Churches (PCEC). Would you know anything about it?
    Response: The ICCC was organized by McIntire, although McIntire was a Presbyterian but a Bible Presbyterian who had taken a strong stand on separation, working together with the General Association of Regular Baptist Churches in America (GARBC). So here in the Philippines, the AFBCP was the product of ABWE missionaries, the Association of Baptists for World Evangelization, had a working relation in America with the GARBC. So here the AFBCP worked together with the missionaries of ABWE because that is where the ABWE started way back in 1933.

19. **Question:** In a book written by Rev Nacita, he mentions that the churches planted by the ABWE, BBSI, and DBBI organized themselves in the AFBCP in 1948 with seven regional associations. You mentioned this a while ago . . . the Association of Baptist Churches in Northern Luzon, the Association of Baptist Churches in Central Luzon, etc.

    Response: These were the original regional councils under the ABCP (later renamed AFBCP). This is the association of Baptist Churches in Northern Luzon, actually the name of this was the Fellowship of Fundamental Baptist Churches in Northern Luzon. Then this one the Association of Baptist Churches in Luzon. Then [the third regional council's] original name was Samahan ng mga Iglesya Baptista sa Timog Luzon, then [after the schism of Rev Ormeo's group those who did not join the ABCLVM] later transferred to [the Samahan ng Iglesya Baptista Fundamental] sa Katagalugan (SIBFK).

20. **Question:** Do you know anything about Pastor Ormeo? His background? Like educational attainment?

    Response: You should ask Nacita, he is more knowledgeable since Rev Ormeo is his father-in-law.

21. **Question:** Do you know if Pastor Ormeo taught in Silliman University?

    Response: I don't think so. After the War (World War II), his [Rev Ormeo's] first church was the Bethel Baptist Church in Malaybalay, Bukidnon. When he resigned from the Bethel Baptist Church in Malaybalay, because he was called to be the first [Filipino] pastor of the First Baptist Church in Padre Faura which is now Manila Baptist Church. The First Baptist Church was pastured by Pastor Ormeo until another problem arose on account of [the ownership of] the property. The property was owned by ABWE. Then the building was destroyed during the war. Then after the war because of the Japanese reparations, the amount taken from the Japanese reparation was the amount spent for the building of the new church building which is in Pennsylvania and Padre Faura. So that's where Pastor Ormeo became the pastor after Richard Durham who was the last ABWE missionary to be pastor of that church. Then later on, when Rev Ormeo's [group] lost the case, they transferred to Quezon City. And then ABWE took over again the property and then later on the church was formed and renamed the Manila Baptist Church.

[There were some irrelevant discussions regarding the founding of certain seminaries and their relationship with each other.]

22. **Question:** Did you ever meet a Pastor Honeywell from FEBIAS?
    Response: Yes. At the very beginning, Honeywell was the president of FEBIAS.

23. **Question:** Someone told me that he was a fundamentalist Baptist pastor?
    Response: I think that there was no question of about their being fundamentalist in their doctrine, only that there is no specific stand on separation from modernists. Their philosophy was to work inside [the liberal churches] hoping to remedy and rescue. But penetration does not work.
    [there were some discussion on the beginnings of ABWE which was ABEO in the 1920s and '30s by Dr R. Thomas]

24. **Question:** How about you pastor? How did you become a Christian? Were you saved in the Doane?
    Response: I was in the army and was involved in the guerilla movement during the war. Then after the liberation, I joined the Philippine Scout and then I was assigned in a group that was assigned in Okinawa for two years. Then when I came back in 1949, I attended the church in that First Baptist Church [which] now the Manila Baptist Church in Padre Faura. And in that meeting then, the pastor there was Rev Bernard Bancroft. Then one of the meetings in the evening, way back in 1949, I think it was the last Sunday of November or the first Sunday of December, when I received Jesus Christ as my savior. I became a member of that church. But I studied at Baptist Bible Seminary (BBSI) for my theological studies. [Baptist Bible Seminary was formerly the] MEI, the Manila Evangelistic Institute then after the war it is Baptist Bible Seminary then because of the [expansion] it was again changed to Baptist Bible Seminary and Institute. [That is where] I got my Bachelor of Religious Education and my Master. I had only one pastorate and it was in Malaybalay in 1956. I succeeded Rev Ormeo when he was

called to Manila Baptist Church. I was called by the church in Bethel Baptist Church to become the pastor there from 1956 to 1960. Then in 1960 the BBSI, in that new facilities in Tikling, they called me to join the faculty.

25. **Question:** Where was BBSI before it transferred to its current location?
    Response: It was in Padre Faura [in the FBCM property]. The building now, that was the building erected on account of the Reparation Fund from the Japanese. There was a building then at the back for the seminary, which was totally destroyed. BBSI transferred to its current location in 1960.

26. **Question:** You mentioned that it was Pastor Durham who recommended Rev Ormeo to become the senior pastor of FBCM?
    Response: Pastor Richard Durham recommended Rev Ormeo to be the [first] Filipino pastor.

27. **Question:** Was that [installation of Rev Ormeo] welcomed by all?
    Response: Yes, it was a big step.

28. **Question:** But nobody opposed it?
    Response: *Wala, wala* (Nobody). It was fully recommended.

29. **Question:** Before he came [to FBCM], you said that he was with the Bethel Baptist Church?
    Response: Yes. After the war, some of the students of Doane concentrated their ministry in Mindanao. Some went to Davao. Rev Ormeo was the one [who worked] in Bukidnon. And he started reorganizing the war-torn Bethel Baptist Church. (Rev Leones recalled an ABWE missionary named Rev Payton) Peyton was a missionary who did not believe in tithing. So there was a conflict between him and Pastor Durham.

30. **Question:** What was his stand on tithing?
    Response: He just believe in offerings [give what you want as opposed to the mandatory 10 percent]. He believed that tithing was an Old Testament practice not a New Testament [practice].

31. **Question:** Why was the separation issue a big issue among the fundamentalist churches?

    Response: In the first place, the issue of fundamentalism. The Scripture, because of the "age of reason" that penetrated the seminaries, the Scripture could no longer be considered as the total [Word of God]. [For the liberals] it contains the Word of God, it is not the Word of God. So if you read the Bible now and it blessed you that is the Word of God. But the following day you read the same Bible, the same passage, and it does not bless you then it is no longer the Word of God. It is more subjective. Then the issue of the Virgin Birth, the issue of the deity of Christ. The issue of the atonement of Christ. The resurrection of Christ. And the issue of the return of Christ.

32. **Question:** Do you remember when these became a big issue in the Philippines?

    Response: At the very beginning, this was already the issue of Dr Thomas.

33. **Question:** Did you believe that some churches were compromising in the 1960s?

    Response: Yes. As far as our churches were concerned, we were united in the separation stand. Our issue was against those who do not make the stand. There are those who do not take the stand because of their liberalism, their modernism. And there are those who were working with those apostate groups.

    (At this point, Pastor Leones appeared to be tired.)

34. **Question:** Thank you *po* pastor for your help and patience with my questions.

    Response: Is ok. My only condition is that before you publish this, can you give me a copy of its draft so that I can check it.

35. *Opo* (yes), pastor. I will gladly do it.

END

APPENDIX F

Interview with Eliseo Capile

(Interview took place at Higher Rock Baptist Church, Malabon City, June 17, 2010.)

1. **Question:** *Naalala niyo yung umpisa kung sino sino ang mga nakasama sa unang meeting* (do you remember the beginning [of PCEC], who were in the very first meeting)?
   Response: *Hindi po eh* (no, I don't). *Kami kami lang ang nag usap* (it was among us). *Parang may representative kami sa meeting ng PCEC* (we had a representative in the PCEC meeting).

2. **Question:** *Anong taon po kaya* (what year would that be)?
   Response: *Baka mga '72 pa yan e* (probably in 1972).

3. **Question:** *A ito na yung bandang huli po nung pahiwalay na* (oh, so this was towards the end, when they (i.e. the fundamentalist and the evangelicals) were about to separate from each other)?
   Response: *Oo* (yes). *Yung sa pangalan pa lang hindi na kami nagkasundo e* (they weren't even able to agree on the name for the council). *Yung fundamental ayaw nila e* (they didn't want the word "fundamental"). *Ewan ko kung bakit ayaw nila* (I don't understand why they didn't like it).

4. **Question:** *Bakit po sa pananaw niyo* (in your opinion, why was this so)? *bakit mabigat yun na tinanggal nila* (why was this such a serious matter that they wanted the name to be removed)?
   Response: *Alam niyo pagka* (you know, when you're) . . . As fundamentalist, *dapat kung anong sinabi ng Biblia e* (you follow what the Bible says). *Kung ano ang sinabi ng Biblia, yun* (whatever the Bible says, that's it). *Hindi natin icocompromise* (we can't compromise what the

Bible says). *Hindi natin palalabnawin* (we can't water it down). *Ganun e* (that's how it is). *Alam nyo sa ngayon ang napupuna ko ang preaching ng maraming pastor ngayon, prosperity gospel* (you know, I have been noticing that there's a lot of pastors who are preaching the prosperity gospel). *Yan po ang napupuna ko* (that's what I have been noticing). *Kaya ang mga tao, pagdating ng problema at pagsubok, hindi maintindihan kung ano ang gagawin* (that's why when people experience problems and trials, they don't know what to do).

5. **Question:** *Yung panahon po ng paghihiwalay, sabi po niyo around 72 yun, ano po iyong parang . . . sino po talaga ang nagsabing "humiwalay na tayo"* (during the time of separation in 1972, who actually said that "we should leave [PCEC]")?
Response: *Kami po . . .* (we did).

6. **Question:** *Nagmeeting po kayo ng hiwalay* (did you have a meeting to discuss the separation)
Response: *Nung tanggalin yung salitang "fundamental," hindi na kami sumama* (when they removed the word "fundamentalist," we didn't join them anymore). *Nabuo na yan* (it was already formed).

7. **Question:** *Naalala niyo po ba yung nangyari kay McIntire* (do you remember what had happened to McIntire)?
Response: *Matandang missionary yan* (he was an old missionary). *Mga 30's pa yan* (he was from the 1930s).

8. **Question:** *Ano po ang ano niya* (what was his affiliation)? *ABWE po ba* (was it with the ABWE)?
Response: ABWE.

9. **Question:** *Yung parang sinasabi dun sa isang nababasa ko, nabastos yata si Mcintyre sa Lausanne yata. Kaya nung umuwi siya, dun na nagsimula yung parang hidwaan e* (I read somewhere that McIntire was disrespected in Lausanne, and when he had returned from that conference, that's when the separation started).
Response: *Hindi ko po naalala yan* (I don't remember that particular detail).

10. **Question:** *Kung ikukumpara niyo po yung faith ninyo sa faith ng mga Baptist sa PCEC, ano po sa tingin nyo ang pagkakaiba niyo sa kanila kaya nasabi niyong dapat maghiwalay* (when you compare your faith with the other Baptists who are connected with PCEC, what would be the major difference that would make you choose to separate from them)?
    Response: *May compromise po iyan* (they were guilty of compromise).

11. **Question:** *San pong paraan sila nagcompromise* (in what way did they compromise [the faith])?
    Response: *Itong Conservative, kasama sa ecumenical movement yan* (the Conservative [Baptist], they are involved in the ecumenical movement).

12. **Question:** *Tsaka yung Convention Baptist po, member sila ng NCCP* (and the Convention Baptist are members of the NCCP).
    Response: National Council? *Yan po e* (that's it). *Pagka sumama kayo sa hindi fundamental, tiyak na may compromise e* (when you join any group that's not a fundamental, for sure you would be guilty of compromise). *Hindi maaring walang compromise e* (it's not possible that there won't be any form of compromise).

13. **Question:** *Naalala niyo pa po ba kung saan kayo nagmeeting noon at nagbotohan kayo na aalis nalang kayo* (do you remember where you had the meeting when you voted to leave [the PCEC])?
    Response: *Sa First Baptist. Diyan bale yung pinaka HQ namin* (it was in First Baptist [Church of Manila], that was our Headquarters).

[the rest of the interview was about his life and his recollections on how it was in the 1960s]

END

APPENDIX G

Interview with Pio Tica

(Interview took place at Higher Rock Baptist Church, Malabon City, June 17, 2010.)

[Previous discussion was focused on how his church was started. At this point of the discussion, the focus was on his educational background]

1. **Question:** And it is amazing that FEBIAS was founded and started by ex-soldiers.
    Response: Actually, it was started by fundamentals even the doctrines. *Talagang kwan very extreme ang position ng ICCC* (However, ICCC's [doctrinal] position was more extreme). *Kaya nung ako na ang pumasok diyan* (that's the reason why, when I enrolled there [FEBIAS]), it was actually against their will *kasi ako ang pastor ng* (because I was the pastor of an) ABCL Church. *Pero yung anak ni Ptr. Capili* (However, one of the children of Pastor Capili), *nauna sa'akin yun* (enrolled in that school ahead of me) *at saka yung isang member ni* (and also one of the members of) Ptr. Calica [enrolled] *sa* (in) FEBIAS *sa* (she was from the) Fellowship Center Church, she was a student of FEBIAS also. *Dun nag-graduate yun eh* (That's where she graduated). So they have gone ahead of me. *Sabi ko kay Ptr. Ormeo* (I told Pastor Ormeo), "Pastor, *bakit po sila hindi niyo tinitira bakit ako* (why don't you criticize them too, why are you singling me out)?" *eh ang sabi nya maliwanag yung sabi nya* (what he said which was quite clear), "well you are a member of the Board member of ABCLVM." *Sabi ko* (I responded), "it's Pastor Calica who recommended me to go to FEBIAS." *Si Ptr. Calica noon* (Pastor Calica at that time), he was a member of the board of FEBIAS

college of the Bible *kasi ang choices ko* (because my choices were) either BBSI or PBTS. *Kasi mayroon nang college background kaya natanggap ako sa Baguio* (I was accepted by [PBTS in] Baguio because of I had some college background). *Pero ang Davao, malayo* (but Davao was far). So *sabi ni Ptr. Calica* (Pastor Calica said), "*baka masama ka sa* (you might become embroiled in the) conflict." "You will be caught in the middle and I know that you are a fighter. But it think it will not be healthy for you to start studying in that kind of atmosphere."

2. **Question:** Was Pastor Leones connected there that time?
   Response: *sa* (in) BBSI, he was the president.

3. **Question:** At that time?
   Response: [yes], at that time, *kaya* (that is why) he recommended me to FEBIAS college of the Bible. *Kaya sabi ko kay Ptr Ben* (That's why I said to Pastor Ben), "it was Ptr. Calica who recommended me." *Pero pagkatapos nun, member na ako ng board ng ABCL* (I only became a member of the board of ABCL after that), chairman of the board of committee on evangelism *at* (and) President *ng* (of the) National Fellowship of Pastors for Christ. *yung mga* (that's for the) young people. Then I was replaced illegally in 1968 when they had a meeting without my knowledge *at nabalitaan ko na lang* (I simply heard about it) by the end of March *na hindi na ikaw ang Presidente* (that I was no longer the President). *Uy, hindi ko alam yan ah* (Ouch! I didn't know that). *Pero di na ko nakipagaway dun* (I no longer resisted their decision) I think. *parang nasulot lang* (It was taken from me without my knowledge and illegally) . . . as a matter of fact *ang totoo non un ding attitude ko siguro* (the truth is, that was my attitude [I simply accepted their decision]) the Lord blessed the attitude and later on *un iba dun na nagaaral hanggan sa yong natl assembly ng* ABCLVM *diyan sa* (there were others, even members of the National Assembly of ABCLVM that studied there in) FEBIAS College of Bible

4. **Question:** I'm just amazed when you talk about FEBIAS now as of this period, and from most evangelicals when they refer to FEBIAS they never see it as coming from the fundamental they always see it as

neo-evangelical as you would say or inter-denominational *yun ung mga* (that was the common) perspective

Response: We are not associated with them but the early missionaries they see it as very fundamentalist . . . but he [the founder of FEBIAS] was with the Christian Gospel Crusade. *ang tawag sa FEBIAS dati ay* (FEBIAS was formerly called) Bible Institute and Seminary. He was a student from a Baptist University. *tsaka yung ibang kasama nyan* (even his other co-faculty there), they were die-hard fundamentalist in that practice so *hindi sila sumasama sa* (they didn't join the) ecumenical movement that time *kaya nga* (that's the reason) that led the Ptr. Ormeo to challenge these people in organizing an organization that is not connected with the NCCP. *kasi noon ang kinikilala ay* (because at that time, the only recognized [protestant group] was the) NCCP in 1963 when they were organized.

5. **Question:** And this is how PCFC started
   Response: *Oo* (yes)

6. **Question:** [this was] the Philippine Council of Fundamental Churches?
   Response: [Yes], it was actually Ptr. Ormeo who *naalala ko dun sa meeting ng* (I remembered in the first meeting at the) First Baptist [Church of Manila], *ako ay nakatunganga lang* (I was just quietly staring at them) because I was [a] first year Bible school student *galing sa mundo* (from the world). *Makamundo talaga ako nun e* (I was quite worldly at that time). *At* (and) I was not even serious with my calling. This was . . . *sa dulo ng* (at the end of) 1963, actually it was in 1962 when they were having a meeting.

7. **Question:** So in 1962 people were already . . .
   Response: *Pero sila sila lang* (Yes, but it was just them, [among the fundamentalist Baptist] only)

8. **Question:** *Sino po sila* (who were these people that you are referring to)?
   Response: *Sina* (it was) Pastor Ormeo, Pastor Gavino Tica, Pastor Leo Calica, Pastor Manuel Alesna, *at* (and) Pastor Apolinario Apoong. *yan ung lima* (it was those five [pastors]).

9. **Question:** *Ano po ung name nung isa* . . . (what was the name of the other one)?
   Response: Manuel Alesna. *yun ay* (he was the) pastor *ng* (in) Pandacan. *yun ay dating* (he was formerly) . . . he was actually . . . from the *Sakdalan* party *mga member ng Hukbalahap yan nung araw* (members of the Hukbalahap [Hukbong Bayan Laban sa mga Hapon, English: The Nation's Army Against the Japanese], in the past). Manuel Alesna. *Yun isa ay* (the other one is) Apolinario Apoong *nasa* (he is still in) Dagupan *pa ngayong yan* (up to this time). Then of course Dr Leo Calica, Dr Ormeo and Dr Gavino Tica.

10. **Question:** So they were the first to really talk.
    Response: We talk about these things *sa pagkakatanda ko noon sa panahon yung ay* (as I recall those days) . . . Back then, I really thirst for these things . . . I know the Lord has called me. I was a backslider *matagal na yun e* (for a long time). *Gusto kong matuto talaga ano ang tunay na church* (I really wanted to learn what was the true church). Anyway, *sa first meeting nila, ang pinaguusapan nila was the ICCC* (in that first meeting, they were talking about the ICCC). So *nagkakaroon sila ng congress ng ICCC* (they were going to attend an ICCC congress). This was in '62. *ang pinaguusapan nila* (they were talking about several topics such as) the national council, liberalism, ecumenical movement *yung ganon* [those subject matters]. Actually that time *medyo may mga* (they had several) side comments *sila kay* (against) Billy Graham. *kasi nung unang nagcrusade si Graham was* (When [Billy] Graham had his first Crusade [in the Philippines]) in 1957, So *may mga side comments sila on the position ni* (they had side comments [i.e. criticism] on the [theological] position of) Billy Graham.

11. **Question:** So were they offended with Billy Graham?
    Response: Actually, they were.

12. **Question:** *ano yung issue* [what was the issue]?
    Response: because of his [Billy Graham's] close association with and his commendation of the Pope *yun ang talgang kwan* (that was the main issue). I talked personally to Dr Carl McIntire in July of 1974 [when] I was representing the Philippines, *member ako ng* (I was a member of the)

Philipine Delegation *sa* (for the) Lausanne Congress. *Nagkita kami* (we saw each other). He was walking in the aisle. *Nagkasalubong kami* (And we bumped into each other). [McIntire said,] "I know you." *Akala nya ako si* (He thought that I was) Ptr. Gavino, *malaki ang pagkakahawig naming* (we have similar features). "You are a Tica." [I said] "and you are Dr McIntire," "What in the world are you doing here? Let us sit down and have coffee." I asked him, "if you don't mind, Dr McIntire, what are you doing here?" [McIntire responded,] "Well I was here, I want to see exactly with my eyes what is going on here. Who are these people? Instead of just hearing. And what are you doing here?" [I jokingly responded,] "I am an intelligence agent from the Fundamental Baptist." And we laugh togther. *So maganda yung usapang* [So the conversation went well] but he was actually, well *nagrarally sila sa labas e dun sa mismong nilalabasan nun dinadaanan ng delgates* (they were rallying [i.e. protesting] outside the very entrance where delegates [would go in and out of the conference]). Billy Graham, Peter Wagner, *ung nasa Korea ahh . . . pastor . . . basta yun yung tinatawag na Billy Graham ng Korea* (another guy . . . the Billy Graham of Korea), *tatlo sila ano at si* (those three and) Jose Mesna *ng* (of) Africa, *yan ang mga naalala kong mga pangalan diyan sila dumadaaan* (those were the ones that I recall, they would pass by that [entrance]). *Diyan saharapan at talgang meron nakalagay na* (they put up a sign right in front of that entrance where it says), "Billy Graham the Most Ecumenical Person . . . Billy Graham The AntiChrist" *naka ganun matindi* (it was really that bad). *Kaya naman si Billy Graham hindi niya binigyan ng pansin* (However, Billy Graham had simply ignored them).

13. **Question:** He [Billy Graham] should have tried to at least have a dialogue. He did not issue a dialogue?
    Response: *Gusto niya daw makipagusap, daw!* (he [Billy Graham] claimed that he really wanted to have a dialogue, probably!) *sa aming usapan* (that's what he said to us). [On his side, McIntire said,] "I tried to talk but I treated . . . I was not even . . . they did not even open their doors to me."

14. **Question:** *yun ang* (that is the) side *ni* (of) Billy Graham?
    Response: *parang ganyan* (something like that). *Sa atin ibig sabihin e sinupla* (in our local dialect, he was snubbed). He [McIntire] felt he was actually treated shabbily by this group. *sinabi mismo sa akin ni Dr Carl Mcintyre* (this is what Dr Carl McIntire actually said to me). *Sabi ko* (I said), "Why not have a meeting with him" He responded, "I would have been willing to sit down and talked with him."

15. **Question:** *ah si Dr McIntire ang prang inisnab* (so it was Dr McIntire that was snubbed).
    Response: *oo inisnab siya at* (yes, he was ignored) . . . He [McIntire] said, "I was looking for the right person to talk to. I have been here for two days." *yun yung sabi nya* (That's what he said). So anyway *balik siya dun eh* (he just went back [to the US]).

16. **Question:** How old was Dr Mcintyre during that time?
    Response: *Mga 60's na* (Around 60-yrs-old). *siguro yan mga early 60s* (he was probably in his 60s)

17. **Question:** Going back to the '62 meeting with Ptr. Ormeo, Gavino, and then you said Calica . . . and Alesna . . . Apoong . . . so there were just five in the beginning.
    Response: *mayroong isang babae dun na* (there was a lady in the meeting). *hindi ko matiyak ito kung si* (I am not sure if it was) Mrs Himoto *sekretarya ni* (the secretary of) Ptr. Ormeo, or was it Pastor Calica. We use to call her Auntie Leony Martinez. I could possibly remember. *di ko matiyak kung siya pero I am sure she was there* (I am no longer sure is she was the one but I remember that there was a lady). *Pero ang pinaguusapan tungkol dun* (but our topic was about those issues). The only thing that sticks to my mind was Billy Graham and then this congress.

18. **Question:** And this was in Manila Baptist Church (formerly the First Baptist Church of Manila)?
    Response: Yes, this was in the Manila Baptist Church, *isang kwarto . . . sa office* (in one of the rooms . . . an office). *Eh ako naman yung ginagawa ng kapatid ko sa akin* (as for me, what my brother was actually doing was) he was actually training me to just always go with him. [Gavino said

to me,] *"Kung nasan ako basta sunod ka sa akin pra malaman mo yung ginagawa ko at pianguuspan dahil pupunta ako sa America* (Wherever I go, you should follow me so that you would know what I am doing and what are the issues that we are discussing because I will be leaving [you behind] to go to America)." So in 1965, he went to the States. But in 1964 there was a meeting. *Hindi ko matiyak sa iyo kung between '64 and '62 kung nagkaron ng meeting sila ano* (I could not be certain if they had a meeting between 1962 to '64). but in 1964, I was there when they had a meeting of organizing this PCFEC.

19. **Question:** *Ah meron nang "E" yun* (So they had the letter "E" [which stands for "evangelical" in the council's name])?
    Response: *Meron* (yes there was). [He corrected himself], *ay hindi wala pa yung "E"* (oops, there was no "E" [in the name of the council]).

20. **Question:** *Ah, wala pa yung "E"* (so there was no "E" [in the name])?
    Response: Philippine Council of Fundamental Churches. *Dapat talaga makausap mo si Dr Ruivivar, andun siya eh* (you should really talk with Dr Ruivivar, he was there in the meeting at that time.

21. **Question:** He [Dr Ruivivar] says, when I e-mailed him, *kasi may binigay na list si Dr Aragon* (because I gave him Dr Aragon's list [of original convenors of PCEC]) and he was going through each of the name. *Sabi niya* (he said), *"yung pumanaw na si De Jesus* (the De Jesus that had already passed away), he came only in '65."
    Response: *Siya ang pumalit kay kuwan eh* (He was the one who replaced . . . [he corrected himself] *Siya ang actually siya ang kaunaunahang executive director bago si Jun Vencer* (He was actually the very first executive director, the one before Jun Vencer).

22. **Question:** Right. *Pero sabi nga nya* (but he [Dr Ruivivar] said that) he [Florentino De Jesus, Sr] only came around that time [after 1965]. *So sabi nya* (so he [Dr Ruivivar] said that) he [Florentino De Jesus, Sr] was never in the [very first meeting], as part of the conveners. Sabi niya (He [Dr Ruivivar] also said that), "Greg Tingson was never part of PCEC of that early stage." So he was going through each [name] of the list. *Tapos nitong kalaunan, di tinintingnan ko yung e-mail nya sabi ko* (in the end, I notice in his email), *"teka nga pastor, ikaw na lang at si Ptr Ormeo ang*

natitira sa listahan (Wait a minute, the only names left on the list are you [Dr Ruivivar] and Pastor Ormeo." *Tapos sabi niya, "mukhang ganung na nga* (He then said, "I think that that's about right")." *Tapos sabi ko* (then I said), "*sino pa po ba* ([do you remember] anyone else)?" *Tapos sabi nya* (he responded), "*Pasensya ka na, 50 years na ang nakalipas* (pls pardon me, its been fifity years), I cannot remember [all the details]." *Sabi nya parang medyo bold caps eh* (he then replied, as if in bold caps [but he did not]), "I wish that I had kept careful record, but I did not. I wish I could remember these people but I could not." *Tapos sabi ko parang kwan* . . . (then I said to myself, [oh oh, I may have pushed too hard to get the names])

Response: *Doon sa list ni Anne Kwantes* (in the list that was written in the book that Anne Kwantes had been the editor), *nakita ko eh wala si Calica at wala si Gavino dun eh* (I saw that Calica and Gavino were not in the list). *Nagulat ako eh* (I was surprised). *Sabi ko, bakit wala dito* (I asked, why were they not in the list).

23. **Question:** Right.

    Response: *Eh all the time andiyan yan* (they were there in the beginning). *Sa* (in the) initial meeting *I was there hindi ako personal na kasama* (I was not there personally [that is he was not a participant in the discussion]) but I was there as observer. I was not within the room *pero andun ako e* (but I was there). I think they had a meeting *sa* (at) . . . [he was trying to recall] let me see. *hindi sa FEBIAS ito eh* (it was not in FEBIAS), *baka sa* (it was probably in) Capitol City [Baptist Church].

24. **Question:** Ah ok. So that meeting that is written down by Avarell is the one already much later?

    Response: [looking at the list] *Kwan to mas later na* (this was much later). *Pero yung initial na meeting nila* (but the very first meeting that they had), *ang pinagpasiyahan nila diyan* (what they were discussing then), as I could remember is *una yung pangalan* (the first issue was the name). *Pangalawa, yung Securities and Exchange Commission* (the second issue was on the registering the council at the Securities and Exchange Commission). *Pero nagcommission sila ng* (but they already commissioned) a constuitutional convention chaired by Gadiel Isidro.

25. **Question:** That was in Sampaloc?
    Response: *Sa* (It was in the) Fellowship Center Church

26. **Question:** Right and that was from . . . I have based on an article, I came up with a timeline. *At yung nga ang problema ko* (and that is my problem), double checking the timeline, *parang iba iba ang infromation na nakukuha ko* (there are some inconsistencies with the information that I am getting). For example, the drafting of the Constitution was 23 November.
    Response: Somewhere here, 1964.

27. **Question:** *Tama po ito* (is this right)?
    Response: *Tama yung initial meeting nila, ay 1964* (this is correct; their initial meeting [with other churches who were not Fundamentalist Baptist] took place in 1964). *Pero sabi ko '62 pinaguusapan na ito* (but what I am saying is that as early as 1962, they were already talking about this [the possibility of a merger]). *Iyan lang di nila alam dahil ang talagang nagtulak nyan paradiyan para iorganize ng Philippine Council of Fundamental Churches* (the reason that they don't know about it [the meeting in 1962 was that it was just among fundamentalist Baptist], it was Pastor Ormeo, the person who really pushed the formation of the Philippine Council of Fundamental Churches is Pastor Ormeo). *Siya ang nag initiate ng meeting na yan* (he was the one who initiated the meeting). *Kasi nga ang kinikilala ng Gobyerno at that time is NCCP* (because the only protestant body that was recognized by the Philippine Government was the NCCP). *Masyadong hiwa-hiwalay* (the fundamentalist and the evangelicals were so fragmented at that time). *Hindi ko alam kung sino ang kumontak sa mga tao* (I don't know who called up the leaders of the other groups). *Pero I assume na yung secretary niya ng kumontak sa kanila para matupad yung meeting na iyon* (but I assume that it was his secretary who called them up so that the meeting could take place). So there was a meeting.

28. **Question:** That's the meeting that Magbanua remembers.
    Response: *Ito* (this one), *nandoon ako pero di ako kasama sa official* (I was there but I wasn't there officially). *Nanonood lang ako sa kanila at ang deliberation, matitindi ang deliberation* (I was only observing them and

the deliberations, they had intense deliberations). *Ang aking natandaan sa discussions nila is the need: "kailangan natin ng isang maiidentify yung Evangelical"* (what I remember the most in their discussion was the need, "we need to have one [council] that can be identified as truly evangelical"). *Ang laging binabanggit dito hindi* "fundamental" (what was repeatedly mentioned was not the word "fundamental"). *Kapag kay Ormeo, "Fundamental"* (when Ormeo speaks, he uses the word "fundamental"); *Calica, Tica, "Fundamental"* (when Calica or Tica speaks, they use the word "fundamental"). *Tapos kay Magbanua, Ruivivar, Evangelical naman* (But when Magbanua or Ruivivar speaks, they use the word "evangelical"). *Pero hindi muna ikinabit yung Evangelical* (but they didn't attach the word "evangelical" [in the name of the council] in the beginning).

29. **Question:** But at this time in '64, so the first meeting was in First Baptist Church?
    Response: Yes

30. **Question:** But I think this is '62 not '64?
    Response: *Hindi* (no). *Tama itong '64 na ito na andito na yung ibang leaders* (1964 is correct, this is the meeting with the other [denominational or non-fundamentalist Baptist] leaders). *Pero yung '62, sila sila lang yan* (but the 1962 [meeting] was just among themselves [the fundamentalist leaders]). *Parang ito yung mga officer ng ABCLVM* (This was among the officers of the ABCLVM [Association of Baptist Churches of Luzon, Visayas, and Mindanao]).

31. **Question:** Right. *Parang ito yung initial* (so this was the initial [meeting]) . . .
    Response: *Wala na ngang ABWE diyan eh* (ABWE was no longer represented in that meeting). *Kasi nag-separate ang ABCL at ABWE* (because ABCL and ABWE had separated from each other). *Ang ABCL, that time it was ABCL wala pa yung VM* (at that time, it was ABCL, the V and the M were not there yet). In 1962 *ang* (the) Association of Baptist Churches in Luzon, *ito ang mga leaders niyan* (these were its leaders).

32. **Question:** Ok. ABCL . . .
    Response: *Yung VM naidagdag na lang in 1963 siguro* (the VM was added probably in 1963 [I am not certain]).

33. **Question:** *Yung* VMF (the VMF)?
    Response: Visayas Mindanao Fellowship. Association of Baptist Churches in Luzon, Visayas, Mindanao.

34. **Question:** *Tapos* (then) there is that meeting. *Sabi nga ni Ptr. Magbanua, he remembers si* (Pastor Magbanua said that remembers) Charles Hufstetler.
    Response: *Meron pang isang amerikano dito eh* (there should be another American in this list).

35. **Question:** [was it] Frank Allen?
    Response: [yes] *Mayroon pang isang amerikano* (there is still one more American). *Tatlo ang natatandaan ko dito eh* (I remember that there were three of them in the meeting).

36. **Question:** *Hindi po si Dr Honeywell* (wasn't it Dr Honeywell)?
    Response: *Parang taga FEBC yun eh* (that person [Dr Honeywell] is from FEBC).

37. **Question:** *Si Spahr* (Was it Rev Spahr)?
    Response: *Yun Edwin Spahr sa* (Yes, its Edwin Spahr from) Grace Academy of Manila.

38. **Question:** He was there in the FEBIAS meeting?
    Response: Yes, *tatlo silang natatandaan ko na amerikano* (I remember that there were three Americans).

39. **Question:** And that was PCFC *na* (already)?
    Response: *Oo* (yes). *Doon nila inadopt yan ang* (that's when they adopted the name PCFC [Philippine Council of Fundamentalist Churches]).

40. **Question:** One of the things that I plan to do by next week is to go the SEC to just check . . .
    Response: *yung date at incorporator* ([check] the date and the persons who incorporated it). *Sino sino yung incorporators ng PCFC* (who were the incorporators of PCFC).

41. **Question:** Right. So [do] you remember that PCFC was incorporated under SEC?

    Response: Then there was a revision of that. *Sa aking pagkakatanda, pero dalawang . . .* (what I remember was that there were . . . [two other meetings]). *Kasi bago naincorporate yan* (because before it was incorporated), *yung another meeting sa* (there was another meeting in the) Conservative Baptist [probably Capitol City Baptist Church]. *doon yata ipinasok yung "E" Evangelical* (that was were the "E" for "Evangelical" was inserted [in the name]).

42. **Question:** "Evangelical" [Philippine Council of Fundamental Evangelical Churches]?

    Response: [yes] *At iyon ang nalagay sa* (and that was [the name] that was given to the) SEC. *Yung PCFC, parang hindi na incorporate yun* (I don't think that the PCFC was incorporated). *Pero tingnan mo rin kasi nung napagusapan ang final incorporation with the doctrines, 8 or 10 different major doctrines ang nailista nila* (Go ahead and check it, because I remember that when they were finalizing the process of incorporation, they already had 8 to 10 major doctrines listed). *Alam mo naman si* (you may know that) Gadiel Isidro he is theologian. *Very strict siya sa* (he was very strict when it came to) theology. *Nagkasundo sundo sila doon pero ang natatandaan kong pinagusapan na matagal e yung second coming: pretrib post trib ba* (they were able to agree in a lot of things, but I remember that one of the issues that took a lot of discussion was on the doctrine of the Second Coming: where you a Pre-Trib[ulationist] or where you a Post-Trib[ulationist])? *Eh may halo halo nun* (there were a lot of different opinions on the matter), *sabi niya* (he said), *parang si Fred na tumayo na huwag muna nating pagusapan yan* (I think it was Fred [Magbanua] who stood up and said that the discussion on the matter should be done later). *Ang pinakamahalaga* (what is important is that), we know that Jesus Christ will come again. *Yung second coming* (that was [the discussion] on the Second Coming). *So siguro yun ang nalagay sa* (so I think that it was included in the) doctrinal statement. We believe in the visible return of the Lord Jesus Christ.

43. **Question:** *Pero walang* (but there were no) specification?
    Response: *Walang specification kung pre trib o post-trib dahil nga sa binubuo pa* (there was no specification whether the [council upheld] that it was Pre-Trib or PostTrib since it was still being discussed). *Pero may nagsabi nga "pag pinagusapan natin, magkakahiwalay kaagad tayo"* (someone did say, "if we persist on talking about the issue, that we will part ways soon).

44. **Question:** *Ang sabi ni Dr Ruivivar* (Dr Ruivivar said [in an email]), he remembers that there were no Pentecostals in those early years.
    Response: *Wala* (there were none), *walang AG* (there was nobody from the AG [Assemblies of God]

45. **Question:** *Wala yung AG, Foursquare . . .* (so there were [no official representative] from the AG and the Foursquare Church)?
    Response: *pati si Ferrez* (Ferrez was not [in the official list of participants]).

46. **Question:** *Pero may sinabi siya* (but he [Dr Ruivivar] said that), there was one assembly . . . I don't know if you were there *na may nag speak na Pentecostal* (when a Pentecostal [pastor] spoke). And from that, *parang naging favourable at inimbitahan na nila . . .* (the Council members looked favourably upon them and invited them to [join the council]
    Response: *Dun na sa PCFEC* (in the time of the PCFEC), *sa pangalawang assembly sa* (in the second council held at the) Capitol City Baptist [Church] and that was the debate. *Kasi ayaw pumayag sina Ptr. Ormeo* (because Dr Ormeo would not agree to it [letting the Pentecostal pastor speak]). *Wala na ang kapatid ko in 1965 wala na siya eh* (my brother was no longer involved in 1965, he was no longer here [in the country]).

47. **Question:** [how about you,] Were you still attending around that time?
    Response: *Isa lang ang nadaluhan ko diyan* (I only attended one more [Assembly]). *Ang nadaluhan ko yung debate nila sa issue sa* (I attended the one where they had a debate on the issue of) Liberalism.

48. **Question:** *Ang nakausap ko si* (I was able to talk with) Dr Tano, he mentions another pastor, I forgot the name *or a teacher daw* (or he was probably a teacher). *Sabi nga nya* (he also said that), "One of the debates,

centered on whether the name 'fundamental evangelical' is redundant." *The argument nung person ay ung* (his main arugument is that) the term "fundamental" is a subset of evangelical, not the other way around. They said, "why should we put something like that?" They were arguing back and forth about it. *Si Dr Magalit naman* (Dr Magalit on the other hand), he remembers one meeting and it is in Caloocan Bible Church, *kung saan* (where) Ptr Isidro was the pastor of that church at that time. *Doon daw po mainit na yung usapan* (there was a heated discussion at that time). *Kasi* (because) they were really going back and forth, should the title be PCFEC or PCEC. *Pero the breaking point yata was in '74* (but the breaking point was really in 1974).

Response: Actually *nung* (by) '74 *yun na talaga wala si Ptr Ormeo* (Pastor Ormeo was already out [of the council]). *Kahit na wala na yung fundamental* (even when the name "fundamental" was taken out [of the council's name]), he was still a member of the board. *Hindi siya nagreresign* (he did not resign) but it was 1974 *yung kanilang assembly na nagresign si Ptr. Ormeo* (in their national assembly that Pastor Ormeo resigned) on the issue of Dr McIntire. *Kasi pinagusapan namin yan* (because we talked about that).

49. **Question:** *Yun pong, kasi nakausap ko si* (I was able to talk with) Pastor Capili, he remembers the meeting in '72 or '74, *pinulong daw sila ni* (there was a meeting led by) Pastor Ormeo and the discussion centered around shall we continue with PCEC or not? and then *sabi nga nya* (he said that), the term Fundamental was already dropped by that time. And I think *inadopt na yata PCEC na* (they were already using the name PCEC) by that time. Then they withdrew. One thing that confuses me, when did Pastor . . . [Ormeo resigned from PCEC] you said Ptr Ormeo continued as a member of the board *pero yung church niya was* (but his church was) the ABCLVM

Response: *ABCL pa din yun pero hindi na ganun kaactive* ([He was the leader of the] ABCL[VM] at that time, but they were not actively supporting [PCEC activities])

50. **Question:** [When] Did they pull out?

Response: After the 1974 meeting. *Dahil* [because] when they removed the word fundamental with finality, *parang si Magbanua ang* *tumayo* (it was probably Pastor Magbanua who stood up) in favour of [evangelicalism instead of fundamentalism], so *yun yon* (that was it). *Sa tono ng meeting na yon* (that was the tone of that meeting when) it was announced.

51. **Question:** That the issue has already been decided. And the decision was made by just Ptr. Ormeo or with Gavino?
    Response: *Wala si Gavino, pero hindi siya umattend kasi meron siyang pinagsalitaan* (Pastor Gavino wasn't able to attend since he had a speaking engagement elsewhere). So I was the one who represented the fundamentalist.

52. **Question:** Where was this meeting? In First Baptist Church?
    Response: No, *hindi naman malaking* (this was not a big) assembly. *Yung malaking assembly, parang isang, kasi meron yang rally every month* (they had meetings which were like rally each month). *Pero iyon* (but there it was), it was already announced that we are no longer members of the Philippine Council of Fundamental Evangelical Churches *kasi inalis yung* (because they had dropped the word) "fundamental." *Si Ptr. Raymundo yung mga matatapang na nagalit sa PCEC nun* (Pastor Raymundo was one of those strong-willed leaders who were offended by PCEC's action [of removing the word "fundamental"]). *"Bakit inalis?"* ([he asked], "why was it removed?"). *yung voice talagang* (his voice was really) sharp. *Ang problema, kaya hindi ako masyadong natigatig, parang ako nasa middle ground* (as it was, the reason why I was not greatly affected was that I held a middle ground). *Dahil graduate ako ng* (because I was a graduate of) FEBIAS *nagsasalita ako sa mga* (I often spoke in) evangelical churches. *Lahat ng denominational group, napagsalitaan ko* (I was able to speak in almost all of the different evangelical denominations). *Evangelistic, pati ABCOP, lalo na ang ABCOP* (among the evangelicals, including ABCCOP [Alliance Bible Christian Communities of the Philippines], especially ABCCOP). *Noong dati . . . Pinagsama ang FEGC tsaka OMF Churches sa Batangas, Laguna, Mindoro Marinduque, at Cavite* (it was formed when the churches established by the FEGC and OMF in Batangas, Laguna, Mindoro Marinduque, and Cavite were merged). *Ang nangyari dyan, pag may major evangelistic meeting ako ang speaker nila sa mga lugar na ito hanggang sa Mindoro hanggang sa Marinduque*

(it so happened that whenever they would have a major evangelistic meeting that they would ask me to speak in these areas from Mindoro down to Marinduque). I was the one who . . . As a matter of fact when I graduated from FEBIAS, I was invited to be the national evangelist of FEGC. In which [I declined] *hindi ko maiwanan yung church sa Tanay na bago pa lamang magsisimula* (I could not abandon the newly planted church in Tanay which was just starting). *Kaya I chose the small group na hindi ko alam kung bakit noon kaysa dito sa isang malaking grupo na malaki naman ang offer* (I didn't know why but I ended up choosing this smaller group instead of the bigger one which had better and bigger offer). But anyway, *yun ang nangyari doon* (that is what had happened). *Pero dito, maraming meeting siya na wala na ako* (but there were a lot of meetings that Pastor Ormeo had attended which I was no longer included). *Noong 1971, nagkaroon ng split ang Gavino tsaka Ormeo* (because in 1971, there was a schism between Gavino and Ormeo). *Ibig sabihin, humiwalay kami* (in other words, we had already separated from them already).

53. **Question:** That is representing ABCL?
Response: We went out of ABCL *at nagtayo kami ng* (and we started the) Baptist Intl Mission of the Philippines. *Kasi itong* (because this) BIMI *ay isang malaking organisasyon yan sa buong mundo na ang office sa* (was a bigger worldwide organization with its headquarters in) Chattanooga Tennessee. So he was the first missionary there. *Noong magkakaroon kami ng* (when we had our schism) . . . *may mga tsismis na kumalat na ina-undermine ni kuya Vino si Ptr. Ormeo* (there were rumors that my brother Pastor Gavino was trying to undermine Pastor Ormeo) which is not really true. *Ang kaso, nadala siya doon kasi mga young people naman, naging madikit sa amin* (sadly, he believe it since the young people were closer to us). *Dahil ako nga yung nasa youth eh natural lang na sa age group, yung mga anak niya nasa Doane sa Iloilo* (this was due to the fact that I was connected with the youth since I was closer to their age group, while Dr Ormeo's children [who could have established relationship with the youth] was still studying at the Doane [Baptist Bible Institute] in Iloilo). *So wala siyang anak dito kaya nandiyan ako para tumulong* (so he didn't have any children here, that is why I was there to help.).

And God knows *na hindi naming inundermine, wala kaming plano na gawin yun* (we had no plans or intention to undermine [Dr Ormeo's leadership]). But anyway, *nagkaroon ng final meeting noon* (we had our final meeting then). *May samaan ng loob at mga binitiwan si Ptr. Ormeo na hindi maganda* (there were hard feelings and some words that Pastor Ormeo said that were hurtful), *dahil siguro yung pressure na din ng tao so nag split kami ng 1971 pero hindi pa rin naman ako umaalis sa ABCL* (it was probably the pressure from the insinuations of other people that we separated from them in 1971 but we never really walked out of the ABCL). In other words *meron pa akong ibang churches na pinagsasalitaan diyan at di naman nagagalit si Ptr. Ormeo* (I still spoke in some of the churches in ABCL and I never heard that Pastor Ormeo resented it). *Kasi Ninong ko yun eh, magkaibigan pa rin kami* (he was my wedding sponsor and we were still friends). *Si Loida kaibigan ni Mrs Tica* (his daughter Loida is still a friend of Mrs Tica). *Nakakapunta pa din ako sa First Baptist Church sa mga meetings nila nandun ako* (I would even attend some of the meetings that they held at the First Baptist Church [of Manila]). *Sa isang meeting nga nila sa isang youth rally, may announcer* (there was even a youth rally, where there was an announcer). *Pero yung meeting na sinasabi ni Ptr. Capili wala ako doon 1974 na yon* (but I was not in the meeting in 1974 that Pastor Capili mentioned).

54. **Question:** So by that time, *naghiwalay na kayo noon* (you had separated from each other)?
    Response: *Nabalitaan na lang naming na yung gulo na dahil diyan sa PCFEC na yan tsaka yung pagiging Liberal, sabi ni Ptr. Ormeo* (we later heard from Pastor Ormeo what had happened to the debacle in PCFEC and its direction towards becoming liberal). *Later on yun naman ang . . . sa mga usapan noon magiging member ito ng isang* (later, this is what we had discussed about PCEC, how it became a member of an) evangelical fellowship which is ecumenical. *Ang isyu nya talaga is ecumenism eh, hindi doktrina* (the issue was really about ecumenism not doctrines). *Kundi yung ecumenical relationship ng evangelical sa mga* (how the evangelicals could have ecumenical relationships with) watered down groups. *Hanggang sa 1978* (even until 1978), *panahon ng Jun Vencer yun e nang maging member ng* World Evangelical Fellowship [WEF]

ang PCEC (during the time of Jun Vencer, [the fundamentalists did not approve of PCEC] becoming a member of the WEF.

55. **Question:** Someone mentioned, I think I do not want to be misquoted *pero* (but) it was either Magbanua or Magalit. They were saying how Ptr. Ormeo . . . one of his motivations is to see whether some of these churches could be affiliated with ICCC.
Response: That is really true. *Napaguusapan naming yun* (we had talked about it). *Ang gusto nya talaga* (what he really wanted was), *kung pwede lang itong PCFEC or PCFC madala as member ng* (if it was possible for PCFEC or the PCFC to become a member of) ICCC.

56. **Question:** But who were opposing it? *sila Magbanua* [was it Magbanua and his group]?
Response: *Sila* (It was) Gadiel Isidro, Magbanua. *Si Ruvivar although opposed siya don, hindi ganon ka strong ang voice niya compared dito sa dalawa* (Although he opposed it, Ruivivar wasn't as passionate as the other two). *Pero sabi nila ang katwiran nila dyan bakit . . .* (but they said that their reason was why . . . [should we join the ICCC]) *Eh masyadong* (it was extremely) hyper-fundamentalist group and they were attacking Billy Graham left and right. *Nag-iisue ng statement . . . FEBIAS is a part bagamat hindi ito member ng PCFC perse* (although FEBIAS was not a part of PCFC, they were issuing statements against its involvement with the council [since they considered FEBIAS's non-denominationalism as another form of ecumenism]). *Mga individual lang ang naging member niyan pero as a group noong PCEC na saka naging member ang FEBIAS* (at first, it was just individuals who were connected with FEBIAS who had joined the PCEC but later when the PCEC was established, FEBIAS joined as an institution).

57. **Question:** Going back to the '62 meeting, you said *kanina* (a while ago) that one of the issues is that the PCFC as it was being formed or discussed, *sila* (the group of) Ptr. Ormeo, Ptr. Gavino, as they were talking about this you said *na inaano nila yung* (that they were talking about the) ecumenical movement that was happening and the voice of Christians that are not being heard. Was there any doctrinal issue that are very pertinent to them as you remember which caused to be the

dividing line? I know you said that you were not connected to NCCP at all obviously. But were there doctrinal issues that are clearly stated *kaya hindi magsasama yung dalawa* (that kept the two groups apart)?

Response: *Ang issue diyan ay yung Bible eh* (one of the issues pertained to the Bible). Bibliology *ang issue* (was the issue). *Kasi sa* NCCP nandiyan sina Nacpil (because Nacpil was a member of the NCCP), *ewan ko lang kung nagbago ng view si Bishop Nacpil* (I don't know if Bishop Nacpil has changed his view [on the Bible]). *Tapos andiyan din yung isang namatay na from ECP ang kanilang view diyan ay parang* (and there was that person who was from the Episcopalian Church of the Philippines that recently died who exemplified their doctrinal stance as similar to the) NeoOrthdoxy by Karl Barth. *Tsaka yung question ng verbal plenary of inspiration. So ayun talaga ang basic principle* (and the question regading the doctrine of Verbal Plenary inspiration, that was another basic principle [that they disagreed upon]).

58. **Question:** I remember *nga* (too) when I was a young Christian, one of the discussion was: *kapag kausap mo ang UCCP* (when you talked with a UCCP*), sa kanila* (for them), *sa atin kasi* (for us) the Bible is the Word of God, *sa kanila* (for them) the Bible contains the word of God.
Response: the Bible is the Word of God *depende* (depending on certain circumstances). *Para kumbaga sa layman language, depende* (its like in their layman's language, it depends). *Pero sa atin walang depende* (but for us, there are no conditions).

59. **Question:** *Sa kanila, meron pa ngang isa eh* (there is another way that they see it). *Parang* (it's like) it's like a fruit you have to dig deep until you find the seed. The seed then is the word of God. But then, you don't get it as a seed *lang* (only), you get it as a fruit. *Yun yung point nya in arguing kaya may error sa Bible* (that's their main point, that there are errors in the Bible).
Response: *Tsaka yung* (another point is the) issue of separation

60. **Question:** Issue with?
Response: with the world. *Kasi ang view ng ABCL, parang ABWE galing sa ABWE yan eh* (The view [theological, etc] of ABCL is similar to the

ABWE because we came from the ABWE). *Mga 19 . . .* ([ABWE has been here] since 19 . . .).

61. **Question:** They were here from 1930s
    Response: *Si Ptr Ormeo kasi* (it is because of Pastor Ormeo), he was a very staunch active leader *ng* (of) ABWE *na naging* (that became) PABWE, *dati pang World evangelism tapos naging pang Pilipinas* (it used to be for world evangelism, now it has its own national body). *At siya yung leader* (and Dr Ormeo was its leader). *Tiga-Bethel Baptist siya from Bukidnon* (he was from the Bethel Baptist Church in Bukidnon). He was called in 1957 when he was called to pastor the First Baptist Church which is the main church *ng* (of the) ABWE *dito sa* (here in) Manila

62. **Question:** *Kaya talagang* (so that is why) even from the beginning *very strong talaga* ([you had] a very strong stand [on matters regarding doctrine and practice]).
    Response: Very strong [indeed]. *Talagang yung separation stance against the world like smoking and drinking and dancing and the worldly music* (we have a very strong separation stand against the world like in smoking, drinking, dancing, and worldly music). *Yun yung issue ng separation yan ay clearly defined* (that is the main issue of separation which we have clearly defined). And then there was the question about the blood of Christ. *Pero hindi masyadong nakalutang* (but it is not much emphasized). *Ang nakalutang talaga* (the one that is much talked about) is the verbal plenary of the Bible *at yung separation* (and regarding separation).
    [there were some discussions on the differences among the churches involved within the NCCP]

63. **Question:** Between '64 and '71 do you recall [of] any other meetings or events that took place between fundamentals and the PCEC people?
    Response: *well sa fundamental, sa PCEC wala na eh* (there were still meetings among the fundamentalists but between the fundamentalist and the people of PCEC, there was none). *Maski nung nag mi meeting sila there were meetings na hindi na dumadalo si Ptr. Ormeo* (Pastor Ormeo no longer attended the meetings held by the PCEC leaders) although he was still considered as member of the board.

64. **Question:** *Parang nag wi-withdraw na siya unti unti* (so was he slowly withdrawing himself from the group)?
Response: *Physically withdrawing ng siya* (he was withdrawing physically) *at pumutok nga iyan noong kay McIntire na hindi maayos yung trato sa kanya sa Lausanne* (and [he finally left] when the issue of the shabby treatment of McIntire took place in Lausanne). *Kung saan talagang siya ay inapi* (where he [McIntire] was really mistreated there). *Inapi yung mama doon* (the man was mistreated). *nakita ko naman kung paano* (I saw how it was done). *andun ako eh* (I was personally there). *Ang totoo may rally nagjoin ako sa kanya pero hindi sa front* (and the truth is that I joined their rally against the Lausanne [although I was an official delegate] but I stood at the back). *Sabi nga nitong sina si Valmike, "bakit nandiyan ka"* (the late Valmike [Apuzen] asked me, "why are you joining them")? *Pero ibig sabihin non walang major meetings non* (but this means that there were no longer major meetings [that discussed the issues between the evangelicals and the fundamentalist]). *Ang huling huli, noong alisin yung word na fundamental* (the final straw was when they removed the word "Fundamental" [in the council's name]). *Nagkaroon ng mainit na mainit na debate diyan, nagcause ang ABCL na ma-solidify* (this resulted in a very heated debate which caused the ABCL to solidify). *Pero kami naman* (but as for us), *kami ay nag-move out from ABCL at nagtayo ng BIMI pero sa dulo niyan, hindi na kami naging very close ni Ptr. Ormeo* (we moved out of ABCL and formed the BIMI and in the end, we were no longer close to Pastor Ormeo). *Tuwing pupunta ako doon, sa lahat ng fundamentalist, ako ang pinagkalooban ng Panginoon ng laya na tumayo in between* (whenever I attended the meetings, among the fundamentalist, God has given me the freedom to stand in the middle). *Andito yung ABCL at BIMI at ako ang nasa gitna* (the ABCL will be in one end while the other end will be occupied by BIMI, and I will be in the middle). *Yung mga leaders hindi, pero yung mga churches nagkakaroon ng fellowship like basketball sa ibang lugar* (while the leaders avoided each other, among the churches, there would still be basketball games between the churches). *Diyan sa Rizal* (There in Rizal) we started the eastern Rizal Baptist Association *sama sama ang ABCL at BIMI churches doon* (the churches from the ABCL and the

BIMI were together) *Tapos yung PCEC tapos itong mga fundamentalist* (and between the PCEC and the fundamentalist), I was in the middle not because I am a compromiser or what. but because we belong to one body. *Tsaka mga kaibigan ko andun eh* (and because I had friends on both sides). I was invited by Ef Tendero to join the PCEC. *Pero sabi ko, "kapatid marami akong makakaaway pag ako nasama sa PCEC"* (but I said, "brother, you know that I will have much opposition if I joined PCEC"). *andiyan naman ako eh* (but I am there with you). Technically I was there. A Simple Prayer Life Seminar was established in 1982 *at ako ang chairman nun so technically andun naman ako* (and I served as its chairman so technically I was there [and part of PCEC]). *Pero yung maging member ka hindi magiging maganda kasi VP ako sa malaking body ng Bible Bap* (but to become an official member of PCEC would not be good since I am the Vice President of one of the largest Bible Baptist churches in the country). *So wala nang masyadong meeting* (so there were no more meetings afterwards). *Ang isa sa aking heartaches diyan na* (one of the heartaches that I had with what happened) I feel and I said I told the fundamental group *nasabi ko* (I said to them) let us be very conscious of the fact that the Holy Spirit might be departing from our group. *Ang mga* (as for the) fundamentalist, *nandiyan na tayo* (we are already there) very strong in the tradition of the doctrine and so forth but our churches are not growing. And one of the greatest problem of the lack of growth is the church. *Wala naman tayong problema sa kulto, katoliko* (we have no problems dealing with the cults or the Roman Catholics). *Ang problema natin kapag lumalaki, nag aaway yan may split* (our problem is when we become big, we start fighting among each other which results in a split). *Kaya nasasaktan ang Panginoong Diyos* (and God is hurt as a result). *Tingnan niyo ang mga* (look at the) evangelical *at* (and the) charismatic they are the biggest church *diyan nagpupunta ang mga tao hindi dahil sa tama yan* (people go to these churches, not because they are right) but because they saw the love. *Sa atin* (as for us), *sa ating pagiging fundamentalist yung ating doktrina, tama* (in our being fundamentalist, our doctrines are correct). *Pero hindi ma feel ng general community ang pagmamahal natin* (but the general community do not feel the love that we have with each other). *Andun tayo nakatago sa ating mga* (there we are, hiding in our) comfort zones *sa ating mga paniniwala* ([hiding] behind our beliefs), *hindi progresibo ang utak natin* (but our minds are not progressive). As we open our eyes, there is a little bit of success *dahil sina Abante, close na close yan malign Baptist yan eh* (because of people like Abante, who is a very conservative Baptist and who have been maligned). *Ngayong kung magsalita sila, don't ever think na tayo lang ang ligtas* (now they are engaging themselves in dialogue, don't ever think that we are the only ones who are saved). Outside the fundamental Baptist *may mga iba pang ligtas* (there are others who are also saved/redeemed). *May mas ligtas pa nga sa atin eh* (there are those who even look and act more redeemed than us). *Yung ang nangyari hanggang sa itatag ang ABC ang* (that has been the case until the ABC had been established, the ABC is the) Alliance Baptist Council *so lahat ng Baptist kasama diyan* (so that all the Baptist could be together in that group). Yan naman ay (that is the) loose association *ng* (of) ABC

[there was further discussion on the current improbability of a union between the fundamentalists and the evangelicals at this time, among the reasons given is their own American supporters and affiliations, and other issues]

END

APPENDIX H

Interview with Ebenezer Nacita

(Interview took place at First Baptist Church of Manila, Quezon City, 22 April 2013.)

1. **Question:** Can you tell about his background? Hometown, family? Who were the first Christians in his family? Any Christian influence that led him to the Lord?
   Response: Dr Ormeo was born in 1913 and died in 2005. Home town: Kabankalan, Negros Occidental. Educational or ministry training: Doane Evangelistic Institute (DEI, later renamed Doane Baptist Bible Institute) in Iloilo operating under the ABWE since 1927–28 had graduates who were pastoring in Negros Occidental. ABWE was formerly called the Association of Baptists for Evangelism in the Orient (ABEO); the name change took place after World War 2. Pastor Antonio Ormeo got saved and studied in Doane to become a pastor. The whole family came to know Christ as savior together in the late 1920s.

2. **Question:** How did he come to know the savior? Who shared the gospel? Any details?
   Response: He was saved through the ministry of Kabankalan Baptist Church under Pastor Epifanio de la Pena. This church had contributed to the growth of the immediate family and many relatives in the area.

3. **Question:** Where did he get his ministry training?
   Response: In 1930, Rev Ormeo completed his ministry education from Doane Evangelistic Institute in Iloilo City.

4. **Question:** What was Rev Ormeo's ministry like before he became the pastor of the First Baptist Church of Manila (FBCM)?
   Response: Before he became the pastor of FBCM, he was the Pastor of Bethel Baptist Church in Bukidnon. After he completed his studies in the DEI, he became the pastor at Pontevedra since Pastor De La Pena was the pastor of the church in Kabankalan. He joined the guerilla movement during the war and also continued ministering despite the conflict. As the Baptist pastors fled to the different provinces during the war, they began to minister to these areas. After the war, these converts acknowledged these pastors and formed the Baptist churches all over the country. Wherever you "landed" during the war, that is where you pastured. After the war, with the help of ABWE missionaries, the Baptist began to enter territories that were assigned to other denominations and groups by the Comity Agreement. As part of their tradition, the Baptist pastors were aggressive in evangelism and church planting.

5. **Question:** How did he meet Dr McIntire?
   Response: He probably met Dr McIntire during his involvement with ABWE, since ABWE, the General Association of Regular Baptist Churches (GARBC), and the Bob Jones University were connected to McIntire's ICCC. Their friendship and working relationship started at the Far Eastern Council of Christian Churches (FECCC) in 1951 where Rev Ormeo served as the first President of FECCC.

6. **Question:** What was the relationship like?
   Response: Dr McIntire thought highly of Rev Ormeo and saw him as one of the key leaders of fundamentalism in the Philippines through the AFBCP (Association of Fundamentalist Baptist Churches in the Philippines). McIntire was impressed because of his knowledge of Fundamentalist Baptist distinctive, of missions, of his perception on indigenous policies, of the economy of the church, and of his commitment to become financially independent. On the issue of financial independence, Rev Ormeo was convinced that local churches should no longer depend on foreign aid and funding, instead the Filipino churches should depend on their own collections through the tithes and offerings. He launched a campaign within the AFBCP on this topic of financial independence and indigenization. His efforts and perspectives

were not welcomed; in fact, these issues were also raised against him in the biennial conference in 1965. When Ormeo left the AFBCP, he continued this policy of financial independence in the Association of Baptist Churches in Luzon, Visayas, and Mindanao (ABCLVM). In fact, everything that the First Baptist Church of Manila (FBCM) owns is through local funding – tithes and offerings. Even after Rev Ormeo's break with the AFBCP, McIntire continued to work with him. In fact, Rev Ormeo and pastors from the ABCLVM were invited as official delegates to the international conferences sponsored by ICCC since Dr McIntire did not know the new leaders of AFBCP. This continued for several years which caused further tension until this was resolved in 1979 when the ABCLVM became a member of ICCC through my [Rev Ebenezer Nacita] leadership and initiative.

7. **Question:** How about their convictions? Did they fully agree?
   Response: In the fundamentals of the faith and the practice of Biblical Separation from worldliness and Liberalism/Apostasy, Yes. In church government and other issues on Baptism and the Lords Supper, No. Dr McIntire was Presbyterian.

8. **Question:** What led to the formation of the PCFC? Who came up with the concept?
   Response: In the biennial conference in Kabankalan, Negros Occidental in 1965, Rev Ormeo (First Baptist Church of Manila) and two other pastors (Rev Leo Calica of the Fellowship Center Church in Sampaloc, Manila and Rev Gavino Tica of the Mandaluyong Baptist Church) were charged with violating the separation stand of the AFBCP. The issue of separation became a major issue in the early 1960s. There were several issues raised in this meeting. One of these was FBCM's involvement in a Sunrise Easter Resurrection Sunday celebration sponsored by the Far East Broadcasting Company (FEBC). In their defense, it must be noted that Rev Ormeo merely attended since he was invited to the said celebration and it was just an annual event not a regular involvement or membership. Besides, their attendance was important since they represented the fundamentalist Baptist in this important Christian celebration. Another issue raised was FBCM's involvement with the Billy Graham Crusade in the Philippines in March 1963. In their

defense, those who got involved with the Crusade were not official church delegates nor representatives sent by FBCM to the event. What happened was that the coordinators of this event had broadcast on FEBC for individuals to join a 1,000 voice choir for the Crusade in Manila. Several members went and wrote down their names, church-affiliation, and pastor's name. When the list was published, Pastor Ormeo and the FBCM was listed as one of the participating churches to the Billy Graham Crusade. It should be noted that these individuals were not applying for membership to the Billy Graham Crusade but merely volunteers to the said event. Despite efforts to explain their involvement, the three pastors and their churches were expelled from the AFBCP during the AFBCP conference in Kabankalan, Negros Occidental in 1965. More than forty Baptist churches from Luzon, Visayas, and Mindanao disagreed with this decision of the AFBCP. They pulled out of the conference along with the expelled pastors and met in Pontevedra, Negros Occidental where they discussed their next option, extending their stay for two more days. At end of this impromptu conference, they had formed the ABCLVM from among the churches that sided with the three pastors. By the time that they had returned to Manila, they had already formed their organizational setup. The ABCLVM became independent from the AFBCP as a separate fundamental Baptist movement which were spearheaded by Pastor Ormeo of the FBCM. The meeting in 1965 between Ormeo, Calica, Tica, Alesna, and Apoong were Rev Ormeo's effort to prevent further schism among those who left the AFBCP. In fact, Rev Apoong had started a totally independent Baptist church in Pangasinan and the Tica brothers (Gavino and Pio) had started their own group. Thus, PCFC was an effort by Rev Ormeo to keep these churches together and maintain their relationship with the ICCC. The council that was in the minds of the Pastor Ormeo and the ABCLVM leaders was to form the Philippine Council of Fundamental Christian Churches (PCFCC). It was their intention to affiliate this council with the ICCC. Pastor Ormeo was already a member of the executive committee of the ICCC since 1956. In fact he was the first President of the Far Eastern Council of Christian Churches (FECCC) when it was organized here in First Baptist Church of Manila that year. At that time,

FBCM was still a member of the Association of Fundamental Baptist Churches in the Philippines. In 1965, the ABCLVM was organized as a separate Fundamental Baptist Association which became a constituent member of both the ICCC and the FECCC. Some time in 1971, several Pastors and leaders of the ABCLVM churches planned to organize the Philippine Council of Christian Churches to affiliate it with the FECCC and the ICCC. At the time of organization the original officers who were mostly from the Fundamentalist movement started to open the application for membership to other churches and associations. Some CBAP, FEBC, Baptist General Conference etc. joined. As the group continued to accept membership, controversy over the issue of Biblical separation grew. The Fundamental Baptist group (ABCLVM) led by Pastor Ormeo decided to withdraw. With Pastor Ormeo's groups together with some original officers out, a new set of officers were elected and the council renamed to PCEC.

9. **Question:** What was Rev Ormeo's relationship to CBAP? FEBC? FEBIAS? Etc.?
   Response: None. They came later when PCFC was expanded to include these groups and the council was changed from PCFC to PCFEC (Philippine Council of Fundamentalist and Evangelical Churches).

10. **Question:** How long did he remain connected to the council?
    Response: Right after the withdrawal, Pastor Ormeo's group terminated their involvement with the PCEC.

11. **Question:** Any circumstances that you know that led to the break-up with the council? Details? Dates? Was the break-away abrupt?
    Response: When churches and pastors who were in the neo-evangelical and ecumenical circles joined, the fundamental/separatist group (Ormeo's) broke away quite abruptly. Nothing heard about problems that followed.

12. **Question:** What did Rev Ormeo do after PCFC? Did he form other groups beyond ABCLVM? Was there any effort to form other councils? NONE.
    Response: As far as the relationship of Rev Ormeo and the leaders of the AFBCP, from 1965 to 1976, the schisms and the disagreement

between the AFBCP and the ABCLVM were intense. At times, the disagreement was so sharp that for a time, these former colleagues and friends did not talk to each other. In fact, when Nacita became part of the FBCM in 1973, he tried to reconcile both parties but it would take several years before both parties were able to reconcile in 1997 in a conference in Bukidnon.

13. **Question:** You mentioned that there has been some continuing controversy and criticism to Rev Ormeo's involvement with PCFC/PCEC. Can you describe them in detail?
    Response: Other Fundamental separatist groups use this unfortunate event – Organizing the PCFC which became the PCEC after he left, to criticize Pastor Ormeo as the organizer of the PCEC. The PCEC did not continue because of issues on Biblical separation questioned by other member churches and leaders. As far as the issue of the stand for Biblical separation, from 1961 to 1965 the issue flared up and was never resolved by ABWE. This doctrine of separation was not clearly taught by the American Missionaries of ABWE. Thus, it was left to the locals to determine what exactly the doctrine entails. They failed to give a strong persuasion to support this doctrine. There were other issues such as social, charismatic movement, and ecumenism. But the main issue in the 1960s was the issue of separation. It became such a big issue that several churches were expelled as a result of this stand. Among the first that were expelled was Rev Ormeo and the two other pastors. But they could not sustain their accusation since the three pastors continued to practice the doctrine of separation. In the 1970s, another issue that was added to the controversies was the use of the King James Bible. This was a major issue among the churches in the ABCLVM. The issue was brought by the Trinitarian Bible Society that flooded the FBCM with the materials that defended the KJV over the modern versions. So the issues now were the following: indigenization, foreign aid, associational control, anti-charismatic, anti-ecumenism, and anti-modern version. As far as the issue of associational control, the ABCLVM was against this and maintained that each local church was free to decide for itself and not control by the denomination. So these issues were never resolved and in some places continues. To clarify, we do not insist that the only

version used should be the KJV but it is our preference. There are some efforts to come up with a new and reliable translation based on the Greek text but its initial enthusiasm has waned as a result of lack of funding and manpower for the work of translation.

14. **Question:** You mentioned that AFBCP was formed in 1948 as a result of the efforts of ABWE + BBSI + DBBI, can you give some details as to the circumstances of this merger? Who led the initiative? What was its purpose? What is its current conditions? Was Rev Ormeo involved in AFBCP?
    Response: I have already explained this in detail in my History of the ABCLVM and FBCM. Please review it.

15. **Question:** Was the AFBCP a response to the formation of UCCP in 1948? If so, what was its purpose?
    Response: No. The AFBCP was formed as the umbrella organization to the regional associations (Northern Luzon, Central Luzon, Southern Tagalog, Palawan, Visayas, Bukindon, Davao) forms out of the churches pioneered by the Graduates of the BBS&I, Doane Evangelistic Institute, Mindanao Baptist Seminary. The organization the World Council of Churches (WCC) in 1948 and the ICCC a month earlier, in Amsterdam, the Netherland was more or less a mutual response that these two world religious bodies made with their own concerns and priorities. Both have their own representation here in the Philippines.

16. **Question:** FECCC was formed in 1951 (1956), can you give the details of this council? Who led the initiative? What was its purpose? Was it a response to any specific need of Christianity in the Phils., in Asia, etc.?
    Response: 1956 was its formation. Biblical separation from Apostasy was the concern – same as that of the ICCC.

17. **Question:** FCCC (1951) was definitely ahead of NCCP (1960's) and PCFC (PCCC – 1971) (1963?), so why was there a need to form the PCFC-(PCCC)?
    Response: The FCCC is Asian Region including Japan, Australia, China and Korea, Philippines etc. PCCC is Philippines. The AFBCP at that time was no longer active with the ICCC. Also because Pastor Ormeo and the ABCLVM broke fellowship with the AFBCP. A new

representation with the FCCC and ICCC was thought of to be more practicable and necessary. But it did not come true.

18. **Question:** What is the current condition of FECCC? What was its relationship with ICCC?
    Response: The present situation of the ICCC and FECCC are no longer known to me. FBCM and I are no longer actively involved with both.

19. **Question:** Who were the key leaders of the AFBCP during the 1960s?
    Response: Rev Ormeo was just among the many leaders of AFBCP, which represented more than 2,000 fundamentalist Baptist churches in the Philippines. As I recall, the following were the leaders of AFBCP in 1950s and 1960s Luis and Zacharias Cometa, Alesna, Manuel Lunes (or Mariano Leones?), the American missionaries of ABWE, Leo Calica, Mandoriao, Gavino Tica, Antonio Ormeo. These were the leaders of the Fundamentalist Churches in the Philippines who were very strong in their separation stand. They would never seek to fellowship with those that they consider as compromisers. You can also include the faculty of the Fundamentalist seminaries as being key influencers as well.

20. **Question:** You mentioned the split between VFFBC which formed the AGC, what is the doctrinal stance of AGC? Can you give some more details of the schism? Does AGC still exist?
    Response: It is in the write up. The AGC was only an accredited foreign mission society in the ICCC. I don't know its present status.

21. **Question:** You mentioned that ABCLVM was the result of the sympathy of several churches to the expulsion of Rev Ormeo, Rev Calica, and Rev Tica.; can you give some details as to why they were voted out? It has been mentioned that it was connected to a "Billy Graham Crusade"?
    Response: Its explained in the history. It is explained in my write up.

22. **Question:** Was the formation of ABCLVM before, during, or after Rev Ormeo's involvement with PCFC?
    Response: 1965 was way before the PCCCC 1971

23. **Question:** It has been mentioned in Dr Aragon's account of the Formation of PCEC that Rev Ormeo officially left PCEC in 1974; that he had continued to serve as a member of PCEC's board and that

the ABCLVM was affiliated to PCEC until their departure after the Lausanne conference. What are you thoughts on this matter?
Response: None . . . I came to FBCM in June 1973 and I know Pastor Ormeo was no longer involved with the PCEC. You may have to look at other sources. I would know since he would have sent me or one of the pastors here as his representative since he was engaged with the problems of FBCM with regards to the property in Padre Faura. If Rev Ormeo was no longer involved prior to 1974, is it possible that it was another group that was formerly identified with ABCLVM that continued to be a member of PCEC? For example, you mentioned that the Tica brothers had started their own group which was connected but semi-independent with ABCLVM, is it possible that they were the ones being referred to by Dr Aragon's book. It is possible. The Ticas had pulled out of ABCLVM around 1972. The Tica's had affiliated themselves with the BIMI, and around twenty churches from Baras, Teresa to the south of Manila had joined them and separated from Rev Ormeo to form their own group. You can expect that since they have pulled out of our group that they would probably continued with their affiliation with PCEC. I think that Pastor Ormeo had pulled out of PCEC by 1972 the year that I married his daughter, Loida. Although I do recall there were meetings in 1972 where they continued to discuss the issues pertaining to PCEC. But by the time that I joined the FBCM in 1973, I do not recall any discussions, meetings, or anything that suggested that Rev Ormeo continued to be interested and involved with PCEC. In 1973 the FBCM was evicted from Padre Faura, Rev Ormeo was so busy trying to rehabilitate the FBCM in its new location here in Project 6, QC. He had no time to deal with other issues. I joined the FBCM and left AFBCP out of compassion and the burden to help them with their crisis. The ABCLVM would not be connected at all to PCEC, especially when the Baptist Conference of the Philippine in Cebu, Swedish Baptist, Back to the Bible, FEBIAS, and the groups of Ruivivar. The separation lines were drawn. It maybe possible that it could have been the Ticas, definitely not Rev Leo Calica since he had left for the US in 1969. When I became the pastor of the Fellowship Center Church (FCC) in 1973, I do not recall any meetings or any

contact with the PCEC people or churches. Although I do recall that when I was still courting Loida around 1971 that PCEC had meetings in the Fellowship Center Church. When I became the pastor of FCC in 1973, Pastor Macasiano (FCC's former pastor) left the church and joined the Back to the Bible where he was involved in the Back to the Bible Broadcast in FEBC. However, when I left FCC, Pastor Macasiano returned to the church and it is possible that he and the church would continue to relate with PCEC.

END

APPENDIX I

Correspondence with Faustino Ruivivar, Jr (6 June 2010)

From: fruivivarjr@aol.com
Sent: Sunday, June 06, 2010 4:26:29 AM
To: rg1965@msn.com

Dear Dr Go,

Thanks for your e-mail. I will try to answer all your questions as I have opportunity. For now I would like to make a few corrections about the names of people who attended the first assembly of PCEC. I am positive the following people were **not** among the convenors of the first PCEC assembly:

Florentino de Jesus Sr. He was in Mindanao; I did not meet him until a few years later, after we invited him to be PCEC's first "executive director."

Eli Javier and Don McGregor. There were no Pentecostals present. It was I who suggested, later, that we invite Pentecostals to participate in PCEC.

Nene Ramientos, Edwin Spahr, Rudolfo Parreno were **never** involved with PCEC. Roger Baldemor was a good friend of mine. I don't recall seeing him at the first assembly.

Antonio Ormeo was the convenor of the first assembly (which was called the Philippine Council of Fundamental Churches). At the next assembly, we voted to change the name to Phil. Council of Fundamental Evangelical Churches. The name lasted one year; at a subsequent assembly we voted to change the name to Philippine Council of Evangelical Churches. Rev Ormeo and his small denomination eventually left PCEC and formed their own "international council" affiliated with Carl McIntire. I don't know if *that* council really got established.

Averell Aragon's informants were misinformed. I was heavily involved in PCFC/PCFEC/PCEC from the outset. I was always on the board (until 1986), served as secretary for several years, and president/chairman for 7 years (1973 to 1980). Jun Vencer, when he was "general secretary" recommended that the title of president be removed. I remember **joking** to Rev Ernie Lagasca (another good friend), who replaced me after I resigned, that I was no longer interested in the position because of the loss of the title "president."

This will do for now.

I think your project is noteworthy. I wish you great success with your dissertation.

Your brother in Christ,

Faustino Ruivivar Jr.

-----Original Message-----
From: Raymond Go <rg1965@msn.com>
To: fruivivarjr@aol.com
Sent: Fri, Jun 4, 2010 10:12 pm
Subject: (no subject)

Dear Dr. Faustino,

Thank you so much for your willingness to help me at this time. I got your email address from Ptr Leandro Danganan of Caloocan Bible Church. As he may have mentioned to you, my name is Raymundo Go and i am a full time faculty member of the International Graduate School of Leadership (www.glg-igsl.org). i am presently doing some research for materials for a potential doctoral dissertation on evangelical christianity in the Philippines. You name was mentioned as part of those who met in 1964 at the first meeting on the formation of the PCEC. i was wondering if you could help me get some more information that i could use. i have written down some questions below. please feel free to change the questions or add info as you see fit. i have also enclosed the article written by Averell Aragon on PCEC as a reference point.

i know that i am asking a lot with your busy schedule (as Ptr Leandro warned me) so i would understand if you would not be able to give as much information on the matter. however, my desire in writing this dissertation is to put together a cohesive account of our history and to have it in written form so that the future generation of Filipino christians can read, study and appreciate our history. thank you so much and i look forward to hearing from you.

God bless po,

Ptr. Raymond Go

Information that I need:
1. can you describe (give a historical background) evangelical Christianity in the late 1950's and 1960's?
2. How did you become a Christian? Where were you trained? Religious and Theological training/education. more for background and connections.
3. What is your connection with the Convenors of PCEC? (see the list below and the enclosed pdf file) friends? Ministry partners? Etc.
4. Why were you chosen to be the representative of Every Home Crusade? or was it that you were personally invited and that it was incidental that you were with Every Home Crusade at that time?
5. Why did they (the convenors) initially decide to form the PCEC instead of joining the NCCP?
6. How was the relationship between the evangelicals and NCCP (or PFCC) back then? Where they trying to recruit the evangelicals to join the PFCC? what was their prevailing attitude towards evangelicals back then?
7. Did you and your organization readily join PCEC? Were there some hesitation? Especially with some of the more Fundamental Baptist members.

8. Are there other issues that were critical that kept you from joining the NCCP?
9. do you anything that you can add (details or other information) that was not mentioned in Aragon's article?

The following are the names of the convenors of PCEC as provided by Aragon's article:

Gadiel T. Isidro, pastor of the Caloocan Bible Church;
Faustino Ruivivar, Jr., of the Every Home Crusade;
Florentino de Jesus, Sr., of the Christian and Missionary Alliance Churches of the Philippines (CAMACOP);
Eleazar (Eli) Javier of the Assemblies of God;
Eustaquio (Nene) Ramientos, pastor of Faith Bible Church (UCCP);
Greg Tingson, founder and honorary pastor of Faith (Convention) Baptist Church;
Frederico (Fred) Magbanua of Far East Broadcasting Corp. and Capitol City Baptist Church;
Franklin W. Allen of the Far East Gospel Crusade;
Rogelio (Roger) C. Baldemor of the Fellowship of Baptist Churches in Southern Luzon (Conservative Baptist);
Donald McGregor of the International Church of the Foursquare Gospel;
Edwin Spahr, pastor of the Grace Bible Church;
Rudolfo P. Parreño of the Inter-Varsity Christian Fellowship; and
Antonio F. Ormeo Sr, who had convened the meeting at the First Baptist Church of Manila.[1]

---

1. Isabelo F. Magalit, interview by author, tape recording, Asia Theological Seminary, Quezon City, 22 March 1999. Magalit was an observer at the first PCFC national assembly in 1965, representing the Inter-Varsity Christian Fellowship. Antonio Ormeo was pastor of the First Baptist Church of Manila at that time.

APPENDIX J

Correspondence with Faustino Ruivivar, Jr (7 June 2010)

From: fruivivarjr@aol.com
Sent: Monday, June 07, 2010 10:26:01 AM
To: rg1965@msn.com

Dear Dr. Go,

I did not mean to confuse you, but yes–**definitely there were two previous assemblies** before the Council became PCEC. The convenor of the first one was Rev. Antonio Ormeo, a fundamentalist who was closely allied to Dr. Carl McIntire. He wanted to form a fundamentalist council in the Philippines that would be affilated with McIntire's "international council" (I'm ot sure of the official name). I was informed that Rev. Ormeo was a "vice president" of McIntire's organization.

I distinctly remember the evolution of the council (from PCFC to PCFEC to PCEC.

After we discarded the name "Fundamental," Ormeo's group lost interest in the Council. His group lost out because the great majority of those involved said they preferred the name "Evangelical" to "Fundamental," which we saw as having negative connotations. After the Lausanne Congress on Evangelism in 1974, at a meeting of the PCEC board, Rev. Ormeo said he was withdrawing from PCEC in protest against the Lausanne Congress's "shabby treatment" of Carl McIntire.

I remember seeing McIntire in Lausanne. He was not a participant; he was there to picket and condemn the Congress. I remember his "interview" of a participant from Cuba. McIntire: "Do you approve of your government?" The man answered, "Yes." (What else could he say?) McIntire said: **"You're a communist!"**

In 1973 I appealed to our mission, World Literature Crusade (sponsor of Every Home Crusade), to sponsor a monthly magazine for PCEC. The first issue came out in May (?) of 1974. I was the founding editor of the magazine, *Evangelical Thrust*. EHC subsidized the magazine's operation, and I served as editor without pay, for 13 years.. It is now named *Evangelicals Today*, a name I suggested to Jun Vencer.

I'm not surprised that some people do not recall the first two years when we had those name changes. Apparently they only got involved after the Council had become PCEC.

I *am* surprised that people who were *never* involved with PCEC were mentioned as being "convenors."

In Christ,

Faustino Ruivivar Jr.

-----Original Message-----
From: Raymond Go <rg1965@msn.com>
To: Dr. Faustino Ruivivar Jr. <fruivivarjr@aol.com>
Sent: Sun, Jun 6, 2010 3:32 am
Subject: RE: (no subject)

Dear Dr. Ruivivar,

Thank you for you prompt response. Knowing that you are busy, i really appreciate the fact that you took the time to answer.

However, i am very much intrigued and confused with the info that you gave me. does this mean that there was an earlier meeting that took place in 1964 before the meeting where the others (those that you mentioned were not in that first meeting, e.g., Eli Javier) attended? if so, where and when was this very first meeting? And what prompted it?

again, salamat po for the willingness to help. by the way, i was able to interview Pastor Eli Javier, he is sick and on semi-retirement. he is presently undergoing dialysis 3 x a week since his kidney failure 6 years ago. also, i am trying to set up an appointment with Bishop Magbanua and Dr. Vencer.

Thank you po, and may God bless you on your endeavors.

Yours in the Harvest,

Ptr. Raymond

APPENDIX K

Correspondence with Faustino Ruivivar, Jr (8 June 2010)

From: fruivivarjr@aol.com
Sent: Tuesday, June 08, 2010 11:06:30 AM
To: rg1965@msn.com

Dear Dr. Go,

It was a long time ago. Almost 50 years ago. I cannot recall if **Isidro, Magbanua** and **Allen**--were at the first assembly convened by Ormeo. **For sure they did get involved later**. But I'm almost positive **Greg Tingson was not there**. I knew Greg Tingson fairly well. I met him and even stayed at his home in Kabankalan, Negros Occidental, for about two days--in **1957**, when I was a missionary with New Tribes Mission Philippines. Greg was always a dominant figure in gatherings in which he was involved. I think I would remember if he was there. In fact, **I do not recall** Greg Tingson being involved in **any** PCEC activities at all. He lived mostly in Negros Occidental and only visited Metro Manila occasionally. The last I heard (in 2009?), he was quite old and feeble. He is in his 90s now.

If you can contact Isidro and Magbanua, they can shed more light for your research. Magbanua is still very active in Christian circles in Metro Manila. Isidro, who was widowed only recently, lives in Cebu. Engineer/Pastor **Victor Manlapaz**, national coordinator of the National Prayer Breakfast, can put you in touch with Isidro. He has printed or published a book or two for Isidro in recent years.

In Christ,

Faustino Ruivivar Jr.

-----Original Message-----
From: Raymond Go <rg1965@msn.com>
To: Dr. Faustino Ruivivar Jr. <fruivivarjr@aol.com>
Sent: Sun, Jun 6, 2010 7:26 pm
Subject: RE: (no subject)

Dear Dr. Ruivivar,

Thank you once again for your prompt response. your info is really new and i have not heard those details but i'm glad to get these info because most people are unaware of the two previous assemblies that you were referring to.

Just to confirm from the previous emails that you sent, the following were at the very first meeting for the formation of PCEC (then the PCFC):

Antonio F. Ormeo Sr., who was the one who had called for the assembly, and the first meeting was at the First Baptist Church of Manila

Gadiel T. Isidro, pastor of the Caloocan Bible Church;

Faustino Ruivivar, Jr., of the Every Home Crusade;

Greg Tingson, founder and honorary pastor of Faith (Convention) Baptist Church;

Frederico (Fred) Magbanua of Far East Broadcasting Corp. and Capitol City Baptist Church;

Franklin W. Allen of the Far East Gospel Crusade

Where there others whose names were not listed below? When was this very first meeting and was it really in the First Baptist Church of Manila (in Padre Faura, Manila)? Any other details that you may recall (length of the meeting? was it heated or light-hearted? Etc.)

From my research, Rev. Ormeo was part of the International Council of Christian Churches (ICCC) and that they were insisting that PCFC become a part of it.

thank you once again and i pray that God would bless you po.

Ptr. Raymond Go

APPENDIX L

Correspondence with Faustino Ruivivar, Jr (9 June 2010)

From: fruivivarjr@aol.com
Sent: Wednesday, June 09, 2010 2:32:52 AM
To: rg1965@msn.com

Dear Dr. Go,

I wish I could recall who all were present at the first meeting. I'm sorry, I **cannot**. I wish I had carefully kept records. I left the Philippines in September of 1987 and could not bring with me all my books and records.

I do not recall meeting Gavino Tica or Leo Calica until sometime **after** the first meeting. Gavino is another one who would not be quiet if he were there. I doubt if he can give you any information now. He has been unable to speak for many years now. His younger brother, Bishop Pio Tica, was probably just "a kid" during those first few years before PCEC got established.

I'm sorry to hear that Eli Javier is very sick. I'm **positive** there were no Pentecostals involved with PCEC in the beginning. As I told you, I was the one who advised the PCEC board to invite the Pentecostals. I told them I had been blessed listening to Rev. Paul Pipkin's messages at my home church, Kalimbas Evangelical Church in Manila. Pipkin was an Assemblies of God missionary. We did invite him to speak at a PCEC assembly. After that we invited the Assemblies of God and the Foursquare people to join PCEC. Later, a few more Pentecostal groups became involved.

I remember that after Ormeo left PCEC, we elected Fred Magbanua as our president/chairman. He served as president for 7 years, while I served on the board as secretary. After Fred stepped down, in 1973, I was elected to replace him. If you can get back copies of *Evangelical Thrust* magazine you can gather much material about PCEC, but of course that magazine did not come into existence until 1974.

If I remember any more details, I will share them with you. **I do want you to get your facts straight.** I'm sorry that some people are not very careful with details. That's why some individuals were listed as "convenors" when **they were not even there!**

One person who may have information about the first meetings is Dr. Leo Calica, who lives in San Francisco, California. He was a close associate of Rev. Antonio Ormeo during those early years . . . .

Blessings!

Faustino Ruivivar Jr.

-----Original Message-----
From: Raymond Go <rg1965@msn.com>
To: Dr. Faustino Ruivivar Jr. <fruivivarjr@aol.com>
Sent: Tue, Jun 8, 2010 2:41 am
Subject: RE: (no subject)

Dear Dr. Ruivivar,

Thank you for the clarification. i was able to interview Bishop Magbanua this morning

(June 8). He also had some difficulty in recalling the details of the very first meeting. What he (Magbanua) recalls is a meeting at Febias where the Fundamentalist Baptists (i.e., Antonio Ormeo, Gavino Tica, Leo Calica), Febias people (i.e., Frank Allen, Charles Hufstetler) and some others attended but he does not mention the Pentecostals in that meeting. he also does not remember Greg Tingson as being present in that meeting. He does remember that it was your written articles that galvanized them to take action and unify since you called to their attention the Liberal theology of the NCCP and that there was a need for another council that will accurate represent the sentiments of the evangelicals.

my problem is that in looking at the original list, with the process of elimination, only you and Ptr Ormeo are left as being definitely in the first meeting. was Gavino Tica and Leo Calica in that meeting? pasensya na po if i am being meticulous. it is unfortunate that no one remembers the details of the first meeting except that it took place in First Baptist Church with you and Ptr. Ormeo. i will try Ptr. Jun Vencer if he can remember, to help shed light to this.

I was able to piece together a timeline of PCEC but i'm not sure if it is accurate.

Some related news and information; Ptr Eli Javier is still alive but he is undergoing dialysis 3 x a week for the last 6 years, Ptr Gavino Tica is bed-ridden and according to Bishop Magbanua is probably unable to recall any of the details, and Ptr. Greg Tingson is now with the Lord, he had a heart-attack on April 24 at his hometown in Negros.

Thank you po ulit and God bless po.

Ptr. Raymond Go

PCEC Timeline:

1963 – NCCP is established from the PFCC
1964 – First meeting to discuss possible union to form the PCFC (in First Baptist Church of Manila)
 – PCFC is formed (in Febias)
 – Nov. 23; Drafting of Constitution and By-Laws of PCFC (in Fellowship Center Church in Sampaloc, Manila)
1965 – Statement of Faith established
 – July 9 & 10; First National Assembly – discussion was focused on the concern over NCCP being the only voice of evangelicalism (in Capital City Alliance Church)

1968 — May 1; Second National Assembly – discussion is on the Fundamentalist- Evangelical debate, compromise position PCFC renamed PCFEC, Fred Magbanua becomes President

1969 — Third National Assembly – PCFEC is renamed PCEC by majority vote

1970 — Aug. 1; Florentino de Jesus becomes first Executive Director of PCEC, Magbanua is President of the Board

1971 — Mar. 3; PCEC is registered with SEC

1973 — Magbanua steps down as President and Dr. Ruivivar, jr. becomes President of PCEC board

1974 — PCEC joins the WEF
— July; Antonio Ormeo resigns from PCEC Board; ABCLVM withdraws from PCEC

1975 — De Jesus steps down as Executive Director

1978 — Feb. 25; Atty. Jun Vencer becomes General Secretary (this is the same position as Executive Director) of PCEC

1980 — Dr. Ruivivar steps down as PCEC President of the Board and Ernie Lagasca (Foursquare) takes his position, The title President of the Board is replaced with Chairman of the Board
— Nov.; PHILRADS was established and DAWN 2000 is launched.

1985 — Ernie Lagasca steps down as Chairman of the Board

1993 — Jun Vencer steps down and Ptr. Tendero becomes CEO (same title as General Secretary and Executive Director)
— National Ecumenical Consultative Committee (NECCOM) was established by Pres. Cory Aquino; PCEC was asked to take leadership.

1994 — Investiture of Tendero, Magbanua changes the title of CEO to Bishop

1999 — Felipe Ferrez Jr. becomes Chairman of the Board of PCEC

APPENDIX M

Correspondence with Faustino Ruivivar, Jr (12 June 2010)

From: fruivivarjr@aol.com
Sent: Saturday, June 12, 2010 9:11:38 AM
To: rg1965@msn.com

Dear Dr. Go,

New names have turned up, I see. That meeting at Caloocan Bible Church may have been a second or third. I knew **Pastor Leones**, but I don't remember sseing him at those early meetings. **Dr. Magalit** is probably right, because Leones was one of the pastors from Ormeo's group. **Valmike Apuzen** was probably the rep. from the CAMACOP. He was involved in those early meetings. **De Jesus Sr.** did not come to Manila until after we invited him to be PCEC Executive Director.

I don't recall meeting Dr. Pablo until much, much later. But **Bishop Saturnino Garcia** was heavily involved with PCEC in those early years and even beyond--as a board member and officer. Pablo and Garcia are from the Wesleyan Church.

Dr. Honeywell may have been there too. He did attend some of our early meetings.

Tino Ruivivar

-----Original Message-----
From: Raymond Go <rg1965@msn.com>
To: Dr. Faustino Ruivivar Jr. <fruivivarjr@aol.com>
Sent: Thu, Jun 10, 2010 10:19 am
Subject: RE: (no subject)

Dear Dr. Ruivivar,

Greetings once again from the Philippines. let share some of the information that i gathered since the last time i emailed you.

i was able to talk with Dr. Magalit, and he remembers a meeting that took place at the Caloocan Bible Church around 1964 or 65 where there was a heated argument on the name. He mentions a Ptr Leones from BBSI who was with the Baptist group.

i also had a quick chat with Pio Tica and he remembers the meeting at FEBIAS that Bishop Magbanua mentioned before. he said that he was there since his brother brought him along. he also mentions that while Ptr Florentino De Jesus was not there, he remembers that there was a representative from the CAMACOP, he thinks that it could be Valmike Apuzen. also he mentions that he thinks Ptr. Honeywell was there.

so far these are the new info that i got, hope i could get more as the days go by. i am also trying to meet with Dr. Pablo (Wesleyan) who is still alive and is healthy.

thank you po and God bless po.

Ptr. Raymond

APPENDIX N

Correspondence with Faustino Ruivivar, Jr (19 June 2010)

From: fruivivarjr@aol.com
Sent: Saturday, June 19, 2010 4:35:57 AM
To: rg1965@msn.com

Dear Dr. Go,

I will try to answer your questions here.

1. Yes, I was at the first meeting presided over by Rev. Ormeo. (Unless there was an earlier one in which only ABCLVM people were present.)

2. I don't recall theological discussions, except in the case of Divorce. It was the time the government was thinking of formulating a law on Divorce. I remember presenting a paper on the subject; Dr. Tano was the chairman of our theology commission.

One thing I appreciated about the PCEC leaders was their willingness to overlook doctrinal differences. I considered all of them--Pentecostals and non-Pentecostals--as true brothers and sisters in Christ. For my part, I purposely avoided discussing doctrinal matters--except our differences with liberal theology. Personally I enjoyed being friends with all the PCEC board members, including Pentecostals like Ernie Lagasca, Jun Ferrez, Eli Javier, Don McGregor, and others. Also those in the non-Baptist groups like the CAMACOP, the Wesleyans, et al. I will always remember with pleasure and gratitude my participation in the PCEC board and in the assemblies.

Tino Ruivivar

-----Original Message-----
From: Raymond Go <rg1965@msn.com>
To: Dr. Faustino Ruivivar Jr. <fruivivarjr@aol.com>
Sent: Thu, Jun 17, 2010 8:25 am
Subject: RE: (no subject)

Dear Dr. Ruivivar,

Greetings from a hot, humid and rainy Metro Manila. i was able to visit some people and had some more info gathered.

Bishop Pio Tica recalls that there was actually an earlier meeting in 1962 among the ABCL Baptist led by Pastor Ormeo, with Gavino Tica, Calica, Manuel Alesna, Apolinario Apoong. they were concerned with the growing influence of NCCP and UCCP. this meeting took place in First Baptist Church in Manila. where you there in that meeting?

I also met Pastor Juanito Danganan from FIFCOP (he said that it was unfortunate that he was not in the meetings of PCEC). he said hello po and to give his regards to you. i met him in Bishop Tica's church.

I also talked with Dr. Vencer and we talked about his time as the PCEC Gen. Secretary. He mentions that during the 2 years when Pastor De Jesus stepped down and before Dr. Vencer became Gen. Sec. that you were providing leadership to PCEC.

Finally, Dr. Tano suggest that i could focus my doctoral dissertation on the "centris" approach of PCEC on theology (how PCEC avoided extremes to provide a wider "room" for fellowship among different denominations). could you recall some of the early theological debates that were a possible dividing issue among the early members of PCEC?

Thank you po.

Ptr. Raymond Go

APPENDIX O

Correspondence with Faustino Ruivivar, Jr (16 August 2010)

From: fruivivarjr@aol.com
Sent: Thursday, August 16, 2012 9:04:00 AM
To: rg1965@msn.com

Dear Brother Go,

I'm happy to give you the facts as I remember them. History is so much better when the facts cited are accurate. People's memories are often faulty. I'm well-informed about the early history of the Council because I was involved from the very beginning. But please don't ask me for specific **dates....**

It's true that Rev. Antonio Ormeo was the initiator of the first meetings of the council that would eventually become PCEC. But most of us from the non-Ormeo group would not be willing to be involved with Carl McIntire's international council. We accepted Ormeo's invitation to join the early committee because we *were* interested in seeing the Evangelicals united in concrete ways.

At the first assembly Rev. Ormeo succeeded in getting the name **Phil. Council of Fundamental Churches** adopted. At the second assembly, many of the participants succeeded in getting the name changed to **Phil. Council of Fundamental Evangelical Churches (PCFEC)** because most of us preferred to be called Evangelicals rather than Fundamentalists. I think it was at the *third* assembly that we succeeded in deleting the word "Fundamental" from the Council's name.

Rev. Ormeo had no choice but to withdraw his group from the Council. The reason he cited at a PCEC board meeting was that Dr. McIntire had been "shabbily treated" at the Lausanne Congress in 1974. I remember that meeting well, and I recall Pastor Ormeo's words vividly. it was a parting of ways that was inevitable because oil and water cannot mix.

As you are aware, PCEC has really grown to the point of representing most of the Evangelical denominations and churches in the country--for which I praise and thank the Lord. Our affiliation with the World Evangelical Fellowship was a highlight of PCEC's history.

At one point I suggested to the PCEC board that we invite the Pentecostals to join PCEC. I don't recall any objection to my suggestion; we voted to extend the invitation to the leaders of the Assemblies of God and the Foursquare Churches to join PCEC. They gladly accepted. The rest is history. I can honestly say that I have never had cause to regret suggesting opening the door to our Pentecostal brethren. In the pursuing years I have personally enjoyed the friendship of the leaders of their groups. PCEC is richer and stronger because of their participation in PCEC.

Blessings to you and yours.

With love in our Lord Jesus,

Tino C. Ruivivar

-----Original Message-----
From: Raymond Go <rg1965@msn.com>
To: Tino Ruivivar <fruivivarjr@aol.com>
Sent: Tue, Aug 7, 2012 6:06 am
Subject: some clarifications

Dear Dr. Tino,

Greetings in the name of Jesus.

Can i ask some questions about PCEC?

Correspondence with Faustino Ruivivar, Jr (16 August 2010)

I was checking some of the dates and there seems to be some confusion. It seems that Dr. Ormeo's main goal in establishing the PCEC (at that time it was the Phil Fundamentalist Churches of the Philippines) was to create a council that would be connected with the ICCC. However, by 1969, it was clear that it would not be solely a fundamentalist group as you and the other leaders of PCEC (e.g., Dr. Gadiel Isidro) chose to be more evangelical. according to Dr. Aragon's research, Dr. Ormeo continued to stay with PCEC until 1973/74 as part of the board. but why would he stay if his goals were no longer possible and the composition of PCEC was clearly non-fundamentalist at this time. it does not make sense. also, Rev. Nacita (the son in law of Dr. Ormeo) insist that Dr. Ormeo would not stay in such an organization and that after the vote to change the name to PCEC, Dr. Ormeo disassociated himself with your group. can you clarify this point? thanks.

Ptr. Raymond Go

APPENDIX P

Correspondence with Felipe Ferrez, Jr (11 June 2013)

From: jrferrez@gmail.com
Sent: Tuesday, June 11, 2013 10:10:54 PM
To: rg1965@msn.com

Hi, Raymond -

I've just arrived from the US after attending the Foursquare convention there. I got a chance to sit down with Don McGregor and showed him the Appendix A from Averell Aragon's work where his name appears.

Don may not be able to communicate with you by email, so I'm passing on to you what I was able to get from him:

Foursquare Philippines under Don McGregor was very much interested in being a part of PCEC from the start because our mother denomination in the US was already then an active member of the National Association of Evangelicals (NAE), with our denominational vice-president, Dr. Howard P. Courtney, serving on the executive staff of NAE.

And so, chronologically, Foursquare was in PCEC ahead of the Assemblies of God, thus McGregor is listed as one of the initiators for the formation of PCEC. However, he was first interviewed to qualify as an initiator by a panel of four: Florentino de Jesus, William Simons and Arthus Beals (Conservative Baptist missionaries, and Antonio Ormeo.

Whatever hesitancy there may have been in accepting the Pentecostals as full-fledged PCEC members (at the time, there were even stringent requirements for Pentecostal MKs to enter Faith Academy) was finally overcome with the visit in 1962 or 1963 to the Philippines of Dr. Clyde Tayllor, NAE Executive Secretary who endorsed the inclusion into PCEC of the Foursquare Church and, by extension, of the AGs and other pentecostals.

This is all that I was able to gather from Don and I hope it helps a little in your project. God bless you,

Jun Ferrez

APPENDIX Q

Interview with Agustin B. Vencer

(Interview took place at Katipunan, Quezon City, 17 June 2010)

1. **Question:** Can you tell me about the early years of PCEC?
   Response: During my term the issue with the fundamentalist group was not as debated as it was in the earlier years. The issue was more on Liberation Theology in Latin America having this. In the 1970s, the issue was for evangelicals embracing a more holistic doctrine. What does the actual doctrine mean to them? And then at that time you are going to say that theology appears like a pendulum; one time it moves to the Fundamentalist section – evangelism only, and then it moves to the other direction – social action only. And then you come to the center of that which is the balancing of evangelism and social action. And my era (as PCEC General secretary) would be more towards synthesizing the two extremes, getting the best of both worlds. We were not denying evangelism, we were not denying social concern; what we are saying is that evangelism and church planting are non-negotiable but social action [only, without evangelism] is not an option either of the church. So the 70s in many ways was exciting because of the Lausanne Covenant which I believe was one of the most historic, [producing one of the] most influential document that was written in the last thirty years or so. So the Lausanne Covenant has significantly influenced the thinking of the evangelicals at that time. For example when I came to PCEC part of my concern was why were we not involved in social concern and the early part of that I was suggesting that we form a relief organization for children. At the very start many of the leaders were closed towards that [or unwilling to consider it] because social action was somehow seen as

a mark [or indication] of liberal theology and I felt at that time that we were relinquishing what in fact is Biblical because of our fear that we can be swayed to the other extreme at the neglect of evangelism. Also you are talking about the agenda of Marxism and you also have the era of Vietnam War that time and again you have missionaries coming back out of that problem. At that time, we lump the idea that if you are Liberal then you do not believe in evangelism and that you are a missionary [of] Marxist in your organization. The real apprehension at that time was should we [evangelicals] moved into that direction which was at the center of that debate. But the leadership at that time was prepared to think outside of the box and at that time I was very insistent that we take a look at the agenda. And I remember at the assembly, they agreed to table that for a year to allow us to think through the issue.

2. **Question:** Which assembly *po iyon* (was it)? What year?
   Response: I cannot remember but if your data here, you say that PHILRADS came up somewhere in 1980 then that is where my recollection is 1980. We can check the document on that and the registration of PHILRADS. But among the issue there, the registration date you should look back a year before that. That was when the initial debate was made. When the registration took place, that was when the approved it so it was subject to the original today. Part of those issues on one side is the fear of social gospel, the second part of that is the issue that we don't have resources and the resources that we may have should be focused on evangelism and church planting rather than dilute our attempt with the components of the social gospel. But the leadership was open and eventually they agreed that we should approve PHILRADS and allow me to hold the two positions to ensure that the balance will be there. It was also the years of Marcos so there was that apprehension.

3. **Question:** [in the] 1980s
   Response: Yes, 1980s

4. **Question:** The closing years of the Marcos era?
   Response: Yes, So there were a number of pastors that were in there which at the same time could be part of the ripeness factors of that time, why the theological discussions on transformation and holism was really

at the top of our list. Well fortunately they have approved it. Indeed we don't have money but we didn't give up, and in five years we became a very significant movement and the result of that was we were helping thousands and thousands of Filipino families every year. At one time I think we were helping 35,000 families a year. We became a multi-million organization in the 1980s towards the early 1990s. So the one side of the development was engaging the public square that was one of the main issues at that time and the divided between the National Council of Churches [in the Philippines] and the Philippine Council of [Evangelical] Churches was not only theological but there are issues that in many ways have really resulted in a cold "cold war" situation where we were very civil with each other but at the same time we were not actually in active participation in national issues. Until one day, I called up Laverne Mercado, Bishop Mercado, the General Secretary of that time and I said, "Laverne let us have lunch together" and Laverne said, "what is the agenda?" and I said, "well let us have lunch first then I'll tell you." And during the meeting he asked, "what is the agenda?" and I said, "I want to find out how liberal you are and I want you to find out how narrow I am." So we had fun together that day and we began to realize that the saying is true "until people meets nothing happens really you look at each other through the lens scopes of stereotypes" and that is a very unhealthy situation. Until you see each other face-to-face and listen to each other, you will never know what to expect and in that case, we were both surprised at what we discovered about each other and then it started us meeting, then our execom started meeting and before long we were dialoguing as a group already then Marcos was toppled down. Eventually PCEC was no longer considered marginal. We were not really recognized by the government at that time. For once, maybe we deserve it we were divided as evangelicals and we were not match in the public square agenda type of things. So the most we were looked up us proselytizers rather than contributors to the public well-being. So when Cory came in power, she wanted to form an organization of church leaders that would give her feedback in terms of policies in her administration. I suppose, coming from a revolutionary government she wanted also the validation of the larger church community. And at that time, when she became the President, I invited her to meet with the evangelicals and expectedly we were refused, our request was denied because at that time it would be alright to speak to the Catholics but to the evangelicals, that was not heard of yet at that time. So one time I was in Bangkok and I met Prof. Derida Romero. She was my law-reviewer at that time years ago and I said, "professor, you are close to the president. Can you remind her that she is the president of all Filipino people?" "What is happening?" "well we invited her to speak to us but we were denied." So she said, "let me find out what I can do." And a few weeks later, Malacanang agreed to speak to us. So for the first time, the president addressed the evangelicals as evangelicals at that time. But it was our desire to put not only the concept of social concern – helping the poor, responding to the emergency situations in the country and you know we have a lot of that: 7–9 typhoons a year, fire, drought pestilence, you can scan that on calendar every year and you know they will come and so the start of the pain that you will know these expectations and yet you are not prepared to do anything about it. Maybe in fairness we did something but it was not in a way so systematic that you really would like to care for them through churches. But at that time our idea really was not only to go into social concern and action, and balance that with evangelism but also to seek government recognition that we are a significant voice that we can contribute to national well-being and so it was part of the issue we had. We decided to begin with relating with the National Council of Churches because at that time they were really the voice at that time. The Evangelicals were quite late when it comes to the area of social action. If you take a look at that, the issue of public square was there with the National Council with World Council of Churches. The fundamentalist council their national fundamental council, the World Evangelical Fellowship, they were not as active in those areas at that time. Understandably, you will note that the early leaders of the country themselves were from the National Council where the significant Filipino leaders who came into the limelight. People like Salonga, Fidel Ramos, they were part of the National Council of Churches. But we evangelicals were not there because in many ways . . . although not really written in our text . . .

our leaders were not really encouraging the young men to move into politics and business because they were the domains of compromises and the domains of evil. So in that sense, you could not that we were trying to prepare a generation of employees rather than employers. We were not really stimulating the minds of younger Evangelicals to move into entrepreneurship, to move into occupying leadership of responsibilities, to become industrialist, to become heads of government. We were not there intentionally at that time. And that was part of the pain that we had. So when Aquino wanted the leaders of the churches to come together, they have met for quite some time and the discussion was should PCEC be part of that because you have Catholics, Iglesia ni Kristo, Muslims, you name it . . . evangelicals, Fundamentals, accidentals. You are wondering whether we should be part of that. So we argued and I said wait a minute, you cannot salt the earth unless you get in touch with it. We were blessed with a new board at that time that we were hoping to explore new possibilities so I was authorized to attend the meeting when I was invited. When I was invited, I found out that the discussion was so heated, how can we work together? And obviously because we were religious leaders, religion was part of the agenda and I said, "wait a minute, we are citizens who are here who happen to be religious with different persuasions." So I requested that I draft a document and I drafted the document and two weeks later, we met again and after two hours of discussion, they approved the document that I submitted to them. Few weeks later, we were in front of President Aquino and we were inducted into office as members of NECCOM. NECCOM today is still alive after so many Presidents changed its name. But it is still there. The purpose of NECCOM was to meet with the President for every three or four months and we can designate any cabinet or we can request any cabinet member or anyone in the government to meet with us and discuss issues and that was quite interesting. So at least at that time we have started the journey. Not just to talk about holism – the weddings of evangelism and social action, but even going beyond that, most evangelicals were really thinking that it is alright to help victims of calamity but we were not dealing issues of causes of poverty and corruption we were not in advocacy at that time. We were not into social justice at that time, yet. In fairness to the evangelical, we were young group; much younger than the NCCP. We were a fragmented group. I remember when I came in there were only 1,200 churches and we have no money. In fact when I came in, we were at the mercy and the grace of the Conservative Baptist church who gave us an office at the basement floor of the church. That is why in my acceptance speech I said, "thank God we cannot go down anymore, we are at the basement floor and by his grace we can only go up." And sure enough, after ten years when I left the office there were thirty-four full time employees and a four-story building and the Lord has been very good on that. But we were young and people were asking "why are we to help you? What are you doing to help us?" so the classic argument of chicken and egg was there. And you can argue until your face turns blue by saying the reason we cannot help you is that you are not giving money, well they said we cannot give you money because you are not doing anything to us anymore. So in that sense our idea that salvation is free, goes into the practical side that if salvation is free then why is PCEC expensive. If salvation is free then everything is free. Again that was reflective of our own history, that we were recipients of finances from the West and some other sources of wealth. Our mentality at that time were perhaps influenced by that as well, I don't know. But it takes some kind of process again to make our people realize that well we need each other and the Marcos regime is pulling us together. The Aquino Regime also even drew us stronger still and the theological climate has changed so the bonding was closer and closer. We became also a significant player in the development of National Evangelical Fellowships in Asia. I do not know the parts because they have heard of Philippines as well and we are significant partner in the development and eventually the World Evangelical Fellowship where I was invited to serve as a member in the Intl Council in somewhere in '89 or '88. But the point is we were beginning to be recognized at that point. So the journey from social action then we moved in to advocacy part of putting again the question of justice in the agenda of the evangelicals and Ef [Tendero] have continued that process to my delight. I'm very glad that he did. He brought into PCEC to a new kind of strength. He is much more of a networker than I am. I am more of a reflector and I deal issues along those lines and tackle it myself. So those were the years that I recall about PCEC. The other side of that is the introduction of a system management into the work of PCEC itself. Because of my background from World Vision and other para-church organization, and my own interest in my organization, I wanted to ensure that there is a structure for growth. You know, when God created the world, he created creational structures. Often times, we overlook the maze or the concept of structure in creation and so we operate as an amorphous network that are incoherent somehow. But you look at creation, the universe, there are structures visible and invisible and if we are not preparing organization with those structure for growth, we may limit our own growth. So I introduced system management into PCEC and organizational restructuring to allow the whole organization to grow as much as they can. Training our leaders, allowing delegations and putting standards of performance in their entire action plan. And that is one of the reasons why we have grown. At one point we were managing the works of about seventeen organizations in the country. So you have structural growth, a very strong system management program, leadership capabilities so on and so forth and shifting theologies. I think this all part of the excitement that I had when I was in PCEC

5. **Question:** I remember, I was in college at that time, one of my cousin in-law actually worked with PHILRAD; *si* (her name was) Ethel Obordo
   Response: I remember Ethel.

6. **Question:** She would tell us about PHILRADS and we would say, what is that? What is PHILRADS? It is the concept of social work for evangelicals when I was growing up it was foreign. I understand what you are talking about how the concept of social work was strongly identified with socialism and that any effort to do something to that effect *parang* (it's like) people were saying "are you watering down the Gospel?" *Ganon po iyon* (it was like that), I remember that. Was it already in your period *yung* (the) FOSIG or that was more of Ptr Ef
   Response: FOSIG was much later. I was already in WEF when that happened. But towards the tail end of my term, FOSIG started to develop. I might say that I'm supportive of it. At least it is an attempt

of Christians in government to really take a look at the justice issue. How effective it is, only time can tell that because I'm not so sure how many have been convicted in this country and the issue of corruption is not easily resolved because corruption has to deal with research, context, laws, a lot of other things are involved in it. So much so that the corrupt are with the non-corrupt as well. But undeniably, it is an issue that I'm glad FOSIG is dealing with, struggling with. It is an issue that has to be dealt with, corruption. The Muslim scholar would say, "the root of corruption is the love of luxury." And hardly can you find a corrupt leader who is not engaged in luxurious living; from mansions to women, to you name it. But the Muslim scholars in the eleventh century would say that the reason of corruption is bad laws and bad men and I think it is more direct to the point. They are really true and corruption is systemic so in that sense, it can not be deterred easily. It has a life of its own. In that sense it is very dangerous, it can cost your life. So corruption is there and we have to deal with that we are not suggesting that there is an easy way to do that but we are hoping the government will take a look at that. In recent years we have been, evangelicals, when I was with WEF for example and with ASIA, I was trying to open up the issue of confirmation again. That we Evangelicals love to talk about evangelism and church planting but in reality, how do you measure the Great Commission. So my struggle was how do you measure performance? How do you what a discipled nation looks like? Are other books around and you can hardly find books dealing with that. And yet we have been doing that for two millenniums so what are we really trying to do. Because if we do not have standard of performance and if we don't have an idea of what a discipled nation looks like, so can you evaluate anybody?

7. **Question:** I agree.
Response: you cannot. I was on a plane with a missionary to Manila and I was told that he is going to plant a church, I asked him a question, "what would the town look like ten years from now because you have planted a church there?" and he never answered a question. And up to now very few pastors would answer the question. And so, it was in this that in the latter part of my ministry when I started struggling with

that. Until I began to realize that the Lord Jesus taught more of the Kingdom of God in the Gospels and only twice I think he mentioned the church in Matthew. So it comes to reason for me that the Great Commission must be looked at through the eyes of the Kingdom of God. In other words, the Kingdom of God serve as hermeneutic for the Great Commission. Otherwise, it would be very hard to evaluate our work in the Great Commission. So at least we know that the Kingdom of God has some indicators that and we call that the "Daily Vision Now" a church course that we are teaching already around the world. We believe that if the Kingdom is present in the church then the church should be concerned with the economic sufficiency for the people. It must deal with social things not just peace with God but peace with your neighbor. It must deal with the issue of labor, racial harmonies, ethnicities, and civility. It must deal with things with the environment. Romans 8, groaning for children of light. Yet evangelical are not even in the forefront or too spoken about ecology, global warming. Gore was just here and we love to listen to him. There are issues in the data that he is raising but nevertheless, at least he is raising the right question and undeniably some data are incontrovertible. There are maybe some that may raise question I'm not so sure that he is off the mark that far. The other part of that is you must deal with public justice. Jesus Christ, the foundation of God's throne justice and righteousness. So if its righteousness that we have to deal, we have to take a look at culture, the values that we have; how does the church impact in this area? So in many countries where I have been to, especially with PCEC, the question is not so much the number of churches. Particularly with DAWN, we are very much concerned with planting a church in every village and that in people group. And that is right, concern about numbers, yes. But by and large, you have to ask the question about impact; not just number but impact of churches. So before we do that, we started evaluating the curricula of Bible Schools and Seminaries. Do we have enough to allow our graduates to think in an integrated way, in other words, how many discipline/diplomas will a seminary or a church give? After graduation, are they linking with each other? Are they integrating their knowledge so that they can contribute significantly towards the convergence of the national vision of a church or are we just going our separate ways? I will go to my church, or I'll go to an office and do counselling or I'll look for a church or a young people group. Where do we integrate ourselves in terms of moving towards the national vision. And this was a part of a question that they were raising that the day of just social action and social and evangelism. Yes, they are still valid. More and more we should think in terms of conjunctive theology. How do we really transform a nation beginning with our churches? Where are we now in terms of our impact, are we in the public square? The election is just over, again we are divided; others don't want pastors to be in politics, others have no problem with that. So we are still a long way and I'm not sure if we can resolve that until the Lord's return but the fact is that, we are still there. So PCEC in my opinion are moving into that. Significantly, PCEC now under Ef, under the administration of Arroyo, had been recognized center. I think it is timely as well because when she came in 2004, somehow, the major groups have detached. The Catholic Church have withdrawn their support, the INC, the NCCP, the other group and she turned to PCEC and we were able to meet or accommodate her and eventually we were at the center stage. So our leaders were already at the center. And that was to a certain extent, significant as well although we may have paid a price for that as well but at least we were recognized. And that process must go on in my opinion.

8. **Question:** Well I think regardless of what we do, we will be hated. *Ganon naman po talaga eh* (that's how it is).
Response: *Ang malaking problema talaga diyan* (the bigger problem there) is not that we are much hated. But the question is, "have we arrived to a point where we can be free in making a decision?" *Sabi ko nga sa mga tao* (that's what I say to some people), *yung* (the) 3-S movement *na yan, maganda yan* (that is good); self-supporting, self-governing, self-propagating. *Ang dapat diyan na idagdag yung pang apat na S* (What must be added is a fourth S): self-theologizing. *Dapat ang mga* (it should be that the) nationals should be able to act on the basis of their own theologizing already. *Kasi marami na tayong napag aral ng* (because there are already a lot who have gained their) Masters *at* (and) PhD *e para ano yun* (so what is it for)? *Dapat ngayon alam na nating*

magtingin sa salita ng Diyos (now we should be able to understand the Word of God) and at the same time how the word can interact to the changing context of the Filipinos. I think the Filipinos are positive theologians and leaders who reflect the word of God and apply them. That is perhaps where our hopes in. There are now younger leaders and theologians that are emerging that I am happy about. I think they are raising the right questions; I know the answers will not always be clear. I don't know if anyone can pontificate any right answer but I think when we put the answers together, you will be surprised to that there are lots of convergence as well that can make the church move ahead faster than we wanted it or faster than the reality is.

9. **Question:** In my class, sometimes I would talk about . . . I remember teaching "Christianity and social trends" and I would tell my students one of the problems of Christians is *yung* (the) "Visa Theology." *Yun bang* (its like this) "I got my US-visa therefore I don't care what happens in the Philippines because I am going to the US." In the same way, most Christians have that perspective: "I am going to heaven and I don't care if earth and my country goes to hell." If I am going to heaven, and my church and my people are saved, [then my responsibility is over]. So that is as far as I can see. So I tell my students, "if that is what you are looking at, *talagang* (then truly) your impact would be curtailed *kasi* (because) you cannot see beyond and all that you can see is that perspective: I'm going to heaven, *tapos* (it's finished). Nothing beyond that point.

Response: A part of that, the problem of biblical text that we are struggling will on one hand, the situation that we are in will become worse and worse but we are promised with a millennial reign of righteousness and peace. If you take the extreme, people would simply say, "well if it will go worse from worse regardless of what we will do, why do it anyway? Why not focus on evangelism?" well if on the other hand, the reign is coming, then whatever we do, no one can stop that let us just cooperate with the whole issue of preaching the gospel and so on and so forth. So theologically since we have not settled our selves in terms the holiness of God and the concept of obedience to the Word of God. I think a few Foundations have done a research on that: Tensions among Evangelicals. That is why in general, those pre-millennialist are strong in evangelism but weak in social concern. While the postmillennialist are very strong in social concern but weak in evangelism. So the theology does determine the study. I think the question that you are raising is valid. But now, the question of "visa theology" is going to change. With the economic meltdown in 2008 and the shifting of gravity towards Asia, especially China, there will be a lot of preaching the visa theology. Because I think that the gospel has moved where the powers are. And it seems to me that North America and Europe are melting. But the powers of China, Russia and the Mid East will be here. So I think the center of activity will shift to us whether we like it or not. And I think that would be an exciting possibility. I think the evangelicals shall perform that, at the turn of the enlightenment period followed by the high criticism of the Bible, we have really denied the authority of the Scripture already. We have shifted to science and in that sense, unless proven it cannot be true. Which is a thesis in itself is easily disproved. My point simply is, if the Bible is true in affirming that there are powers and principalities that there is Satan, then perhaps what is Paul Hiebert was suggesting to return to the excluded middle is a valid proposition. At the same time, if there is any one group of people that can significantly contribute to the transformation of nations and to deal with corruption, then the evangelicals and their theological formulation should be able to guide our people. Because there are two ways, we can take a look at that. In the book of Habakkuk, Idolatry is the basis for corruption. If there is no God, there is no law, if there is no law, there is no guilt; no guilt no conscience; no conscience no shame. So you can be naked, you can be drunk, you can plunder, you can kill, you can do whatever you want. So at one point, godlessness, idolatry in that sense is true. It is something that we have to deal with and the evangelicals are very rooted in that. But the other side of that is, if in fact Satan is the ruler de facto of this world, and they significantly influence structures like government and all that. Then if you adapt Romans 3:23, "all have sinned." You should take a look at the fact that this are sinners are in power and they are the ones who dictate the policies of the nation and the policies of business, then why are you surprised about corruption? But at the helm of that is Satanic influence on both sides. And the evangelicals in my opinion, have the unique indispensable contribution of sharing the gospel so that those in the domain of darkness can move in the domain of light. And they are the only one who can bind Satan and his minions casting them out they are authorized by Jesus to do that anyway in the Great Commission itself. And they can change public policy and law. That is why I am very much concerned in that we move out from simply responding to disaster to move into justice and advocacy issue but beyond that to intentionally plant so that the next generation of evangelicals will not have only a burden of souls but also will have a burden for the well-being of souls saved in the community that we prepare them not only to be saved but to be leaders, policy makers and to ensure that powers of structures will be changed, and therefore reform. As a lawyer, the powers of corporation is defined by its corporation, by-laws and articles of incorporation. Whatever the articles of incorporation, or by-laws is the grant of power to you as a corporation. If you violate that and then you are beyond your power. So that is true with the government, our Constitution, our laws grants power to the government. If our laws are bad, corruption will take place but who can be in the right position to impact our governors in terms or policy and laws? I am not saying that only evangelicals can do that because the doctrine of the image of God still allows unbelievers to significantly contribute to the national well-being and I'm glad for that. The concept of common grace, the concept of providence is still there. But the evangelicals have a unique contribution at least we enforce what the non-believers are already thinking about. I think in that we should not make any apology but rather prepare the next generation to move into the future. And that is what I think is evangelicalism is all about. Even when I was with the WEF that was the message

10. **Question:** *Actually po ang ministry ko ngayon* (Actually, my ministry at this time) is inside the PNPA working with cadets and trying to prepare to think more critically. *Kasi* (because) one of the training that they get is obey blindly regardless of what orders are. But now I'm trying to help them understand there are legal orders and there are illegal orders and the Christian must be able to distinguish between the two. Suffice to say the time to get to us, they have been shaped already by their churches.

But some, they catch the idea. Our only hope is for every generation that comes at least we impact two or three of this cadets that are coming through our church. And hopefully they can have more impact. It is a strategic ministry and I can also see in the military some are moving in. I'm excited I am one of those choir members there.

Response: Every year we conduct an institute for selected people not more than thirty-five people per institute. Its an intense institute for eight days and we focus on issues on Church and State, Transformation, Structuralism, Anatomy of Corruption. What are the minimal theological themes that the church must really deal with if it wants to move in transformation ministry. We had fun in fact the last time we had, we had two pastors from PMACF

11. **Question:** *Sino po si* (Was it) Erwin Luga?

    Response: Yes and there, we have Commodore Mumar who attended. We had Gen Gudani before, Gen Razon before. And slowly we are looking at some of them. We had a Consul in the last session. The next class we had we have the Senate President from Guyana coming in from the Caribbean to attend the training. He is very much interested in what we are teaching.

12. **Question:** Can I ask another question, when PCEC was formed many of the things that were written was it was formed more for fellowship, more for a common voice, but what you are introducing is not just simply *parang* (like) that one is more of lets come together and to protect ourselves. But what you are talking about now is moving into society and coming together united to transform society.

    Response: I think that was part of the natural development of PCEC itself. It was evolutionary in that sense.

13. **Question:** Was it in the beginning?

    Response: In the beginning the whole issue was unity. In the beginning the issue was survival where we wanted to affirm that we are a distinct religious Christian community and at that time preservation of our values, the gospel so on and so forth. I think those were necessary beginnings but in due time as they began to feel their unity and began to grow together, the context around them changed as well and the evolutionary process of PCEC took place quite naturally. I think at the very start, in the case of PCEC, we started asking the question because again we understand that the Lausanne covenant was part of the document at the early start as well.

14. **Question:** That was in '74 *po* (sir)?
    Response: and many of the evangelicals were part of that process and they were influenced by that document.

15. **Question:** Who the General Secretary was it still Ptr. de Jesus or *kayo na po* (or was it you already)?
    Response: No. I came in quite late in '78.

16. **Question:** So that was still the era of Pastor de Jesus.
    Response: there was a hiatus of two years I think '74–'76, de Jesus was there until 1976 and the position was vacant for two years. I was a young lawyer who was always attending the Assembly. You talk too much, that's how you get noticed. The Billy Graham Crusade came in '77. There were a number of events that intensified the influence on the mindset of the evangelicals. The Lausanne in '74, the Billy Graham in '77 the preparation starting with '75–'76. Again these theological frameworks simulating the minds and are being cascaded in the new mindsets as well. So those were fertile years of development of the mind and the theology of the evangelicals.

17. **Question:** *Kasi* (because) during that time, there was the group of McIntire who strongly opposed the Lausanne meeting and people refer to that as an incident. But what is the deeper motivation, why were they so opposed to the Lausanne? Should they considered it as something to celebrate that finally people are really coming together?
    Response: Well there is one thing about unity. It is a paradox and it is a very difficult paradox to capture. On one hand, we cannot create unity and we know that. It is a given. What you are in part, you are one in the body. So there is a sense in which we are never divided regardless of how we call ourselves because from a theological perspective, we were never divided anyway. From the practical perspective, we see manifestations of this division. Even again in my early years with PCEC, the one that helped me was basically Paul Hiebert. His concept of bounded and

centered set. Centered set: it does not matter how far we are from the center as long as our direction is Christ. So as long as the focus of our hearts is Christ, then we should be one. You maybe near but if your focus is not on Christ then you are really off. But the bounded set was really fascinating because we tend to take western categories and define ourselves in that category and many times those categories are way beyond the fundamentals of the gospel. For example, you might say, what are the common denominators of being an evangelical Christian? The trinity, the word of God, salvation by faith in Christ, the unity of the church, the coming of Christ. I mean you can come up with a few more . . . if you believe in the trinity, you believe in the word of God, you believe in salvation through faith in Christ, then regardless of what the others believe, one body, one church then we are one already. Number 5, I think the need to evangelize, the need to proclaim the gospel. The moment you say "proclaim the gospel," do you begin to cite the gospel you are proclaiming and that has divided the church again and again. But we go beyond those categories; we want to talk about the second coming, we want to talk about the rapture, we want to talk about the millennium, we want to talk about this and that. When you start increasing your parameters beyond those basics and will not tolerate any differing theological interpretation, *madi-divide talaga kayo* (you will really divide with each other). So at that point there are those who believe as the fundamentals would say that the Bible is only the King James version. *Pagka hindi ka* (if you are not using the) King James Version *lagot ka na* (then you are in trouble). *Wala na kayong* (you don't have any) point of contact, *maghiwalay na kayo* (you will separate from each other). There are those who believe evangelism, there are those who believe that you can't deal with government, you cannot relate with your brother who is not of this complete belief with you. In effect what you are trying to do is that you are creating of an image of who a Christian is from your own theological and denominational perspective. And that was very difficult to understand. Billy Graham was talking about social concern and action . . . and so he is compromising in that sense so they were really opposed to that and Billy Graham would work with as wide a spectrum of Christian whether World Council or World Evangelical

Fellowship, or you name it and they could not accept that. The concept of a purist pastor is there and it is a good idea except that good ideas exist in heaven but not in our part of existence. So Billy was accused of ecumenism in that sense, and to the fundamentalist, ecumenism is a no-no. You can see why he's opposed to Billy Graham at that point.

18. **Question:** Back in '74, were you a lawyer back then or a chairman?
    Response: I was a young lawyer working our denomination, the CAMACOP.

19. **Question:** And you said you started speaking *kaya kayo napansin* (that is how you got noticed).
    Response: Yes because at that time, most of my clients were mission agencies and some denominations and I was with PCEC as well attending the assemblies in behalf of my denomination. I was close to the leaders among others. In '77 I was invited to serve as office manager in the Billy Graham Crusade so I began to know the denominational leaders of both sides of the council. I think because of that, it gave me a higher profile among leaders to invite me to become the Secretary of PCEC which from the start I was not really excited.

20. **Question:** Who invited you [to lead PCEC]?
    Response: The Board [of PCEC]

21. **Question:** Through Pastor Fred Magbanua?
    Response: [No] At that time it was Ruivivar. I remember one missionary friend who said, "how in the world did you get invited?" well you know, blame it on one of your friends in the board. I will not tell you his name. And then my wife was praying and my wife was more inclined to accept helping the church more religious in nature, and me I was trying to get out of my poverty cycle because I came from a poor and broken family. My concern was how can I make enough money so I can ensure that my children would not experience the same hardship that I had. And my wife have other ideas. It's a very good lesson to us when your wife is praying differently from yours, something normally happens. So the Lord is good. In retrospect, I never regretted that we followed him and we went into PCEC. It was a good ministry indeed.

22. **Question:** They would say that in the era of de Jesus. Florentino rather. It was more on he brought the prestige and it helped unify the fledgling and struggling evangelical church. If you were to put a word in your era, what would it be? Most people say that you were really the one who established the DNA of PCEC.
    Response: Basically, my era was more putting PCEC in a more transformational path to engage the totality of our world and I think that was basically what I did, I put structure to it and provided a theological framework where we can engage our society today. You know we opened the church to the rest of the world.

23. **Question:** If I were to say, I see you more on really putting as the saying goes, where the rubber meets the road where Christianity is no longer on the spiritual realm per se but having its hands and feet engaged in the world. I think Bishop Ef as you mentioned, the period now is more on expansion, and furthering its influence and finally gaining a voice. *Yun yung nakikita namin na* (that's what we see) as observers in church history. And so we really appreciate your period pastor. Was there, as you mentioned in the beginning, you talked about opposition within you the body of PCEC about the direction you are taking then.
    Response: It was more of a caution I think

24. **Question:** Not a division per se?
    Response: not a division. It was not to an extent that we were divided. For example during martial law and the revolution itself, at that time were just beginning to pick up our unity. We were just beginning to make our coalition and move into the center stage and then the revolution took place. But if you take a look at the preparation of our leaders at that time, the curriculum of the Bible Schools that they came from were not really holistic or transformational in terms of their learning. So there are those on our side, still from the fundamentalist group and there are those on our side who are moving towards the social action group and so, you are caught in between . . . By the time I left there are were already 9,072-10,000 churches but we begin with 1,000 also. I mean constantly you stretch your arm like that holding to both extreme because both are prepared to speech and spin off. And yet you're holding them together it's like being crucified constantly. In the council

there is a microcosm of that division on the world itself. On one hand there are those who do not want EDSA. There are those who believe, let's go there. My role was to ensure that the council will not splinter but to bring them together to a common unity. And that is not something that you can decide and makes you a monolithic or you are empowered with a dictatorial power. This is the word, I'll do it. *Hindi naman tayo* (we are not) theocratic in nature. We are democratic in nature. So you have to get the feedback of in fact those were difficult times because sometimes I would write the position paper of the council but the theology commission could hardly meet and you have to meet with few people that ok this is what we need to do but we need to say something. If you wait for the regular process of convening commission, *ay patay na yung kabayo siguro* (the horse would already be dead) [referring to an old Filipino proverb . . . *"aanhin pa ang damo kapag patay na ang kabayo"* – what's the use of grass when the horse is already dead]. So I was forced to research and study because of that. And I'm glad that there were members of the commission that backed me up like Constancio Amin of ATS, Jun Ferrez, Dr Pablo.

25. **Question:** *Si* (was it) Dr Pablo *ng* (of the) Wesleyan?

    Response: *Oo* (yes). But at that time *ang feeling ko naman* (what I felt was), if we can come to a point where you can secure understanding and acceptance of all and making a decision without destroying the council, that would be good. So the night before, the day before, the EDSA ended, we met in Capital City Alliance Church about 3 o'clock in the afternoon. We gathered there. The debate was so intense, should we join or should we not. So what I did as head of PHILRADS, I already sent relief assistance to the guy on the field, we already assisted in giving medicine, rice, kerosene. [we thought that] it was a long siege so *may mga nabili na kaming* (we had already bought) material for the long siege. So in the end, *sabi ko naman sa kanila* (what is said to them), "the issue is do we have . . . does Marcos have the legal right or the moral right to rule?" Now the question of legality is a justice question and therefore it has to be decided by the court. But our position was, he had no moral basis to rule so we are saying what the Catholics were saying that he had no moral basis to rule and on that basis I said, "I think it is time to identify ourselves with our people and to be in the streets." So in the end *nag-decide ang council na those na hindi magpunta doon* (the Council decided that those who could not go to EDSA), will you please just pray for those who will go there but do not oppose those who are going. Don't give your blessing because you say "*sa aming policy, hindi kami pwede* (in our policy, we can not join you)." Ok fine, we will honor that as well. So on that basis, *nag agree kami* (we agreed). So the means is multi-practice. There were those who are free to go there, and free to remain in the church but pray. But the freedom was there so the decision was ok, we will not do this and multi-track. So that afternoon, we were there. *Mga leaders pumunta na roon* (Several leaders went there [to EDSA]). And we were prepared for a long siege, [however] the following day *natapos* (it was over).

26. **Question:** I remember that because I was in the Lord's church and there was much debate among the youth and the young pro because many of them were from UP and so the pastor was Jun Castro was that time and he was more on the side of "let's go." *Pero* (but) the board who were older, the wise, kept saying "separation of church and state, submission to all authority." Endless debates and finally they came to that consensus that those who want to go, you go; those who want to pray, you pray. But let us not divide ourselves. I remember that was a Sunday afternoon.
    Response: In fact I heard over the radio [what was happening in EDSA]. *Sabi ko* (I said), those who would like to go, go; those who would like to stay in churches understands and pray for those who will be going. So at the same time we believe the administration has no more moral right to rule. So let the people decide. *Masaya yun pero* (it was exciting times but) I started looking at the comments of people and they were not very fair with issues with PCEC at that time.

27. **Question:** [This was] After the incident?
    Response: yes they were not accurate. And those who wrote from the distance and they did not ask. So the accounts were not as accurate as they think they are. It was misleading. But it was a good time because . . . *sinugod pa ako noon sa* (people confronted me in my office in) PCEC. *Sabi nga di Dr Tano, di minomonolithic yung position ninyo* (Dr Tano

defended PCEC's choice by saying that our stand was not monolithic). You are dealing with a diverse organization like PCEC

28. **Question:** Where was PCEC at that time? Did you have the new building at that time?
    Response: *wala pa ata* (I don't think we had one yet). We did not have the new building. Well the new building was an effort to reach out *talaga* (really). We thank God for the World Relief for that and the Tear Fund they were the major donors.

29. **Question:** I was quite young in the faith at that time when all of this were happening. *Kaya nga* (that is why) as of now as I was interviewing people, I am also getting me in touch of my past *kasi* (because) I was more of a child seeing the elders work and many times your actions were not, as you said, properly understood many times. But I could see the wisdom of God in all these and where we are now as a result
    Response: *Naalala ko din yung mga years na yun* (I also remember those years). *Mag isa ako sa kwarto* (I was alone in the room). *Nakaluhod na lang ako* (I was down on my knees). *Wala na e* (there was nothing more [I could do]). *yung grupo mo may fundamentalist na separatist talaga ang background* (in the group there were those whose background was fundamentalist that were separatist), *mga ABWE talaga ang background* (they background was really with ABWE) and all that. You know *ang hirap . . . nakakatakot* (it was hard . . . it was scary). Those were the days of prayer . . . sometimes *nagtatanong ako* (I ask), "Lord, *bakit nandito ako sa ganitong kapanahunan* (why am I here, at a time such as this)." Maybe I could have enjoyed my life in another way. *Ikaw ang focus: if you act patay ka; if you don't, patay ka* (You [Vencer] was in the crosshairs: if you do something then you get into trouble, if you don't do anything then you are also in trouble). Everybody is shooting at you until that Sunday *natapos* (it ended). So *mabuti naman na* (it was good that) despite of that work, in a very special way, they have come to an understanding: alright it is time to move PCEC. They granted PCEC the right to decide so they agreed to my proposal that those who will stay, pray. Those who will go, go. But let us not divide the council. So I think that was major victory.

30. **Question:** Actually, among the evangelicals I remember the discussion was, the moment we get involved was really the turning point. *Kasi* (because) thereafter *dun na pumasok yung American* (that's when the Americans intervened), the phantom jets that flew, the leaflets that were falling from the sky, *yun na yun* (that was it); the beginning of the end. *Pero* (but) I really remember many of the leaders were saying, "It's because the church began to speak and moved the hand of God," I remember the criticism back then *na gaya gaya lang tayo sa Catholic* (we were only copying the Roman Catholics). I believe that it was because we started trusting God and that is when God started to move.
    Response: just before we adjourned to walk towards EDSA, the prayer was so intense

31. **Question:** That was in CCAC *po*?
    Response: yes *doon nangyari yon* (that is where it took place) and then we started moving.

32. **Question:** And this was a meeting of how many leaders?
    Response: *maraming mga* (there was a lot of) denominational leaders. It was really much like an assembly.

33. **Question:** Who were in that meeting?
    Response: CAMACOP, Foursquare, I mean *alam ko marami* (I know there was a lot). I sure may ABCCOP *at andun si Mauro Brion* (and Mauro Brion was also there). I think he is there at that time. So I'm not sure but the leaders were there. But the amazing thing was, it was not a debate whether or not we should be involved because we been teaching that already. In our board meetings we were teaching about Mindanao. Even subsequently the question of separation, it was an intense building up. The Marcos era was only the beginning of that after that, *mga* (the) MILF, terrorism, NPA, *pagpatay ng* (the killing of) pastors *kasama yan sa issue na hinaharap ng PCEC nuon* (those were some of the issues that confronted the PCEC then). So *nagbuild up na yon* (those things escalated). Those were the years when I would attend church-military liaison committee, *sinasabi na nila na baka tumulong ka sa NPA, aarestuhin ka nila* (they said that if you help the NPA that they will arrest you). *Sabi ko kaming mga* (I said that we) evangelicals

we are on the business of stopping the dying and when we help needy people we don't ask them to show their ID if they are pro Marcos or pro Marxist. Then we were part of a church committee, where the idea was to protect the missionary and the pastors *na bago nila arestuhin, ipaalam muna nila sa PCEC* (that before they arrest them, that they should clear it first with PCEC). *Kasi may mga kinukuha na sila na mga pastor na pinapatay na nila* (because they had abducted and killed several pastors already).

34. **Question:** This was at the tail end of the Marcos era?
    Response: *Tail end na yan* (that was at the tail end). *Mabuti naman na nag agree* (it was good that they agreed to our request) and to my knowledge *wala namang nadala* (there were no more abductions). Our role is to protect the missionaries and pastors. Our immersion really until we were recognized by Aquino. Aquino was the first president to recognize the evangelical as a distinct body. Later on, with Ramos, *ok lang yon* (it was ok). Ramos was still very much involved because *may Protestant background siya* (he had a Protestant background). When Estrada came, that changed. *Wala na ako pero ang* (I was no longer there but) NECCOM was still there but not as active anymore. Then, Gloria under Ef and Ef did a good job under Gloria's administration in my opinion in terms of extending our influence.

35. **Question:** I think the "I am sorry" was the major point when Arroyo came up and said I am sorry, there was a news of evangelical leaders backing her up. As you were saying, many of the Catholic Church, CBCP were beginning to pull out and the evangelicals were the one's extended forgiveness. *Kasi nag- ask siya ng forgiveness* (because she did ask for forgiveness).
    Response: When they asked me that, I was no longer with PCEC anymore. My position is she is sorry for what?

36. **Question:** That is a good question
    Response: she never specified that. And we were just so eager to forgive and I said, when you forgive, you cannot hide the truth under the rock. What is she sorry for and that was never answered.

37. **Question:** I think that was the question of the hour *na tinatanong ngayon* (that is still being asked nowadays). You mentioned an attorney that reviewed you before.

    Response: *Si* (it was) Flerida Romero from UP, she became a justice in Supreme Court. Brilliant woman. She was the one who led us to President Aquino and eventually *pumasok sina Atty. Daway* (Attorney Daway got involved in the process). *Yun ay may mga Christian background na noon* (he had a Christian background). They were at Malacanang at that time. They were the link that we had with them

38. **Question:** And that is how NECCOM came to exist?

    Response: They were already helping us. One of the sidelights was that I became a bishop. All the religious leaders in the committee where bishops. They were all wearing clerical collars but *ako, palaging naka-barong* (I was always wearing a barong). In one meeting, it was suggest that I change my title. They jokingly said that this group was only for bishops and "Vencer is not a bishop" *kaya* (that is why) the President was always "*malayo sa'yo* (far or distant from you)." *Mula nuon palagi na akong umuupo malapit sa presidente* (from then on I would always sit near or beside the president) and I referred to myself as bishop. But I think, in retrospect *sa ating mga kristiyano* (as far as us Christians were concerned), part of the issue was . . . the issue of . . . yes we want to be engaged, but do we have the right to be misunderstood when we make moves with the liberals, Muslims and Catholics and so on. We were working with Bishop Deogracias Iñiguez. *Yan ang mga kasama ko nuon talaga* (Those were my colleagues at that time). I told him one time, "I never realize that I can appreciate a Catholic Bishop," he responded and said, "I never realized that I can also like a Protestant leader." But Iñiguez was a man who had the right perspective. I think his heart was right. But the question was can we work with them? I think at that point the cultural tradition of trust came in. they trusted leaders. I think I'm glad from my board who trusted me. That I can work with them and not compromise in anyway what we believe and I can represent them in any forum whether national, regional or global. I'm grateful for PCEC for that.

39. **Question:** Just to clarify, in your period there is no longer any major theological issue in terms of the identity of Christ.
    Response: the question of Christ was not an issue with us. The issue was more on the social gospel.

40. **Question:** One of the confusion, this just a thought, I met with Bishop Tica and he said back in '62, it was Pastor Ormeo who was beginning this concept of PCFC with the perspective that this will become part of ICCC of McIntire. That is why when that did not go through, they went out at the end of the day. *Pero ang question ko* (my question is), would you remember the very first coming together of the convenors of PCEC?
    Response: I think there was really an attempt. When the fundamentalist and evangelical leaders came together, they were hoping against hope that they can really consolidate their forces so to speak and provide a counter-voice to NCCP and even to the Catholic Church at that time. But the theological distinctive in some ways, debated publicly, but in some ways hidden so not all the issues were discussed openly because there was that civility among them. At one time the name was Philippine Council of Fundamental Evangelical Churches so the time to marry the two was the key. That was an attempt to accommodate both sides but it did not work either and eventually, Ormeo's group left. Again, part of that also is that Evangelicals around the world are beginning to define the church. What was happening has seen an influence of thinking because most of our missionaries came from North America and Europe. When the National Association of Evangelicals started to develop they have a strong lobby office in Washington DC then Billy Graham emerged as an outstanding evangelical figurehead and he is already ecumenical in his outreach. There are the influences and then Lausanne came to picture. But the others said about that is this: if the realization that if you would take a look of this picture the liberals on one side and the fundamentalists on the other side, there are certain issues that can be discussed; Polarities so to speak. This one is more heavenly, this one is more earthly. You can talk about this is more spiritual, this one is more human . . . spiritualization or humanization. If you take a look at the reality that at the center of this is a converging group called the

Evangelical. Which really the neo-evangelicals lead by Harold Ockenga, Billy Graham, Carl F. Henry. So that group in there is a wide circle that embraces some liberal and embraces some fundamental. Again, the boundaries between the evangelical, fundamentals and liberal, they are blurred boundaries. I think it is wrong to say that the walls are so clear. It is not clear. It is so amorphous. So you cannot say evangelicals are only PCEC, no. There are evangelicals in the NCCP and other groups even many other fundamental churches and there are also fundamentalism in the other side as well as the social gospel. So I think the emerging evangelical-ecumenical movement, worldwide as well that was also preparing us for the option of the Vietnam war and Korean war and all of the other things. I think these issues have to be taken into context. I think PCEC responded in a way that is thinking outside of the box. It was a slow process how we wished that we probably could have shortened it but you can never just shorten a process. When you alter a DNA of a movement, it is very hard. You cannot just do that overnight. It takes some time.

41. **Question:** You mentioned "ecumenism" and in some places, its like a four-letter word.
Response: That's precisely our problem also that we evangelicals, we tend to surrender good words. Just because it is being used by the other side, "oh don't use that anymore because if you use that, then you're identified with them." But those words were contained inside of the Scripture. Why are we surrendering those good words or should we recapture the words and put the meaning that scriptures had intended it to have.

42. **Question:** It comes from the Greek workd, *oikomene*.
Response: Exactly! *tayo na lang lagi ang nagre-react na humahanap ng alternate words* (we are the ones who react and end up looking for alternative words). *Nakukuha nila yung* (they got those) biblical words. *Tayo hanap ng kung anong gagamitin yan* (We look for substitute words). Why do we have to capitulate on those issues. If those words are biblical then we need to be context with that and live it out.

43. **Question:** Even the word evangelical is also a debate because the word evangelical is being used by the liberal and you would see it in their documents that they refer to themselves as evangelicals. I think it was Ormeo who said "why do we use such a word because it is so identified with them?" I'm not sure whether it was Isidro or Ruivivar or one of them, "why do we sacrifice, why do we give these names to them as a title?"

    Response: the leading thinkers of that time of the formulation was Isidro, Ruivivar, Magbanua. Those three voices were prominent in the dialogue there were others but the three were there. The others came much later.

44. **Question:** *Sabi din ni Dr Tano* (Dr Tano says the same thing).

    Response: *Later na sina Dr Tano* (Dr Tano and the others came later). I did not find their names in the history notes. See I looked at the minutes of the PCEC as far back as I could but they are now lost *kasi nabaha na yun* (because we got flooded) at one time. The three leading voices was Isidro, Ruivivar, Magbanua. Ruivivar came from a more "right side" [fundamentalist]. Isidro was centrist as well as Magbanua but Magbanua's background was CBAP so in that sense, *talagang mga* (they were really [trying]) . . . *kung madala mo sila sa sentro* (if you could bring them to the center), *malaking development na yun from this side* (that was already a big development). And at that time most of the evangelical was more from this side to the center. At that time, they were "right of the center" [meaning, they were leaning towards fundamentalism but was strongly in the middle]

45. **Question:** I'm in email with Dr Ruivivar and he just saying about the early convenors of PCEC. *Ang naalala niya nalang* (what he remembers) is himself, Ptr Ormeo who already passed away. *Sabi niya* (he said), "how I wish I could still remember." He was talking about the early '64 *kasi* the one that most books referred to is sometime in November or late 64. The one that took place in FEBIAS I think which had *parang yun na yung* (probably the one where these groups) coming together. But the discussion even before. From what you know about Dr Ruivivar *kasi* (because) I'm doing checking about him well I find him his Every Home Crusade and the he graduated from FEBIAS *pero* (but) he seems

to be in the middle of everyone. He is a friend of Ormeo, a friend of the Pentecostals. I see that as I have been doing my research.

Response: Ruivivar came from a more evangelism side. He came from ABWE side. So he is close to Ormeo in that sense. Ruivivar that time intellectually understands social action but he would he would not openly fight for it. But he would go for social ministry like relief and all that. But in dealing with the public square, I think the Ruivivar when I came was just beginning to open up to that. So that was my analysis of him. On the other spectrum, Ormeo was an outstanding voice. He was genuinely reaching out to the evangelicals perhaps regretfully, not to a point where he can hold the tension and move ahead

46. **Question:** What would you say is his reason or motivation for that? *Kasi* (because) it's always been said "because he wanted people to become part of ICCC." Was there any other motive apart from that?

    Response: that I don't know. The issue of council loyalty is probably there but I'm not so sure that was the only reason why he reached out . . . I'm not sure. I think if the . . . for the most that was the one that perhaps stopped the initiative that he had. But I'm not so sure if there are any other reason although you can extrapolate by saying that they were the one that stopped it so that may be the primary reason. But I think its much more that.

47. **Question:** *Kasi* (because) in my research with Bishop Pio Tica, he mentions that there are five people in the beginning: Ptr Ormeo, Gavino Tica which eventually they split with each other, there was another person and two more and the name Manuel Alesna and Apolinario Apoong.

    Response: I'm not sure about the last two that you mentioned. Gavino Tica was known already when I came in. I was a young leader. I got save 1968. So my own involvement started with the 70s, '72, '73, '74. The leaders were already from the evangelical side *sina* (they were) . . . Bel Magalit, Dr Canlas were the guys then Ruivivar, Magbanua, Isidro. But at that time the one who is most respected was Florentino de Jesus. I think, at the very start the credibility of PCEC is also in large link to the reputation of his holy life.

48. **Question:** Whose reputation? Pastor Florentino?

    Response: *Oo* (yes). Because the issue of holiness at that time was not as well not debated although that was foundational in the whole process in terms of what does holiness really mean and the different definitions can be divisive. One word that divides. But I think Florentino had given the [PCEC] credibility as well so that it could start.

49. **Question:** That is the observation of Dr Aragon that it was really the credibility, the reputation and the perception of *Tatay* (father) de Jesus as a unifying figure in all these things *pero* (but) that was from the interview I had this morning, by that time the fundamentalist were already one foot outside at that time. They have really been outright frustrated with the discussion of the fundamental evangelical. From the interview that I had from some of them, they would say, that questioning the word "fundamental" or even the suggestion to drop it . . . that was when it started the question for them whether "should we stay or not?" when they started questioning its [the word fundamental] presence. Dr Tano said that . . . you mentioned the name the teacher of ATS anyway he did say that there is such a thing as what is fundamental and what is evangelical and his argument was fundamentalism is a subset of evangelicalism. So *parang redundancy yung* (it was redundant) having the both names in the title. With the word evangelical, it is more inclusive . . . representing both the fundamentalists and non-fundamentalists.

    Response: and yet the term fundamental perhaps was the more recognized term with the . . . as a term to respond to the social movement, the thesis of Machen on fundamentalism. The word fundamentalism was the emerging marching banner at that time because to discuss it is like the Hegelian process: thesis, anti-thesis and synthesis . . . and the anti-thesis to the thesis was fundamentalism. So you bring to the extreme side of it that you believe in the Bible, the word of God, etc. etc. and my reading is that evangelical came as a synthesis in the middle when used by the others. And yet, having said that, from a historical perspective, then you move from the discussion from a missiological and historical perspective into what the word of God really says then the word evangelist is pre-eminent in all these.

50. **Question:** And it seems to me from my analysis that evangelicalism is more on returning to the basics. Its really . . . the extreme point which was liberalism and the other extreme point which fundamentalism, evangelicalism tried to say let us return to what is first century Christianity in its purest form or from its essence. *Pero ngayon din po* (but even now), the word fundamentalism is now an F word in some places or a four-letter word in some circles.

    Response: the evangelicals in many ways have taken the center stage

51. **Question:** And they themselves . . . I was talking with Bishop Tica this morning. *Sabi niya* (he said) if there is one thing that was a regret is the gut aspect that somehow . . . *sabi nga niya* (he really said) "did we in our passion drive away the Holy Spirit." *Sabi nga niya* (he really said), yes we are the champion of the fundamentals of the faith and yet in its consequence our churches died or lessened in its membership. They divided and split into faction.

    Response: But I think also has been made in the development PCEC and evangelicalism that just after the World War II the coming of the charismatic-Pentecostals have added dimensions to the newness that was in the circulation of what we understand as evangelical today. After the Second World War, the word evangelical, especially in my term from the Pentecostal, there were voices already from Ernie Lagasca to Felipe Ferrez. They were significant voices in terms of newness that God was bringing into the whole framework of PCEC and evangelicalism. I think in that sense the word evangelical is more inclusive. Although you go to certain places and those words . . . fundamental and evangelical are no longer used in many churches. You go to Latin America and other places and the word evangelical and Pentecostals are is still coined together. It will take time because Pentecostals are majority in number and they don't want to drop the word Pentecostal for the sake of evangelical because the evangelical has a history of looking at the Pentecostal from another perspective. When I was in WEF that issue was very strong in Germany and I have to go to Germany to meet the believers about Pentecostalism around the world. But the evangelical-Pentecostal controversy is another chapter by itself. Unfortunately, in the Philippines and in the Asia, that happy understanding as if were not a merger but the happy understanding of others view and acceptance with each other had taken place. While it is still there in some extremes but I think basically we can say that we have learned to expand our understanding of the two groups

52. **Question:** I think the AG and foursquare they are the ones that represent the Pentecostals but they are more centrist.
Response: Eli Javier did a good job on that. In my term, Eli Javier was among the theologians that really contributed to that as well.

53. **Question:** I already met Ptr Eli Javier. He is now undergoing dialysis thrice a week. Still alive and strong but it has been six years.
Response: It is hard to talk about evangelicalism without talking about Eli Javier and his contribution. He was one of the foremost leader of the era as well. Me, I was an unknown card. I did not come from the traditional academic environment. So I was an unknown card, I was a hitting target, suspected by everyone. But I'm glad that in many ways that was what was needed to start thinking outside of the box. I was not bound by any theological presupposition that was so strong I could not think outside of the box. That is why Carl Henry, I appreciate him very much when he came [to] Manila. I said "I'm excited about taking MTh at ATS because you are there." By that time, he was familiar with my life, he said, "my suggestion is that you don't go to the seminary."

54. **Question:** Why [did he say that]?
Response: he said, no doubt you can learn much and no doubt we need the seminary. But once in a while there are some people who have the capacity of reflection who can look at the word and the world and interact with it. We think that you [Vencer] was one of them. So during those early years, whenever I would write, I would send him my materials and say to him "Carl, would you comment?" and that old man will always send back with the manuscript and say "go ahead and print it" But his mentorship is really amazing to me. So much so that *ang* (the) last letter *niya sa akin* (he wrote to me) was, "Jun, the twilight years has come and I have turned over your works to the seminary." I wish I kept that letter and *yung mga* (those) manuscript *na may mga changes ibinigay na niya sa isang seminary sa US* (that had his corrections and

changes had been donated to a seminary). But Carl Henry was one of the mindshapers of evangelicalism in the 60's 70's. He was behind Billy Graham and was behind John Stott in Europe and Carl Henry in North America. These were some of the prominent names of evangelicalism at that time. I am glad that God gave me the opportunity to interact with some of the mind changers of that time from Ron Siders to Andrew Kirk of England and Philip Cosme from Croatia so my own understanding of the issue were caused by the practical interaction with some of these guys who struggled with their own culture.

55. **Question:** I'm also thinking Dr Vencer, could it be also that had you been a pastor, not just talking about the theological constraints but if you had been a pastor of one denomination, that in itself will restrict you from the leadership direction where you are taking the PCEC because it will always be having a suspicion "are you doing this for a vested interest of a denomination?"

    Response: that is a very good observation. I think that's part of that because I was viewed as a layman, as a lawyer, I was free. And many of the denomination that were under PCEC were my client. I was consultant to them and I know the mission agencies connected to them as I also was a consultant to them [these agencies]. So I know the leaders on first name basis. Sometimes [when I had worked for them], they would ask "how much will I pay you?" "I don't know, just give send me some books." As a result, I finally developed one of the largest theological library in the country I think because of that. But my point is just you are right. Maybe that is one of the reasons why God has placed me at that time and I'm grateful but I did not understand it then. But in retrospect I'm glad that God has allowed me to be part of that.

56. **Question:** And probably the fear that you can always sue them. Because being a lawyer . . . but it's really amazing. Now I see *kasi kami* (because) we are looking from hindsight is 20–20 and I see the wisdom of God just the right people at the right time, placing the right people. You mentioned that was a two-year hiatus of leadership. Who led PCEC at that time? The board?

    Response: Ruivivar as the board through Ruivivar. Ruivivar and I at the start were very civil but as we worked together I began to realize that this man who was once influenced the more fundamentalist theology was a man whom the Spirit of God was also speaking to. I could not remember a time when I would recommend anything that he would not support. In that I am grateful to the board. The only time when I introduced PHILRADS. But even that, the agreement was to table it for one year and the following year . . . I'm just grateful that God gave me the needed support that I need for the change that was taking place. But I have always been that way. Perhaps I'm not popular in the sense that I'm a very civil person when I deal with issue. When I deal with issues there are black and white so you have to take sides. Either you will like me or hate me. But I deal with those issues like that. I don't want to be ambiguous. This is the way that we should go, period. I think the evangelicals by and large denominations have learned that. They can accept a man like that as well. But I think I was catering also to the younger generation of leaders at that time who were also beginning to think outside of the box. They have seen someone who can perhaps speak outside of their denominational constraints. Maybe in that sense they were excited as well that someone is talking speaking in tongues.

57. **Question:** And the withdrawal of the Fundamentalist had opened the door. *Kasi* (because) had they stayed, they would have checked every move you move thereafter. *Kasi* (because) they would always debate, not speaking against them, it is just the reality that their convictions are very strong in some areas.

    Response: I would think so and I wouldn't deny that. Although some of them in some ways have known them in very civil way but we have not felt ill of each other. I have always respected them. As Jesus Christ had said, "those who are not against us are for us." And we need them because there is always the strong pull of the other extreme and they anchor us towards the fundamentals and we respect that as far as we can but whether you like it or not, you know the anchor, the foundation of what the word of God is, the gospel is all about, evangelism is all about, and I'm glad that in many ways they remind us that, "hey don't forget that the Gospel very old not just 21st century." I think they serve a purpose that is very important but on the other hand the other guys [the liberals] serve us on the extreme that "guys, you are not really looking at human needs the way God is looking at human needs." And in that sense, the whole issue of obedience is one issue that we have to deal with as evangelicals. We tend to obscure the concept of obedience by the very boundaries of our policy, so sometimes without knowing it, our policies became more authoritative than the word of God. Although you can argue that our policies are commentary, that places the authority issue upside down.

58. **Question:** And sometimes *nakakalimutan na natin* (we forget) that the situation is more of our opinion rather than the word of God.
Response: *maski nga sa selection nito e magmensahe ako sa kanila sabi ko huwag niyong kalimutan na ang loyalty natin ay kay Kristo hindi sa pulitiko* (even in their choice, I sent them a message that we must be loyal to Christ alone and not to the politicians). *Huwag naman tayo madala diyan* (let us not get carried away by them).

59. **Question:** Actually this last election the church is quite divided. But the choices then are also except for Eddie Villanueva but still that is a hot issue among many. I don't want to comment on the politics of it. Thank you very much I have taken much of your time.
Response: I hope it helped.

Yes it has opened many areas of thought especially the centrist perspective.
END

Glossary

Denominations A group or association of churches that share a common doctrinal, experiential, or organizational heritage. Denominations are either formed through the merger of churches, schisms within a larger ecclesiastical body, or through missiological reproduction (often referred to as church planting).

Evangelical A person or a group of individuals who belong to a movement which began in the mid-twentieth century within the fundamentalist movement in North America which sought to balance doctrinal orthodoxy with social relevancy.

Fundamental/fundamentalist A person or a group of individuals who belong to a movement which began in the late 1900s within Protestantism which reacted to the emphasis and the direction of the modernist/liberals. Their emphasis and commitment is to what they consider as the fundamentals of the faith (e.g. the authority of the Bible, nature and identity of Jesus Christ, the need of a salvation which is appropriated by faith, etc.).

Modernist/Liberal A person or a group of individuals who belong to a movement within Protestantism that began in the mid-nineteenth century in North America which was heavily influenced by German higher criticism, Darwinism and other perspectives which were part of the outcome of the enlightenment period; where rationalism and science becomes the final arbiter of truth.

Selected Bibliography

Books

Ahlstrom, Sydney E. *A Religious History of the American People.* New Haven; London: Yale University Press, 1972.

Anderson, Gerald H., ed. *Biographical Dictionary of Christian Missions.* Grand Rapids: Eerdmans, 1999.

———, ed. *Studies in Philippine Church History.* Ithaca, NY: Cornell University Press, 1969.

Anthony, Michael J., ed. *Evangelical Dictionary of Christian Education*, Baker Reference Library. Grand Rapids: Baker Academic, 2001.

Apilado, Mariano C. *Revolutionary Spirituality: A Study of the Protestant Role in the American Colonial Rule of the Philippines, 1898-1928.* Quezon City, Philippines: New Day, 1999.

Aragon, Averell U., ed. *Making Missions Practical: A Compendium of the Regional Consultation in Missions.* Davao City: Mindanao Challenge, 1990.

Arcilla, José S. *Recent Philippine History 1898-1960.* Manila: Office of Research and Publications, Manila University, 1990.

Armstrong, Maurice W., Lefferts A. Loetscher, and Charles A. Anderson. *The Presbyterian Enterprise.* Eugene, OR: Wipf & Stock, 2001.

Bromiley, Geoffrey W. *Historical Theology: An Introduction.* Grand Rapids: Eerdmans, 1978.

Brown, Arthur Judson. *New Era in the Philippines.* New York, NY: Fleming H. Revell, 1903.

Cairns, Earle E. *Christianity Through the Centuries: A History of the Christian Church.* 3rd ed., revised and expanded. Grand Rapids: Zondervan, 1996.

The Church: Volume 4, Issue 4. N.p.: Church Publication Company, 1897.

Commons, Harold T. *Heritage and Harvest: the History of the Association of Baptists for World Evangelism.* Cherry Hill, NJ: Association of Baptists for World Evangelism, 1981.

Davis, Jim. *From Carryall Beginnings to Crossing Borders: A 50-Year Journey of Conservative Baptist Ministries in the Philippines.* Manila: LifeChange, 2006.

Deats, Richard L. *The Story of Methodism in the Philippines.* Manila: G. Rangel & Sons, 1964.

Dillow, Joseph C. *Speaking in Tongues: Seven Crucial Questions.* Grand Rapids: Zondervan, 1975.

Dollar, George W. *A History of Fundamentalism in America.* Greenville, SC: Bob Jones University Press, 1973.

Elwell, Walter A., ed. *Evangelical Dictionary of Theology.* Baker Reference Library. 2nd ed. Grand Rapids: Baker, 2001.

Erickson, Millard J. *Christian Theology, Unabridged.* 1 volume edition. Manila, Philippines: Christian Growth Ministries, 1995.

———. *The Evangelical Left: Encountering Postconservative Evangelical Theology.* Grand Rapids: Baker Books, 1997.

Foster, Douglas A., Paul M. Blowers, Anthony L. Dunnavant, and D. Newell Williams, eds. *The Encyclopaedia of the Stone-Campbell Movement.* Grand Rapids: Eerdmans, 2004.

Fuller, Daniel P. *Give the Winds a Mighty Voice: The Story of Charles E. Fuller.* Waco, TX: Word Books, 1972.

Fuller, W. Harold. *Global Crossroads: Focusing the Strength of Local Churches.* Mandaluyong City: World Evangelical Fellowship [printed by OMF Literature], 1998.

———. *People of the Mandate: The Story of the World Evangelical Fellowship.* Grand Rapids: Baker, 1996.

Graham, Billy. *Just as I Am: The Autobiography of Billy Graham.* San Francisco: HarperCollins, 1997.

Grant, Fern Babcock, Domini Torrevillas-Suarez, and Leon O. Ty, eds. *Enrique C. Sobrepeña: His Life and Work.* Quezon City: Sponsorship Committee, 1975.

Grudem, Wayne A. *Systematic Theology: An Introduction to Biblical Doctrine.* Grand Rapids: Zondervan, 1994.

Hartendorp, A. V. H. *The Japanese Occupation of the Philippines.* Manila: Bookmark, 1967.

Hiebert, Paul G. *Anthropological Reflections on Missiological Issues.* Grand Rapids: Baker, 1994.

Honeywell, Russell, and Betty Honeywell. *Faith under Fire.* Manila, Philippines: self-published, 1974.

Jocano, F. Landa. *Filipino Social Organization, Traditional Kinship and Family Organization. Anthropology of the Filipino People.* Vol. 3. Metro Manila: Punlad Research House, 1998.

Kane, J. Herbert. *Understanding Christian Missions*. 4th ed. Reprint. Grand Rapids: Baker, 1991.
Kennedy, Elaine J. *Baptist Centennial History of the Philippines*. Makati City: Church Strengthening Ministry, 2000.
Kwantes, Anne C., ed. *A Century of Bible Christians in the Philippines*. Manila, Philippines: OMF Literature, 1998.
———, ed. *Chapters in Philippine Church History*. Manila: OMF Literature, 2001.
———. *Presbyterian Missionaries in the Philippines: Conduits of Social Change (1899-1910)*. Quezon City, Philippines: New Day, 1989.
———, ed. *Supplement to Chapters in Philippine Church History*. Manila, Philippines: OMF Literature, 2002.
Larsen, Timothy, ed. *Biographical Dictionary of Evangelicals*. Downers Grove, IL: InterVarsity Press, 2003.
Latourelle, René, and Rino Fisichella, eds. *Dictionary of Fundamental Theology*. Makati, Philippines: St. Pauls, 1994.
Leiffer, Murray H. *An Introductory Study of Methodist and Other Protestant Churches: Greater Manila 1965 with Notes on Self-Study Program for a Local Congregation*. Manila, Philippines: Methodist Headquarters, 1965.
Marsden, George M. *Fundamentalism and American Culture: The Shaping of Twentieth-Century Evangelicalism, 1870-1925*. New York: Oxford University Press, 1982.
McGavran, Donald A. *Understanding Church Growth*. 3rd ed, revised and edited by Peter C. Wagner. Grand Rapids: Eerdmans, 1970.
Mead, Frank S., and Samuel S. Hill. *Handbook of Denominations in the United States*. New 9th ed. Nashville: Abingdon, 1990.
Montgomery, James, and Donald McGavran. *The Discipling of a Nation*. Santa Clara, CA: Global Church Growth Bulletin, 1980.
Moreau, A. Scott, ed. *Evangelical Dictionary of World Missions*. Baker Reference Library. Grand Rapids: Baker Books, 2000.
National Council of Churches in the Philippines. *A Public Faith, A Social Witness: Statements and Resolutions of the National Council of Churches in the Philippines*. Vol. 1. Quezon City: National Council of Churches in the Philippines, 1995.
The New Encyclopaedia Britannica: Micropaedia Ready Reference. Vol. 10, 15th ed. Chicago: Encyclopaedia Britannica, 1994.
Osias, Camilo, and Avelina Lorenzana. *Evangelical Christianity in the Philippines*. Dayton, OH: United Brethren Publishing House, 1931.
Pannenberg, Wolfhart. *Systematic Theology*. Vol. 2. Translated by Geoffrey W. Bromiley. Grand Rapids: Eerdmans; Edinburgh: T & T Clark, 1994.

Petillo, Carol Morris. *Douglas MacArthur: The Philippine Years.* Bloomington, IN: Indiana University Press, 1981.

Pierson, Paul E. *The Dynamics of Christian Mission: History through a Missiological Perspective.* Pasadena, CA: William Carey International University Press, 2009.

Pollock, John. *Billy Graham Evangelist to the World: An Authorized Biography of the Decisive Years.* San Francisco, CA: Harper & Row, 1979.

Rodgers, James B. *Forty Years in the Philippines: A History of the Philippine Mission of the Presbyterian Church in the United States of America, 1899-1939.* New York, NY: Board of Foreign Missions of the Presbyterian Church in the USA, 1940.

Sandeen, Ernest R. *The Roots of Fundamentalism: British and American Millenarianism, 1800-1930.* Grand Rapids: Baker Books, 1970.

Schumacher, John N. *Readings in Philippine Church History.* 2nd ed. Quezon City, Philippines: Ateneo de Manila University, 1987.

Shelley, Bruce L. *Church History in Plain Language.* Updated 2nd ed. Nashville, TN: Thomas Nelson, 1995.

———. *A History of Conservative Baptists.* Wheaton, IL: Conservative Baptist Press, 1981.

Sire, James W. *The Universe Next Door: A Basic Worldview Catalog.* 5th ed. Downers Grove, IL: InterVarsity Press, 2009.

Sitoy, T. Valentino, Jr. *Comity and Unity: Ardent Aspirations of Six Decades of Protestantism in the Philippines (1901-1961).* Quezon City, Philippines: National Council of Churches in the Philippines, 1989.

———. *Several Springs, One Stream: The United Church of Christ in the Philippines.* Vol. 1, *Heritage and Origins (1898-1948).* Quezon City, Philippines: United Church of Christ in the Philippines, 1992.

Suarez, Oscar S. *Protestantism and Authoritarian Politics: The Politics of Repression and the Future of Ecumenical Witness in the Philippines.* Quezon City, Philippines: New Day, 1999.

Sunquist, Scott W., ed. *A Dictionary of Asian Christianity.* Grand Rapids; Cambridge, UK: Eerdmans, 2001.

Trinidad, Ruben F. *A Monument to Religious Nationalism.* Quezon City, Philippines: Evangelical Methodist Church in the Philippines, 1999.

Tuggy, Arthur L. *The Philippine Church: Growth in a Changing Society.* Grand Rapids: Eerdmans, 1971.

Tuggy, Arthur L., and Ralph Toliver. *Seeing the Church in the Philippines.* Manila: OMF, 1972.

Tye, Norwood B. *Journeying with the United Church of Christ in the Philippines: A History.* Quezon City, Philippines: United Church of Christ in the Philippines, 1994.

Vencer, Agustin B., Jr. *A Biblical Framework for an Evangelical Response to the Current Socio-Political Unrest in the Philippines.* Quezon City, Philippines: Philippine Council of Evangelical Churches, 1983.

Vencer, Agustin B., Jr, and John Allan. *Poor Is No Excuse: The Story of Jun Vencer.* Dagupan City, Philippines: Alpha Printing Press, 2011.

Von Oeyen, Robert R., Jr. *Philippine Evangelical Protestant and Independent Catholic Churches: An Historical Bibliography of Church Records, Publications and Source Material Located in the Greater Manila Area.* Bibliography Series no. 1. Quezon City, Philippines: Asian Center, University of the Philippines, 1970.

Woodbridge, John D., ed. *More Than Conquerors: Portraits of Believers from All Walks of Life.* Quezon City, Philippines: Pick Source, 2003.

Electronic Storage

Christian History: The Entire Collection of "Christian History and Biography" Magazine. CD-ROM. Carol Stream, IL: Christianity Today International, n.d.

Internet

Alliance of Bible Christian Communities of the Philippines. "About Us: History." Accessed 27 May 2010. http://abccop.org/history/.

Association of Baptists for World Evangelism. "Our History." Accessed 28 April 2010. https://www.abwe.org/our-history.

Apostolic Archives International. "Agnes Ozman - My Personal Testimony." Apostolic Faith April, 1951. Accessed 6 July 2018. http://www.apostolicarchives.com/articles/article/8801925/ 173171.htm.

Christian Aid Mission. "Home: News: Philippines: Greg Tingson Goes Home to Glory." Accessed 15 August 2013. http://www.christianaid.org/News/2010/mir20100430.aspx.

De Guzman, Lawrence. "Philippines Still Top Christian Country in Asia, 5th in World." *Philippine Daily Inquirer*, 21 December 2011. Accessed 4 September 2012. http://globalnation.inquirer.net/21233/philippines-still-top-christian-country-in-asia-5th-in-world.

Doane Rest. "About Us: ABWE-Philippines." Accessed 28 April 2010. https://doanerest.com/abwe-philippines/.

Febias College of Bible. "History." Accessed 10 July 2018. http://www.febias.edu.ph/index.php/about-fcb/history.

"Federal Council of the Churches of Christ in America Record, 1894-1952." Accessed 25 June 2103. http://www.history.pcusa.org/collections/findingaids/fa.cfm?record_id=NCC18.

Fletcher, Dan. "A Brief History of NBC." *Time Entertainment*, 4 December 2009. Accessed 3 July 2013. http://www.time.com/time/arts/article/0,8599,1945408,00.html.

General Council of the Assemblies of God. "History." Accessed 27 May 2010. https://ag.org/About/About-the-AG/History.

GMA NewsTV. "Council of Churches Urges Filipinos to Become 'Instruments of Peace.'" *GMA NewsTV*, 24 December 2007. Accessed 31 may 2010. http://www.gmanews.tv/story/74056/council-of-churches-urges-filipinos-to-become-39instruments-ofpeace39.

Gugliotta, Guy. "How Radio Changed Everything." *Discover*, 31 May 2007. Accessed 3 July 2018. http://discovermagazine.com/2007/jun/tireless-wireless.

Harmon, Tim. "Who's In and Who's Out? Christianity and Bounded Sets vs. Centered Sets." *Transformed*, 17 January 2014. Accessed 10 July 2018. https://www.westernseminary.edu/transformedblog/2014/01/17/whos-in-and-whos-out-christianity-and-bounded-sets-vs-centered-sets/.

ICCC.Org. "A Short History of FECCC." Accessed 27 May 2013. http://www.iccc.org.sg/FECC.html.

Lausanne Movement. "1966 World Congress on Evangelism." Accessed 20 May 2011. http://www.lausanne.org/berlin-1966/overview.html.

———. "The Lausanne Covenant." *Lausanne Movement*. Accessed 21 September 2013. http://www.lausanne.org/en/ documents/lausanne-covenant.html.

McIntire, Carl. "A Critique of the World Council of Churches by the International Council of Christian Churches." Speech given in August 1948, *CarlMcIntire.org*. Accessed 6 July 2018. http://www.carlmcintire.org/speeches-critique.php.

Myers, Jeremy. "Bounded Sets vs. Centered Sets." *Redeeming God*. Accessed 10 July 2018. https://redeeminggod.com/ bounded-sets-centered-sets/.

National Association of Evangelicals, "History." Accessed 15 April 2011. https://www.nae.net/about-nae/history/.

OMF International. "Resources: CIM/OMF History." Accessed 4 May 2010. http://www.omf.org/omf/us/resources__1/omf_archives/china_inland_mission_stories/cim_omf_history.

Philippine Council of Evangelical Churches. "About Us: Core Values." Accessed 11 May 2010. http://www.pceconline.org/about/corevalues.htm.

———. "Commissions: League of Philippine Evangelism." Accessed 15 August 2013. http://pceconline.org/commissions/lpe.htm.

———. "Commissions: Commissions and Networks." Accessed 11 May 2010. http://www.pceconline.org/commissions/index.htm.

Quirino, Carlos. "Nicolas V. Zamora." In *Who's Who in Philippine History*. Manila: Tahanan Book, 1995. Accessed 3 October 2009. http://www.nhi.gov.ph/downloads/rel0017.pdf.

Religious Tolerance.Org. "Cooperation between Roman Catholics and Conservative Protestants." Accessed 15 May 2011. http://www.religioustolerance.org/chr_caev.htm.

SEND International. "History." Accessed 10 July 2018. https://www.send.org/about/history.

Suico, Joseph. "History." *Philippine General Council of the Assemblies of God*. Accessed 27 May 2010. http://pgcag.wordpress.com/about/.

Tendero, Efraim M. "The Philippines Model-Efraim M. Tendero." Accessed 28 February 2019. http:// www.ad2000.org/ gcowe95/tend.html.

Toril Capital Alliance Church. "About Us: CAMACOP." Accessed 27 February 2019. http://www.torilcapitalalliancechurch.org/about-us/camacop.

Virtual Museum of Protestantism. "The 1910 World Missionary Conference, Which was Held in Edinburgh." Accessed 5 July 2018. https://www.museeprotestant.org/en/notice/la-conference-missionnaire-mondiale-edimbourg-1910/.

"Wheaton Declaration." Wheaton, IL, 9–16 April, 1966. *Billy Graham Centre Archives*. Accessed 20 September 2013. https://www2.wheaton.edu/bgc/archives/docs/wd66/b01.html.

———. *Biblical Training*. Accessed 21 September 2013. https://www.biblicaltraining.org/library/wheaton-declaration.

World Council of Churches. "United Church of Christ in the Philippines." Accessed 10 July 2018. https://www.oikoumene.org/en/member-churches/united-church-of-christ-in-the-philippines.

Annual Reports

Advancing the Gospel Towards 2000. Souvenir Program at the 23rd AFBCP Biennial Conference. Malaybalay, Bukidnon, Philippines, 5–8 May 1997.

"Amended By-Laws of the PCEC." *Philippine Council of Evangelical Churches, 22nd National Assembly: Empowering The Churches*. Souvenir Program at the 22nd National Assembly. Christian Development Centre, Tagaytay City, 15–18 July 1997.

"GS Report." *Philippine Council of Evangelical Churches, 22nd National Assembly: Empowering the Churches*. Souvenir Program at the 22nd National Assembly. Christian Development Center, Tagaytay City, 15–18 July 1997.

The Light, 1956 (Doane Evangelistic Institute Yearbook for 1956). Illoilio City, Philippines.

Nacita, Ebenezer T. *Celebrating God's Mercy and Grace Through the Years . . . and Beyond: Church Anniversary Program*. Quezon City, Philippines: n.p., 2003.

Philippine Council of Evangelical Churches, 29th National Assembly: Churches Transforming Communities: Working Together Toward National Transformation. Souvenir Program at the 29th National Assembly. Christian Development Centre, Tagaytay City, 12–15 July 2011.

Tan, Paul Lee. "Official History of GCC." In *Grace Christian Church, 40 Years of God's Grace: Onto Greater Heights*. Souvenir Program at the 40th Anniversary. Quezon City, Philippines, 27 April 2009.

Tendero, Efraim. "National Director's Report (July 2001-June 2003)." *Philippine Council of Evangelical Churches, 25th National Assembly: Developing Healthy Churches for National Transformation*. Souvenir Program at the 25th National Assembly. Christian Development Centre, Tagaytay City, 8–11 July 2003.

———. "PCEC Accomplishment Report, June 1993 – May 1995." *Philippine Council of Evangelical Churches, 21st General Assembly: That the World May Believe*. Souvenir Program at the 21st General Assembly. Brokenshire Resource Center, Davao City, 20–23 June 1995.

Journals

Cunningham, Floyd T. "Diversities within Post-War Philippine Protestantism." *Mediator* 5, no. 1 (October 2003): 42–144.

Isidro, Gadiel T. "Participation? Yes! Political Party? No!" *Evangelical Thrust* 13, no. 1 (January 1986): 10.

"News Roundup: Evangelists Visit President Marcos." *Evangelical Thrust* 12, no. 10 (October 1985): 26–28.

Ruivivar, Faustino, Jr. "Do You Have a Question? Can a Christian Become a Soldier?" *Evangelical Thrust* 12, no. 1 (January 1985): 21.

Vencer, Agustin B., Jr. "The Evangelicals in the Philippines: A Brief History of the Philippine Council of Evangelical Churches." *Evangelicals Today and Asia Ministry Digest* 21, no. 8 (August 1994): 16–17.

———. "The Evangelicals in the Philippines: A Brief History of the Philippine Council of Evangelical Churches." *Evangelicals Today and Asia Ministry Digest* 21, no. 9 (September 1994): 14–16.

———. "The Evangelicals in the Philippines: A Brief History of the Philippine Council of Evangelical Churches." *Evangelicals Today and Asia Ministry Digest* 21, no. 10 (October 1994): 25–32.

———. "Guest Editorial: As the Election Draws Near . . . Participate . . . and Pray (Condensed from an appeal by the PCEC General Secretary)." *Evangelical Thrust* 13, no. 1 (January 1986): 2–3.
———. "PCEC Update." *Evangelical Thrust* 12, no. 1 (January 1985): 26–28.
———. "PCEC Update." *Evangelical Thrust* 12, no. 4 (April 1985): 24–25.
———. "PCEC Update." *Evangelical Thrust* 12, no. 5 (May 1985): 24–25.
———. "What Kind of Christian Workers Should We Prepare in Times of Crisis?" *Evangelical Thrust* 12, no. 1 (January 1985): 7–9, 14.

Dissertations

Aragon, Averell U. "A Study on the History and Development of the Philippine Council of Evangelical Churches and Its Contribution to the Growth of Protestantism in the Philippines." ThM thesis, Asia Graduate School of Theology, 1999.

Bickert, Robert A. "Perception and Response to Receptivity: The History and Growth of the Wesleyan Church in the Philippines 1932-1994." D. Miss. dissertation, Asbury Theological Seminary, Wilmore, Kentucky, 1996.

Jalando-on, Francis Neil Gico. *A History of Philippine Baptist Pastors, 1898-2002.* IATS Series Vol. 2. Iloilo City, Philippines: Religion, Ecumenics, Mission and Society, 2003.

Uayan, Jean Uy. "A Study on the Emergence and Early Development of Selected Protestant Chinese Churches in the Philippines." PhD diss., Asia Graduate School of Theology, 2007. (Published by Langham Monographs, 2017, under the same title).

Public Documents

Republic of the Philippines. Securities and Exchange Commission. *Articles of Incorporation of Association of Fundamental Baptist Churches in the Philippines, Inc.* Mandaluyong City, Philippines, 1964.

Langham Literature, with its publishing work, is a ministry of Langham Partnership.

Langham Partnership is a global fellowship working in pursuit of the vision God entrusted to its founder John Stott –

to facilitate the growth of the church in maturity and Christ-likeness through raising the standards of biblical preaching and teaching.

Our vision is to see churches in the majority world equipped for mission and growing to maturity in Christ through the ministry of pastors and leaders who believe, teach and live by the Word of God.

Our mission is to strengthen the ministry of the Word of God through:
- nurturing national movements for biblical preaching
- fostering the creation and distribution of evangelical literature
- enhancing evangelical theological education

especially in countries where churches are under-resourced.

Our ministry

Langham Preaching partners with national leaders to nurture indigenous biblical preaching movements for pastors and lay preachers all around the world. With the support of a team of trainers from many countries, a multi-level programme of seminars provides practical training, and is followed by a programme for training local facilitators. Local preachers' groups and national and regional networks ensure continuity and ongoing development, seeking to build vigorous movements committed to Bible exposition.

Langham Literature provides majority world preachers, scholars and seminary libraries with evangelical books and electronic resources through publishing and distribution, grants and discounts. The programme also fosters the creation of indigenous evangelical books in many languages, through writer's grants, strengthening local evangelical publishing houses, and investment in major regional literature projects, such as one volume Bible commentaries like the *Africa Bible Commentary* and the *South Asia Bible Commentary*.

Langham Scholars provides financial support for evangelical doctoral students from the majority world so that, when they return home, they may train pastors and other Christian leaders with sound, biblical and theological teaching. This programme equips those who equip others. Langham Scholars also works in partnership with majority world seminaries in strengthening evangelical theological education. A growing number of Langham Scholars study in high quality doctoral programmes in the majority world itself. As well as teaching the next generation of pastors, graduated Langham Scholars exercise significant influence through their writing and leadership.

To learn more about Langham Partnership and the work we do visit **langham.org**

www.ingramcontent.com/pod-product-compliance
Lightning Source LLC
Chambersburg PA
CBHW052011290426
44112CB00014B/2204